LIFE SCIENCES UNICORNS

FROM A CHINA INVESTMENT PERSPECTIVE

DA LIU

The Commercial Press (Singapore) Limited

About the Authors

MAIN AUTHOR: MR. DA LIU

Da LIU started his professional career as a clinical pharmacist in the State of New York, the U.S. and transitioned into the positions of a pharmacy manager, a healthcare corporate executive, and finally, a global life sciences investment PE/VC fund manager over the past 20-plus years. Liu's international work experience spans New York, Beijing, and Hong Kong. The unique combination of Liu's clinical expertise and investment experience, backed by his well-rounded industrial and cross-cultural experience in the past decades makes him a successful life sciences investment fund manager.

Liu published the first book on life sciences investments in Hong Kong in 2021, which has been well received by professionals from investment banks, asset management firms, law firms, and more. Liu is a strong believer that through the promotion of a greater understanding of life sciences amongst the industry players, investors and the public, this sector can thrive, and humanity will benefit as a whole. He therefore devotes much time to promoting the life sciences industry to stakeholders and the public. He frequently gives presentations to college students, professionals and the public about the life sciences industry and investment knowledge.

Liu believes that the purpose of life sciences investment is to help people live longer and healthier, to 100 years old and beyond. To achieve this purpose, he focuses on not only innovative products and technologies but also on products that would help alleviate global healthcare inequalities.

Liu has successfully invested in leading life sciences companies, such as GenScript, Legend Biotech, New Horizon Health, MiRXES, Eye Yon Medical, and more. Many of them are considered life sciences unicorns.

Liu is frequently invited to be a speaker or panellist at global life sciences summits organized by BioCentury, BioEquity, SGX etc. He is currently based in Hong Kong and is an advisor to the Government of Hong Kong SAR on life sciences.

Co-AUTHORS

1. CHAPTER 5: CHINA MARKET OPPORTUNITIES FOR INTERNATIONAL PHARMAS
by Justin WANG & L.E.K Consulting

Justin WANG

Wang is a Partner of L.E.K. Consulting based in Shanghai, China. He is the Head of L.E.K. China and a leader in the firm's Healthcare and Life Sciences Practice.

Wang has 20 years of experience in strategy consulting, advising Chinese and international clients in pharmaceutical, medical technology, and healthcare service sectors. Wang has extensive experience in growth strategy, commercialization, pricing and market access, M&A and licensing transaction support, and international expansion.

Wang graduated from Fudan University in China, majoring in International Finance.

L.E.K. Consulting

L.E.K. Consulting is a global strategy consultancy working with business leaders to seize competitive advantage and amplify growth. Their insights are catalysts that reshape the trajectory of their clients' businesses, uncovering opportunities and empowering clients to master their moments of truth. Since 1983, their worldwide practice — spanning the Americas, Asia Pacific, and Europe — has guided leaders across all industries from global corporations to emerging entrepreneurial businesses and private equity investors.

2. CHAPTER 6: CHINA CAPITAL MARKET FOR BIOTECH INVESTMENT
by Jens EWERT & Deloitte China

Jens EWERT

Ewert is the Senior Partner with Deloitte China, has over 30 years of working experience in professional services, based in Shanghai since the end of 2002 he has been a member of the Deloitte China Eastern Region Management team since then. Jens is the national leader for Deloitte China Life Sciences &

Health Care Industry, leading a dedicated industry team comprising over 1000+ partners and professionals. He also covers our multidisciplinary service offering to Multinational Clients in China.

Ewert received the 'Magnolia Silver Award' from the Shanghai Government in September 2021, recognizing foreign business leaders for their special and outstanding contribution to the City's development. He is also a Board member at the EUCCC Shanghai and the National Vice-Chair of the Investment Working group at the EU Chamber in China.

Deloitte China
Deloitte China provides integrated professional services, and it is a globally connected firm with deep roots locally, owned by its partners in China, determined with long-term commitment and being a leading contributor to China's reform, opening-up, and economic development.

With currently over 20,000 professionals across 30 Chinese cities, we provide it clients with a one-stop shop offering world-leading audit & assurance, consulting, financial advisory, risk advisory, business advisory, and tax services.

The Deloitte brand originated in 1845, and its name in Chinese (德勤) denotes integrity, diligence, and excellence. We serve with integrity, uphold quality and strive to innovate. With the professional excellence, insight across industries, and intelligent technology solutions, it helps clients and partners from many sectors seize opportunities, tackle challenges and attain world-class, high-quality development goals.

3. CHAPTER 12: OVERVIEW OF THE CROS AND PHARMA SERVICES SECTOR
by Miron LILA

Miron LILA
Lila is the Head of Capital Markets and Investor Relations for Caidya (formerly known as dMed-Clinipace), a global mid-sized clinical CRO. Lila has 15 years of healthcare corporate finance experience. Prior to joining Caidya in July 2021, Lila spent 13 years as a healthcare-focused investment banker in both London as well as Hong Kong and was last co-head of Citi's Asia healthcare investment banking team. During his time in banking, he successfully closed over 30 deals

across all products (US$15 billion in aggregate deal value), including multiple landmark transactions in the Asia biopharma space. Since July 2022, Lila has been appointed to the Listing Committee member of the Stock Exchange of Hong Kong.

Living in Hong Kong since January 2011, Lila is deeply committed to supporting biopharma innovation in the Greater China region. Lila graduated with a BSc. degree from the London School of Economics and Political Science.

4. CHAPTER 13: ONCOLYTIC VIRUS (OV) by Fang HU & Zhijun CAI

Fang HU

Hu is the founder and director of the board of ConVerd, a leading Oncolytic Virus company in China. He served as the CEO of Shanghai Sunway Biotech Co., LTD., and a visiting professor at Cancer Hospital Chinese Academy of Medical Science and Cancer Hospital Peking Union Medical College. Hu built the Sunway R&D team and accomplished H101 (Oncorine®)'s bench-to-bed milestones, which is the first Oncolytic Virus product on the market approved officially by China SFDA in 2005. Hu earned his master's degree in Shanghai Second Medical University (Now Shanghai Jiaotong University, School of Medicine), Postdoctoral fellow, University of California San Francisco, in the U.S.

Zhijun CAI

Cai serves as Vice President of ConVerd and has 15 years of international experience in the pharmaceutical industry. His work encompasses innovative drug R&D, innovative drug financing, introducing original research projects and pharmaceutical marketing management in 3 countries. He helped achieve more than RMB200 million in financing for ConVerd. Cai earned his master's degree in business and administration from Zhejiang University, China.

5. CHAPTER 14: QUANTIFYING CIRCULATORY miRNA FOR DISEASE EARLY DETECTION by Lihan ZHOU

Lihan ZHOU

Zhou co-founded and serves as CEO of MiRXES, a Singapore headquartered, RNA-centric life sciences company with the mission to improve and save lives through early, actionable, and personalized diagnosis. Zhou oversees MiRXES group's overall strategy and global operations in Singapore, USA, China, and Japan with a team of 360 staff.

Under Zhou's leadership, MiRXES was named Singapore's Most Promising Start-up in 2016, Singapore's Fastest Growing Companies in 2018, 2019 and 2020. MiRXES has successfully raised US$130 million in venture funding since 2016, which is among the highest raised by an Asia-based genomics company.

Zhou was recognized by the *MIT Technology Review* as a member of the Innovators Under 35 (2015). He was also presented the A*STAR Scientist-Entrepreneur Award together with his co-founders in 2017, the NUS Outstanding Young Alumni Award and the EY Entrepreneur of The Year™ Singapore awards (Overall Winner & Biotechnology category) in 2021. Zhou has been serving on the Board of Enterprise Singapore since April 2022.

Zhou obtained his Ph.D. in Biochemistry from Yong Loo Lin School of Medicine, National University of Singapore. He has authored and co-authored more than 25 peer-reviewed publications and several patent applications.

6. CHAPTER 15: 3D PRINTED PHARMACEUTICALS by Senping CHENG

Senping CHENG

With 12 years of entrepreneurial experience in both China and the U.S., Cheng founded Triastek in 2015, serves as CEO of this company. As a global leader in 3D printing of pharmaceuticals, Triastek is also pioneering the implementation of digital pharmaceutical solutions.

Cheng obtained a Ph.D. degree in toxicology at University of Kentucky and is an adjunct professor at University of the Pacific. She has published 20 papers and submitted 122 patent applications. Cheng has been named to the 2022 Forbes 20 Potential Women in Chinese Business and 2022 Forbes Top 50 Women in Tech in China.

7. CHAPTER 17: HKEX CHAPTER 18A LISTING by Paul CHAU

Paul CHAU

Chau is Managing Director, Head of Investment Banking & Global Capital Markets at Ping An of China Capital (Hong Kong) Company Limited. Chau was appointed a member of the Listing Committee of The Stock Exchange of Hong Kong Limited ftom 2015 to 2021, and proactively contributed to the policy-making of the biotech company listing regime in Hong Kong.

8. CHAPTER 18: VALUATIONS ON LIFE SCIENCES PROJECTS by Glenn HOU & Luke LIU

Glenn HOU

Hou is the Founding Partner at China Insights Consultancy (CIC), a leading industry consulting firm providing market entry, feasibility study, market expansion, commercial due diligence, competitor intelligence, and IPO industry consulting services. Hou has over 18 years of experience and an extensive understanding of the healthcare industry. Hou is the lecturer for Hong Kong Stock Exchange and Securities and Futures Commission's internal training and participated in the preparation of Hong Kong Chapter 18A.

Luke LIU

Liu is the Executive Director at CIC. He is responsible for strategy consulting projects, IPO projects, and commercial due diligence projects in the healthcare industry.

Liu holds a master's degree in applied economics and biostatistics from University of Minnesota, Twin Cities, and a bachelor's degree in mathematics from Carnegie Mellon University. Prior to joining CIC, he had worked at Federal Reserve Bank of Minneapolis in the U.S.

Liu has successfully executed dozens of healthcare and life sciences consulting projects, such as CanSino Biotech, United Imaging, MGI Tech, Genor Biopharma, Sirnaomics, Burning Rock, Kangji Medical, JW therapeutics, New Horizon Health, Transcenta Holding and more.

9. CHAPTER 19 - LEGAL DUE DILIGENCE OF BIOTECHNOLOGY COMPANIES BEFORE INVESTMENT
by Charles CHAU & Jones Day

Charles CHAU

Chau is a Partner of the international law firm Jones Day and a seasoned life sciences lawyer in Hong Kong. He has more than 20 years of extensive experience and regularly advises life sciences and healthcare companies on M&A, capital markets, joint ventures, and other corporate and commercial transactions, including the IPOs and/or secondary offerings of Sinopharm, GenScript Biotech Corporation, Legend Biotech and BBI Life Sciences. He also advises institutional investors on their investment in life sciences and healthcare companies. Chau is a member of The BayHelix Group and HK Bio-Med Innotech Association. He is also an advisor of Y-Lot Foundation, a non-profit organization supporting the development of frontier science and technology. Chau obtained a Master of Laws degree from the University of Cambridge and a Bachelor of Laws (1st Class Honors) degree from the University of Hong Kong.

Jones Day

Jones Day is a global law firm with more than 2,400 lawyers in 40 offices across five continents. The Firm is distinguished by a singular tradition of client service; the mutual commitment to, and the seamless collaboration of, a true partnership; formidable legal talent across multiple disciplines and jurisdictions; and shared professional values that focus on client needs.

Jones Day's clients tap the experience and knowledge of Jones Day lawyers on complex transactions, high-stakes litigation, cybersecurity, capital markets activities, intellectual property rights, regulatory compliance, tax issues, and virtually every other type of legal matter potentially impacting the modern national or multinational corporation.

Every Jones Day lawyer in every practice has made exceptional client service a Firmwide priority. Year after year, Jones Day's high standards continue to earn accolades from industry groups and publications, acknowledgment from peers, and recognition from both new and established clients.

Recommendations

I wish to congratulate Liu on his very informative book. We have more access to innovative technologies than any period in history. These technologies have given us exciting possibilities for detecting and curing human diseases. Geopolitically, we have entered a new era seemingly characterized by de-globalization and protectionism. Hence, while technological developments seem to be giving us more diversified possibilities, geopolitical issues seem to somehow constrict these. Using his vast experience in life sciences and commercialization, Liu's book offers a bird's eye view guiding potential investors in life sciences through this nexus. Liu's insightful perspective on the development of the life sciences industry in China is particularly useful for this important market.

Dr. Y. M. Dennis LO
Winner of the 2022 Lasker DeBakey Clinical Medical Research Award
President of Hong Kong Academy of Sciences

Liu typifies the trustworthy scout for the path to use science and knowledge, guided by morality and compassion, to reshape the life sciences investment scene into what it can become to make sure that health care is of ever-increasing value, better for patients, better for health, through wise investment in impactful technology. Liu is an expert above all who knows how to read the map and point us in the right direction. His excellent book is full of insights gained from an extremely successful career in life sciences investments. It is clearly written, comprehensive and gives us a view from both sides of the negotiating table. It is particularly strong, of course, on China and the enormous potential of this scientific powerhouse and the challenges inherent in establishing new companies on its leading stock exchanges. I thoroughly recommend this book to investors, analysts, university tech transfer officers, entrepreneurial academics, and governmental policymakers, all of whom will benefit from access to this excellent book.

Dr. David KERR
Former President of European Society for Medical Oncology 2010–2012
Professor of Cancer Medicine, University of Oxford

Liu is a long-term friend of the Research, Innovation and Enterprise (RIE) ecosystem in Singapore, particularly in life sciences and diagnostics. He was instrumental in leading a major investment in one of the leading In Vitro Diagnosis (IVD) companies in the ASEAN countries, MiRXES. Additionally, he is actively promoting Singapore's life sciences sector to global investors. I would be happy to continue working with him for the benefit of society.

Dr. Wanjin HONG
Winner of Singapore President's Science and Technology Award
Professor & Executive Director
Institute of Molecular and Cell Biology (IMCB), A*STAR

Liu has extensive experience in strategic research and project investment, both in the United States and China. This makes his book very useful and serves as a much-needed contribution to our understanding of the experiences, and challenges of investment and funding in the life sciences and technology field that we should pick up and apply where relevant. I would like to congratulate Mr. Liu on this excellent book and recommend it to those who are interested in becoming a fund manager.

Dr. Hazri KIFLE
Vice Chancellor and President
Universiti Brunei Darussalam

As a successful investment fund manager and an active member of the Hong Kong Life Sciences Ecosystem, Liu shares his first-hand experiences with life sciences investment. Moreover, he devotes his time to promoting fundamental life sciences knowledge to students and the public. Liu has well-rounded business experience and global industry connections, shaping him as a valuable and trustable business partner. This is a must-read for people with ambitions for high achievement, follow the instructions in the book to identify life sciences' unicorns.

Professor Yuk Lam LO BBS
President of HK Bio-Med Innotech Association

Liu is instrumental in bringing life sciences companies to go public on the Hong Kong Stock Exchange and has the rare ability to identify life sciences unicorns. He actively promotes and teaches the art of investing in life sciences. In 2021, Liu wrote a Chinese book on life sciences investment and how to capture the next life sciences unicorn. It had a great impact on the Chinese life sciences community. In this new English version, he continues to do an excellent job, ever-more extensively revealing the life sciences developments happening in Asia and China, which are currently the fastest-growing life sciences economies in the world. The book is a must-read item if you want to understand how life sciences are being developed in the eastern part of the world. It is a compelling read to investors; clearly presenting the spectacular rise of the life sciences sector in China, deep analysis of the industry policies and investing strategies, and insights into the definitive Asian view on life sciences and life sciences investment.

Professor Albert Cheung-Hoi YU, JP
Chairman
Hong Kong Biotechnology Organization

Liu, who has an extensive experiences and international background as a pharmacist and life sciences investor, has a strong global view and deep local knowledge of the Chinese life sciences industry. As a successful fund manager, he has brought a disciplined and systematic approach focusing on technological breakthroughs. We share his view that with international cooperation, science and radical innovation can improve patients' lives and help clinicians treat their patients more effectively.

Philippe POULETTY
Chairman of France Biotech (2001-2009)
Managing Director and CEO of Truffle Capital of France

Liu's description of the drug industry and life sciences unicorns is truly fascinating. It shows that the commercialization of scientific discoveries for humanity is a many-faceted and thrilling voyage of life, with which I concur. He described the shared common elements and distinctive features of venture investment in the U.S. and China. His passion and philosophy of investing for humanity first and the return-on-investment coming after are jumping through the pages. Liu offers a roadmap and direction for recognizing and taking advantage of China's fastest-growing life sciences sector and identifying Chinese companies with a global vision might well reinvent 21st-century medicine and give patients a reason to hope for cures, as well as provid more economically sensible medications to people in need.

Dr. Sujuan BA
President and CEO of the U.S. National Foundation for Cancer Research

I have known Liu since I joined the Hong Kong Science and Technology Parks Corporation (HKSTP). He is a valuable contributor to us who provides enriching assistance in building business collaborations between HKSTP and the rest of the world. He has great passion and foresight for enhancing Hong Kong as a global life sciences innovation center with a sound ecosystem from solid capitals, global companies, and world-class academia. It is truly a pleasure to work with him, and I believe this book will be a very pleasant read for all stakeholders in the life sciences realm.

Albert Hak-Keung WONG
Chief Executive Officer
Hong Kong Science and Technology Parks Corporation

There is always someone who grasps opportunities when desperation takes the rest down; there is always someone who searches for truth when the fake fools the rest.

Walking with those who seek truths and running from those who think they have found them, we have seen more speculators than real investors.

Liu persistently stands out as a real investor in the healthcare and life sciences space. In this book, he inspires his readers with his rich 30 years of experience.

Yang LIU
Chairperson & CIO
Atlantis Investment Management Limited

As Liu's second publication, this book continues to chronicle the evolvement of Chinese life sciences companies and explore this global forward-looking industry. Liu is particularly felicitous due to his prolonged background in healthcare corporations and practical experiences in the capital market. I am highly confident that this book allows an all-rounded and systematic review for both public, practitioners in our realm as well as capitalists, guiding and fostering the future development of the life sciences industry which in turn serves the greater goal of delivering longer and healthier lives to all mankind.

Jian-ge MENG
Chairman of the Board & Executive Director
GenScript Biotech Corporation (1548.HK)

Liu's fund was the lead investor in the Pre-IPO financing round of New Horizon Health. The due diligence process was truly gratifying as he is professional in the field, he is decisive as a Fund Manager, and helpful in adding value to our company. Both his local and global connections and networks give us a cutting edge in our strategic expansion in Hong Kong. This book exemplifies his thought-out investment logic and unique critical thinking in the life sciences investments, which will for sure be of great success.

Yeqing ZHU
CEO, Chairman & Founder
New Horizon Health Ltd (6606.HK)

I have known Liu for several years. We both are passionate about promoting life sciences collaborations and cross-border investments between China and Europe. This book is a great investment guide on China-related life sciences companies. I recommended it to investors, start-ups, students and any professional within this industry.

Sven AGTEN
Managing Partner of Agio Capital of Belgium
Author of *Adventures in the Chinese Economy: 16 Years from the Inside*

As a fund manager and a pharmacist, Liu's book is an excellent resource for anyone interested in getting into the fast-moving life sciences sector. Readers can learn about the companies which are successfully treating diseases that were previously untreatable, as well as the technologies that will likely break through in the near future. What makes this book unique is its insight into China's life sciences sector, such information is scarce, especially in the English language. It is an essential reading for all professionals in life sciences, from investors to practitioners, as well as those who find themselves curiously drawn to this fascinating sector.

Al CHALABI
Director of CASP-R Limited of Hong Kong
Co-author of *Cracking the Code: Understand and Profit from the*
Biotech Revolution That Will Transform Our Lives and Generate
Fortunes; **and** *Juvenescence: Investing in the Age of Longevity*

Foreword

My first book *Reflections on Life Sciences Investment* was written in Chinese. It was the first ever book about life sciences investment published in Hong Kong. As Hong Kong becomes the largest life sciences fund raising market in Asia, the book received much attention from professionals, namely investment bankers, lawyers, and accountants, who provide services to these listing companies. Another interesting group of readers is the clients of major asset management companies, they see my book as an introductory guide to investing in this area.

Ever since I shared my first book on LinkedIn, my friends, who do not read Chinese, have been encouraging me to write one in English. Benefiting from my life and working experiences in both China and the U.S., I am more than delighted to share my 30 years of observations and thoughts in clinical pharmacy, retail pharmacy, healthcare corporation and global life sciences investments. I genuinely believe that a better understanding of the industry will lead to more successful and prosperous businesses and a win-win situation for everyone. Therefore, here we are, reading this English book. I hope readers will share the same view as I have: encourage global collaboration, focus on scientific advancement, do more business and help people with medical needs.

BACKGROUND

Time flies

In the early 1990s, my parents bought me a one-way ticket on the American Airline to New York City to pursue the so-called "American Dream", even though back then I had no idea what it meant. George H.W. Bush[1] was the 41st president of the U.S. at that time. Since then, many significant historical moments took place, changing the world and the industry, to name a few here:

The Soviet Union collapsed on December 31, 1991,[2] which shocked the entire world. The U.S. became the only left Superpower – I began my time in the U.S.

---

1   https://www.whitehouse.gov/about-the-white-house/presidents/george-h-w-bush/

2   https://www.britannica.com/event/the-collapse-of-the-Soviet-Union

Mr. Clinton became the president of the U.S. at the age of 46 in 1993.[3] The first lady, Hillary Clinton, was put in charge of the Clinton Healthcare Reform Plan. Its goal was to provide a universal and comprehensive healthcare plan for all Americans, which was a cornerstone of the Clinton administration in the first-term agenda. The plan ended up in controversy and defeat. – I was in the college of pharmacy.

Between 1995 and the peak in March 2000, the NASDAQ Composite stock index rose 400%, only to fall 78% from its peak by October 2002, giving all the gains during this historical **Dot-Com bubble**.[4][5]

In October 2001, the **Enron Scandal** made the world's headlines and Enron declared bankruptcy, it was the largest bankruptcy reorganization in the U.S. history at that time. Along with it, Arthur Anderson, which was one of the global top five audit and accountancy firms was dissolved. Enron was once the darling on Wall Street, its stock price at peak was US$90.75 per share in mid-2000, down to less than US$1 by the end of November 2001. As *Time* magazine stated in 2021, the Enron Scandal deeply altered American business forever: the Americans lost trust in the stock market, and this scandal was a big blow to the credibility of the U.S. market.

In June 2002, **WorldCom Scandal**, then the second largest long-distance company, overstated its earnings and assets to maintain stock price. At that time, this was the largest accounting fraud in the American history – I was in an MBA program.

911 attacks[6] happened in 2001, which shocked the entire world and the U.S. changed ever since then – I was in the U.S.

Financial crisis of 2007-2008,[7] was also called subprime mortgage crisis that originated from the U.S., as the result of the collapse of the local housing market.

---

3   https://www.whitehouse.gov/about-the-white-house/presidents/william-j-clinton/

4   https://www.investopedia.com/terms/d/dotcom-bubble.asp

5   https://www.thestreet.com/dictionary/d/dot-com-bubble-and-burst

6   https://www.britannica.com/event/September-11-attacks

7   https://www.britannica.com/event/financial-crisis-of-2007-2008

It threatened to destroy the international financial system, several major banks and insurance companies failed. It is the worst financial downturn since the Great Depression in 1929.

Patient Protection and Affordable Care Act,[8] **also known as Obamacare**, was signed into law on March 23, 2010. The major provisions came into force in 2014. By 2016, the uninsured share of the population had halved, and an estimate of 20 to 24 million people were insurance-covered. It was indeed a courageous move since Medicare and Medicaid in 1965. However, up till 2021, there are still roughly 30 million people without healthcare insurance, given the fact that the U.S. has spent the highest budget across the globe.

All the above mentioned directly and indirectly impacts the life sciences industry and investments. Financial crisis, stock market crashes, healthcare reforms, geopolitical tensions, globalization, have more and great impacts on this industry, which make it the most complicated yet regulated industry among all industries. However, one message is clear that globally the existing model does not function well. A paradigm shift will take place soon.

MY BOOK

Part 1 Learning from the Past, Investing in the Future consists of three chapters, which analyze the industry history of the past 40 years. I apply the terms "paradigm" and "paradigm shift" from the well-known publication *The Structure of Scientific Revolutions* by Thomas Kuhn. The common terminologies and concepts in this part include blockbuster drugs, first-in-class, best-in-class, paradigm and paradigm shift, as well as unicorn companies. Many cases in the book combine both pharmaceutical science and business knowledge. Moreover, I detail some business development transactions so that readers can comprehend deeper on how this industry works. By knowing the past, we can identify present and future patterns and trends, so that we deduce more precise predictions about the future, especially when uncertainties become the new norm.

---

8   https://www.congress.gov/bill/111th-congress/house-bill/3590

Part 2 The Right Place at the Right Time consists of four chapters, which are related to China. The rationale is that, for one to make a sound judgment, it is better to take views from different perspectives. Therefore, I invite L.E.K. Consulting and Deloitte China to contribute their thoughts. Followed by the chapter "China Unicorns and Beyond", which illustrates the successful Chinese life sciences company cases. These companies are primarily listed in Hong Kong or New York or generate a large portion of their business revenue outside China. Readers can easily access their legal documents filed on stock exchanges, or company websites. Moreover, readers can compare the developments of China-based companies, to those based in the U.S., the U.K., Germany, Japan or other countries.

Part 3 Stay Humble, Stay Foolish[9] consists of four chapters, which are "Rare Diseases and Orphan Drugs", "Viruses and Vaccines", "Vision Health", and "Precision Cancer Medicine". These chapters systematically analyze each sector's history, global players, China market and leading companies. The stress is that although humankind has made great technological advancements, we are still in the disadvantaged position in the fight against diseases. Acknowledging human beings' limitations, we may become less arrogant and ignorant.

Part 4 Looking into The Future consists of four chapters, which are written individually by successful entrepreneurs. They are also the Key Opinion Leaders (KOL) in their fields, namely, "Overview of the CROs and Pharma Services Sector", "Oncolytic Virus (OV)", "Quantifying Circulatory miRNA for Disease Early Detection", "3D Printed Pharmaceuticals". Authors are unique in their journalistic styles, and their valuable experiences and insights are first handed. I salute them for their knowledge, persistence, and courage to take risks.

Part 5 Hong Kong, A Rising Global Star in Life Sciences is my contribution to Hong Kong. I have lived and worked in three global metropolitans, New York, Beijing, and Hong Kong. By far, I appreciate and favor Hong Kong the most. This part consists of four chapters, a snapshot and introductory information from three key opinion leaders in investment banking, legal services, and marketing analysis. They represent Ping An, Jones Day and China Insights Consultancy (CIC). These KOLs are willing to spend time and

---

9   https://wisdomquotes.com/stay-hungry-stay-foolish/

share insights with other professionals. I truly treasure their valuable input.

Hong Kong Stock Exchange is a major capital raising center in global life sciences. Consequently, professional services are competitive strengths of Hong Kong by any worldwide standard.

Part 6 Appendix consists of four chapters including "Chinese Life Sciences Pioneers", "Life Sciences Fund Investment Logic", "Recommended Reading" and "References". China had been much more advanced than these European countries before 16th century. This chapter exemplifies exemplarities of Chinese contribution, along with sections of Chinese history, so that readers can better understand what has happened. This book encourages further reading, thinking, and exploring, that is how these references and recommended books play a convenient role.

Throughout this book, I emphasize on facts, data and logic. Readers are free to draw their own conclusion. During my writing, I deeply realize the boundary of my knowledge and limitations of my intuition. Even though I have been in this industry for 30 years, and as a wide reader, I still find out it is very challenging to finish this book, as many new sciences and technologies emerge. Therefore, I welcome any feedback and comments, please email lifescienceunicorn@gmail.com. I sincerely thank you for reading this book, and I hope you benefit from it.

Let us work together, to live in health and longevity!

Contents

■ **PART 4** Looking into the Future

■ **PART 5** Hong Kong, a Rising Global Star in Life Sciences

■ **PART 6** Appendix

Acknowledgments   380

PART 1

Learning from the Past, Investing in the Future

Chapter 1

The Chemical Drug Paradigm

The modern pharmaceutical industry has a history of more than a century, with Bayer's Aspirin being the first industry-recognized landmark drug. Bayer obtained the registered trademark for Aspirin on March 6, 1899. In the U.S., China, and Europe, Aspirin from Bayer is still widely used even today. It comes to 325 mg and 81 mg tablet dosage forms, which are used for pain relief, inflammation, fever and preventing Myocardial Infarction (MI), respectively. Aspirin is a very rare drug that has been around for over a century.

Although some classic drugs, such as Penicillin, Amoxicillin, and Warfarin, were developed and widely used, modern pharmaceuticals were accompanied by a series of "blockbuster" drugs in the last quarter of the century. The dawn of the chemical Golden Era has arrived: Tagamet® set a milestone and signaled the rapid advancement of modern chemical medicine. The launch of Lipitor® which became the world's first "mega blockbuster" drug with annual sales of more than US$10 billion in 2004, signaled the pinnacle of the chemical drugs' era. The peak annual sales of Lipitor® of more than US$13 billion made it the industry's most profitable medicine at that time. Its patent in the U.S. market expired in November 2011. Since generic drugs flooded the market soon after, the sales of Lipitor® nosedived, and dropped out of the top ten global sales list. This historic event signaled the end of the Golden Era of chemical drugs.

Using "blockbuster" drugs as a critical criterion allows for an in-depth examination of the chemical drug paradigm. Firstly, the author illustrates various perspectives of pharmaceutical industry and presents a whole picture of it. Secondly, the author combines science and business. Thirdly, this section is not an exhaustive list of all therapeutic areas, it will not be specifically mentioned, for example, birth control pills, Attention Deficit Hyperactivity Disorder (ADHD) medications for children, and antibiotics. This, however, does not imply a lower significance of these areas. Fourth, the author focuses on the height of this golden era of chemical drugs while providing industry's updates until present.

Noteworthy examples are summarized by their respective therapeutic areas,

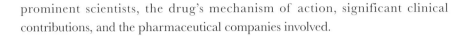
prominent scientists, the drug's mechanism of action, significant clinical contributions, and the pharmaceutical companies involved.

1. CASE ONE: HISTAMINE H2 ANTAGONIST AND PEPTIC ULCER DISEASES

Gastric acid is required for protein and fat digestion. After being degraded by gastric acid, food enters the small intestine, where nutrients are absorbed, and non-biodegradable substances are excreted. Inadequate gastric acid can result in a variety of discomforts, but excessive gastric acid can result in heartburn and ulcers.

Prior to the introduction of Tagamet®, the primary treatment options for peptic ulcers included rest, a light diet, and surgery in severe cases. Patients conventionally take antacids such as Alka-Seltzer®, Maalox®, Mylanta®, Pepto-Bismol®, Tums®, and Gaviscon®, among others. While neutralizing gastric acid can alleviate symptoms within minutes, the curative effect is brief, typically lasting only for a few hours. Due to the constant presence of gastric acid, the medicinal effects of these Over the Counter (OTC) products treat the symptoms but may cause some side effects if used in excessive amount.

1) Cimetidine

Under the brand name of Tagamet® among others, Cimetidine is a histamine H2 antagonist, or H2 blocker. Its mechanism of action includes competitive inhibition of histamine at H2 receptors of gastric parietal cells, which inhibits gastric acid secretion and gastric volume. Its successful development has resulted in a paradigm shift in the treatment of diseases associated with gastric acid secretion, such as duodenal and gastric ulcers, acid reflux, and dyspepsia. A *Lancet*[10] study showed that the number of ulcer operations performed in the U.S. decreased by 30% within 12 years after the launch of Tagamet®.

Cimetidine was the culmination of a project at Smith, Kline & French (SK&F) Laboratories in Welwyn Garden City, the U.K., led by James W. Black and Robin

---

10   https://www.thelancet.com/: a leading journal in sciences

Ganellin and others. This was one of the first drugs discovered using a Rational Drug Design approach. James W. Black was awarded the 1988 Nobel Prize in Physiology or Medicine for his discovery and development of Propranolol and Cimetidine.[11]

Cimetidine was synthesized in 1972 and evaluated for toxicology in 1973. In 1976, Cimetidine was first marketed in the U.K., and approved in the U.S. in 1977, as a tablet formulation. It took 12 years from the initiation of the H2 antagonist program to commercialization. By 1979, Cimetidine was sold in more than 100 counties. The commercial name of Tagamet® fused the two words "antagonist" and "Cimetidine". In 1986, Tagamet® reached a significant milestone of exceeding annual global sales of US$1 billion, making it the world's first blockbuster drug.[12]

SK&F had been a small unknown American pharmaceutical firm based in Philadelphia until the landmark success of Tagamet®, transforming the firm into one of the largest pharmaceutical companies in the world, ranking the ninth in terms of revenue then.

The patent for Tagamet® would expire in 1994. SK&F began clinical trials in the second half of 1980 to obtain approval for the OTC version from the U.S. FDA to open another sales channel and expand their market share. The wisdom of this strategy became evident as the Tagamet® sales plummeted from US$600 million in 1993 to US$400 million in 1994 after it lost patents exclusivity. Other drug-makers copied this strategy as a method to combat patent cliff.

Tagamet® has two major drawbacks. One is that the drug's half-life is two hours only, requiring it to be taken four times daily thus lowering medical adherence. Another issue is that some patients experience mild skin rashes as a side effect.

2) Ranitidine

Under the brand name Zantac® among others, Ranitidine was first developed by

---

11 https://www.nobelprize.org/prizes/medicine/1988/black/facts/

12 A blockbuster drug commonly refers to a drug with annual global sales exceeding US$1 billion.

Allen and Hanburys, part of the British company Glaxo, in the U.K. Zantac® was marketed in the U.K. in 1981, and in the U.S. in 1983, as a tablet formulation. It has a longer half-life, only requires twice administrations daily, and has fewer side effects. As a later comer, Glaxo took the following strategies: 1) aggressive pricing strategy, charging 50% more for Zantac® than for Tagamet®, 2) formed partnership with Hoffman-La Roche and increasing U.S. sales force from 400 to 1,200 professionals, 3) invested the additional revenue into marketing. Consequently, the sales of Zantac® exceeded US$2 billion in 1986, turning into another blockbuster drug. More importantly, it became the world's best-selling drug in 1987.

Due to the revolutionary discovery of H2 Blocker and the enormous success of Tagamet® and Zantac®, other pharmaceutical industry giants followed and entered this area and eventually succeeded, examples include Yamanouchi of Japan, and Eli Lilly of the U.S. Yamanouchi developed and launched Famotidine, under the brand name Gaster® in 1985. One year later, Yamanouchi co-marketed with Merck, under the brand name Pepcid® in the U.S., becoming the world's third H2 Blocker. Eli Lilly developed and launched Nizatidine, under the brand name of Axid®, the fourth H2 Blocker, in the U.S. in 1988.

These patents did not last: SmithKline Beecham's Tagamet® expired in 1994, Merck's Pepcid® expired in 2000, Glaxo's Zantac® and Eli Lilly's Axid® expired in 2002. They all subsequently turned to selling on the OTC market by lowering drug dosage strength.

3) Afterwards

SmithKline Beecham merged with Glaxo Wellcome in a stock swap worthy of US$76 billion in 2000,[13] and created GlaxoSmithKline (GSK), the largest drug company in the world at that time, holding 7.3% of the world pharmaceutical market. Consequently, GSK owned both Tagamet® and Zantac® brands.

Later, Ranitidine was superseded by the more effective Proton-Pump Inhibitor (PPI) class of drugs, with Omeprazole becoming the biggest-selling drug for many years.

---

13 https://money.cnn.com/2000/01/17/europe/glaxo_deal/

In September 2019, the probable carcinogen N-Nitrosodimethylamine was discovered in ranitidine from several manufacturers, resulting in recalls.[14] In April 2020, Ranitidine was withdrawn from the U.S. and suspended in the Europe and Australia. This is the result that no one would have imagined 30 years ago.

2. CASE TWO: PROTON-PUMP INHIBITOR AND GERD

1) Omeprazole and Esomeprazole

Under the brand names Prilosec®, Losec® and among others, Omeprazole is a medication used to treat Gastroesophageal Reflux Disease (GERD), peptic ulcer disease, and Zollinger-Ellison syndrome. Its mechanism of action is to inhibit the hydrogen/potassium ion ATPase (H+/K+ ATPase) in gastric parietal cells, which is more effective than H2 blockers. Their dosage forms are delayed-released capsules. Losec®, Nexium®, and other "me-too" drugs such as Prevacid®, Protonix®, and Pariet® can effectively prevent excessive gastric acid secretion, with nearly 90% of patients experiencing a complete relief. These medications have a long half-life, and once daily dosing is sufficient.

The huge success was credited to both hard work from worldwide scientific collaborations and business strategies: 1) a research team led by Austria-born George Sachs established that hydrogen/potassium ion ATPase was a Proton-Pump involved in the transport of gastric acid through the mucosa and parietal cells,[15] 2) chemists at the Sweden-based company Astra Hassle made significant contributions to its molecular structure, culminating in the creation of Losec®, 3) the Swedish regulatory agency approved the drug to treat duodenal ulcer and reflux esophagitis in 1988, 4) in the U.S., Merck co-developed the medication and sold under the brand name Prilosec®. Omeprazole was a game changer in the treatment of gastric ulcers, with sales exceeding US$6 billion in 1999.

On April 6, 1999, the Swedish pharmaceutical company Astra AB, and U.K. based Zenaca Group plc merged and became AstraZeneca, one of the largest

---

14 https://www.theguardian.com/business/2019/oct/09/zantac-in-global-recall-over-unacceptable-levels-of-potential-carcinogen

15 https://www.gastrojournal.org/article/S0016-5085(20)30618-1/fulltext

European mergers ever. Upon the completion of the merger, Astra shareholders held 46.5% share of the combined company, while Zeneca shareholders owned 53.5%. The global headquarters located in the U.K., and the R&D headquarters were to be in Sweden.[16]

Astra Hassle began researching backup compounds in 1987 and eventually developed Esomeprazole, under the brand name Nexium®, which was approved in Sweden and the U.S. in 2000 and 2001 respectively. Nexium® was one of the most controversial drugs in the early 2000s, and the concept of "Chirality" was introduced. Esomeprazole's predecessor, Omeprazole, is a mixture of two mirror-imaged molecules (Esomeprazole and R-omeprazole). Critics said that the company tried to evergreen the patent and marketed aggressively to doctors that Esomeprazole is more effective than the mixture. Between the launch of Esomeprazole in 2001 and 2005, the drug made US$14.4 billion revenue for AstraZeneca.[17] These two blockbuster drugs set a solid foundation for AstraZeneca as a global pharmaceutical giant.

In October 2019, AstraZeneca turned the global commercial rights of Omeprazole over to German pharma Cheplapharm at the price of US$243 million, except for four countries namely the U.S., China, Japan, and Mexico,[18] putting an end to AstraZeneca's Omeprazole legend.

Omeprazole's success drew attention from other pharmaceutical companies to develop similar drugs, named "me-too". A few turned out to be successful:

2) Pantoprazole

In 1984, SK&F and the German-based company Byk Gulden (later became part of Altana Pharma AG) agreed to collaborate on the development of a Proton-Pump Inhibitor (PPI), leading to the discovery of Pantoprazole. Due to its high solubility and stability in water, it was the first injectable PPI. Pantoprazole was

---

16 https://www.pharmaceuticalonline.com/doc/astra-zeneca-to-merge-0001

17 https://pharmaphorum.com/views-analysis-sales-marketing/a_history_of-_astrazeneca/

18 https://www.astrazeneca.com/media-centre/press-releases/2019/astrazeneca-divests-rights-for-losec-to-cheplapharm-01102019.html#

originally marketed in Germany in 1994. U.S. based Wyeth Pharmaceuticals licensed the U.S. patent from Altana and obtained marketing approval from the U.S. FDA in 2000 under the brand name Protonix®. In March 2001, the U.S. FDA approved Protonix IV® for patients with GERD, and used it as an alternative to patients who are not able to take Protonix Delayed-Release Tablets.[19] In 2004, the worldwide sales of Pantoprazole were US$3.65 billion, about half of which were in the U.S.

In 2007, Altana's pharma business was acquired by Swiss-based Nycomed at the transaction amount of €4.6 billion.[20] Later, Nycomed was acquired by Japanese company Takeda in 2011, at the transaction amount of US$13.7 billion.[21] The patent protecting the drug was set to expire in 2010, but Israeli Teva Pharmaceuticals filed an Abbreviated New Drug Application (ANDA) in 2007. Wyeth and Nycomed sued Teva for patent infringement. The litigation between Teva and Pfizer/Takeda was settled in 2013, with Teva paying the patent holders US$2.15 billion for early launch.[22] In December 2012, the U.S. government officials and Wyeth announced the settlement that Wyeth paid US$55 million plus interest for promoting off-label use of Protonix®.[23]

3) Lansoprazole

It was discovered by Takeda Chemical Industries of Japan.

In the U.S., Takeda partnered with Abbott to establish a joint venture called TAP Pharmaceuticals (TAP) in 1977. The purpose of this partnership was to get Takeda-developed products approved and marketed in the U.S. markets. This strategy was strongly supported by the Japanese government at the time to assist

---

19 http://test.pharmabiz.com/news/wyeth-receives-us-fda-approval-of-new-formulation-for-protonix-iv-21309

20 https://www.altana.com/press-news/article/altana-ag-completes-sale-of-pharmaceuticals-business-to-nycomed.html

21 https://www.reuters.com/article/us-takeda-nycomed-idUSTRE74I15620110519

22 https://www.pfizer.com/news/press-release/press-release-detail/pfizer_obtains_2_15_billion_settlement_from_teva_and_sun_for_infringement_of_protonix_patent

23 https://www.medpagetoday.com/washington-watch/washington-watch/36469

its national economy to compete globally.

Two of the most lucrative products from TAP were Lansoprazole under the brand name Prevacid®, and Leuprorelin under the brand name Lupron®. Lansoprazole, approved in 1995, was the second PPI marketed in the U.S. Prevacid® hit US$3 billion in sales in 1999.

In 2001, the U.S. Department of Justice and TAP Pharmaceutical settled criminal and civil charges against TAP related to federal and state Medicare fraud as well as illegal marketing of Leuprorelin. TAP paid a total of US$875 million, a record at the time.[24] TAP was dissolved in 2008.

4) Rabeprazole

It was discovered by Eisai of Japan, under the brand name of Aciphex® among others. Rabeprazole was patented in 1986, and approved for medical use in Japan in 1997, in Europe in 1998, and in the U.S. in 1999. In the U.S., Rabeprazole was co-promoted by Eisai and PriCara, part of Ortho-McNeil-Janssen Pharmaceuticals.[25]

5) Bacteria and peptic ulcer disease

In 2005, Australian pathologist Robin Warren and physician Barry Marshall jointly won the Nobel Prize in Physiology or Medicine for their discovery of the role of Helicobacter Pylori in gastritis and peptic ulcer disease.[26] This discovery was significant in understanding a causal link between Helicobacter Pylori infection and stomach ulcer disease, resulting in the current standard treatment plan for Helicobacter Pylori infection, further advancing the treatment of gastric ulcers.

---

24   https://www.justice.gov/archive/opa/pr/2001/October/513civ.htm

25   https://www.eisai.com/news/news200842.html

26   https://www.nobelprize.org/prizes/medicine/2005/press-release/

3. CASE THREE: ANTIHISTAMINES AND ALLERGY TREATMENT

Allergy is one of the most prevalent chronic diseases worldwide: allergic rhinitis affects between 10%–30% of the world's population. Sensitization (IgE antibodies) to foreign proteins in the environment is present in up to 40% of the world's population. Sensitization rate to one or more common allergens among school children is approaching 40%–50%.[27]

Allergies are primarily caused by pollen, food, dust mites, or animals. Pollen allergies peak in the spring season. Some suffer from allergies to seafood, peanuts, and other foods. Allergies are characterized by symptoms such as itches, swellings, redness of the skin, sneezes, runny nose, and watery eyes.

Scientists have been looking for solutions by delving into the mechanism of action of allergies. In 1937, the Swiss-born Italian pharmacologist Daniel Bovet discovered antihistamine, which blocks the neurotransmitter histamine. The antihistamines Phenbenzamine and Pyrilamine were subsequently launched in 1942 and 1944 respectively. Bovet was, for such, awarded the 1957 Nobel Prize in Physiology or Medicine.[28] Antihistamines of the first generation primarily worked by inhibiting H1 receptors. However, because of their high lipophilicity, these drugs can easily cross the Blood-Brain Barrier (BBB) and cause related side effects, including drowsiness, sedation, dizziness, and memory loss.

Diphenhydramine, under the brand name of Benadryl® among others, is a well-known first-generation antihistamine that is still widely used even today. George Rieveschl,[29] a chemistry professor at the University of Cincinnati in the U.S., invented this medication in the early 1940s. He worked with pharmaceutical company called Parke-Davis to test the compound and the company licensed the patent from him. Diphenhydramine is also widely used for other indications, including motion sickness, seasickness, and antiemetics under the equally famous brand name Dramamine®.

---

27 https://www.aaaai.org/About/News/For-Media/Allergy-Statistics
28 https://www.nobelprize.org/prizes/medicine/1957/bovet/biographical/
29 https://www.nytimes.com/2007/09/29/business/29rieveschl.html

1) Terfenadine

Under the brand name Seldane® among others, manufactured by Hoechst Marion Roussel (now part of Sanofi), was the first product of non-drowsiness antihistamine, also known as the second-generation antihistamines. Compared to its predecessors, its side effects are significantly reduced, owing to its reduced ability to penetrate the BBB. Terfenadine acts as antagonist of the histamine H1 receptor. It is a pro-drug, metabolized in the liver by the enzyme cytochrome P450 3A4. Terfenadine was synthesized in 1973 as a potential tranquilizer. In 1985, Terfenadine was launched in the U.S. and became the best-selling prescription drug in the same year. It once held 80% of the market for allergy drugs.[30] Unfortunately, Terfenadine was withdrawn from worldwide markets in 1997 due to the risk of a particular type of disruption of the electrical rhythms of the heart.[31]

2) Loratadine and Desloratadine

Schering-Plough, headquartered in New Jersey, the U.S., had a history of discovering, manufacturing, and marketing antihistamines prior to its 2009 acquisition by Merck.[32] It developed Chlor-Trimeton®, which was widely used in cold and allergy medications, first as a prescription drug, then as an Over the Counter (OTC) medication after 1976.

Frank Villani,[33] a chemist at Schering-Plough, slightly improved the first-generation product and developed Piriton®. This medication had a longer half-life and required one daily dosage only. It witnessed tremendous success, and up till present, the active ingredient Chlorphenamine is still widely used in OTC medications for anti-influenza and allergy medications.

Frank Villani discovered Loratadine in 1970 and filed patents in 1980. According to the patent, Loratadine displayed negligible to no sedative effect. Loratadine

---

30 https://www.wsj.com/articles/SB883416339908496500

31 https://www.latimes.com/archives/la-xpm-1997-01-14-mn-18552-story.html

32 https://www.nytimes.com/2009/03/10/business/10drug.html

33 https://www.newjerseyhills.com/mr-frank-j-villani-81/article_a54b93e8-47bd-5cab-8aee-915821ec2aef.html

was finally approved by the U.S. FDA in 1993 under the brand name Claritin®.

The U.S. FDA relaxed its regulations on prescription drug advertising in 1997.[34] In 1998 and 1999, Schering-Plough spent US$322 million on marketing, far more than any other drug brands. Claritin® increased its annual sales from US$1.4 billion in 1997 to US$2.6 billion in 2000. It accounted for nearly 30% of Schering-Plough's annual revenues.[35]

To address the patent cliff created by the patent expiry of Claritin®, Schering-Plough developed Clarinex® and marketed it in 2002. Clarinex® is the active metabolite ingredient of Claritin®. Both patients and academia had debate and doubts over this strategy.[36] Regardless, Claritin® and Clarinex® made Schering-Plough one of the biggest pharmaceutical companies in the world.

In March 2009, Merck and Schering-Plough announced merger at the deal worth of US$41 billion.[37]

4. CASE FOUR: BLOOD THINNERS

Blood is primarily composed of red blood cells, white blood cells, platelets, and plasma. Red blood cells are responsible for transporting oxygen to various organs. White blood cells are responsible for resisting the invasion of bacteria and viruses. Platelets are a sticky and minute component of the blood, accounting for approximately 1% volume and aids in blood clotting, a process called coagulation. Hemophilia is a condition in which individuals lose their ability to clot blood. These patients require regular coagulation factor injections. However, excessive platelets cause blood thickening, which can result in blood clots and other cardiovascular and cerebrovascular diseases. Population groups particularly susceptible to Deep Vein Thrombosis (DVT) include passengers of frequent long-haul flights since they are confined to a small space for an extended period

---

34 https://www.fda.gov/regulatory-information/search-fda-guidance-documents/
    prescription-drug-marketing-act-pdma-requirements-questions-and-answers

35 https://www.nytimes.com/2001/03/11/magazine/the-claritin-effect-prescription-
    for-profit.html

36 https://www.science.org/content/blog-post/claritin-and-clarinex

37 https://www.fiercepharma.com/pharma/merck-nabs-schering-plough-41-1b-deal

and are sedentary, or professionals that stand for a long period of time such as pharmacists. The term "embolus" refers to a blood clot that migrates through the body's circulatory system and causes obstruction. It is a potentially fatal symptom. Blood thinners are the first line of defense and treatment of thrombosis and embolism.

1) Heparin

Discovered in 1916 by Jay McLean, then a second-year medical student and his mentor professor William Henry Howell,[38] at Johns Hopkins University in the U.S.,[39] Heparin is one of the earliest known classic drugs which is still widely used today. It is safe and effective. Heparin is a glycosaminoglycan anticoagulant found in nature which is stored as a must in hospitals for use in hemodialysis, vascular surgery, and organ transplantation, among other procedures. Additionally, it is used in stents, which have saved the lives of millions of patients. Heparin is manufactured by a variety of pharmaceutical companies worldwide, which means no single brand dominating the market. Moreover, it must be administered via injection.

2) Warfarin

Warfarin is a widely used antithrombotic medication in clinical practice such as clinical anticoagulation therapy. Unlike Heparin, it is an oral medication. It works by inhibiting the activation of vitamin K-dependent coagulation factors (II, VII, IX, X). Although it is inexpensive and taken orally, there are significant concerns about the medication's efficacy and safety. Its efficacy can be influenced by a variety of food, medications, and diseases. To ensure the treatment's safety and effectiveness, frequent blood sampling and monitoring are required in addition to constant dosage adjustments. Pharmaceutical companies have developed Novel Oral Anticoagulants (NOACs) in response to Warfarin's numerous shortcomings. Such drugs do not require frequent monitoring for adverse effects. As a result, the use of Warfarin is gradually narrowed in the treatment of certain indications. At

---

38 http://www.nasonline.org/publications/biographical-memoirs/memoir-pdfs/howell-william.pdf

39 https://www.nature.com/articles/nrcardio.2017.171

the same time, the two most widely used NOACs are Eliquis® by Btistol Myers Squibb (BMS) and Pfizer, and Xarelto® by Johnson & Johnson (J&J) and Bayer.

3) Apixaban

Under the brand name Eliquis® and among others, Apixaban works by reversible direct inhibiting free or clot-bound factor Xa. Factor Xa catalyzes the conversation of prothrombin to thrombin, the final enzyme in the coagulation that is responsible for fibrin clot formation. It was approved for medical use in the European Union in May 2011. On December 28, 2012, Apixaban was approved to reduce the risk of stroke and systemic embolism in patients with nonvalvular atrial fibrillation. Atrial fibrillation is the most common type of irregular heartbeat, which affects approximately 5.8 million people in the U.S. alone and resulting in a five times greater risk of stroke.[40] In August 2014, Apixaban was approved by the U.S. FDA for the treatment of Deep Vein Thrombosis (DVT) and Pulmonary Embolism (PE), and the reduction in the risk of recurrent DVT and PE following initial therapy. In the U.S. alone, 900,000 patients are affected by DVT and PE every year.[41] It comes in 2.5mg or 5mg tablets, taken twice daily.

Bristol Myers Squibb (BMS) discovered the medication. Pfizer and BMS jointly developed and commercialized it, they shared profits and losses equally. Eliquis® crossed the blockbuster threshold in 2015 and ranked the fourth among the world's best-selling drugs in 2020, with annual sales totaling US$9.17 billion.

4) Rivaroxaban

Under the brand name Xarelto® and among others, Rivaroxaban was initially developed by the German company Bayer. In the U.S., it is marketed by Janssen Pharmaceuticals (part of Johnson & Johnson). It is selective direct factor Xa inhibitor with an onset of action of 2.5 to 4 hours. Rivaroxaban was patented in 2007, and approved for medical use by Health Canada, and the European

---

40 https://www.pfizer.com/news/press-release/press-release-detail/update_with_multimedia_u_s_fda_approves_eliquis_apixaban_to_reduce_the_risk_of_stroke_and_systemic_embolism_in_patients_with_nonvalvular_atrial_fibrillation

41 https://www.pmlive.com/pharma_news/fda_approves_bmspfizers_eliquis_in_dvt_and_pe_594363?SQ_DESIGN_NAME=2

Commission in September 2008. In November 2011, Rivaroxaban was approved to reduce the risk of stroke and systemic embolism in patients with nonvalvular atrial fibrillation.[42] In May 2015, Xarelto® was approved in China by the China Food and Drug Administration.[43] The most popular dosage forms are 15mg or 20 mg tablets, taken twice daily. On March 25, 2019, Bayer and J&J settled the U.S. Xarelto® litigation for US$775 million over side effects lawsuits.[44] In 2021, Xarelto® netted in US$7.5 billion for Bayer and J&J globally.

5) Aspirin

The German chemist Felix Hoffman[45] was credited with synthesizing Aspirin while working at Bayer.[46] It has been used for more than a century as an analgesic, antipyretic, and anti-inflammatory substance. It is considered one of the classic drugs in the history of pharmaceutical industry. The mechanism of action of this drug was not fully understood until 1971, when John Robert Vane revealed that acetylsalicylic acid worked by inhibiting the formation of prostaglandin. In 1976, he discovered the Prostacyclin prostaglandin, which expanded the smallest blood vessels, inhibited the formation of platelets that caused blood to coagulate. His works led to new treatments for heart and blood vessel disease and introduction of ACE inhibitors. John Vane shared the 1982 Nobel Prize in Physiology or Medicine with Sune Bergstrom, and Bengt Samuelsson for their discoveries concerning prostaglandins and related biologically active substances.[47]

In 1985, the Secretary of Health and Human Services of the U.S. announced to the public that a daily dose of 81 mg Aspirin would help prevent secondary

---

42 https://www.jnj.com/media-center/press-releases/fda-approves-xarelto-rivaroxaban-to-reduce-the-risk-of-stroke-and-systemic-embolism-in-patients-with-nonvalvular-atrial-fibrillation

43 https://www.fiercepharma.com/pharma-asia/bayer-s-xarelto%C2%AE-approved-china-for-stroke-prevention-patients-non-valvular-atrial

44 https://www.reuters.com/article/us-bayer-xarelto-idUSKCN1R61O8

45 https://www.bayer.com/en/history/felix-hoffmann

46 https://www.sciencehistory.org/historical-profile/felix-hoffmann

47 https://www.nobelprize.org/prizes/medicine/1982/vane/facts/

myocardial infarction.[48] Since then, Aspirin can be seen in medications boxes in every household. However, in 2022, New Guidance from the U.S. Preventive Services Task Force suggested people aged 60 or above not to take low-dose Aspirin daily to prevent cardiovascular events, like strokes and heart attacks.[49]

6) Ticlopidine and Clopidogrel

Sanofi, the French pharmaceutical giant founded in 1973, was a spin-out of Elf Aquitaine (an oil company). However, its pharmaceutical business rooted back to Labaz group, a pharmaceutical company formed in 1947. In 1999, Sanofi merged with Synthelabo, and formed Sanofi-Synthelabo.[50] In 2004, it again merged with Aventis at the price of US$65 billion and renamed into Sanofi-Aventis.[51] This deal attracted great attentions and debates from both industry and academia.

Chemist Jean-Pierre Maffrand[52] assisted to transform Sanofi into a world-class pharmaceutical company with the introduction of two blood thinners, Ticlid® and Plavix®. Both are tablets and taken orally.

Sanofi chose to partner with Bristol-Myers Squibb (BMS) in the U.S. in 1993 to develop, and market clopidogrel. The U.S. was and still is the largest pharmaceutical market in the world, despite its 330 million population out of 8 billion people worldwide.[53] BMS was the number four drug company in the world at that time, with leading position in cardiovascular area. BMS discovered the first Angiotensin Converting Enzyme (ACE) inhibitor Captopril, under the brand name Capoten®,[54] in 1978 for hypertension. By 1992, Capoten® was a

---

48 https://academic.oup.com/book/40666/chapter-abstract/348352142?redirectedFrom=fulltext

49 https://www.npr.org/sections/health-shots/2022/04/26/1094881056/older-adults-shouldnt-start-a-routine-of-daily-aspirin-task-force-says

50 https://www.pmlive.com/pharma_news/a_look_back_at_sanofis_merger_with_synthelabo_477146

51 https://www.wsj.com/articles/SB108291923112092711

52 https://www.sciencedirect.com/science/article/pii/S1631074812000938

53 https://worldpopulationreview.com/countries/united-states-population

54 https://www.bms.com/trademarks.html

blockbuster drug.

Clopidogrel differs from Aspirin in its mechanism of action, allowing it to selectively inhibit platelet ADP receptors and thus inhibiting platelet aggregation. The results of a large-scale clinical trial, CAPRIE[55] manifested that Clopidogrel is more effective than Aspirin and shows fewer gastrointestinal side effects. Sanofi and BMS filed an application in the U.S. in April 1997 and were granted priority review. Clopidogrel was approved for marketing in the U.S. in November 1997 under the brand name Plavix® for the prevention and treatment of high platelet aggregation-related heart, brain, and other arterial circulatory disorders. Plavix® was prescribed to over three million patients in the U.S. alone within its first year of approval. It was the second best-selling drug in the world in 2007 and reached annual sales of US$6.6 billion in 2009.

7) Prasugrel

Prasugrel was developed by Japan-based Daiichi Sankyo. In the U.S., it was marketed in cooperation with Eli Lilly. Its brand name is Effient® in the U.S., and Efient® in the European Union (EU).[56] It was approved for use in the EU in February 2009, in the U.S. in July 2009. This is a "me-too" drug that has a better safety performance than Clopidogrel.

8) Ticagrelor

Developed by AstraZeneca, it was approved for medical use in the EU in December 2010, in the U.S. in July 2011, under the brand name Brilinta®.

AstraZeneca invested the estimated US$5.4 billion in sunk costs in Brilinta®. Unfortunately, it is unlikely to turn a profit on this blood thinner as the generic version expected to hit the market in 2024.[57]

---

55 https://www.thelancet.com/journals/lancet/article/PIIS0140-6736(96)09457-3/fulltext

56 https://www.ema.europa.eu/en/medicines/human/EPAR/efient

57 https://www.fiercepharma.com/pharma/astrazeneca-has-dumped-billions-into-brilinta-r-d-but-will-it-ever-pay-off

One research on global antiplatelet sales trend with a focus on P2Y12 inhibitors from 2008 to 2018 by the University of Hong Kong concluded: despite the fact that current guidelines and recommendations prefer Ticagrelor and Prasugrel for the prevention of atherothrombotic complications in patients with an acute coronary syndrome, Clopidogrel remains the highest sales volume among the P2Y12 inhibitors from 2008 to 2018.[58]

5. CASE FIVE: ANALGESIC, ANTIPYRETIC, ANTI-INFLAMMATORY, AND COX-2 INHIBITORS

Pain has accompanied mankind through history since the documentation, and it is frequently associated with fever and inflammation. Traditionally, there had been two classes of medications for painkillers.

Non-Steroidal Anti-Inflammatory Drugs (NSAIDs)[59] was one of the classes. Willow Bark,[60] which dates to 1500 B.C., is a source of Aspirin. Felix Hoffmann, a chemist from German Bayer, prepared and synthesized it in 1897. The early versions of Aspirin had gastrointestinal side effects, which had since been properly addressed by enteric coating at a later stage. Another example, Ibuprofen, is a common active ingredient in OTC medicines for children's colds and used to treat menstrual cramps as well. Other medications in this class include Naproxen, Indomethacin, Diflunisal, and Diclofenac Sodium were popular medications used for arthritis.

Another class was Acetaminophen,[61] or Paracetamol, which is marketed under the brand name Tylenol® among others. Acetaminophen is one of the most common active ingredients in medicines against the cold, and it comes in a variety of dosage forms for children such as drops and syrups. The U.S. FDA recommended that adults consume no more than 4 grams per day due to the risk of liver damage from overdosing. In the history of pharmaceutical industry, Johnson & Johnson (J&J)'s prompt handling of the Tylenol® safety incidents had

58 https://www.sciencedirect.com/science/article/pii/S2666602221000185

59 https://my.clevelandclinic.org/health/drugs/11086-non-steroidal-anti-inflammatory-medicines-nsaids

60 https://www.healthline.com/health/willow-bark-natures-aspirin#forms-and-dose

61 https://www.drugs.com/acetaminophen.html

been regarded as a case study of public relations crisis, which greatly boosted J&J's brand image.[62]

There are two types of cyclooxygenases, COX-1, and COX-2. COX-1 protects the gastric mucosa and promotes vasodilation; COX-2 is found primarily in inflammatory cells and tissues and is activated during acute inflammation. As a result, anti-inflammatory drugs that target COX-2 are both safer and more effective. COX-2 inhibitors shifted the therapeutic paradigm, Celebrex® by Pfizer and Vioxx® by Merck. Both have gone on to become blockbuster drugs but ended in unequal fates.

1) Celecoxib

The first COX-2 inhibitor was discovered and developed by Searle, part of Monsanto, where Phillip Needleman[63] oversaw the COX-2 research project. Celecoxib was approved by the U.S. FDA on December 31, 1998,[64] initially for osteoarthritis and rheumatoid arthritis. Monsanto and Pfizer co-promoted the drug under the brand name Celebrex®. It is in capsule form and taken twice daily orally. In 2003, Pfizer merged with Pharmacia, which merged previously with Searle,[65] Pfizer therefore indirectly owned Celebrex®. It reached annual sales US$2 billion in 2006 and remained to be one of the Pfizer's top selling drugs until 2014 when generics moved into the market.[66]

2) Rofecoxib

The second COX-2 inhibitor was discovered and developed by Merck & Co. In the U.S., it was approved in 1999 under the brand name Vioxx® for the treatment of osteoarthritis and rheumatoid arthritis.

---

62 https://knowledge.wharton.upenn.edu/article/tylenol-and-the-legacy-of-jjs-james-burke/

63 http://www.nasonline.org/member-directory/members/15537.html

64 https://www.news-medical.net/health/Celecoxib-History.aspx

65 https://www.pfizer.com/about/history/pfizer_pharmacia

66 https://www.fiercepharma.com/sales-and-marketing/pfizer-s-billion-dollar-celebrex-patent-loss-has-mylan-actavis-revving-up

From its launch to identification of its potential risks, around 80 million people were prescribed with Rofecoxib. In 2003, Vioxx® reached US$2.5 billion in annual sales, contributing to 11% of Merck's total annual revenue.[67]

Surprisingly, the VIGOR clinical trial conducted by Merck exemplified that when compared to patients taking Naproxen,[68] the incidence of cardiac infarction in Vioxx® patients increased 4-fold, despite the risks of gastrointestinal toxicity less than Naproxen. As a result, Vioxx® was voluntarily recalled from the market on September 30, 2004, only five years after launching. It was one of the most widely used drugs ever to be withdrawn from the market. Consequently, Merck's market value dropped by US$30 billion in just a few months, heavily damaging its reputation as a trustable and innovative company. In 2007, Merck settled Vioxx® lawsuits for US$4.85 billion.[69] Both sides claimed victory, and Merck did not admit causation or fault. In 2016, Merk reached US$830 million settlement in the long-running litigation, finally put this seemingly never-ending saga into close.[70]

3) Valdecoxib

Valdecoxib was developed by Pharmacia and received the U.S. FDA approval on November 20, 2001[71] for the treatments of arthritis and menstrual cramps. Pharmacia jointly promoted Bextra® with Pfizer. Later in 2003, Pfizer and Pharmacia merged into one group.

On April 7, 2005, Pfizer voluntarily withdrew Valdecoxib on recommendation by the U.S. FDA, citing the increased risks of myocardial infarction and severe skin

---

67   https://www.thepharmaletter.com/article/merck-co-pulls-2-5-billion-year-blockbuster-drug-vioxx-on-safety-fears

68   https://www.npr.org/2007/11/10/5470430/timeline-the-rise-and-fall-of-vioxx

69   https://www.reuters.com/article/us-merck-vioxx-settlement-idUSL0929726620071109

70   https://www.fiercepharma.com/regulatory/merck-reaches-830m-settlement-long-running-vioxx-litigation

71   https://www.thepharmaletter.com/article/update-pharmacia-gets-us-approval-for-celebrex-follow-up-bextra

allergies.[72] On September 2, 2009, the U.S. Department of Justice announced that Pfizer agreed to plead guilty and paid US$2.3 billion for fraudulent marketing of Bextra®, the largest healthcare fraud settlement in its history.[73]

Amongst all COX-2 inhibitors, only Celebrex® remains on the global market. Nonetheless, before the advent of biopharmaceuticals for the treatment of autoimmune diseases, COX-2 inhibitors were the standard for arthritis treatment.

6. CASE SIX: SSRIS AND ANTIDEPRESSANTS

Depression is a common mental illness worldwide, estimated 3.8% of the global population is affected which is equivalent to 280 million people, including 5% among adults, and 5.7% among adults aged above 60. In severe cases, depression can lead to suicide. Each year, over 700,000 people die due to suicide and suicide is the fourth leading cause of death in 15-29 years old.[74]

During the 1950s, Tricyclic Antidepressants (TCAs) were the most used drug class for depression. While they relieved symptoms, few undesirable side effects occurred such as drowsiness, constipation, and blurred vision. Mono-Amine Oxidase Inhibitors (MAOIs) was another class of commonly used medications; however, they raised the serious risk of drug-drug interactions.

In 1988, the American pharmaceutical company Eli Lilly introduced Fluoxetine, a new class of antidepressant known as Selective Serotonin Receptor Inhibitors (SSRIs), which was safer and more effective than the previous categories. Three scientists, Ray Fuller, David Wang, and Bryan Molloy were well-known for the discovery of Fluoxetine, under the brand name Prozac®, as well as Cymbalta®, Zyprexa® and Strattera®.[75] SSRIs give good drug stability, long half-life and exhibit fewer side effects, particularly to the central nervous system, thus are used as alternative treatment options for bulimia nervosa or Obsessive-Compulsive Disorder (OCD).

---

72 https://money.cnn.com/2005/04/07/news/fortune500/bextra/

73 https://www.justice.gov/opa/pr/justice-department-announces-largest-health-care-fraud-settlement-its-history

74 https://www.who.int/news-room/fact-sheets/detail/depression

75 https://newsinfo.iu.edu/news/page/normal/20732.html

1) Fluoxetine

Under the brand name Prozac® and Sarafem®, among others, Fluoxetine first appeared and launched in Belgium in 1986, then in the U.S. in 1987. It is used for the treatments of major depressive disorder, OCD, bulimia nervosa, panic disorder, and premenstrual dysphoric disorder.

In 1992, it reached global annual sales of US$1 billion, and became a blockbuster drug. In 1999, Prozac® was named one of the "Products of the Century" by the *Fortune* magazine.[76] Its sales peaked at US$2.3 billion before the patents expired in 2003, accounting for one-third of Eli Lilly's total annual revenue. Eli Lilly became a leader in the therapeutic of antidepression because of this drug, and its followers Cymbalta®, Zyprexa®, and Strattera®. It is taken orally once a day in capsule formulation.

Sarafam® is a higher dosage form of Fluoxetine, but only taken weekly. It was introduced to the market by Eli Lilly, the move, however, greatly harmed its reputation as an innovative company. The diagnostic category of Premenstrual Dysphoric Disorder (PMDD) was controversial when it was proposed in 1987. Eli Lilly was criticized for inventing a disease to make money and seeking ways to continue making money from existing drugs.[77] There were debates over aggressive marketing and PMDD by academics and public.[78]

2) Paroxetine

Under the brand name Paxil® or Seroxat® among others, Paroxetine was developed by the British pharmaceutical company GlaxoSmithKline (GSK). In 1992, it was approved by the U.S. FDA for major depressive disorder, social anxiety disorder, premenstrual dysphoric disorder, premature ejaculation, and hot flashes due to menopause. Its peak sales reached US$2.7 billion, becoming a blockbuster drug. Its patents in the U.S. expired in 2006. On July 2, 2012, the U.S.

---

76 https://www.nature.com/articles/nrd1821

77 https://www.washingtonpost.com/archive/politics/2001/04/29/renamed-prozac-fuels-womens-health-debate/b05311b4-514a-4e65-aaa5-434cb2934271/

78 https://californiahealthline.org/morning-breakout/sarafem-marketing-barrage-sparks-debate-over-pmdd/

Department of Justice announced that GSK pled guilty and paid US$3 billion to settle unlawful promotion of certain medications, failure to report certain data, and alleged false price reporting practices. The resolution was the largest-ever penalty by a drug company.[79]

3) Sertraline

Invented and developed by scientists at Pfizer, Sertraline was approved in the U.K. in 1990, and in the U.S. in 1991, under the brand name Zoloft®. Zoloft® is the first-line treatment for depression and OCD, it may work better for some subtype of depression. It reached the peak sales of US$3.3 billion in 2005.[80] Sales of Zoloft® plugged 80% after its patent expired in 2006.[81]

4) Citalopram and Escitalopram

Forest Laboratories (Forest) was founded in 1956 as a small laboratory service company. In 1967, it became a public company via an initial public offering. Later, Howard Solomon became the chief executive officer of the company. Forest licensed in the U.S. rights of three central nervous system medications from the renowned Danish company, Lundbeck. Both Forest and Lundbeck were relatively small players, these two antidepressants gave them fame in the pharmaceutical industry.

Citalopram had been the best-selling antidepressant in eight European countries before its approval in the U.S. in July 1998, under the brand name of Celexa®.[82] One of its key features was low tendency for drug-drug interactions. In August 2002, the enantiomer version, called Escitalopram, received the approval from the U.S. FDA, under the brand name of Lexapro®. At height, Celexa® won nearly 10% of the American antidepressant market. Forest started the campaign by pricing the drug lower than Prozac® and Zoloft®, and by paying the doctors to

---

79   https://www.justice.gov/opa/pr/glaxosmithkline-plead-guilty-and-pay-3-billion-resolve-fraud-allegations-and-failure-report

80   https://money.cnn.com/2006/04/04/news/companies/antidepressants/

81   https://www.wsj.com/public/resources/documents/info-pp-070420-Zoloft.html

82   https://www.thepharmaletter.com/article/citalopram-launched-in-usa-by-forest

prescribe the drugs.[83] Both Celexa® and Lexapro® were blockbuster drugs.

On July 1, 2014, Actavis announced the completion of Forest acquisition in cash and equity at the valuation around US$28 billion.[84]

5) Venlafaxine

Under the brand name Effexor® among others, Venlafaxine was the first antidepressant in the class of drugs known as Serotonin-Norepinephrine Reuptake Inhibitors (SNRIs). It was originally developed and marketed by Wyeth Pharmaceuticals, until Pfizer merged with Wyeth in 2009. Venlafaxine was first approved in the U.S. for the treatments of general depressive disorders in 1993, and later its extended-release version Effexor XR® received approval in 1997. Both formulas contain the same active ingredient, Venlafaxine.

Effexor® became a blockbuster drug, and sales peaked at US$3.9 billion dollars in 2008. The U.S. FDA approved its first generic version in 2010, and Effexor® sales plummeted to US$440 million in 2013. Today, only Effexor XR® and generic Effexor® are available in the market.

6) Common side effects of SSRIs

Two common side effects of SSRI antidepressants are suicide and sexual dysfunction. The U.S. FDA requires all antidepressants to carry a black box warning on possible suicide risk. The likely sexual dysfunctions include loss of libido, lack of vaginal lubrication, and erectile dysfunction, etc.

7) Summary

As mentioned in one of *Barron's* articles, for the pharmaceutical industry, the 1990s was the decade of depression.[85] Between 1991 and 2001, the global sales of antidepressants rose 10-fold, to over US$11 billion, making this sector the

---

83 https://www.barrons.com/articles/SB1021686885462923040?tesla=y

84 https://www.allergan.ca/en-ca/news/list/actavis-completes-forest-laboratories-acquisition

85 https://www.barrons.com/articles/SB1021686885462923040?tesla=y

drug industry's main profit driver in the decade. Simultaneously, the U.S. became Prozac Nation.[86]

7. CASE SEVEN: HMG-COA REDUCTASE INHIBITORS AND HYPERLIPIDEMIA

Hyperlipidemia is defined as an abnormally high level of lipids in the blood, which results in an increase in the blood's viscosity. These lipids will deposit on the lining of the blood vessel wall and progressively form tiny clumps that obstruct the blood vessels, resulting in slowed or stopped blood flow. It can lead to coronary heart disease, cerebral apoplexy, renal arteriosclerosis, and a variety of other induced disorders, depending on the clumping location. Blood lipids are formed mostly of cholesterol, triglycerides, and lipids, with the former two being the most clinically relevant. According to the World Health Organization, hyperlipidemia is a major disease burden in both developed and developing countries, as it is a risk factor for ischemic heart disease and strokes. In 2008, the global prevalence rate of the total cholesterol among adults was 37% for males, and 40% for females.[87]

There are many classes of medications for the treatment of hyperlipidemia, each with its own mechanism of action, but the most successful and widely recognized class is statins.[88] Statins revolutionized the prevention and treatment of coronary heart disease. Numerous large-scale clinical trials have demonstrated that statins can particularly lower cholesterol synthesis. The mechanism of action is by inhibition of HMG-CoA reductase, which results in a decrease in Low-Density Lipoprotein Cholesterol (LDL-C) levels in the blood.

Michael Brown and Joseph Goldstein of the University of Texas were awarded the 1985 Nobel Prize in Medicine or Physiology "for their discoveries concerning the regulation of cholesterol metabolism".[89] Their achievement led to new principles for treatment and prevention of atherosclerosis. They also won the

---

86   https://www.fiercepharma.com/sales-and-marketing/pfizer-forest-and-lilly-dominate-top-10-ranking-of-psych-meds

87   https://www.who.int/data/gho/indicator-metadata-registry/imr-details/3236

88   https://www.nhs.uk/conditions/statins/

89   https://www.nobelprize.org/prizes/medicine/1985/summary/

1985 Albert Lasker Basic Medical Research Award for their work.[90]

A Japanese biochemist, Akira Endo, discovered the relationship between fungi and cholesterol biosynthesis. In 1973, he isolated Compactin from Penicillium citrinum, and began the proceeding research on Statins.[91] His contribution was recognized globally, Endo won the 2006 Japan Prize,[92] the 2008 Lasker Clinical Medical Research Award, and others.[93]

1) Lovastatin and Simvastatin

Merck isolated Lovastatin in 1978 and commenced clinical trials in 1980. The U.S. FDA approved Lovastatin only ten months after its application, near record time, under the brand name Mevacor® in 1987. This was a semi-synthetic Statin and held significance as the first-in-class drug.

Due to large patients population, ease of usage, and the influence of direct-to-consumer advertising, Lovastatin earned estimated US$260 million in its first year in the market, the highest sales ever for any prescription drugs by then. In 1990, Mevacor® dominated the anti-lipemic market in both the number of prescriptions dispensed and the total retail pharmacy sales in the U.S.

Bristol-Myers Squibb and Daiichi Sankyo Pharmaceutical co-developed a "me-too" drug for Pravastatin, under the brand name Pravachol® in the U.S. It is less effective at reducing cholesterol than Lovastatin, but priced 5–10% less, making it more accessible to managed care plans and price-sensitive patients. It captured 20% of the statin market shares in 1994.[94]

Merck scientists continued to work on a better agent, eventually Simvastatin

---

90 https://laskerfoundation.org/michael-brown-and-joseph-goldstein-receptor-mediated-endocytosis/

91 https://www.japanprize.jp/data/prize/2006/e_2_achievements.pdf

92 https://www.japanprize.jp/en/prize_prof_2006_endo.html

93 https://laskerfoundation.org/winners/statins-for-lowering-ldl-and-decreasing-heart-attacks/

94 https://www.bostonfed.org/publications/regional-review/2003/quarter-1/too-much-of-a-good-thing-can-be-bad.aspx

which is more effective than both Lovastatin and Pravastatin, came to the market at the end of 1991 under the brand name Zocor®. With both Zocor® and Mevacor®, Merck had been dominating this market for the next six years. In 1997, Merck claimed that Zocor® was the market leader in terms of global sales in cholesterol lowering market.

In 2004, the U.K. Department of Health announced the permission Over the Counter (OTC) of low dose, 10-mg formulation of Simvastatin to people at the moderate risk of coronary heart disease. *The Lancet* published its view and believed that OTC statins approval was a bad decision for public health.[95]

2) Atorvastatin

Bruce Roth at Warner-Lambert synthesized an experimental compound in 1985, later called Atorvastatin. In 1996, Warner-Lambert signed a co-developed agreement with Pfizer, then an important, middle-sized company originated from Brooklyn, New York.

Lipitor® was approved in the U.S. market in 1997. Warner-Lambert and Pfizer took aggressive marketing strategies to promote Atorvastatin: 1) selling it cheaper than even less-potent statins, 2) training 2,000 sales representatives to pay visits to over one million doctors in the first year after launch, 3) offering millions of free samples as a temptation to write prescriptions, 4) direct-to-consumers marketing to encouraging patients to pressure doctors. The Lipitor® launch was so successful that it even took the two companies by surprise, and they had to acquire a new factory to meet the demand.

In 1999, Warner-Lambert agreed with a friendly takeover by American Home Products.[96] Pfizer responded the next day with a move unseen in the drug industry, a hostile, yet ultimately successful bid at the valuation of US$90 billion.[97] The Federal Trade Commission of the U.S. gave consent order to allow this

---

95 https://www.thelancet.com/action/showPdf?pii=S0140-6736%2804%2916284-3

96 https://www.pharmaceuticalonline.com/doc/warner-lambert-and-american-home-products-to-0002

97 https://www.pharmaceuticalonline.com/doc/pfizer-warner-lambert-agree-to-90-billion-mer-0001

merger by asking them to divert some pharmaceutical and healthcare products.[98]

Lipitor® became the first mega blockbuster in history with annual global sales over US$10 billion. From 1996 to 2012, Atorvastatin contributed US$125 billion, making it the best-selling medication of all time.

3) Rosuvastatin

Under the brand name Crestor®, Rosuvastatin was launched by the Europe-based AstraZeneca in the U.S. in 2003. It is more potent and has longer half-life. AstraZeneca budgeted US$1 billion for the promotional campaign in the first-year launch.[99] In 2015, Crestor® was AstraZeneca's bestselling drug, achieved global sales of US$5 billion out of the company's annual revenue of US$23.6 billion. It quickly plummeted in 2016 due to its generic version drugs.[100] In 2020, AstraZeneca sold the former blockbuster Crestor® for an upfront payment of US$320 million to a German pharmaceutical company Gruenenthal.

4) Afterwards

After two decades of Statins, the Proprotein Convertase Subtilisin/Kexin 9 (PCSK9) was identified for the first time in 2003. It took less than a decade from conceptualizing its mechanism of action on an atomic level to the actual launch of the corresponding drug. Clinical trials have demonstrated that PCSK9 inhibitors can significantly lower blood LDL-C levels. The European Medicines Agency (EMA) and the U.S. FDA approved Amgen's Repatha® for marketing in July and August 2015 respectively.[101] Praluent®, which was co-developed by Sanofi and Regeneron, was also approved for marketing by the U.S. FDA and EMA in

---

98 https://www.ftc.gov/legal-library/browse/cases-proceedings/0010059-pfizer-inc-warner-lambert-company

99 https://www.thelancet.com/journals/lancet/article/PIIS0140-6736(03)14669-7/fulltext

100 https://www.nytimes.com/2016/07/21/business/generic-crestor-wins-approval-dealing-a-blow-to-astrazeneca.html

101 https://www.amgen.com/newsroom/press-releases/2015/08/fda-approves-amgens-new-cholesterollowering-medication-repatha-evolocumab

July and September 2015 respectively.[102] Unlike Statins, which are chemically synthesized drugs, PCSK9 is a monoclonal antibody with a high degree of specificity. However, biologics are more expensive to produce, their intrinsic high price tag negatively impacted sales. Nonetheless, treatment guidelines recommend PCSK9 inhibitors or combined statins as viable options for patients with statin intolerance or those who show elevated LDL-C levels after being administered a high dose of statins.

8. CASE EIGHT: RESPIRATORY DISEASES AND ADVAIR®

Respiratory diseases are among the most prevalent diseases in the world, with Chronic Obstructive Pulmonary Disease (COPD), asthma, and allergic rhinitis being the most common.

According to the World Health Organization, COPD is the third leading cause of death worldwide, causing 3.23 million deaths in 2019, over 90% of deaths aged under 70 occur in low- or middle-income countries.[103] The incidence rate tends to increase in countries with high smoking rates and aging populations. There is no cure for COPD currently, however, early diagnosis and treatment are important to slow the progression of symptoms and reduce the risks.

Asthma is a major non-communicable disease, affecting both adults and children, and it is the most common chronic disease among children. Asthma affected estimated 262 million people in 2019 and caused 455,000 deaths.[104] With proper disease management and inhaled medications, asthma can be controlled, and patient can enjoy a normal and active life. Most asthma-related deaths occur in low and middle-income countries, where diagnosis and treatment are still major challenges.

Allergic rhinitis, or hay fever, is triggered by allergens, which can be found both indoors and outdoors. It happens when we breathe in substances we are allergic

---

102 https://investor.regeneron.com/news-releases/news-release-details/regeneron-and-sanofi-announce-fda-approval-praluentr-alirocumab/

103 https://www.who.int/news-room/fact-sheets/detail/chronic-obstructive-pulmonary-disease-(copd)

104 https://www.who.int/news-room/fact-sheets/detail/asthma

to, and the nose becomes inflamed and swollen. Sinusitis is inflammation of the lining inside the sinuses, which can be acute and chronic. Allergic rhinitis and sinusitis are interrelated to each other, and both are non-communicable diseases.[105] Allergic rhinitis has been increasing in prevalence over the last few years, with close ties to the environment, seasons, and various allergens.

Clinical treatment is primarily based on inhaled medications which are available in four dosage forms: nebulizers, dry powders, aerosols, and nasal sprays. Among them, dry powder is the most widely used formulation.

Throughout the history of developing respiratory inhalers, GSK, AstraZeneca, and Germany-based Boehringer Ingelheim have maintained unmatched positions. Ventolin®, GSK's first asthma medication, was launched in 1969. Alupent®, Atrovent®, and Berodual® were launched on the market by Boehringer Ingelheim in 1961, 1975, and 1980 respectively. In the 1990s, the most frequently prescribed medications were AstraZeneca's Pulmicort®, GSK's Beconase AQ®, and Flovent®. These medications all contain a single active ingredient, and their auxiliary respiratory device is relatively simple.

1) Advair Diskus® / Seretide®

Developed and invented by GSK, Advair Diskus® is ranked among the top ten global bestselling drugs before its generic version was introduced to the market. In an article from *Fierce Pharma*, Advair® was ranked the fourth best-selling U.S. drugs over 25 years.[106]

Advair® was first approved for medical use in the U.S. in 2000. The first generic version by Mylan was only approved 19 years later in 2019.[107] The following factors made Advair® very different to copy: 1) Advair® is the combination of Fluticasone and Salmeterol, two active ingredients at fixed dosage form.

---

105 https://www.who.int/news-room/questions-and-answers/item/noncommunicable-diseases-allergic-rhinitis-and-sinusitis

106 https://www.fiercepharma.com/pharma/from-old-behemoth-lipitor-to-new-king-humira-u-s-best-selling-drugs-over-25-years

107 https://www.fda.gov/news-events/press-announcements/fda-approves-first-generic-advair-diskus

Fluticasone is one type of corticosteroid used as anti-inflammatory, which decreases the inflammation in the lung and helps breathing. Salmeterol, a long-acting beta agent, treats constriction of the airways. 2) its unique and patented device, Diskus™ built another entry barrier for generic versions. 3) it is a combination of drug and device. For any generic version, it must meet both requirements. 4) only until 2013 did the U.S. FDA issued a draft product-specific guidance on Advair®, providing bioequivalence, and formulations and device considerations.

Mylan claimed that the company invested US$700 million to produce these generic versions, and its stock was up 7% upon the approval news.[108] Mylan's Wixela® was given approval as "substitutable" generic, which means pharmacists can recommend it to patients as a replacement of Advair®. The Israeli company, Teva, had previously introduced a Fluticasone and Salmeterol combination called AirDuo RespiClick® but it did not gain the substitutable status.[109]

As Advair® struggled, GSK partnered with Innoviva, and developed Trelegy Ellipta®, which was the first once-daily dosing, single inhaler, and triple therapy for the treatment of COPD in appropriates patients. It was approved by the U.S. FDA in 2017.[110] In September 2020, the U.S. FDA added new asthma indication to it.[111] However, EMA refused the asthma label indication expansion.[112] Trelegy® contains Vilanterol, Umeclidinium, and Fluticasone.

Respiratory inhalers are progressing from single active ingredient, two active ingredients to three active ingredients in one inhaler. However, the most used ones are still these drugs developed many years ago.

---

108 https://www.pharmaceutical-technology.com/news/mylan-advair-generic-approval/

109 https://www.reuters.com/article/us-teva-pharm-ind-asthma-idUSKBN17M2K8

110 https://www.gsk.com/en-gb/media/press-releases/trelegy-ellipta-approved-as-the-first-once-daily-single-inhaler-triple-therapy-for-the-treatment-of-appropriate-patients-with-copd-in-the-us/

111 https://www.drugs.com/history/trelegy-ellipta.html

112 https://www.pharmaceutical-technology.com/news/ema-gsk-trelegy-asthma-refusal/

9. CASE NINE: PDE5I AND ERECTILE DYSFUNCTION

Erectile Dysfunction (ED) is defined by persistent inability to obtain or maintain an erection to have a satisfying sexual life for at least three months. It is difficult to study the epidemiology of ED. According to a 2019 survey in Massachusetts, the U.S., the prevalence rate amongst men aged 40 to 70 is 52%; in China, an ED survey in 11 cities reveals that men aged over 40 are at high risk, with an incidence rate exceeding 40%.

The aetiology of ED is very complex, with contributing factors such as psychological discomfort (anxiety, tension, and sadness), cardiovascular diseases (hypertension, hyperlipidaemia), diabetes, and depression and other diseases caused by neurological problems, abnormal testicular development or injury, and adverse drug reactions. ED brings along negative impacts on self-esteem, personal relationships, and potentially leads to family discords. Unfortunately, there is no cure for ED at present.

Before the emergence of Viagra®, ED received little attention for three reasons. 1) it involved personal privacy, and it was embarrassing for patients to open on this issue. 2) there had been no effective and safe methods to help treat erectile dysfunction. The mostly used methods were unsafe and painful, including direct injection into the shaft of the penis, complex surgery, vacuum-assisted penis pumps, or prosthetic implants. 3) people did not have sufficient understanding on ED.

Robert Furchgott, Ferid Murad, and Louis Ignarro shared the 1998 Nobel Prize in Physiology or Medicine "for their discoveries concerning nitric oxide as a signalling molecule in the cardiovascular system".[113] This discovery played a critical part in the understanding of mechanism of action of this class of medication.

1) Sildenafil

Under the brand name Viagra® and among others, Sildenafil was launched in

---

113 https://www.nobelprize.org/prizes/medicine/1998/press-release/

the U.S. on March 27, 1998.[114] Dubbed as the "the little blue pill", it marked a milestone in the history of pharmaceutical industry, people considered it as revolutionary move for sex lives.[115] The discovery was simply a coincidence by the chemists in American company Pfizer's research facility in Kent, the U.K. The original study was for the treatment of hypertension and angina pectoris. After clinical phase one, researchers found out that it had little effect on angina, but it could induce penile erections. Pfizer patented this drug in 1996. This is a typical example of drug re-positioning.

Sildenafil enhances the effect of nitric oxide by inhibiting Phosphodiesterase type 5 (PDE-5), which is responsible for degradation of cyclic Guanosine Monophosphate (cGMP) in the corpus cavernosum. When sexual stimulation causes local release of nitric oxide, inhibition of PDE-5 by Sildenafil causes increased levels of cGMP in the corpus cavernosum, resulting the smooth muscle relaxation and blood inflow. Sildenafil is taken orally, it is a diamond-shaped, 50mg tablet originally. Later, 25mg and 100mg tablets and injection came to the market. The U.K. was the first country to make a particular brand "Viagra Connect" and it has been sold over the counter since early 2018.[116]

The publicity and attention that Viagra® received were unprecedented in the history. One of the most famous public figures, Bob Dole, the former republican head at the U.S. Senate, was on TVs, newspaper etc. to promote Viagra®, even though this is a prescription medication.

Viagra® is to be taken 60 minutes before sexual activity. It will not result in an erection without sexual stimulation. However, there is no clinical evidence that it works as libido. The effective rate was about 70%, and 50% of people stopped using it within one year.[117] People who are on nitrates medication should not use any PDE-5 inhibitors, because serious drug interactions may occur.

---

114 https://www.history.com/this-day-in-history/fda-approves-viagra

115 https://www.theguardian.com/lifeandstyle/2017/dec/03/viagra-25-years-sex-virility-drug-male-impotence

116 https://www.fiercepharma.com/marketing/otc-viagra-pfizer-snags-nod-for-non-prescription-sales-uk

117 https://www.theguardian.com/science/2019/jun/09/race-to-replace-viagra-patents-erectile-dysfunction-drug-medical-research-cialis-eroxon

The sales of Viagra® reached US$1 billion in the first year after its launch, making it a blockbuster. At the time of approval, Viagra® experienced the fastest initial sales growth for any prescription product launch. It was sold over US$1 billion annually for 17 years, with peak sales of US$2.1 billion in 2012.[118]

2) Tadalafil

Like Viagra®, the discovery of Cialis® was made by somewhat an accident, as ICOS tried to work on a compound for cardiovascular disease. ICOS's original partner, Glaxo, chose to focus on other drugs and lapsed the agreement with ICOS in 1996.[119] In 1998, Eli Lilly paid ICOS an upfront fee of US$75 million and formed a 50/50 joint venture to share costs and profits. Tadalafil was approved by the U.S. FDA in 2003, under the brand name of Cialis®. In July 2005, Cialis® was marketed in over 100 countries, resulting in US$1 billion global sales milestone, becoming a blockbuster drug.[120] In 2007, Eli Lilly bought out ICOS's interest in Cialis® for US$2.3 billion. In 2011, its indication also expanded into treatment of benign prostatic hyperplasia, caused by an enlarged prostate gland, and resulting in frequent need to urinate.

Cialis® has a prolonged duration about 36 hours, and it is not affected by moderate alcohol consumption. It was originally approved as 10mg and 20mg tablets.

According to Nielsen,[121] Eli Lilly spent US$248 million in 2014 to promote Cialis® directly to consumers, making it the most expensive advertising drug in the world. Based on IMS Health's data, the sale of Cialis® sale in its largest market, the U.S., was up 88% from 2010 to 2014, even as the number of prescriptions only raised up 8%. That means Eli Lilly raised the price over the period, which was a very common pricing strategy for pharmaceutical companies.

---

118 https://www.pharmaceutical-technology.com/comment/viagra-competition-q3-sales/

119 https://www.ibj.com/articles/57284-for-cialis-glory-days-are-over

120 https://investor.lilly.com/news-releases/news-release-details/lilly-icos-cialisr-tadalafil-reaches-1-billion-global-sales

121 Nielsen is a renowned advertising firm specializing in drug industry.

Time magazine included Cialis® on the list of the Best Inventions of 2003.[122] In 2005, Cialis® became a blockbuster drug. Since its inception, it has generated more than US$20 billion for Eli Lilly.

10. AUTHOR'S INSIGHTS

i.   Blockbuster drugs become a key indicator of success in the pharmaceutical industry.

ii. Successful pharmaceutical companies must possess either first-in-class or best-in-class innovative drugs.

iii. A pre-requisite for ranking as one of the Global Top 20 Pharma was to have strong market position in at least one therapeutic area.

iv. Countries such as Germany, Japan, the U.K., and the U.S. were leaders in chemical drugs paradigm owing to their solid foundations in the chemical industry.

v.   Successful "head-to-head" clinical trials are critical, especially if you want to stand out in the same class of medications. However, it is also a double-sided sword.

vi. The therapeutic effect of a drug does not necessarily signify its commercial success. The latter was powered by strong marketing capabilities and massive spending on advertising.

vii. Mergers & Acquisitions are proven to be the only option for pharmaceutical companies to quickly expand their market position.

viii. Globalization drives cross-borders market expansion and mergers.

ix. Most of these blockbuster drugs are widely prescribed for mass populations, for general medicine, or called primary care. They all revolutionize their therapeutic areas and create a new paradigm within each class.

x.   "Patent cliff" creates panic for pharmaceutical executives, resulting in decisions with dubious consequences, such as mega-merger, off-labelling marketing, medication pricing, etc.

---

122 https://content.time.com/time/specials/packages/article/ 0,28804,1935038_1935081_1935220,00.html

Chapter *2*

The Biopharmaceutical Paradigm

1. FOREWORD

This chapter introduces the 40-year history of biotech and biopharmaceuticals from the 1980s to the present. Compared with chemical drugs, the technology and manufacturing process of biopharmaceuticals are more important and complicated as they directly affect cost and quality of the final products.

What is biotech? Biotech is a short form for "biotechnology", which is a generic umbrella term covering technology related to living organisms, it also refers to the studies and research related to biology. Biotech makes medicines from living organisms, such as living cells.

What is the difference between a biotech company and a biopharmaceutical company?

- A biotech company is one still in research, pre-clinical or clinical stage and none of its products has been approved by any national regulatory agency for commercialization yet.
- A biopharmaceutical company is one with a product approved for commercialization, also referred as biopharma. Biopharmaceuticals are the result of biological processes. For example, Amgen was defined as a biotech company at first until its product EPO was sold in the market, it is then called a biopharmaceutical company.

What is the difference between a pharmaceutical company and a biopharmaceutical company?

- Traditionally, pharmaceutical companies develop medicine from chemicals or natural products. Biopharmaceutical companies make medicines from living organisms, such as cells and viruses.

On January 25, 2009, Pfizer announced a landmark merger and acquisition of Wyeth at US$50.19 per share with a total transaction amount of approximately

US$68 billion. The combined company would be one of the most diversified companies across the globe, creating the world's premier biopharmaceutical company.[123] This is the first time that a leading industry player identified itself as a biopharmaceutical company. This is also the crucial milestone that shifted the industry paradigm from chemical to biopharmaceutical.

Depending on the innovative properties, biopharmaceuticals can also be categorized into novels and biosimilars.

A comparison table between chemical drugs and biopharmaceuticals is as follows:

	Chemical Drugs	Biopharmaceuticals
Molecular Size	Small, 500–900 Da	Large, 4,000–140,000 Da
Structure	Well characterized	Complexed 3D structure
Production	Less impacted by process	Synthesized by living cells, difficult in reproducibility and scaling
Stability	High	Low
R&D Time	Short, 3–5 years for typical generic drug	Long, 8–10 years for typical biosimilar
R&D Cost	Low, US$1–5 million for typical generic drug	High, US$100–200 million for typical biosimilar
Manufacture Process	Simple	Complex

Below sets out the success and development of industry leaders, including Genentech and Amgen, as well as how other large pharmaceutical companies such as Eli Lilly, Novo Nordisk, Pfizer, Merck, and Abbott Laboratories entered this field.

The development of protein replacement therapies began in 1982 and reached a standstill in 2015. By contrast, therapeutic proteins encoded by antibodies have entered a Golden Era of development because of technological advancements.

Orthoclone OKT3® was the world's first monoclonal antibody drug approved

---

123 https://www.fiercebiotech.com/biotech/pfizer-to-acquire-wyeth-creating-world-s-premier-biopharmaceutical-company

for treatment of immune rejection following organ transplantation in 1986. This paved the way for the incorporation of antibody-based drugs into modern medicine. From the late 20th century to 2015, the number of antibody drugs approved by the U.S. FDA and the European Union every five years was relatively consistent. However, between 2015 and 2020, the number of antibody drugs approved for marketing in Europe and the U.S. increased more than double. In terms of the composition of the approved innovative drugs, antibody drugs accounted for more than half of all biopharmaceuticals approved for the first time, surpassing their previous proportion of 27% between 2010 and 2014.

2. PROTEIN REPLACEMENT THERAPIES

1) Case One: Insulin

Three kingdoms: Eli Lilly, Novo Nordisk, Sanofi

In 1921, Frederick Banting and Charles Best at the University of Toronto, Canada, designed series of experiments to identify how the pancreas was involved in carbohydrate metabolism. They published their work based on findings from the past 40-50 years and demonstrated that the pancreas was key for what is commonly known as type 1 diabetes. Their study has also led to the identification of insulin.[124] Banting and J.J.R. Macleod were awarded the 1923 Nobel Prize in Physiology or Medicine for their work in identifying insulin.[125] They shared this prize with their colleagues, Charles Best and James Collip. This is a historic milestone because there had been no treatment for diabetic patients before insulin was discovered.

In 1922, George Clowes, the Director of Biomedical Research at Eli Lilly, an Indianapolis-based pharmaceutical company, met the researchers from the University of Toronto and negotiated an agreement for the mass production of insulin. In 1923, Eli Lilly began selling the first commercially available insulin under the trade name of Iletin® in the U.S. market. Insulin, being one of the most important drugs in the history, positioned Eli Lilly as one of the major

---

124 https://www.nature.com/articles/d42859-021-00004-3
125 https://www.nobelprize.org/prizes/medicine/1923/summary/

pharmaceutical manufacturers globally.

While in Europe, the Denmark-based Nordisk Insulin Laboratory began mass-producing insulin in 1923 and exported it to various European countries bordering Denmark. Similarly, having derived its insulin technology from the same source, Novo Therapeutics was able to expand at a rapid pace.

Since the 1920s, insulin production had been requiring an enormous quantity of animal pancreas, generally from cows and pigs. The public also quickly recognized its short-acting nature and inconvenient usage.

Additionally, protein yields extracted from natural sources were low, as evidenced by the allergic reactions in patients. Porcine insulin was a frequently used first-generation insulin due to its minor divergence in amino acid sequence when compared to human insulin. However, it may elicit immune responses in patients, resulting in subcutaneous fat atrophy or hyperplasia at the injection site. Over the next 40 years, Nordisk, Novo, and Eli Lilly have each overcome technical obstacles in the development of long-acting insulins. For instance, Nordisk developed Neutral Protamine Hagedorn (NPH) insulin in the 1930s, and Novo manufactured insulin zinc in 1952.

In 1978, scientists at City of Hope[126] and Genentech developed a method for producing biosynthetic human insulin using recombinant DNA (rDNA) technology in a unique multiple-step process. As a result, Genentech was the first biotech company to be able to successfully use this technology and produce high-purity recombinant human insulin using E. Coli.

Genentech was founded in 1976 by Robert A. Swanson, a venture capitalist, and Professor Herbert Boyer, the inventor of rDNA technology. This cross-disciplinary partnership serves as an exemplar of how ventures can flourish the biotech industry, it has been a role model for generations of scientists and venture capitalists. The advent of rDNA technology truly ushered in a "paradigm shift" in biopharmaceuticals and fostered the evolution of a "biopharmaceutical era".

---

126 https://www.cancer.gov/research/infrastructure/cancer-centers/find/
      beckmancityofhope

Eli Lilly signed an agreement with Genentech to use rDNA technology in making human insulin commercially available. Eli Lilly had been an industry expert in the purification, laboratory testing and clinical trials of human insulin. rDNA had the potential to produce unlimited quantities of human insulin using bacteria. On October 28, 1982, after a record time of mere five months of review, the U.S. FDA approved Humulin®, the first biosynthetic human insulin product and the first approved medical product of any kind derived from rDNA technology.[127] Back then, the average approval time for new drugs was 30.5 months.

Humulin® has structural similarity to naturally secreted human insulin and has lower allergic reactions when compared to animal insulin. rDNA insulin is regarded as the second-generation insulin.

The production costs of Humulin® have decreased significantly due to technological advancements, thereby allowing the second-generation insulins to take the place of their predecessors. In 1989, the two Danish companies Novo and Nordisk announced their merger to establish Novo Nordisk A/G, marking the birth of another influential global leader in the insulin market.[128]

In 1985, Novo launched the first insulin pen injector.[129] It has improved the quality of life for diabetic patients by avoiding the trouble of using glass syringes and enhancing the accuracy of self-administration. NovoPen® family has significantly improved the position of Novo Nordisk in the global market.

On June 9, 2000, the European Medicines Agency approved the launch of the long-acting modified insulin under the brand name Lantus® by Sanofi-Aventis Germany. It is used once daily via injection under the skin. This medicine was also approved in the U.S. market in 2000. Lantus® made the European-based Sanofi the third leader in the global insulin market.

Since the 1990s, the public has been acquiring a deeper understanding of the structure and properties of insulin. Additionally, with technological advancement,

---

127 https://www.acsh.org/news/2019/10/28/record-time-fda-approval-human-insulin-1982-when-genetic-engineering-came-age-14362

128 https://www.novonordisk.com/about/our-heritage.html

129 https://www.novonordisk.com/about/insulin-100-years.html

it has become possible to modify the properties of drugs by altering the structure of natural human insulin through modifying the insulin peptide bonds, altering the specific amino acid sequences on natural human insulin, and manipulating the polymerization tendency. The resulted refined insulins are referred to as the third-generation insulins, as they more closely mimic the natural insulin secretion mechanism in human bodies in terms of the onset of action, peak times, and duration of action. There are various types of insulin available in the market today, which are called analogues, including ultra-long-acting, fast-acting, short-acting, and even inhalable insulin.

The insulin industry is dominated by three undisputable behemoths: Eli Lilly, Sanofi, and Novo Nordisk. They together produce 71% of human insulin and 92% of insulin analogues worldwide.[130]

Sanofi has a longstanding history in the insulin market, with its leading products Lantus®, Toujeo® (long-acting insulin glargine) and Soliqua®. However, on December 9, 2019, its CEO, Paul Hudson, announced a significant change in the future strategy of the company: to terminate diabetes research and focus more on oncology and genetic therapy products.[131]

Inhalable insulin and Pfizer's failure

San Francisco-based Nektar Therapeutics developed a technology to convert insulin into inhalable small particles, which was subsequently licensed to Pfizer. The Ireland-based Alkermes has also developed an inhaled insulin delivery device licensed to Eli Lilly.

Lipitor® contributed US$13 billion in 2006, accounting for 27% of Pfizer's annual revenue. However, its patent was due to expire in 2011 in the U.S. market. Therefore, Pfizer was desperate to find a successor and it held great expectations for Exubera®. Pfizer spent US$1.3 billion to acquire all of Sanofi-Aventis' shares

---

130 https://www.iqvia.com/insights/the-iqvia-institute/reports/understanding-insulin-market-dynamics-in-low-and-middle-income-countries

131 https://www.pharmaceutical-technology.com/comment/sanofi-terminates-diabetes-research-following-struggle-to-remain-competitive/

to gain full control over Exubera®.[132] Finally, Exubera® was approved by the European authorities in 2006, followed by the U.S. FDA one day after. It is the first inhaled insulin to be granted marketing approval. More importantly, it offers a novel route of insulin administration ever since the 1920s.[133]

Dramatically, in October 2007, after 11 years of efforts and only one year since its approval, Pfizer announced that it would cease its production and take US$2.8 billion charges. It was one of the most expensive failures and losses ever in the history of the pharmaceutical industry. Pfizer disclosed that Exubera® only generated revenue of US$4 million in the last quarter,[134] shocking the entire industry and sparking heated debates in both the industry and academia.

In principle, human lungs offer a route for the delivery of peptides which can be rapidly absorbed due to the large respiratory area. This delivery also provides painless administration and is especially suitable for patients with needle phobia. Common side effects include hypoglycemia, increased risks of respiratory infection, coughs and other conditions related to respiratory tract. Yet, a 2007 systematic review concluded that inhaled insulin appears to be effective, but not better than injected short-acting insulin in therapeutic effect despite its much higher additional cost. In the U.K., the cost is reimbursed by the National Health Service (NHS) only for people with needle phobia. In the U.S., it is not reimbursed by any insurers. Other related debates include the design of device, marketing practices, physician detailing, acceptance level of patients, etc.

Another question was raised about Pfizer's striking lack of research productivity. It spent US$55 billion in ten years to deliver nine medicines, and only one became a blockbuster generating sales of more than US$1 billion annually.

Alarming the failure of Exubera®, Novo Nordisk and Eli Lilly halted similar research on inhaled insulin. However, these setbacks did not deter Mannkind

---

132 https://www.fiercebiotech.com/biotech/pfizer-to-pay-1-3-billion-for-sanofi-s-exubera-rights

133 https://www.fiercebiotech.com/biotech/fda-approves-pfizer-s-inhaled-insulin

134 https://www.forbes.com/2007/10/18/pharmacuticals-pfizer-exubera-biz-sci-cx-mh-1018pfizer.html?sh=199d56cc1040

Corporation,[135] and research on its inhaled insulin product Afrezza®, which later received approval from the U.S. FDA in June 2014.[136] Nearly a year after launching Afrezza®, Paris-based Sanofi returned the rights to the drug to its developer, Mannkind.

A comparable product from Highland Pharmaceuticals, Dypreza®, was also approved in 2013 and 2016 in Europe and the U.S. respectively. However, Dypreza® was recalled in 2018 due to safety concerns regarding long-term insulin absorption through the lungs.

2) Case Two: Erythropoietin (EPO)

Rise of a biopharmaceutical from patent disputes: Amgen, and Johnson & Johnson

Erythropoietin is a glycoprotein hormone secreted by the kidneys that are responsible for red blood cell production in the body, synthesized through rDNA technology and collectively referred to as Erythropoiesis Stimulating Agents (ESAs). ESAs are mainly used to treat anemia, which is commonly associated with kidney failures or cancer treatments.

Amgen, one of the most successful biotech companies in history, was established in 1980, and headquartered in Thousand Oaks, California. George Rathmann was the co-founder and the first Chief Executive Officer (CEO) until 1988. Gordon Binder was the second CEO and the author of a book titled *Science Lessons*, an illustration of Amgen's early years in terms of its discovery, Initial Public Offering (IPO), and legal disputes.

Fu-Kuen Lin and his team at Amgen identified and isolated the EPO gene on chromosome 7 from 1.5 million human genome fragments. He chose to clone it using cells derived from the ovary of a Chinese hamster. His novel approach has laid groundwork for the company's first drug.

---

135 https://mannkindcorp.com/

136 https://investors.mannkindcorp.com/news-releases/news-release-details/mannkind-corporation-announces-fda-approval-afrezzar-novel-rapid

After an eight-year investment of US$300 million, Amgen finally received the U.S. FDA approval for the first recombinant human erythropoietin product, Epoetin alfa, under the brand name of Epogen® among others for the treatment of anemia associated with chronic kidney failure. It was an orphan drug.

Interestingly, EPO was also marketed under the brand name of Procrit® among others, which meant the same drug under a different trade name, pursuant to a product license agreement. Amgen was in the despite needs of funding and licensed its oncology indication to Johnson & Johnson.

The *Fortune* magazine named Epogen® as the number one product of 1989,[137] a year in which Amgen's profits rose more than triple to US$19.1 million, and in 1990, its profits nearly doubled to US$34.3 million. Epoetin alfa constituted the single drug with the greatest expenditure incurred by the U.S. Medicare system for years. Epogen® was the most successful biotech drug in history then, a solid proof that a biotech firm could commercialize a billion-dollar product.

Aranesp® was approved on September 17, 2001. It is a glycosylation analogue of EPO containing two additional N-linked carbohydrate chains. Aranesp® has a longer serum half-life and a higher potency than Epogen®. However, there were not significantly clinical differences in safety and efficacy.[138]

Amgen took a massive marketing approach, including Direct-to-Consumer (DTC) television advertisements, to promote the use of EPO in treating fatigue associated with cancer treatments. In 2006, Aranesp® was the 6th bestselling drug in the world, with US$5 billion. Together, Epogen® and Aranesp® contributed US$7.1 billion in sales, constituting 50% of Amgen's total revenue in 2006 and dominating this market sector.

Nature Biotechnology Editorial has expressed concerns over Aranesp® safety and has criticized Amgen's aggressive promotion of EPO in the oncology market, which might jeopardize its renal therapeutics market.[139]

---

137 https://pharmaphorum.com/views-and-analysis/a_history_of_amgen/

138 https://www.cancernetwork.com/view/no-clinical-difference-between-epoetin-and-darbepoetin

139 https://www.nature.com/articles/nbt0407-363

3) Case Three: Human Growth Hormone (hGH)

Two rivals: Genentech and Novo Nordisk

Growth Hormones (GH) or somatotropin, also known as human Growth Hormone (hGH), are produced by the pituitary gland in the human brainstem and have a diameter of approximately one centimeter, sizeable to a broad bean. GH is a peptide hormone that stimulates growth, cell reproduction and cell regeneration in humans and other animals. For instance, it controls children's height growth, stimulates lipolysis, promotes protein synthesis, and regulates carbohydrate metabolism and electrolyte balance.

There is a total of 51 amino acids in human insulin, whilst hGH has 191 amino acids. Hence, from a technical standpoint GH is more difficult to produce than insulin. In the early days, Genentech was led by scientists who ambitiously viewed GH and its development as a high-priority pipeline in research, even though the market for GH was only a fraction of that of insulin. Moreover, GH is distinct from insulin in the sense that the raw materials derived from animals are incompatible with humans. Therefore, hGH drugs must be derived exclusively from humans. Prior to the advent of recombinant growth hormones, GH proteins could only be obtained from the human pituitary glands. Hence, the research and treatment would involve donations from the deceased or patients requiring pituitary removal as part of their treatment for other diseases. Due to the small size of the pituitary glands, secretion of hGH and thus extraction of which are limited, the overall supply was very much scarce. In 1960, the U.S. established the National Pituitary Agency to oversee the donation of pituitary glands for distribution. Genentech's venture was motivated to tackle the problem of hGH scarcity. More significantly, from start to finish, the hGH project's success demonstrates the biotech industry's progress.

Firstly, Genentech developed a model for biotech financing that incorporated down payments, milestone payments, and sales commissions. Genentech encountered cash shortage during the early R&D stages of hGH and sold its future interest and rights to KabiVitrum, a pharmaceutical company owned by the Swedish government as well as the world's leading commercial supplier of hGH. GH research was still in its infancy. Hence, to mitigate the risk of enormous transactional losses due to potential failure, KabiVitrum proposed a transfer model that distributed cooperative payments funds from the research stage to commercialization. In specific, KabiVitrum would cash an initial payment to Genentech once both parties had reached an agreement, followed by periodic payments to Genentech in accordance with agreed targets until the project is successfully completed. KabiVitrum obtained exclusive rights outside of the U.S. and shared the U.S. market with Genentech. The two signed the very first agreement between a biotech company and a pharmaceutical company in 1978.

Secondly, Genentech pioneered the use of E. Coli to express pure and biologically active growth hormones. This is the first time a cell line was used to express whole proteins. Genentech published an article in 1979 in *Nature* about the use of E. Coli in the production of hGH. Genentech overcame significant technical obstacles in the process, building the foundation for future biotech development projects.

Thirdly, from the governmental regulatory perspective, Genentech's experience reflected the difficulties and obstacles associated with drug registration approval. Genentech's first-generation product was Protropin®, which not only had lower therapeutic effects than naturally extracted growth hormones, but also posed an increased risk of immune rejection, and thus was not approved by the U.S. FDA for a long period of time. Between the end of 1982 and 1985, Prion viruses were discovered in naturally derived GH, they were subsequently banned in the U.S. market.

On October 18, 1985, the U.S. FDA approved Genentech's Protropin® (somatrem for injection), for children with growth hormone deficiency. It was the first biotech drug to be manufactured and marketed by a biotechnology company. Its production ceased in 2004, and market demand shifted toward its successor, Nutropin® (Somatropin for injection).[140]

As of 2005, the recombinant growth hormone product in the U.S. market included Eli Lilly's Humatrope®, a recombinant human growth hormone product free of excessive amino acid sequences. The U.S. FDA designated it as an orphan drug for the treatment of children with hGH-deficiency and Eli Lilly enjoyed

---

140 https://www.gene.com/media/news-features/25th-anniversary-of-first-product-
approval

exclusivity on it. Therefore, Genentech had to pursue other indications, such as growth retardation in children caused by chronic renal insufficiency, Turner syndrome, and adult growth hormone deficiency. Off-label use also gained popularity as GH indications expanded, for example, in the anti-aging field.

Norditropin® from Novo Nordisk quickly captured a sizable share of the U.S. market. The reason was that Novo Nordisk did not simply provide a medicinal product; it also included an additional product to maximize the effectiveness of drug administration. The injection pen for Novo Nordisk's GH is well-received by children due to its thinner needle and less painful injection. NovoPen® is also welcomed by parents given its ease of use, accurate measurement, and flexible storage conditions. It could be stored without refrigeration for several weeks. Moreover, in collaboration with the medical reimbursement system, dedicated teams have been assigned to customers, thereby significantly improving the user experience, and resulting in increased popularity.

Other hGH products included Genotropin® from Pfizer, and Saizen® from Germany-based Merck Serono.

3. THERAPEUTIC PROTEINS – ANTIBODIES

The success of antibody drugs is not coincidental. In comparison to the conventional chemical drugs, antibody drugs exhibit a higher affinity and specificity for target proteins and a lower level of off-target activity, making them an attractive alternative to chemical drugs. It is quite common that chemical drugs have liver and kidney toxicity associated with metabolic processes. On this basis, antibody-based therapeutics are expected to have superior therapeutic effects with fewer adverse effects.

Antibody drugs have a higher molecular weight and much more complex structure than protein replacement drugs. These compounds frequently require post-translational modifications, one of which is the glycosylation of the structure. The glycosylation of antibody drugs has a significant effect on their efficacy and half-life. As a result, production cell lines such as E. Coli are incapable of producing and handling antibody drugs which are complex and glycosylated. It was not until 1975 that scientists Kohler and Milstein[141] successfully characterized a hybridoma cell line capable of producing monoclonal antibodies, allowing for study, and manufacturing, resulting in rising of antibody drugs. Kohler and Milstein were awarded the 1984 Nobel Prize in Physiology or Medicine.[142]

There were two primary challenges in the discovery and development of antibody drugs: 1) the screening of proteins that could be developed and used as a safe and effective medicinal drug, and 2) the future viability of cost-effective manufacturing scaling-up capability. To meet the large-scale manufacturing requirements, global institutions and scientists actively explored possible manufacturing systems, resulting in numerous approvals granted between 2006 and 2015. Since 2015, mammalian cell cultures have gradually gained prominence, and the development of antibody drug production systems has matured, heralding the start of antibody drug development.

At the forefront of global biotech sector, Genentech made significant contributions to antibody drugs development by successfully bringing multiple classic drugs to the global market, several of which have consistently ranked in the top ten global annual pharmaceutical list, for instance, Rituxan®, Herceptin® and Avastin®. Roche acquired 60% of Genentech's shares in 1990 for US$2.1 billion, rescuing the company from financial distress caused by the severe cash flow shortage due to large R&D investments. Genentech continued to launch blockbuster drugs over the next two decades, demonstrating their huge business value, and resulting in Roche's complete acquisition of Genentech for US$46.8 billion in 2009,[143] over 30 times valuations in 20 years.

1) Case One: Anti-CD20 antibody drugs, Rituxan® in treating blood cancers

Rituximab, under the brand name Rituxan® among others, is a chimeric monoclonal antibody from mice and humans that targets CD20. The CD20 protein is a surface antigen present on B cells and was first discovered by Lee

---

141 https://www.nature.com/articles/ni.3608

142 https://www.nobelprize.org/prizes/medicine/1984/press-release/

143 https://www.fiercebiotech.com/biotech/roche-makes-offer-to-acquire-all-outstanding-shares-of-genentech-for-us-89-00-per-share

Nadler in the Dana-Farber Cancer Institute.[144] Rituximab's mechanism of actions include three major independent mechanisms: 1) antibody dependent cellular cytotoxicity, 2) complement medicated cytotoxicity, and 3) apoptosis.

In 1997, Rituxan® was approved for medical use as the first monoclonal antibody for the treatment of cancer.

Ronald Levy[145] invented Rituximab and co-founded IDEC Pharmaceuticals, based in San Diego, California. William Rastetter, the CEO of the company, repositioned the product development strategy and set IDEC on the path to the development of the monoclonal antibody targeting CD20 antigen on cancerous B-cells. The result was Rituxan®, which received regulatory approval seven years later. The U.S. patent for the drug was issued in 1998 and expired in 2016 and the patent in Europe expired in 2013.

In June 2003, IDEC merged with Boston-based Biogen with the transaction amount of US$6.6 billion. It was a merger of equals, and each company owned a blockbuster drug.[146] IDEC jointly marketed Rituxan® with Genentech. Meanwhile, Biogen faced concerns on heavy reliance on one single drug, Avonex® for the treatment of multiple sclerosis. IDEC shareholders owned 50.5% of the shares of the combined company, and Biogen owned 49.5%. IDEC's long-term CEO became the executive chairman.

The industry has widely adopted the strategy of stratifying orphan drug indications first, then facilitating market penetration and clinical data collection before expanding to other indications. For example, Rituxan® was initially approved as an orphan drug for the treatment of refractory B-cell non-lymphoma Hodgkin's with CD20 positivity. To date, Rituxan® has been approved for treating all types of non-Hodgkin lymphomas, chronic lymphocytic leukaemia, rheumatoid arthritis, and others. In 2016, Rituxan® hit US$8.58 billion in global peak sales.

---

144 https://www.cancerresearch.org/scientific-advisory-council/lee-nadler

145 http://www.nasonline.org/member-directory/members/29324.html

146 https://www.marketwatch.com/story/idec-biogen-in-merger-highlighting-their-reversals

On November 28, 2018, the U.S. FDA approved the first biosimilar Truxima®️ for the treatment of adult patients with non-Hodgkin's lymphoma.[147] Biosimilars caused the sales of Rituxan®️ to fall and became the 10th best-selling drug in 2019, with global sales of US$6.54 billion, and to 17th in 2020, with global sales of US$4.52 billion.[148]

Genentech demonstrated outstanding pipeline development capabilities. A study of Rituximab in Multiple Sclerosis (MS) with superior results was published in the *New England Journal of Medicine* (NEJM) in 2008, which sparked the interest in B cell depletions MS and led to the extensive off-label use of Rituximab to treat primary and relapsing MS. Rituximab is a mouse protein and is immunogenic in humans. Therefore, Genentech decided to focus on a similar but humanized monoclonal antibody Ocrelizumab for the treatment of MS. It targets CD20 marker on B lymphocytes which binds to an epitope that overlaps with the epitope to which Rituximab binds.

Ocrelizumab was granted Breakthrough Therapy Designation, Fast Track Designation, and Priority Review. It received marketing approval from the U.S. FDA under the brand name of Ocrevus®️ among others for the treatment of MS in March 2017 and in the European Union in January 2018. It was the first drug to treat primary progressive MS. Ocrevus®️ commercial success was extraordinary, with sales reaching US$6.41 billion in 2020.

2) Case Two: Anti-VEGF antibodies

Avastin®️ and biosimilars

Bevacizumab, under the brand name of Avastin®️ among others, is a fully humanized anti-VEGF monoclonal antibody that works by inhibiting the growth of blood vessels through binding to Vascular Endothelial Growth Factor A (VEGF-A), subsequently cutting nutrient supply to tumors and eliciting an anti-tumor effect.

---

147 https://www.fda.gov/drugs/fda-approves-truxima-biosimilar-rituxan-non-hodgkins-lymphoma

148 https://www.fiercepharma.com/special-report/top-20-drugs-by-2020-sales

Napoleone Ferrara[149] is an Italian American molecular biologist, who joined the University of California, San Diego. At Genentech, he discovered VEGF. His findings facilitated the clinical development of the first angiogenesis inhibitor, Bevacizumab, which prevents the growth of new blood vessels into solid tumors. This discovery became part of the standard treatment for many tumors. His work has also led to the development of Ranibizumab under the brand name Lucentis® among others, a highly effective drug for prevention of vision loss in intraocular neovascular disorders. In 2010, Ferrara was awarded the prestigious Lasker Prize for his discovery.[150]

Avastin® was first approved by the U.S. FDA in 2004 for the treatment of advanced colon cancer, later approved for advanced lung cancer in 2006 and kidney and brain (glioblastoma) cancers in 2009. It was also approved for metastatic breast cancer in 2008 under the accelerated approval program under which, a drug may be approved based on results of clinical data suggesting its important clinical benefit. However, additional information is required to verify the data.[151]

Avastin® has consistently performed well in the market since its launch. Its sales declined from US$7.1 billion in 2014 to US$6.6 billion in 2017, but rose to US$7.0 billion in 2018, primarily due to the higher sales in China. In 2018, its sales accounted for roughly 15% of Roche's total pharmaceutical revenue.[152]

Avastin® market exclusivity period ended in 2019. On September 14, 2017, Amgen and Allergan received the U.S. FDA approval for their biosimilar Mvasi® which is the first biosimilar in the U.S. for the treatment of cancers.[153] Roche initiated lawsuits against the partnership. In July 2019, Amgen and Allergan launched Mvasi® at a 15% discount on Avastin® brand price. Pfizer launched

---

149 http://www.nasonline.org/member-directory/members/20012448.html

150 https://laskerfoundation.org/winners_name/ferrara-napoleone/

151 https://www.fda.gov/drugs/postmarket-drug-safety-information-patients-and-providers/avastin-bevacizumab-information

152 https://www.nasdaq.com/articles/roches-$7-billion-drug-sales-at-risk-2020-01-21

153 https://www.fda.gov/news-events/press-announcements/fda-approves-first-biosimilar-treatment-cancer

its own counterpart Zirabev® at a 23% discount on Avastin® original price. Additionally, Genentech sued Bioepis for patent infringement, aiming to keep the Korean Samsung Bioepis version of the market. In 2020, Avastin® was ranked as the 14th best-selling drug with global sales of US$5.32 billion, experiencing a 25% decrease from sales in 2019.

VEGF in vision care

Anti-VEGF agents can be used to treat retinal neovascularisation and eye diseases associated with Age-related Macular Degeneration (AMD), which is a common cause of severe and irreversible vision loss in older adults. In the U.S. alone, there are annual 155,000 newly diagnosed patients.[154] Prior to the discovery of anti-VEGF therapy, patients with AMD were doomed to blindness. Ranibizumab is a humanized IgG1 kappa isotype therapeutic antibody fragment developed for intraocular use. According to the U.S. FDA news release, it was the first treatment that, when given monthly, could maintain the vision of >90% of patients with this form of AMD.

Ranibizumab was developed by Genentech, approved by the U.S. FDA in September 2006 under the brand name Lucentis® among others for the treatment of wet AMD. Again in 2010, it was approved for macular edema following Retinal Vein Occlusion (RVO). In 2015, it was the first eye medicine for treatment of Diabetic Retinopathy (DR) in patients with Diabetic Macular Edema (DME). DME affected nearly 750,000 Americans in the U.S. market alone.[155] In 2017, it was approved for the treatment of all forms of DR.[156] DR is the most common cause of blindness and vision loss in patients with diabetes, affecting nearly 7.7 million individuals in the U.S. market. This medication was considered as a milestone in the history of the ophthalmology.

The COVID-19 pandemic disrupted the Lucentis® market in 2020. In the U.S., it generated a revenue of US$1.61 billion. However, Lucentis® faced competition

---

154 https://retinatoday.com/articles/2006-sept/0906_09.html

155 https://www.fiercepharma.com/regulatory/fda-approves-roche-s-lucentis-ranibizumab-injection-for-treatment-of-diabetic

156 https://www.pharmacytimes.com/view/fda-approves-lucentis-for-all-forms-of-diabetes-retinopathy

from both new entrants like Novartis's Beovu®, and biosimilars as it lost market exclusivity in 2021.[157]

Economics concern

Ranibizumab treatment is significantly more expensive than Bevacizumab because it is developed for and is used exclusively in ophthalmology. Additionally, physicians in the U.S., China, and Europe have believed that Bevacizumab was equally effective in treating wet macular degeneration, thereby promoting its use in clinical practice as an off-label substitute for patients with eye diseases to alleviate their economic burden.

The National Eye Institute in the U.S. implemented a study named CATT for comparing Lucentis® and Avastin® in the treatment of AMD. The initial results were published in the *New England Journal of Medicine* in May 2011,[158] exemplifying that the two drugs had equivalent effects on visual acuity when administered under the same schedule. However, adverse effects were more common for patients administering Avastin®.

Eylea® (Aflibercept), also known in the scientific literature as VEGF Trap-Eye, is a recombinant fusion protein, consisting of portions of human VEGF receptors 1 and 2 extracellular domains fused to the Fc portion of human IgG1, and formulated as an iso-osmotic solution for intravitreal administration. Eylea® was developed by Regeneron Pharmaceuticals, based in Terrytown, New York, the U.S. and was approved by the U.S. FDA on November 18, 2011.[159] The initial indication was for the treatment of wet AMD, and its indications later expanded to Central Retinal Vein Occlusion (CRVO) in 2012,[160] DME in 2014,[161] and diabetic

---

157 https://www.fiercepharma.com/special-report/top-10-drugs-losing-u-s-exclusivity-2021

158 https://www.eyedocs.co.uk/ophthalmology-journal-articles-classic/1085-catt-trial

159 https://investor.regeneron.com/news-releases/news-release-details/regeneron-announces-fda-approval-eylea153-aflibercept-injection/

160 https://www.eye.md/2012/11/12/fda-approves-regenerons-eylea-for-crvo/

161 https://newsroom.regeneron.com/news-releases/news-release-details/eylear-aflibercept-injection-receives-fda-approval-treatment/

retinopathy in 2019.[162] In Europe, it was marketed by the Germany-based Bayer.

In February 2015, a 660-participant study, sponsored by the U.S. National Institutes of Health, was published in the *New England Journal of Medicine*. This was the first head-to-head study to compare Eylea® and Lucentis®, which revealed that Eylea® outperformed in treating moderate to severe vision loss in patients with DME.[163]

According to a survey of ophthalmologists from three geographic regions, namely the U.S., Europe (France, Germany, Italy, Spain, and the U.K.), Asia-Pacific (China, Japan, and Australia), most physicians expected the number of patients to be treated with Eylea® to increase over the next two years.[164]

Eylea® achieved global sales of US$8.9 billion and was ranked as the 9th best-selling drug in 2021.[165]

3) Case Three: Targeted Drugs and anti-HER2 antibody solid tumour drugs

Herceptin® and companion diagnosis

Trastuzumab, under the brand name of Herceptin® and others, is a monoclonal antibody targeting HER2. It works by binding to HER2 receptor and slowing down cell replication.

Trastuzumab was fast-tracked and approved by the U.S. FDA for the treatment of HER2-positive breast cancer on September 25, 1998,[166] and by the European Union in August 2000. It can be used alone or in combination with chemotherapy drug Paclitaxel.

---

162 https://newsroom.regeneron.com/news-releases/news-release-details/fda-approves-eylear-aflibercept-injection-diabetic-retinopathy

163 https://www.fiercepharma.com/regulatory/regeneron-s-eylea-beats-roche-s-lucentis-new-head-to-head-study

164 https://www.pharmaceutical-technology.com/comment/eylea-bayer-regeneron/

165 https://www.fiercepharma.com/special-reports/top-20-drugs-worldwide-sales-2021

166 https://www.nytimes.com/1998/09/03/us/drugs-to-fight-breast-cancer-near-approval.html

In the mid-1970s, scientists discovered that certain mutated genes could cause cancers. Therefore, researchers developed the theory that targeting these oncogenes, or the proteins they code for, should prevent the spread of malignancies. The combined work of Alex Ullrich, Dennis Slamon and Michael Shepard culminated in the creation of Herceptin®, the first monoclonal antibody therapy that targets a protein encoded by an oncogene. Their research efforts demonstrated that monoclonal antibodies are effective in treating solid tumors. In 2019, they were awarded the Lasker Award, the prestigious biomedical scientific award in the U.S.[167] A book about Slamon's work titled *Living Proof* was published and subsequently adapted as a film.

On the same day Herceptin® was approved, the U.S. FDA also approved the HER2 gene ex vivo detection kit Hercep Test™, which was developed by DAKO Corporation. This was not a coincidence, but a fruitful result of the complementary joint venture between Genentech and DAKO Corporation. The combination of genotype-specific targeted drugs and interdependent testing methods for the detection of genotypes in patients could ensure the drug effectiveness. The venture opened a new era for targeted drugs, namely the incorporation of companion diagnosis into the target selection process, which leads to an individualized genotype-specific therapy plan. HER2-positive breast cancer patients accounted for approximately 25% to 30% of all breast cancer patients. Patient groups with this indication have since then greatly benefited from the astonishing clinical performance of Herceptin® as opposed to conventional drugs. The industry sees the era of pharmacogenomics upon us.[168]

Herceptin® has been one of the mostly used cancer drugs since its inception.[169] It has been a leader in the breast cancer treatment and reached annual sales of US$7 billion, accounting for 15% of the total pharmaceutical revenue of Roche

---

167 https://laskerfoundation.org/winners/herceptin-a-targeted-antibody-therapy-for-breast-cancer/

168 https://www.bioprocessonline.com/doc/fda-approves-dako-herceptest-for-her2-overexp-0001

169 https://www.pharmaceutical-technology.com/analysis/featurethe-worlds-most-sold-cancer-drugs-in-2015-4852126/

in 2019.[170]

A full treatment course of Herceptin® costs about US$70,000. In November 2017, the European Commission approved Ontruzant®,[171] a biosimilar from Korea-based Samsung-Bioepis, for the treatment of early breast cancer, metastatic breast cancer, and metastatic gastric cancer.

4) Case Four: Autoimmune diseases, anti-TNFα antibody drugs

The legendary Humira®

Adalimumab, under the brand name Humira® and others, is a monoclonal antibody drug targeting TNFα. Its mechanism of action involves inactivating the tumor necrosis factor alpha (TNFα) to trigger immunosuppression and control inflammatory responses. On December 31, 2002, Adalimumab was approved by the U.S. FDA as the first fully humanized monoclonal antibody for the treatment of rheumatoid arthritis to be used alone or in combination with Methotrexate. Humira® was the third TNF inhibitor in the market.

Adalimumab was co-discovered by BASF Bioresearch Corporation from Germany, and Cambridge Antibody Technology from the U.K. in 1993. The drug candidate was named D2E7. It was further manufactured at BASF Bioresearch and developed by BASF Knoll. In 2001, BASF sold off all its pharmaceutical business, which included the D2E7, to Abbott for US$6.9 billion in cash as part of their strategic reorientation.[172]

Analysts forecasted the turnover of D2E7 could reach US$500 million, and BASF quoted potential sales of US$1 billion a year.[173] Both would be hugely surprised by the later outcomes.

---

170 https://www.forbes.com/sites/greatspeculations/2019/08/28/can-roches-blockbuster-drug-herceptins-sales-grow/?sh=73acf81d42e5

171 https://www.ema.europa.eu/en/medicines/human/EPAR/ontruzant

172 https://www.pharmexec.com/view/abbott-acquire-basf-pharma-business

173 https://www.thepharmaletter.com/article/basf-sells-pharma-business-to-abbott-labs-for-6-9-billion-in-cash

After Abbott received the approval for Humira® in 2002 for the treatment of rheumatoid arthritis, its indications continually expanded to many other aspects, boosting its applicability in the market.

In 2005, Abbott launched Humira® for psoriatic arthritis, with sales exceeding US$1 billion, which became a blockbuster drug. Amazingly, Humira® has been the best-selling drug worldwide for nine consecutive years. With worldwide sales of US$20.4 billion in 2020, Humira® is the first medicine to reach annual sales of US$20 billion. Moreover, it made the industry history by being the most lucrative drug ever up till present, generating a revenue of US$200 billion in 20 years since its launch in 2002.[174]

The following factors contributed to the success of Humira® : 1) outstanding therapeutic and safety results, prompting recommendations from doctors and clinical practitioners, 2) active engagement in clinical trials for expansion of its indications, making Humira® applicable to multiple autoimmune diseases, 3) continual research and optimisation of new dosage forms and formulations, prolonging the term of its patent; AbbVie filed about 250 patents, and 4) annual increase of the price of Humira® , for example, the price to Medicare increased by 41% between 2016 and 2020 and this inevitably poses financial strain on the patients and healthcare systems.

In 2012, Abbott split off into two companies in the hope of boosting its valuations. AbbVie owned all the branded drug businesses, such as Humira®, HIV treatment Kaletra®, and prostate cancer drug Lupron®. Abbott owned the medical device business, as well as generic drugs and food supplements.[175]

Remicade®

The first TNF inhibitor in the market was Infliximab, under the brand name Remicade® among others. It seems to work by binding to and neutralizing TNFα, preventing it from interacting with its receptors on the cell. It was originally developed in mice as a mouse antibody. As humans give immune reactions to

---

174 https://www.biopharmadive.com/news/humira-abbvie-biosimilar-competition-monopoly/620516/

175 https://www.reuters.com/article/us-abbott-idUSTRE79I46K20111019

mouse proteins, the mouse domains were replaced with human domains. It is a combination of amino acid sequences in mouse and human antibodies, therefore named "chimeric monoclonal antibody". A biotech company called Centocor developed Remicade®, the first new drug to treat the Crohn's disease in 30 years.[176] It received approval from the U.S. FDA and the European Union on August 24, 1998, and in August 1999 respectively.

On October 6, 1999, Johnson & Johnson announced the completion of merger with Centocor at US$4.9 billion.[177] In 2016, Remicade® reached a historic revenue height of US$6.97 billion. In 2020, its sales were US$4.195 billion, ranking as the 20th best-selling drug globally. Its biosimilars were approved in the EU in 2013, in Japan in 2014 and in the U.S. in 2016. The primarily approved indications include Crohn's disease, ulcerative colitis, rheumatoid arthritis, and psoriatic arthritis, etc.

Enbrel®

The second TNF inhibitor was Etanercept, under the brand name Enbrel® among others. It is a TNF receptor-IgG fusion protein.

The prototypic fusion protein was first synthesized in the early 1990s by Bruce Beutler and was shown to be active and usually stable as a blockade of TNF in vivo. He was awarded the 2011 Nobel Prize in Physiology or Medicine for his discovery in the activation of innate immunity.[178] He patented the protein and sold all rights of its use to Seattle-based Immunex, a leader in inflammation and one of the premier biotech companies. In 1998, Enbrel® was first approved by the U.S. FDA for the treatment of moderate-to-severe rheumatoid arthritis. In 2002, Amgen merged with Immunex for US$16 billion, the largest ever deal at the time, creating a behemoth with a market valuation of US$72 billion.[179] Amgen owned Enbrel® since this acquisition.

---

176 https://www.nature.com/articles/nbt1098-900.pdf?origin=ppub

177 https://johnsonandjohnson.gcs-web.com/news-releases/news-release-details/johnson-johnson-announces-completion-merger-centocor-inc/

178 https://www.nobelprize.org/prizes/medicine/2011/beutler/facts/

179 https://www.wired.com/2001/12/amgen-immunex-in-16b-deal/

In North America, Enbrel® is marketed by Amgen in two formulations, one in powder and another in pre-mixed liquid form. Wyeth is the sole marketer outside of the North America, excluding Japan, where Takeda markets the drug therein.

In 2019, the worldwide sales of Enbrel® reached US$7.2 billion, ranking the 7th in bestselling drugs.[180] In 2020, it was ranked the 11th with worldwide sales of US$6.37 billion.

5) Case Five: anti-IL12/23 antibody drugs, Stelara®

Ustekinumab is a first-in-class, fully humanized monoclonal antibody, targeting Interleukin 12 (IL-12) and Interleukin 23 (IL-23). Both interleukins are naturally occurring cytokines, which are speculated to induce immune-mediated inflammation. Ustekinumab can bind to the p-40 subunit present on both IL-12 (p35/p400) and IL-23 (p19/p40) to trigger an inhibitory effect on the two cytokines, subsequently preventing them from binding to IL12Rβ1 receptor on cell surfaces. This blocks the transduction of downstream pathway signaling, and thus treating immune-mediated inflammatory diseases.

In December 2007, Centocor and Jassen-Cilag International filed a Biologic License Application (BLA) with the U.S. FDA. Almost two years later, in September 2009, Ustekinumab under the brand name Stelara® among others received U.S. FDA approval for the treatment of moderate-to-severe plaque psoriasis. This delay was due to the concern that the immunosuppressant nature of the antibody might increase risks of serious infections and cancers for psoriasis patients.[181]

These indications for Stelara® expanded to Crohn's disease, ulcerative colitis, and psoriatic arthritis.[182]

Since its launch in 2009, Stelara® has grown to be J&J's largest product. In 2021, its worldwide sales reached US$9.1 billion.

---

180 https://www.fiercepharma.com/special-report/top-20-drugs-by-global-sales-2019

181 https://www.evaluate.com/vantage/articles/news/belated-stelara-approval-should-be-worth-wait

182 https://www.fiercepharma.com/pharma/stelara%C2%AE-ustekinumab-receives-fda-approval-to-treat-active-psoriatic-arthritis

6) Case Six: Immunotherapy, anti-PD-1/PD-L1 antibody drugs

Every significant advancement in medical history has been accompanied by a better understanding of the mechanism of actions within the human body. The most recent landmark is the discovery of immune checkpoint inhibitors in cancer treatment. One of the immune system's functions is to distinguish between self-markers and non-self-markers, and to respond appropriately to maintain an organism's normal function. The specific mechanism of the immune system is so complex that despite decades of research, mankind only deciphers a portion of its complexities. T cells are an integral part of the immune system; they are activated when their receptors detect any foreign or abnormal substances. Immune checkpoints are T cell regulators that allow them to tolerate certain specific foreign substances. When T cells identify proteins from immune checkpoints, they classify such proteins as "non-self" and eliminate them. Certain cancers take advantage of this system by expressing immune checkpoint proteins that inhibit T cells activities through binding to their receptors, thereby evading immunological surveillance and resulting in tumorigenesis. Immune checkpoint inhibitors work by inhibiting either immune checkpoint proteins on cancer cells or T cell receptors, thereby preventing them from binding and reactivating the immune system's cancer-killing capacity. Professor James Allision of the University of Texas MD Anderson Cancer Center and Professor Tasuku Honjo of Kyoto University in Japan received the 2018 Nobel Prizes in Physiology or Medicine for their discovery of cancer therapy by inhibition of the negative immune system.[183]

Yervoy®

Ipilimumab, under the brand name Yervoy® or others, was the first immune checkpoint inhibitor monoclonal antibody to receive approval worldwide. It activates the immune system by targeting CTLA-4, a protein receptor that downregulates the immune system. Cytotoxic T Lymphocytes (CTLs) can recognize and destroy cancer cells. Ipilimumab turns off the inhibitory mechanism and boosts the body's immune response against cancer cells.

---

183 https://www.nobelprize.org/prizes/medicine/2018/press-release/

The concept of using anti-CLTA-4 antibody was first developed by James Allison at the University of California, Berkeley. The rights to develop it as a drug, Ipilimumab, were licensed to a small American company, NeXstar Pharmaceutical, in 1995. On March 1, 1999, Gilead Sciences and NeXstar Pharmaceutical merged.[184] The cancer business of NeXstar was sold to Medarex. Bristol-Myers Squibb (BMS) acquired Medarex for US$2.4 billion in 2009.[185]

On March 25, 2011, BMS received approval for Yervoy® from the U.S. FDA for the treatment of adults with unresectable or metastatic malignant melanoma, the deadliest form of skin cancer.[186]

Two rivals: Opdivo® and Keytruda®

PD-1 is another inhibitor of the immune checkpoint expressed on the surface of T cells. Following its inhibition, T cells acquire the ability to recognize cancer cells that express one of the two PD-1 receptors, namely PD-L1 or PD-L2. The rivalry between Opdivo® and Keytruda® is an interesting drama and case study in the biopharmaceutical history.

Opdivo®

Nivolumab was generated in 2005 under intellectual property of PD-1 owned by Japan-based Ono Pharmaceutical and Medarex.[187] Medarex had the rights in North America, and Ono retained the rights for all other countries. Through the research collaboration with Ono, Dr. Changyu Wang, and his team at Medarex invented Opdivo®. The discovery and in-vitro characteristics of the antibody called MDX-1106/ONO-4538 was published in 2014. The initial clinical results were very promising, that caused the excitement among industry and PD-1 became a biological target that is actively pursued.

---

184 https://www.gilead.com/news-and-press/press-room/press-releases/1999/3/gilead-sciences-and-nexstar-pharmaceuticals-to-merge

185 https://www.fiercebiotech.com/biotech/bristol-myers-squibb-to-acquire-medarex

186 https://news.bms.com/news/details/2011/FDA-Approves-YERVOY-ipilimumab-for-the-Treatment-of-Patients-with-Newly-Diagnosed-or-Previously-Treated-Unresectable-or-Metastatic-Melanoma-the-Deadliest-Form-of-Skin-Cancer/default.aspx

187 https://www.ono-pharma.com/sites/default/files/en/news/press/enews20050512.pdf

Ono received approval from the Japanese authorities to use nivolumab to treat unresectable melanoma in July 2014, which was the first regulatory approval for PD-1 in the world.[188]

Nivolumab did not get much attention during the Medarex Merger, as it was still in the early stages.[189] Later, Nivolumab demonstrated promising preclinical results. BMS was very fortunate to acquire Medarex at a favourable price, together with two strong immune checkpoint inhibitors targeting distinct targets. Nivolumab was shown to be more efficacious than Ipilimumab, and BMS had high expectation for it, naming the clinical trials for this pipeline drug candidate the "Checkmate" series.

On December 22, 2014, the U.S. FDA approved Nivolumab, under the brand name Opdivo® among others, for the treatment of patients with unresectable or metastatic malignant melanoma and disease progression.[190] On June 15, 2018, the China NMPA approved Opdivo®, which became the country's first immune-oncology and the first PD-1 therapy. In 2019, with worldwide sales of US$8.06 billion, Opdivo® was ranked 4th on the global top 20 drugs list. In 2020, it was ranked 8th with global sales of US$7.92 billion. In 2021, it was ranked 11th with global sales of US$8.5 billion.

Dramatically, on the same day that Keytruda® was approved by the U.S. FDA, BMS filed a lawsuit that Merck infringed its patents awarded on May 20.[191] In January 2017, Merck reached a settlement with BMS and Ono, by the US$625 million payment and additional 6.5% royalty fees on sales of Keytruda® until December 2023, and 2.5% of royalty fees from January 2024 to December 2026.[192]

---

188 https://www.fiercebiotech.com/biotech/anti-pd-1-cancer-star-nivolumab-wins-world-s-first-regulatory-approval

189 https://news.bms.com/news/details/2009/Bristol-Myers-Squibb-to-Acquire-Medarex/default.aspx

190 https://www.merck.com/news/merck-receives-accelerated-approval-of-keytruda-pembrolizumab-the-first-fda-approved-anti-pd-1-therapy/#

191 https://www.biopharmadive.com/news/bms-sues-merck-over-historic-pd-1-cancer-drug-keytruda/306806/

192 https://www.pmlive.com/pharma_news/merck_settles_pd-1_patent_lawsuit_with_bms_and_ono_1184849

Keytruda®

Pembrolizumab, which was discovered and researched by scientists at Organon in 2006, is a humanized antibody. In 2007, Schering-Plough acquired Organon at the price of US$14.4 billion.[193] Only two years later, Merck merged with Schering-Plough at the valuation of US$41.1 billion in 2009.[194]

In early 2010, Merck decided to terminate the Pembrolizumab development program and began to license it out. Later in the same year, BMS published an article in the *New England Journal of Medicine* highlighting the potential for immune checkpoint inhibitors as treatment for metastatic melanoma. This article alarmed Merck. Although Merck had little experience in oncology and immunotherapy, senior management recognized this opportunity, quickly reactivated this program, and filed its IND by the end of 2010. Merck reallocated significant resources to focus on Pembrolizumab. One of the senior managers with background in oncology even stepped down to lead the clinical development of Pembrolizumab for treating lung cancer.

At the time, Merck's strategy entailed enormous risks. BMS was ahead of Merck in terms of available clinical data; and even worse Merck was suffering from the lack of robust pipelines. Had the gamble not paid off, Merck would not only have diverted resources away from other pipelines but would also have increased the risk of capital rupture.

There are two primary reasons that a latecomer like Merck eventually took the lead.

1) It adopted a more effective clinical trial design. During its development, two options were available: the first option was to combine the drug candidate with a companion diagnostic tool that restricted its use to patients with specific indications and biomarker expression. This corresponds to the expression of PD-L1 genes and proteins in cancer patients when PD-1 drugs are used. This clinical trial design reduces the number of patients

---

193 https://www.fiercebiotech.com/biotech/press-release-schering-plough-corporation-completes-14-43-billion-acquisition-of-organon

194 https://www.fiercepharma.com/pharma/merck-nabs-schering-plough-41-1b-deal

eligible for clinical trials, thereby shortening the overall clinical trial timeline. Additionally, as the biomarker expression is used as a target, this has the potential to increase the response rate and efficacy of drugs to the selected patients, thereby significantly increasing the likelihood of a successful clinical trial. Empirically, such a design significantly limits the scope of applicability of the drug once it is approved for sale, as it benefits only patients with the expressed biomarkers, resulting in reduced sales. Drug manufacturers usually avoid this strategy. The alternative is to abandon companion diagnosis in favor of developing a drug with more indications. Merck chose the first strategy to catch up with BMS's R&D progress, which followed the second strategy. This fact also emphasized the growing importance of precision medicine in the development of future medicine.

2) It undertook a new regulatory pathway called Breakthrough Therapy Designation, which was not well understood at that time. Merck quietly applied for and earned it in 2013. One of the advantages was that the U.S. FDA convened more meetings with drug developers, reducing the regulatory risks and misunderstanding between the developer and regulatory authorities. That was Merck's first use of this designation.

In September 2014, the U.S. FDA approved Pembrolizumab under the Fast Track Development Program for the treatment of unresectable or metastatic adult malignant melanoma and disease progression.[195]

Both companies aggressively expanded the indications for their respective drugs and invested heavily in clinical trials of various combination therapies, resulting in a partially overlapping list of extensive indications for both drugs to date, owing to their shared mechanisms of action.

The second quarter of 2018 was the turning point where Merck took the lead over BMS in terms of PD-1 sales.[196] In 2019, with worldwide sales of US$11.12 billion, Keytruda® ranked 2nd on the global top 20 selling drugs list. In 2020, it maintained its ranking with global sales of US$14.38 billion. In 2021, it ranked

---

195 https://www.merck.com/news/merck-receives-accelerated-approval-of-keytruda-pembrolizumab-the-first-fda-approved-anti-pd-1-therapy/#

196 https://www.biospace.com/article/merck-takes-lead-from-bristol-myers-squibb-for-pd-1-pd-l1/

4th with global sales of US$17.2 billion.

PD-L1 inhibitor: Tecentriq®

Atezolizumab, under the brand name Tecentriq® and others, is a fully humanized IgG1 antibody developed by Genentech. It is the first PD-L1 inhibitor approved by the U.S. FDA. Its mechanism of action involves the interaction of PD-L1 with programmed cell death protein 1 (PD-1) and CD80 receptors. PD-L1 can be highly expressed on certain tumors, and it is believed to lead to reduced activation of immune cells that recognize and attack the cancer cells.

On May 18, 2016, it was approved by the U.S. FDA for the treatment of locally advanced and metastatic urothelial carcinoma.[197] Additionally, Atezolizumab was approved for medical use in the European Union in September 2017. In August 2018, the U.S. FDA updated the prescribing information for Atezolizumab to require the use of an U.S. FDA-approved companion diagnostic test to determine PD-L1 levels in tumor tissue from cisplatin-ineligible people with locally advanced or metastatic urothelial cancer.[198] On October 18, 2016, it was approved by the U.S. FDA for the treatment of people with metastatic Non-Small Cell Lung Cancer (NSCLC) whose disease progressed during or following platinum-containing chemotherapy.[199] The treatment costs on average are US$14,540 per month in the U.S., depending on the dosage schedule.[200] Tecentriq® generated revenue of US$3 billion in 2020.[201]

197 https://www.fda.gov/drugs/resources-information-approved-drugs/atezolizumab-urothelial-carcinoma

198 https://www.fda.gov/drugs/resources-information-approved-drugs/fda-updates-prescribing-information-keytruda-and-tecentriq

199 https://www.gene.com/media/press-releases/14641/2016-10-18/fda-approves-genentechs-cancer-immunothe

200 https://www.drugs.com/medical-answers/cost-tecentriq-3064818/

201 https://www.reuters.com/business/healthcare-pharmaceuticals/roche-aims-tecentriq-early-lung-cancer-after-data-shows-benefit-2021-05-19/

4. VACCINE

Prevnar®

In 2010, the U.S. FDA granted approval for Prevnar 13® pneumococcal conjugate vaccine for active immunization of children aged between six weeks to five years for the prevention of invasive disease caused by 13 Streptococcus pneumoniae serotypes, and prevention of otitis media caused by certain serotypes.[202] Invasive pneumococcal disease includes sepsis and bacteremia, meningitis, bacteremic pneumonia, and empyema.

In 2012, Pfizer received the U.S. FDA approval to extend the use of Prevnar 13® for prevention of Pneumococcal Pneumonia and invasive disease in adults aged 50 or above.[203]

In 2014, Prevnar 13® received key endorsement from the Centers for Disease Control and Prevention (CDC) committee in adults over 65 years of age as routine vaccination.[204] The rollout in that population drove sales for years. Before 2015, the main driving force for sales had been from outside of the U.S. market.

In 2019, Prevnar 13® reached worldwide sales of US$5.95 billion, making it Pfizer's best-selling solo medicine, unlike blood thinner Eliquis®, whose sales were shared with BMS. The revenue generated from Prevnar 13® between 2015 and 2020 exceeded US$35 billion.

On September 20, 2018, Pfizer announced that the U.S. FDA granted Breakthrough Therapy Designation for Prevnar 20® for the prevention of invasive disease and pneumonia in adults aged 18 or above. On June 8, 2021, the U.S. FDA approved Prevnar 20®. This is a major milestone in the vaccine development history.

---

202 https://www.pfizer.com/news/press-release/press-release-detail/pfizer_receives_fda_approval_for_prevnar_13_for_the_prevention_of_invasive_pneumococcal_disease_in_infants_and_young_children

203 https://www.fiercebiotech.com/biotech/pfizer-receives-fda-approval-to-extend-use-of-prevnar-13%C2%AE-for-prevention-of-pneumococcal

204 https://www.cdc.gov/vaccines/vpd/pneumo/hcp/recommendations.html

The size of the market also attracted Merck. In July 2021, Merck announced that VAXNEUVANCE® (Pneumococcal 15-valent Conjugate Vaccine) was granted approval by the U.S. FDA for the prevention of invasive pneumococcal disease in adults aged 18 or older.[205] In June 2022, the indications were approved by the U.S. FDA to expand further to infants and children, making it the first pneumococcal conjugate vaccine approved in almost a decade to help the pediatric population in their fight against the invasive pneumococcal disease.[206] Additionally, the European Commission expanded VAXNEUVANCE® indication to include infants, children, and adolescents in October 2022.[207] This approval once again demonstrated the position of Merck as a global leader in pediatric vaccine development.

5. AUTHOR'S INSIGHTS

i. Traditional global pharmaceutical conglomerates enter the biopharmaceutical field through M&A, which enabled them to secure market position at a rapid pace. For instance, Roche Pharmaceuticals acquired Genentech, Pfizer Pharmaceuticals acquired Wyeth Pharmaceuticals, and Abbott Pharmaceuticals acquired the German BASF's pharmaceutical business.

ii. Quoting from Severin Schwan[208] on how to foster innovation: "Scientific success cannot be programmed, but we can create the conditions that will allow it to happen: being open to new ideas, having the courage to take risks; our researchers need to have the freedom to work on their ideas and all, they need a positive space in which ideas are shared and independent thinking is encouraged." This well-summarized on Roche's success, we shall ponder on these elements and guide on the next unicorns.

---

205 https://www.merck.com/news/merck-announces-u-s-fda-approval-of-vaxneuvance-pneumococcal-15-valent-conjugate-vaccine-for-the-prevention-of-invasive-pneumococcal-disease-in-adults-18-years-and-older-caused-by-15-serot/

206 https://www.merck.com/news/u-s-fda-approves-mercks-vaxneuvance-pneumococcal-15-valent-conjugate-vaccine-for-the-prevention-of-invasive-pneumococcal-disease-in-infants-and-children/

207 https://www.merck.com/news/european-commission-expands-mercks-vaxneuvance-pneumococcal-15-valent-conjugate-vaccine-indication-to-include-infants-children-and-adolescents/

208 https://www.roche.com/about/leadership/severin-schwan

iii. With the Orphan Drug Designation as the starting point, innovative drugs have either expanded their list of indications or found clinical applications in other therapeutic areas to become "Blockbuster" drugs, with some drugs exceeding US$10 billion in global annual sales. Orphan drugs do not mean less sales.

iv. It is common for biotech companies to face shortage of funding during their growth phase. Patents, accumulated knowledge, and insights are their most valuable assets.

Chapter *3*

The Life Sciences Paradigm

1. FOREWORD

The discipline of life sciences and technology concerns all scientific fields that conduct research on all living things (humans, animals, and plants), and related fields, such as bioethics. In this book, this concept only applies to human beings. Although biology is the backbone of this sector, advances in molecular biology and biotechnology have made it a more specialized and multidisciplinary field. "Life sciences and technology", as the name implies, combines both life sciences and technology, emphasizing not only research but also application. The term "biotechnology" is interchangeable with "life sciences and technology" in many literatures. However, the author believes that "life sciences and technology", or simply "life sciences", is a more appropriate term to describe the status quo, for the following reasons:

As predicted in the popular book *The 100-Year Life*, we are living and working in an age of longevity, and all industries must invest and develop products and services accordingly, just like what human beings did for "baby boomers" after World War II. Additionally, we want healthy and quality longevity. In the traditional sense, medical intervention usually consists of three components, namely prevention, treatment, and rehabilitation in the management of diseases. However, the author believes that it is more appropriate to add "anti-aging" as the fourth component today.

At present, the concept of "life" is even more important. People tend to use "patient-centered" to define medical practices. However, these diseases are part of our lives. From the moment that we were born, we received medical treatment, even though we were supposed to be healthy individuals. When we leave this world, we want to be in healthy conditions as well. Therefore, "life-centered" is a more proper definition than "patient-centered".

The industry has experienced an unprecedented level of innovation in terms of both quantity and quality, which is rare in the past century. These innovations include RNAi, message RNA, CAR-T, oncolytic viruses, antibody-drug conjugates, gene editing therapies, tumor vaccines, stem cell therapies, PROTACs, etc. Even though some industry peers call them as "new modalities", the author prefers to call them as "life sciences products or therapies" rather than the traditional meaning of "drugs".

The combined clinical applications of different treatment methods, such as oncolytic virus+cell therapy, oncolytic virus+PD-1/PD-L1 monoclonal antibody drugs, medication+MedTech, etc. have been carried out in many trials around the world, and the combination therapy is becoming the trend in the industry.

Other technologies, such as next-generation sequencing, early cancer screening, artificial intelligence applications, 3D technologies, and quantum technologies in life sciences are constantly emerging. These innovative technologies, along with drugs and therapies, are the building blocks to achieve individualized medicine.

Everything we do is about "life", living longer and healthier. That is what a life sciences fund manager is all about.

2. MAIN BODY

1) RNA interference (RNAi)

Nucleic acids carry the genetic information used for protein transcription and translation and are therefore the most basic component of living organisms and a fundamental topic of biological research. In the past, drug development centered on the protein level, including the discovery of small molecular drugs or macromolecule biological drugs to modulate the function of target proteins. Proteins are crucial building blocks for the structure and function of all organs and systems within the human body. Many human diseases are caused by over-production or under-production of proteins or mutant proteins.

With the advent of molecular biology and the conception of the central dogma of molecular biology,[209] an increasing number of nuclei acid drugs have been

---

209 DNA can self-replicate, its physiological functions are expressed in the form of proteins. DNA nucleotide sequence stores genetic information which generates messenger RNA through the transcription process followed by translation into protein.

developed to regulate the expression of downstream proteins.

RNAi, namely RNA interference, its mechanism of action, was first discovered by two American scientists, Andrew Fire and Craig Mello, in 1998. This discovery won them the 2006 Nobel Prize in Physiology or Medicine.[210] RNAi is a biological process in which RNA molecules participate in the sequence-specific suppression of gene expression by double-stranded RNA, through translational or transcriptional repression. RNAi exists in plants, animals, and humans. In 2001, Thomas Tuschl[211] first presented at a conference in Tokyo that he discovered that tiny double-stranded RNA molecules designed to target a particular gene could specifically block the effect of that gene when introduced into human cells. Over the next few years, global pharma giants entered this field in the form of partnerships or mergers and acquisitions with small biotech companies. The large dollar amount of deal transactions made by them caused irrational exuberance.[212] However, RNAi technology faced a series of setbacks due to an insufficient understanding of the key technologies surrounding the delivery system, leading to a market downturn between 2007 and 2011. Consequently, global pharma giants exited the field one after another. It was until 2012, a year marked a turning point, when major breakthroughs in delivery systems were achieved, laying a good foundation of excellent clinical trials data and technical foundations during the early stage. As of February 2021, 13 drugs have received regulatory approval in the U.S. and Europe. The main RNAi technology platforms include anti-sense oligonucleotides represented by Ionis; siRNA, represented by Alnylam, Dicerna and Sirnaomics.

Growth in this field had been fueled by robust capital trading activity. According to a report by the Boston Consulting Group, the market value of RNAi-listed companies between 2017 and 2020 outperformed the NASDAQ Biotechnology Index by 400% and similar gene editing companies by an average of 215%.

---

210 https://www.nobelprize.org/prizes/medicine/2006/press-release/

211 https://www.technologyreview.com/technology/rnai-therapy/

212 Irrational Exuberance is a term first proposed by former Federal Reserve Chairman Greenspan in a speech at the American Enterprise Institute during the 1996 Internet bubble period. He points out that asset prices are divorced from the fundamental factors that reflect their value. However, the subjective judgments of market participants spurred the continual rise of asset prices.

The world's leading life sciences industry leaders typically had close strategic partnerships with RNAi start-ups. From 2017 to 2020, these companies increased their RNAi investment from US$8.5 billion to US$35 billion.

Notable examples include:

In 2019, Novartis acquired The Medicines Company based in the U.S. for US$9.7 billion,[213] indirectly obtaining rights to Inclisiran, a clinical phase III RNAi drug. On December 22, 2021, Novartis announced that the U.S. FDA approved this medicine under the brand name Leqvio® for the treatment of Atherosclerotic Cardiovascular Disease (ASCVD).[214] This is the world's first-in-class siRNA medicine for cholesterol, and patients only need to take twice a year.

In April 2020, Blackstone, a global leader in private equity, invested US$2 billion in Alnylam, including stock purchases, acquisition of the sales rights of Inclisiran, and participation in business investments related to the cardiometabolic space.[215] Drug indications during clinical trial stages have been gradually expanding to include a wider range of indications as opposed to exclusively rare diseases.

In November 2021, Novo Nordisk, a Danish company, announced its acquisition of RNAi-based therapeutic company Dicerna in cash, at the price of US$38.25 per share, for a total equity valuation of approximately US$3.3 billion.[216]

Below are the major technology platforms and leading players:

Anti-sense oligonucleotides

It is a class of the 15–25 nucleotide single strands that perform complementary

---

213 https://www.forbes.com/sites/brucelee/2019/11/26/why-novartis-is-buying-the-medicines-company-for-97-billion/?sh=60bcfcbc8107

214 https://www.novartis.com/news/media-releases/fda-approves-novartis-leqvio-inclisiran-first-class-sirna-lower-cholesterol-and-keep-it-low-two-doses-year

215 https://www.blackstone.com/news/press/blackstone-and-alnylam-enter-into-2-billion-strategic-financing-collaboration-to-accelerate-the-advancement-of-rnai-therapeutics/

216 https://www.novonordisk.com/content/nncorp/global/en/news-and-media/news-and-ir-materials/news-details.html?id=87435#

binding to the base pairs on targeted RNAs to modulate their function.

IONIS Pharmaceuticals[217] (IONS.US)

The company headquartered in Carlsbad, California, formerly known as Isis Pharmaceuticals, was founded in 1989 by Stanley Crooke, a former head of research of GlaxoSmithKline, with the goal of commercializing antisense therapy.

In 2002, Isis and Genzyme entered a partnership for Mipromersen. The deal included purchase of Isis stock by Genzyme for US$150 million, license fee of US$175 million, as well as milestone fees and royalties.[218] Mipromersen was rejected by the European Medicines Agency in 2012, and again in 2013. However, it was approved by the U.S. FDA in 2013. In January 2016, Ionis terminated the agreement with Genzyme.

In 2007, Isis and Alnylam formed a 50/50 joint venture, namely Regulus Therapeutics,[219] to apply their intellectual property and knowledge in oligomer biotherapeutics to micro-RNA targets.

In December 2015, Isis changed its name to Ionis to avoid being confused with the Islamist militant group known as ISIS.

Ionis is a leading global innovator in RNA-targeted therapeutics. It focuses on two core franchises, which are cardiovascular and neurology. Two of its antisense RNA drugs have been approved in the U.S. market, namely SPINRAZA®[220] and Tegsedi®;[221] and one medicine, Wavlivra®,[222] was approved in the European Union market. Ionis has accumulated extensive knowledge of antisense oligonucleotide technologies and products after 30 years of R&D and global

---

217 https://www.ionispharma.com/about/

218 https://www.fiercepharma.com/pharma/genzyme-isis-solidify-collaboration-agreement

219 https://www.regulusrx.com/about/

220 https://www.spinraza.com/

221 https://tegsedi.com/

222 https://www.ema.europa.eu/en/medicines/human/EPAR/waylivra

collaborations. It currently has eight medicines with ten indications in the clinical phase III.[223] In January 2017, SPINRAZA®, a collaboration between Ionis and Biogen, was approved in the European Union[224] for the treatment of Spinal Muscular Atrophy (SMA), the first drug ever approved for the treatment of this disease.

The use of aerosol inhalation administration allows deep drug penetration into the lungs, and preliminary studies have shown good safety and drug tolerance, but more research is required. Ionis currently has two drugs: IONIS-ENAC-2.5Rx and IONIS-PKK-LRx, which have entered the clinical Phase II trials.

Small interfering RNA (siRNA)

It is a class of double-stranded RNA, usually 20–24 nucleotides base pairs in length. It interferes with the expression of specific genes with complementary nucleotide sequences by degrading mRNA after transcription, preventing translation.

Alnylam Pharmaceuticals (ALNY.US)

Alnylam is a spin-off from the Max Planck Institute for Biophysical Chemistry. Alnylam is named after a star in Orion's belt. In 2002, it was founded by scientists Phillip Sharp, Thomas Tuschl, Paul Schimmel, David Bartel, and Phillip Zamore; and investors Christoph Westphal and John Clarke. It is headquartered in Cambridge, Massachusetts, the U.S. Its founding CEO was John Maraganore, who retired in 2022 and wrote a reflective article on his reflections of his 19-year journey.[225] Alnylam primarily covers the therapeutic areas in genetic diseases, cardiometabolic diseases and infectious diseases.

To strengthen intellectual property protection, it merged with a Germany-based company, Ribopharma AG in 2003.[226] Additionally, Alnylam not only owns

---

223 https://www.ionispharma.com/ionis-innovation/pipeline/

224 https://www.ema.europa.eu/en/documents/overview/spinraza-epar-summary-public_en.pdf

225 https://www.nature.com/articles/s41587-022-01304-3

226 https://www.bizjournals.com/boston/blog/mass-high-tech/2003/07/alnylam-ribopharma-merge-notch-246-million.html

Tuschl's core patent series,[227] but also acquired all the intellectual property rights related to the nucleic acid interference technology, which had been previously acquired by Merck for US$1.1 billion at that time for just US$175 million. Alnylam paid US$25 million in cash US$150 million in stock for this deal.[228] In 2012, it discovered and the GalNAc[229] technology and patented it, signifying a breakthrough in the RNA delivery system.

With its leading edge in intellectual property, Alnylam has successively established cooperative relationships with leading giants such as Hoffmann-La Roche, Novartis, GlaxoSmithKline, and Sanofi, and has generated significant cash income from patent licensing and partnership. In 2014, French giant Sanofi acquired a 12% stake in Alnylam and obtained further rights to several drugs for US$700 million.[230]

On August 10, 2018, Alnylam received a pioneering approval from the U.S. FDA[231] for the first RNAi drug, Onpattro®,[232] for the treatment of a rare hereditary disease, hereditary transthyretin-mediated amyloidosis (hATTR). It affects 50,000 people worldwide. On November 20, 2019, the U.S. FDA granted approval to Givlaari®[233] for the treatment of adult patients with acute hepatic porphyria (AHP), a genetic rare disease.[234] In November 2020, the European Medicines Agency granted approval to Oxlumo®[235] for the treatment of primary

227 In 2001, a team led by Thomas Tuschl, a scientist at the Max Planck Institute in Germany, published a peer-reviewed paper in Nature, discovering RNAi in human cells, and for the first time verifying the possibility of RNAi as a treatment for human diseases. Tuschl has filed multiple patents for RNAi in human cells.

228 https://www.fiercebiotech.com/financials/merck-writes-off-rnai-punts-sirna-to-alnylam-for-175m

229 Capable of linking N-acetylgalactosamine to siRNA.

230 https://www.reuters.com/article/us-sanofi-alnylam-idUSBREA0C07K20140113

231 https://www.fda.gov/news-events/press-announcements/fda-approves-first-its-kind-targeted-rna-based-therapy-treat-rare-disease

232 https://www.onpattro.com/

233 https://www.givlaari.com/

234 https://www.fda.gov/news-events/press-announcements/fda-approves-first-treatment-inherited-rare-disease

235 https://www.oxlumo.com/

hyperoxaluria type 1,[236] a rare metabolic disorder.

On February 27, 2002, Alnylam filed for an IPO, raising US$26 million, and began trading on the NASDAQ stock exchange. Prior to 2018, Ionis and Alnylam had comparable market capitalizations; however, after 2018, the valuations of the two companies diverged, with Alnylam's market capitalization significantly ahead.

Swiss-based Novartis developed Inclisiran, the world's first siRNA medicine, for lowering Low-Density Lipoprotein Cholesterol (LDL-C), which was approved in the European Union and the U.S. under the brand name Leqvio®, for the treatment of adult hypercholesterolemia and mixed dyslipidemia. Inclisiran utilizes natural RNAi processes found within the human body and binds to the PCSK9 protein-encoding mRNA, thereby reducing mRNA levels through RNA interference and preventing the liver from producing PCSK9 protein, enhancing the liver's ability to remove LDL-C from the blood. Unlike statins, which requires daily doses, this innovative medicine requires only two subcutaneous injections per year to achieve lipid-lowering effect. In September 2021, Novartis entered into an agreement with the NHS in the U.K.,[237] and it is expected that 300,000 patients at high risk of cardiovascular disease will be treated with Leqvio® over the next three years. Under the license and collaboration deal with Alnylam, Novartis has obtained the global rights to develop, manufacture and commercialize Leqvio®.[238]

Messenger RNA (mRNA)

Prior to the outbreak of COVID-19 pandemic in 2020, RNA-based therapeutics were widely recognized as an innovative technology platform within the industry, but little was known to the public. However, mRNA technology has come into the spotlight due to continual highlights on the clinical progress of vaccine

---

236 https://www.ema.europa.eu/en/medicines/human/EPAR/oxlumo#authorisation-details-section

237 https://www.fiercepharma.com/pharma/novartis-nhs-england-move-forward-landmark-access-deal-cholesterol-drug-leqvio

238 https://www.biopharmadive.com/news/novartis-alnylam-liver-failure-rna-research/616736/

development in news headlines by mainstream media. Consequently, the stock market value of the two mRNA vaccine companies, U.S.-based Moderna and Germany-based BioNTech, have soared. Pfizer, the global partner of BioNTech, has made great contribution to the discovery, development, manufacture, and distribution of mRNA vaccines. Dr. Albert Bourla, Pfizer's Chairman and CEO, even wrote a book titled *Moonshot*, revealing the nine-month race to make this vaccine. Within just three years since its listing, Moderna's market capitalization peaked at US$200 billion, making it one of the world's largest biotech companies in terms of valuation.[239] *MIT Technology Review* listed mRNA vaccines as one of the top ten breakthrough technologies in February 2021.[240]

A feature article in *Nature* describes the tangled history of mRNA vaccines and concludes that hundreds of scientists had been working on mRNA vaccines for decades before the coronavirus pandemic brought a breakthrough.[241] mRNA vaccines carry genetic information that induces the body to produce specific viral proteins that trigger the desired immune response.

BioNTech (BNTX.US)

BioNTech SE stands for Biopharmaceutical New Technologies, is a Mainz-based mRNA company. It was founded in 2008, by scientists Ugur Sahin, Ozlem Tureci and Christoph Huber, with a seed investment of €150 million from an affluent German family. Its vision is to harness the power of the immune system to develop novel therapies to fight cancer, infectious diseases, and other severe diseases.

Katalin Kariko, who worked on mRNA while working at the University of Pennsylvania in the U.S., joined BioNTech the Senior Vice President in 2013. Her work helped to show that chemical modifications to RNA can smuggle the molecule past the body's immune defenses.

In August 2018, BioNTech entered into an R&D agreement with U.S.-based

---

239 https://www.fiercepharma.com/pharma/moderna-s-unjustifiable-200b-market-value-splits-wall-street-as-it-tops-merck-amgen-and

240 https://www.technologyreview.com/2021/02/24/1014369/10-breakthrough-technologies-2021/#messenger-rna-vaccines

241 https://www.nature.com/articles/d41586-021-02483-w

Pfizer to develop mRNA-based vaccines for the prevention of influenza. In January 2019, French-based Sanofi invested €80 million in BioNTech and extended the mRNA cancer research collaboration between the two companies.[242] Sanofi previously paid US$60 million upfront for the rights to five discovery-stage immunotherapies of BioNTech in 2015.[243] In September 2019, BioNTech received a capital contribution of US$55 million from the Bill & Melinda Gates Foundation.[244]

In October 2019, BioNTech launched an initial public offering (IPO) in the form of American Depository Shares (ADS) on the NASDAQ Global Select Market under the ticker symbol, BNTX. BioNTech raised gross proceeds of US$150 million from this IPO, with a valuation of US$3.4 billion, making it one of the largest biotech IPOs ever.[245]

On March 16, 2020, BioNTech received an investment of US$135 million from Shanghai-based Fosun Pharma in exchange for 1.58 million shares in BioNTech and the future development and marketing rights of the mRNA vaccine BNT162b2 in China.[246] In June 2020, BioNTech received €250 million from Singapore-based Temasek Holdings via the purchase of ordinary shares and four years' convertible bonds. On September 15, 2020, the German Federal Ministry of Education and Research awarded BioNTech a grant of €375 million to accelerate the development of the COVID-19 vaccine.

In 2020, BioNTech partnered with Pfizer to co-develop the world's first mRNA vaccine for the prevention of COVID-19 infections, which at that time offered 91% efficacy in preventing confirmed COVID-19 from occurring at least seven days after the second dose of vaccination. On December 2, 2020, the U.K.

---

242 https://www.fiercebiotech.com/biotech/sanofi-invests-eu80m-biontech-as-cancer-mrna-hits-clinic

243 https://investors.biontech.de/news-releases/news-release-details/sanofi-and-biontech-announce-cancer-immunotherapy-collaboration/

244 https://endpts.com/biontech-partners-with-bill-and-melinda-gates-foundation-scoring-55m-equity-investment-novartis-sells-china-unit/

245 https://www.nasdaq.com/articles/biontechs-ipo-values-it-at-$3.4-billion-in-one-of-the-largest-biotech-listings-of-all-time

246 https://investors.biontech.de/news-releases/news-release-details/biontech-and-fosun-pharma-form-covid-19-vaccine-strategic/

government granted its provisional HMR authorization for vaccination. A few days later, the U.S., Canada, and the European Union approved it for emergency authorization, under the brand name COMIRNATY®.

The COMIRNATY® vaccine has made a historical milestone in human history: it has brought mRNA from vision to reality, the fastest vaccine development in medical history, the first ever approved mRNA therapy, and one of the most successful pharmaceutical launches in history. By the end of 2021, 2.6 billion doses of vaccines were delivered to over 165 countries and territories.

BioNTech believes in global social responsibility and democratizing access to novel medicines. It started construction of the first mRNA vaccine manufacturing facility in Rwanda, Africa.[247] BioNTech has more than 4,000 employees from over 60 countries and has operations in Germany, the U.S., Austria, Turkey, China, Singapore, and the U.K.

Moderna (MRNA.US)

In 2005, Derrick Rossi studied a paper by Hungarian biochemist Katalin Kariko on RNA-mediated immune activation and her joint findings with Drew Weissman on nucleoside modifications that suppress the immunogenicity of RNA. Kariko and Weissman received the prestigious Lasker Award in 2021, America's Top Biomedical Research Prize for their contribution.[248]

In 2010, Derrick, along with Timothy Springer, Kenneth Chien, Bob Langer, and Noubar Afeyan from Flagship Ventures,[249] co-founded "ModeRNA Therapeutics", in Cambridge, Massachusetts, the U.S. In 2011, Afeyan, the largest shareholder of Moderna, hired Stephane Bancel as CEO, who has remained in his position ever since. In 2012, less than two years since its inception, Moderna reached to a unicorn valuation.

In 2013, Moderna and AstraZeneca signed a five-year exclusive option

---

247 https://investors.biontech.de/news-releases/news-release-details/biontech-starts-construction-first-mrna-vaccine-manufacturing/

248 https://www.pennmedicine.org/news/news-releases/2021/september/penn-mrna-scientists-drew-weissman-and-katalin-kariko-receive-2021-lasker-award

249 https://www.flagshippioneering.com/

agreement to discover, develop, and commercialize mRNA for the treatment in the therapeutic areas of cardiovascular, metabolic, and renal diseases and selected cancer targets. The deal included an upfront payment of US$240 million to Moderna, one of the largest initial payments ever in the pharmaceutical industry licensing deal that does not involve drugs that have been already clinically tested.[250] In October 2013, Moderna received an award of up to US$25 million by the Defense Advanced Research Project Agency (DARPA) for the development of mRNA therapeutics.[251]

In December 2018, Moderna became a public listed company via the largest public initial public offering in history, raising US$621 million at US$23 per share for 27 million shares.[252]

In March 2020, the U.S. FDA approved clinical trials for Moderna's COVID-19 vaccine candidate, and Moderna received an investment of US$483 million from the Operation Warp Speed Project sponsored by the U.S. government. On December 18, 2020, mRNA-1273 was granted an Emergency Use Authorization (EUA) in the U.S. and, a few days later, in Canada, the European Union and the U.K., under the brand name, SPIKEVAX®.

Moderna became a commercial company in 2021, and the SARS-CoV-2 virus changed everything. Moderna delivered 807 million doses worldwide. It had 2,700 employees live in 12 countries, primarily G7 countries. Moderna focuses on infectious diseases, Immuno-Oncology, rare diseases, cardiovascular disease, and autoimmune diseases. Its Respiratory Syncytial Virus (RSV) vaccine entered fast into a phase II/III study with 34,000 participants. Its Personalized Cancer Vaccine phase II trial is fully enrolled and is expected to have a readout in 2022.

2) CAR-T Cell Therapy

For over 100 years, the pillars for cancer treatment have been surgery,

250 https://www.astrazeneca.com/media-centre/press-releases/2013/astrazeneca-moderna-therapeutics-cardiometabolic-diseases-cancer-treatment-21032013.html#

251 https://www.fiercebiotech.com/biotech/darpa-awards-moderna-therapeutics-a-grant-for-up-to-25-million-to-develop-messenger-rna

252 https://www.investors.com/news/technology/moderna-therapeutics-biotech-ipo/

chemotherapy, and radiation therapy. Each treatment has its own pros and cons. For example, chemotherapy only works for certain types of cancer; meanwhile, chemotherapy patients usually experience severe side effects, such as nausea, vomiting, hair loss, just name a few. As a result, patients must take other medications to treat side effects. The emergency of "targeted therapy", the fourth pillar, has shifted cancer treatment to the next paradigm. Gleevec®,[253] a breakthrough product in cancer treatment, is an example: Gleevec® was approved by the U.S. FDA for the treatment of Chronic Myelogenous Leukemia (CML) in 2001. Before Gleevec®, the only treatment options were either bone marrow transplantation or daily interferon infusions, both of which have severe side effects and only prolong patients' survival time. Only 30% of patients with CML survived five years after diagnosis. With Gleevec®, this number raised to 89%.

Cellular immunotherapy made cancer treatment enter the next paradigm, becoming the fifth pillar. In 2011, Professor Carl June[254] and his team from the University of Pennsylvania published findings that a new therapy in which patients with refractory and relapsed Chronic Lymphocytic Leukemia (CLL) were treated with genetically engineered versions of their own T cells. This therapy is called CAR-T.[255] Its mechanism of action includes screening and extracting T cells from the patients, then engineering them with chimeric antigen receptors to give T cells the new ability to target a specific antigen, followed by cell expansion and infusion back into the patient. The modified T cells can specifically target cancer cells and qualify as a targeted therapy for main indications including relapsed and refractory leukemia, lymphoma, multiple myeloma, and other hematological tumor-related fields. Unlike traditional drugs in history, this is a therapy. More importantly, CAR-T therapy is customized for each individual patient. This is truly revolutionary. It clearly demonstrated the trend from general medicine to precision medicine or individualized medicine.

The CAR-T cell therapies approved by the U.S. FDA to date target one of the two antigens on B cells, which are CD19 or BCMA. Prior to the development of CAR-T, many adults and children with advanced aggressive lymphomas were

---

253 https://www.nature.com/scitable/topicpage/gleevec-the-breakthrough-in-cancer-treatment-565/

254 https://www.med.upenn.edu/cci/junelab/

255 Chimeric Antigen Receptor T-Cell immunotherapy.

virtually untreatable. The initial focus of CAR-T treatment was on the most common cancer in children, which is Acute Lymphoblastic Leukemia (ALL). Like all other cancer treatments, CAR-T therapy can cause severe side effects, including Cytokine Release Syndrome (CRS), and neurologic effects such as confusion. As physicians and researchers gain more experiences, these side effects become more manageable. Another concern is the cost of therapy, which is typically around a half million US dollars per patient.

On August 30, 2017, Swiss giant Novartis announced that the world's first Chimeric Antigen Receptor T-cell (CAR-T) immunotherapy, Kymriah® suspension for intravenous infusion, received marketing approval from the U.S. FDA. [256]

Two large deals shocked the industry, as global giants were under tight time pressure to acquire CAR-T companies. On August 28, 2017, California-based Gilead Sciences announced its acquisition of Kite Pharma for approximately US$11.9 billion in cash at US$180 per share. [257] Celgene's acquisition of Juno Therapeutics for about US$9 billion at the price of US$87 per share. [258] Both Kite and Juno were listed companies at the time of the merger. However, whether these two deals are worthwhile remains debatable.

Progress is also being made in the treatment of solid tumors with CAR-T. However, the major obstacles are identifying antigens on the surface of solid tumors and tumor heterogeneity, which means solid tumors of the same cancer type may vary molecularly from patient to patient, even within a particular patient. Additionally, preclinical and clinical studies on CAR-NK and CAR-macrophage are also underway.

Between 2021 and April 15, 2022, the number of active cell therapy agents in the global immuno-oncology pipeline increased from 2,031 to 2,756, representing an

---

256 https://www.novartis.com/news/media-releases/novartis-receives-first-ever-fda-approval-car-t-cell-therapy-kymriahtm-ctl019-children-and-young-adults-b-cell-all-refractory-or-has-relapsed-least-twice

257 https://www.gilead.com/news-and-press/press-room/press-releases/2017/8/gilead-sciences-to-acquire-kite-pharma-for-119-billion

258 https://www.celgene.com/newsroom/cellular-immunotherapies/celgene-corporation-to-acquire-juno-therapeutics-inc/

increase of 36%, but it also reflected a slowdown in the R&D of oncology cell therapy compared to 43% and 61% the previous two years. The number of NK cell-based therapies increased sharply by 65%.[259]

Below are the key leaders in the global CAR-T space:

Novartis[260] (NVS.US)

In 2012, in partnership with the University of Pennsylvania in the U.S., Novartis invested US$20 million to establish a laboratory focusing on CAR-T research.[261] Kymriah® (CTL019) was granted priority review qualification and unanimous market approval by an expert panel in August 2017 for the treatment of Relapsed or Refractory Acute Lymphoblastic Leukemia (R/R ALL) in children and young adults up to the age of 25.[262] Adult patients with Relapsed or Refractory Diffuse Large B-Cell Lymphoma (R/R DLBCL) were granted the priority review in both the U.S. and Europe.[263] The product sells for US$475,000 per treatment.

259 https://www.nature.com/articles/d41573-022-00095-1

260 https://www.novartis.com/research-development/technology-platforms/cell-therapy/car-t-cell-therapy-and-beyond

261 https://www.fiercepharma.com/pharma/university-of-pennsylvania-and-novartis-form-alliance-to-expand-use-of-personalized-t-cell

262 https://www.fda.gov/news-events/press-announcements/fda-approval-brings-first-gene-therapy-united-states

263 https://www.fiercepharma.com/regulatory/seeking-to-expand-reach-car-t-novartis-snags-new-regulatory-milestones-for-kymriah

Kite Pharma[264]

Kite was founded in 2009 by Arie Belldegrun, an Israeli American oncologist in Santa Monica, California, the U.S. In 2012, Kite entered into a cooperative R&D agreement with the National Institutes of Health (NIH) of the U.S. In March 2014, Kite announced that the U.S. FDA orphan drug designation was granted for the company's proposed therapy for Diffuse Large B Cell Lymphoma (DLBCL). In December 2015, its lead product candidate, KTE-C19, was granted the Breakthrough Therapy Designation status for the treatment of DLBCL, Primary Mediastinal B Cell Lymphoma (PMBCL), and Transformed Follicular Lymphoma (TFL).

In March 2011, Kite received US$15 million in the Series A investment. In June 2014, Kite obtained gross proceeds of US$146.6 million from its IPO at the price of US$17 per share and was listed on the NASDAQ Global market under the symbol "KITE".[265] It became a life sciences unicorn.

In January 2017, Kite announced that it formed a joint venture with Shanghai-based Fosun Pharma to develop and commercialize its cancer treatment in China.[266] Kite received US$40 million, and regulatory and commercial milestones totaling US$35 million.

Gilead Sciences acquired Kite for US$11.9 billion in September 2017. One month later, Yescarta® (KTE-C19) received the U.S. FDA approval, the first CAR-T therapy for the treatment of adult patients with relapsed or refractory Large B-Cell Lymphoma (LBCL) after two or more lines of systemic therapy. On April 1, 2022, Gilead announced that Yescarta® received the U.S. FDA approval as the first CAR-T cell therapy for initial treatment of relapsed or refractory LBCL, the first LBCL treatment to improve upon standard of care in nearly 30 years.[267] The landmark ZUMA-7 study demonstrated that patients

---

264 https://www.kitepharma.com/

265 https://www.nasdaq.com/articles/kite-pharma-prices-ipo-17-above-range-2014-06-19

266 https://www.reuters.com/article/us-kite-pharma-fosun-pharma-idUSKBN14U1JC

267 https://www.gilead.com/news-and-press/press-room/press-releases/2022/4/yescarta-receives-us-fda-approval-as-first-car-tcell-therapy-for-initial-treatment-of-relapsed-or-refractory-large-bcell-lymphoma-lbcl

taking Yescarta® were 2.5 times more unlikely to have cancer progression or need additional cancer treatment within two years.

Tecartus®, the third CAR-T cell therapy, was approved by the U.S. FDA in July 2020, becoming the first and only CAR-T treatment for relapsed or refractory Mantle Cell Lymphoma (MCL). [268]

Juno Therapeutics

Headquartered in Seattle, Washington, the Fred Hutchinson Cancer Center, Memorial Sloan-Kettering Cancer Center, and Seattle Children's Research Institute collaboratively founded Juno Therapeutics in December 2013.

Juno was launched with an initial investment of US$120 million. In 2014, Juno raised US$300 million through private funding, and further raised US$265 million through its IPO, selling 11 million shares at US$24 per share.[269] The total capital raising amount exceeded US$600 million in just more than 12 months, which is an extraordinary accomplishment in the industry.

On January 22, 2018, Celgene announced to acquire Juno Therapeutics at US$87 per share in cash, a total of approximately US$9 billion.[270] In November 2019, New York-based Bristol-Myers Squibb (BMS) completed its US$74 billion acquisition of Celgene. The combined companies have nine products with an annual sale of more than US$1 billion, all of which are blockbuster drugs and the number one oncology franchise for both solid and hematologic tumors.

On February 5, 2021, the U.S. FDA approved Liso-cel under the brand name Breyanzi®[271] for the treatment of Large B-Cell Lymphomas in adults, who has

---

268 https://www.gilead.com/news-and-press/press-room/press-releases/2020/7/us-fda-approves-kites-tecartus-the-first-and-only-car-t-treatment-for-relapsed-or-refractory-mantle-cell-lymphoma

269 https://www.fiercebiotech.com/r-d/updated-juno-banks-a-265m-ipo-pushing-next-big-thing-oncology

270 https://www.reuters.com/article/us-juno-m-a-celgene-idUSKBN1FB1DB

271 https://www.breyanzi.com/

also received failed alternative treatment options on more than two occasions.[272] Liso-cel was priced at US$410,000.

Legend Biotech[273] (LEGN.US)

Founded in 2014 and headquartered in New Jersey, the U.S., Legend is one of the subsidiaries of GenScript, a biotech company listed in Hong Kong. On December 21, 2017, Janssen entered into a worldwide collaboration and license agreement with Legend Biotech to develop CAR-T therapy for Multiple Myeloma treatment.[274] Multiple Myeloma is an incurable cancer in the bone marrow. Globally, it is estimated that 124,225 patients were diagnosed with and 87,084 people died from Multiple Myeloma in 2015. On August 5, 2020, Legend Biotech announced that the China Center for Drug Evaluation recommended Breakthrough Therapy Designation for cilta-cel, an investigational BCMA CAR-T therapy. On February 28, 2022, the U.S. FDA approved Carvykti®, which was co-developed by Janssen and Legend.[275] Several months later, both the European Union and Japan regulatory agencies approved it as well.

JW Therapeutics (2126.HK)

In 2016, Juno and WuXi AppTec joined forces to create a new CAR-T company in China. This Shanghai-based company was led and co-founded by James Li, the founding general manager of Amgen in China.

In March 2018, JW gained US$90 million for Series A investment from leading global investors.[276] In 2022, JW completed and raised US$100 million in Series B financing, followed by a successful IPO in Hong Kong and raised US$300

---

272 https://www.ahdbonline.com/web-exclusives/fda-approvals/3128-fda-approved-breyanzi-novel-car-t-cell-therapy-for-large-b-cell-lymphoma

273 https://legendbiotech.com/

274 https://www.jnj.com/media-center/press-releases/janssen-enters-worldwide-collaboration-and-license-agreement-with-chinese-company-legend-biotech-to-develop-investigational-car-t-anti-cancer-therapy

275 https://www.reuters.com/business/healthcare-pharmaceuticals/fda-approves-jjs-cell-based-multiple-myeloma-therapy-blood-cancer-treatment-wsj-2022-03-01/

276 https://www.fiercebiotech.com/biotech/juno-wuxi-car-t-china-biotech-jw-therapeutics-gains-90m-series-a

million.[277] Bristol-Myers Squibb still owns 17% of this company after the dilution.

In September 2021, JW's CD-19 CAR-T therapy Relma-cel obtained China NMPA approval to treat Large B Cell Lymphoma after two prior lines of systematic treatments.[278] It is the second approved CAR-T therapy for commercialization, after Fosun-Kite joint venture's Yescarta® was first approved in China.

3) Antibody-Drug Conjugates (ADCs)

ADCs are a combination of monoclonal antibodies and small molecules, and are composed of effector molecules, linkers, and antibodies. This special structure takes advantage of the targeting properties of antibody drugs and the tumor-killing characteristics of chemical drugs. The main advantages include: 1) reducing the specificity of the biological function of the target, thus having a wider choice of tumor targets selection compared to monoclonal antibody drugs, and 2) the bystander effect[279] which destroys cells adjacent to the target even if they do not express the target, giving it certain potential for the treatment of solid tumors.

This technology platform has been increasingly prominent in the field of oncology treatment. Over the past 20 years, scientists around the world have made continuous efforts to synthesize ADC drugs, improve safety, and reduce off-target and toxic side effects. Since 2015, the global ADC clinical trials have increased rapidly, and more than 200 clinical trials are underway so far, with indications shifting from hematological tumors to solid tumors such as breast cancer, ovarian cancer, etc. As of September 2021, 14 antibody-drug conjugates have been approved for marketing globally, mainly targeting CD series, HER2, TROP2, and BCMA. The indications include leukemia, lymphoma, breast cancer and multiple myeloma, etc. Among the approvals, 12 were approved in

---

277 https://www.fiercebiotech.com/biotech/jw-therapeutics-rakes-300m-hong-kong-ipo-to-bring-car-ts-to-china

278 https://www.fiercepharma.com/pharma-asia/juno-wuxi-jv-goes-up-against-yescarta-china-nod-for-car-t-therapy

279 The bystander effect refers to the biological response of a cell resulting from an event in an adjacent or nearby cell.

the U.S. market, one in China market, and one in Japan market.[280] The current global ADC market size has exceeded US$5 billion. According to the Boston Consulting Group, there will be more than 40 ADC drugs on the market by 2026, with combined sales exceeding US$25 billion.

The world's first antibody-drug conjugate, Mylotarg®, (developed by Pfizer/Wyeth) was approved by the U.S. FDA in 2000 for the treatment of relapsed CD 33 Acute Myeloid Leukemia (AML), based on a study with surrogate endpoints. In June 2010, the U.S. FDA forced Pfizer to withdraw it after no clear evidence of benefit but severe toxicity in a clinical phase III trial. Later, the U.S. FDA re-approved it with a lower and fractionated dose in 2017. This drug was also approved in Japan and European markets.[281]

Recent deals involving ADC drugs demonstrate the increasing interest in the industry. On September 13, 2020, Gilead Sciences announced the acquisition of Immunomedics, a publicly listed company, and its lead product, Trodelvy®, at US$88 per share in cash, for a total of US$21 billion.[282] Trodelvy® becomes the world's first commercialized TROP-2 ADC. Its sales in 2021 amounted to US$362 million with an estimated sales in 2022 of US$788 million.[283]

On March 28, 2019, AstraZeneca (U.K.) and Daiichi Sankyo (Japan) signed a US$6.9 billion global development and commercialization agreement for the HER2 ADC drug DS-8201.[284]

On July 27, 2020, both groups further expanded their global collaborations in the ADC area. AstraZeneca paid Daichi Sankyo an upfront payment of US$1

---

280 https://www.eposters.net/poster/adc-drugs-global-sales-of-2021-and-future-prospects#

281 https://www.nature.com/articles/d41573-021-00054-2

282 https://www.gilead.com/news-and-press/press-room/press-releases/2020/9/gilead-sciences-to-acquire-immunomedics

283 https://www.fiercepharma.com/special-report/top-10-antibody-drug-conjugate-contenders-2021

284 https://www.astrazeneca.com/media-centre/press-releases/2019/astrazeneca-and-daiichi-sankyo-enter-collaboration-for-novel-her-2-targeting-antibody-drug-conjugate.html#

billion in staged payments,[285] an additional amount of US$1 billion for successful regulatory approvals, and US$4 billion for sales-related milestones.

On February 22, 2013, the U.S. health regulators approved Kadcyla®, produced by Roche Holdings AG, for patients with late-stage metastatic breast cancer who have failed to respond to other treatments.[286] This is the first ADC ever approved for solid tumors. Its global sales reached US$1.9 billion in 2020 and US$2.2 billion in 2021,[287] which is a blockbuster drug.

Seagen[288] (SGEN.US)

The company was founded in 1997 by Henry Perry Fell, Jr. and Clay Siegall. It is headquartered in Bothell, Washington, a suburb of Seattle, the U.S.

It is a global pioneer in the field of ADCs and has led the way in this revolutionary cancer treatment. Its flagship product, Adcetris®,[289] a CD30-specific monoclonal antibody linked to Monomethyl Auristatin E (MMAE), received an accelerated approval in 2011, as the second ADC entering the oncology market. Approved indications included leukemia and systemic anaplastic large cell lymphoma.[290]

On December 15, 2009, Seattle Genetics received an upfront payment of US$60 million and retained full commercialization rights to Brentuximab Vedotin in the U.S. and Canada, while Millennium (Takeda Oncology Company) and its parent company, Japan-based Takeda pharmaceutical group, retained the commercialization rights covering the rest of the world. Seattle Genetics and

---

285 https://www.astrazeneca.com/media-centre/press-releases/2020/astrazeneca-and-daiichi-sankyo-enter-collaboration-to-develop-and-commercialise-new-antibody-drug-conjugate.html#

286 https://www.reuters.com/article/us-roche-approval-idINBRE91L0N420130223

287 https://www.contractpharma.com/heaps/view/8822/1/377366

288 https://www.seagen.com/

289 https://www.adcetris.com/

290 https://www.fiercebiotech.com/biotech/seattle-genetics-announces-fda-accelerated-approval-of-adcetris-tm-brentuximab-vedotin-for

Takeda Group jointly fund the global development costs on a 50/50 basis.[291]

On September 14, 2020, Merck and Seattle Genetics announced two strategic oncology collaboration agreements. Both companies co-developed and co-commercialized Ladiratuzumab Vedotin globally, and Merck would acquire US$1 billion equity stake in Seattle Genetics' common stock.[292]

In October 2020, Seattle Genetics rebranded its name to Seagen, as its presence expanded out of the U.S. and went global.[293]

On August 9, 2021, Seagen and China-based RemeGen (9995.HK) announced an exclusive and worldwide license and co-development agreement for Disitamab Vedotin.[294]

4) Gene therapy

Gene therapy has unique advantages in specific indications and can address clinical problems at the genetic level. However, some are cautious of the scientific and ethical issues involved, including its irreversibility. It focuses on the genetic modification of cells to produce a therapeutic effect or the treatment of disease by repairing or reconstructing defective genetic material. In 1990, Dr. William French Anderson concluded from a prolonged trial concerning children with ADA-SCID that gene therapy can safely and effectively treat specific patients.

Herein, the author categorizes gene therapy into two classes: 1) Adeno-associated Virus Vector, and 2) gene editing therapies based on CRISPR/Cas9 technology.

---

291 https://investor.seagen.com/press-releases/news-details/2009/Seattle-Genetics-and-Millennium-The-Takeda-Oncology-Company-Announce--Strategic-Collaboration-for-Novel-Late-Stage-Lymphoma-Program--Brentuximab-Vedotin-SGN-35/default.aspx

292 https://www.merck.com/news/seattle-genetics-and-merck-announce-two-strategic-oncology-collaborations/

293 https://www.fiercepharma.com/marketing/seattle-genetics-shortens-name-to-seagen-dropping-local-seattle-as-it-goes-global

294 https://investor.seagen.com/press-releases/news-details/2021/Seagen-and-RemeGen-Announce-Exclusive-Worldwide-License-and-Co-Development-Agreement-for-Disitamab-Vedotin/default.aspx

Adeno-associated Virus Vector (AAV)

Between 2016 and 2019, the number of clinical trials utilizing Adeno-associated Virus Vector (AAV) has increased from less than 10 to 45 globally, with main indications targeting the eyes, liver, muscle, and brain. Most of the clinical trials are Phase I/II trials. However, viral-vector gene therapies have several challenges, including: 1) safety concern posed by the use of viruses, 2) selected patients who naturally possess anti-viral antibodies are not eligible for viral therapy, since the viral drug is quickly rendered obsolete by their immune system upon administration, 3) the efficacy of viral-vector gene therapies significantly decreases after the first dose, as the innate human immune system produces anti-viral antibodies, and 4) AAV vectors have a transgene carrying capacity of 4.7 kb, limiting it to only small nucleic acids sequences.

In 2012, the European Medicine Agency (EMA) approved the first gene therapy Glybera[®],[295] an AAV1 vector carrying the human LipoProtein Lipase (LPL) gene, for the treatment of severe muscle diseases lacking LPL. This is an ultra-rare disease, only one person in one million suffering from it. It was subsequently withdrawn due to poor sales as it was sold at the price of US\$1.2 million per patient while there was a limited number of patients in 2017.[296]

In 2017, Spark Therapeutics developed Luxturna[®], an AAV2 vector carrying the RPE65 gene to treat vision loss caused by rare hereditary retinopathy, marking it as the first gene therapy of its kind that received the U.S. FDA approval.[297]

In July 2021, Bluebird bio (BLUE.US) announced Skysona[®], a single-dose gene therapy which was granted marketing authorization by the European Commission (EC) to treat children under 18 years of age with early Cerebral Adrenoleukodystrophy (CALD). On September 16, 2022, Bluebird announced that it received accelerated approval in the U.S.[298]

---

295 https://www.ema.europa.eu/en/medicines/human/EPAR/glybera

296 https://www.labiotech.eu/trends-news/unique-glybera-marketing-withdrawn/

297 https://www.fda.gov/news-events/press-announcements/fda-approves-novel-gene-therapy-treat-patients-rare-form-inherited-vision-loss

298 https://investor.bluebirdbio.com/news-releases/news-release-details/bluebird-bio-receives-fda-accelerated-approval-skysonar-gene

CRISPR therapy

Clustered Regularly Interspaced Short Palindromic Repeat (CRISPR) therapy is one of the most powerful and transformative technologies in human history.[299]

Three pioneering scientists have made significant contributions in this area. Two of them, Jennifer Doudna of the University of California, Berkeley, the U.S., and Emmanulle Charpentier of the Max Planck Unit for the science of Pathogens,[300] Germany, shared the 2020 Nobel Prize in Chemistry for the revolutionary gene-editing technology. This ended years of speculation about who would be recognized for their work in developing the CRIPR-Cas9 gene-editing tools.[301] Prof. Feng Zhang of the Broad Institute is also widely recognized as a pioneer in the development of CRISPR-Cas9 as a genome editing tool and the use in eukaryotic cells, including human cells, from a natural CRISPR immune system found in prokaryotes.[302]

The institutions of the three scientists are locked in a fierce patent battle over who deserves the intellectual property rights to the discovery of CRISPR. On the other hand, the three scientists shared a few prestigious awards together. They have all founded their own start-ups in the field of gene editing.

CRISPR Therapeutics (CRSP.US)[303]

Co-founded by Dr. Emmanuelle Charpentier,[304] Dr. Rodger Novak and Shaun Foy in 2013, the company is headquartered in Zug, Switzerland with its operation of R&D in Cambridge, Massachusetts, the U.S., Germany giant Bayer is one of its investors. In 2016, CRISPR went public on NASDAQ, raising US$56 million.[305]

---

299 https://www.pharmaceutical-technology.com/comment/crispr-based-therapeutics/

300 https://www.mpusp.mpg.de/

301 https://www.science.org/content/article/crispr-revolutionary-genetic-scissors-honored-chemistry-nobel

302 https://mcgovern.mit.edu/profile/feng-zhang/

303 https://crisprtx.com/

304 https://www.nobelprize.org/prizes/chemistry/2020/charpentier/facts/

305 https://www.fiercebiotech.com/biotech/crispr-therapeutics-raises-a-56m-ipo-but-patent-battles-potential-stock-drops-loom

Its broad pipeline of ex vivo and in vivo programs spans four franchises: hemoglobinopathies, immuno-oncology, regenerative medicine, and in vivo approaches.

CRISPR published promising data on the use of CRISPR in β-thalassemia and sickle cell disease in the *New England Journal of Medicine.*[306] In partnership with VERTEX, CRISPR has the potential to deliver the first approved CRISPR-based medicine for the treatment of sickle cell disease and β-thalassemia for over 30,000 patients in the U.S. and the EU.

Intellia Therapeutics (NTLA.US)[307]

In 2015, co-founded by Dr. Jennifer Doudna[308] and Nessan Bermingham, Intellia completed Series A investment of US$15 million led by Atlas Venture and Novartis. Novartis funded it due to its interest in applying CRISPR in CAR-T therapy. Intellia was created by Atlas and Caribou Biosciences, in which Dr. Jennifer Doudna is also a scientific advisor. In September 2015, it secured Series B funding of US$70 million. In May 2016, Intellia announced the closing of IPO and raised approximately US$112.9 million.[309]

The initial therapeutic focus is ex vivo applications, which means cells are removed from the body, either from blood or bone marrow, modified to correct disease-causing genes and returned to the patients for therapeutic benefit.[310]

Intellia established collaborations with Regeneron[311] and Novartis,[312] which

---

306 https://www.nejm.org/doi/full/10.1056/NEJMoa2031054

307 https://www.intelliatx.com/

308 https://vcresearch.berkeley.edu/faculty/jennifer-doudna

309 https://ir.intelliatx.com/news-releases/news-release-details/intellia-therapeutics-announces-closing-initial-public-offering

310 https://ir.intelliatx.com/news-releases/news-release-details/intellia-therapeutics-announces-15-million-funding-develop

311 https://newsroom.regeneron.com/news-releases/news-release-details/regeneron-and-intellia-therapeutics-expand-collaboration-develop

312 https://www.novartis.com/news/media-releases/novartis-collaborates-intellia-therapeutics-and-caribou-biosciences-explore-making-medicines-and-drug-discovery-tools-crispr-genome-editing-technology

boosted its ability in drug development and commercialization. On June 1, 2020, Regeneron and Intellia announced their collaboration to develop CRISPR-based treatments. As a result, Intellia would receive an upfront payment of US$70 million, and Regeneron would make an additional equity investment in Intellia of US$30 million at US$32.42 per share.

Editas Medicine (EDIT.US)

In 2013, Editas was co-founded by Feng Zhang, Jennifer Doudna, George Church, David Liu, and Keith Joung, with funding from Third Rock Ventures, Polaris Partners, and Flagship Ventures. Doudna quit in June 2014 over the one intellectual property rights of Cas9. In August 2015, Editas raised US$120 million in Series B funding from Bill Gates and other investors.[313] Editas went public on February 2, 2016, raising US$94 million.[314] In March 2020, Editas, in partnership with Allergan, became the first to use CRISPR and to try to edit DNA inside the human body (in vivo) for the treatment of Leber congenital amaurosis.

5) PROteolysis-TArgeting Chimeras (PROTACs)

All clinicians are facing the drug-resistance problem, which is unavoidable and for which there is currently no solution. Another bottleneck that the industry has is the limited number of drug targets, which represent only 20-25% of all protein targets being studied. A promising and appealing technology, Proteolysis Targeting Chimeras (PROTACs), has attracted great attention from both academia and industry in the hope of solving problems mentioned above.

They are bifunctional small molecule compounds consisting of two ends: a ligand that binds to the target proteins, and a ligand that binds to E3 ubiquitin ligase, while a linker connects the two to form a protein trimer that promotes ubiquitination[315] of the target protein and leads to the ubiquitin-proteasome

---

313 https://ir.editasmedicine.com/news-releases/news-release-details/editas-medicine-raises-120-million-advance-genome-editing

314 https://www.reuters.com/article/editasmedicine-ipo-idINL2N15H366

315 Ubiquitin, a low-molecular-weight molecule selects the target protein molecule and performs specific modifications on it under the presence and action of a series of prerequisite enzymes.

pathway that degrades the target protein.

One of the most significant advantages of the PROTACs technology is that it can convert "undruggable" targets to "druggable" ones. While conventional small molecules bind to active sites on enzymes or receptors, PROTAC can capture the target protein from any direction.

In July 2001, Craig Crews of Yale University and Raymond Joseph Deshaies of the California Institute of Technology co-authored a paper titled Inducing MetAP-2 Protein Degradation Using Peptide-Based Heterobifunctional Small Molecules, which formally introduced the concept of PROTAC. However, peptide compounds have difficulty entering cells, thus putting an end to the development of the first generation of PROTACs.

In 2008, Craig Crews *et al* designed the second-generation PROTACS that can degrade Androgen Receptor (AR) based on the E3 ubiquitin protein ligase MDM2. In 2015, the team also designed a new generation of PROTACs that can reduce the levels of various proteins by more than 90% based on the novel E3 ubiquitin protein ligase VHL and CRBN ligands. In the same year, James Bradner of Novartis published a new generation of PROTAC molecules based on thalidomide analogy. Since then, the global R&D enthusiasm for PROTACs has continued to increase.[316]

PROTACs have undergone rapid development over the past 20 years, but are limited by challenges around its molecular design, including the design of target protein ligand, limited E3 ligase ligands to choose from, and large molecular weight. Protein structure prediction and virtual drug screening technologies provided by AI technology can alleviate this problem and help the search of suitable ligands for the target protein and E3 ligase to a certain extent. According to *Nature*, at least 15 PROTACs will enter clinical trials by the end of 2021.[317]

Although the research of PROTACs is mainly concentrated in the field of tumors, there are many studies in the fields of neurodegenerative diseases, inflammation, and immunology, such as iRAK4, a non-cancer target, which has

---

316 https://www.nature.com/articles/s41392-019-0101-6
317 https://pubmed.ncbi.nlm.nih.gov/35042991/

been proved to be related to arthritis and atherosclerosis, Alzheimer's disease, gout, systemic lupus erythematosus and psoriasis.

Arvinas (ARVN.US)

Professor Crews founded the world's first PROTAC technology start-up in 2013 to turn protein degraders into patient therapies. In late 2016, Arvinas created the first oral PROTAC. As of the third quarter of 2022, the company's pipeline has three programs in clinical trial phase II for the treatment of difficult-to-treat breast and prostate cancers.

In July 2021, Pfizer and Arvinas announced the global partnership to co-develop and co-market ARV-471 for breast cancer. The total valuation of this deal is US$2.4 billion, which includes Arvinas obtained an upfront payment of US$650 million from Pfizer. Additionally, Pfizer would make an equity investment of US$350 million, taking nearly 7% ownership in Arvinas. In addition, Arivnas is eligible for up to US$400 million on meeting regulatory approval milestones, and up to US$1 billion in commercial milestones. The global development and marketing costs and profits on this product will be equally shared by the partners.[318]

6) Genetic testing

With the rapid improvement of human genome sequencing technology, biomedical analysis technology and big data analysis tools, precision medicine has gradually come into the spotlight. Different regions have varying definitions of precision medicine, but there are some commonalities as follows. 1) Precision medicine is a diagnosis and treatment method based on big data, and treatment plans are based on data information of patients, 2) precision medicine has a wider range of applications, as seen by the extensive scope of medical care it covers, including early diagnosis of disease, personalized guidance, genetic risk analysis, and disease detection. In terms of mechanism of action, precision medicine stresses the diagnosis of individual diseases at the molecular level, 3) precision medicine is based on individualization and differentiation, unlike simple interaction between doctors and patients in the past, it focuses on comprehensive and whole-process

---

318 https://www.pharmaceutical-technology.com/news/arvinas-pfizer-breast-cancer/

observation and diagnosis to suggest personalized treatment plans for patients.

Precision medicine captures individual differences in the genome. Genetic testing is based on chromosomal structure, DNA sequence, variation sites or gene expression levels, providing medical researchers with a basis for evaluating diseases, physique or personal traits tied to genetic inheritance. Common methods of genetic testing include fluorescence quantitative Polymerase Chain Reaction (RT-PCR), Amplification Refractory Mutation System (ARMS-PCR), Fluorescence In Situ Hybridization (FISH) and Sanger sequencing (first generation sequencing). Among them, Next-Generation Sequencing (NGS) is the most extensive technology at present. By introducing reversible termination sequencing technology, sequencing by synthesis has the properties of high throughput and short read length which is ideal for high-throughput DNA sequencing and significantly reduces the cost of large-scale sequencing.

The gene sequencing industry chain consists of upstream instrument and consumable companies, midstream service providers providing gene sequencing, downstream bioinformatics analysis companies, and terminal consumer groups. Gene sequencing instruments and consumable reagents companies are in the upstream of the industry chain, with major global companies such as Illumina,[319] ThermoFisher[320] and Roche,[321] and independent China-based companies include BGI [322] and DaAn Gene.[323] Companies providing gene sequencing services are situated in the midstream, while competition is the fiercest among Chinese companies with more than 100 players. Non-invasive prenatal gene sequencing stands out as one of the most mature gene sequencing technologies. Major U.S. companies include Sequenom, Ariosa Diagnostics and Natera,[324] while in China they are BGI and BerryGenonics.[325] Downstream bioinformatics companies are mainly responsible for the storage, interpretation, and application of big data,

---

319 https://www.illumina.com/

320 https://www.thermofisher.com/hk/en/home.html

321 https://www.roche.com/about/business/diagnostics/

322 https://www.bgi.com/global

323 https://en.daangene.com/

324 https://www.natera.com/

325 https://www.berrygenomics.com/cmscontent/211.html

represented by BGI in China. In terms of consumer groups, the largest market share is still in the field of scientific research, but there is a gradual shift towards the field of disease treatment.

The scale of the global gene sequencing market has grown rapidly due to the popularity of genetic testing and technological breakthroughs. As the relationship between diseases and gene mutations are increasingly characterized, the accuracy of genetic testing is improving. On the other hand, with the maturity of sequencing technology, the cost of gene sequencing shows a downward trend year by year, and the decline of sequencing cost will increase the penetration rate of gene sequencing services, thereby promoting the rapid development of the market.

3. AUTHOR'S INSIGHTS

i.   The world's leading industry players participate in technology platforms often through collaborations, such as, RNA interference, cellular immunotherapy, oncolytic viruses, antibody drug conjugates, gene therapy and stem cell therapy. Industry giants provide funding and global infrastructure in development, regulation, manufacturing, and commercialization, etc. Start-ups provide innovative concepts, new technologies and research talents.

ii. Transactions around tens of billions of US dollars occur. That is a benchmark cost of entering a new field or acquiring an innovative medicine or therapy. However, the author questions if it is worthwhile from an investment perspective and socially responsible perspective, as inequity further divides society.

iii. "Breakthrough" and "revolutionary" technologies rarely happen. They come with generations of global research, accumulations of knowledge and clinical experiences, sacrifice of patients, "trial and error", and often "luck". Each time a "breakthrough" or "revolutionary" emerges, the class of therapeutics enters a new paradigm.

iv. The leading players have two advantages to maintain strong positions, namely deep-pocket capital, and legal actions. As present, the top 20 ranking positions barely change, unless technological disruption occurs.

v.   The traditional valuations based on P/E or P/S ratios do not apply to this wave of life sciences start-ups. It becomes more difficult to forecast due to too many uncertainties. Two realistic methods are based on "supply and demand" and "negotiation".

PART 2

The Right Place at the Right Time

Chapter 4

Investing in China, Investing Now

1. FOREWORD

As a fund manager specializing in global life sciences investments, the author believes abundant investments in the fast-growing region significantly raise the probability of success. In global context, China has been and will be the fastest growing region owing to its overall economic strength, huge unmet clinical needs, industriousness and ingenuity of its people and decades of fundamental research experiences.

Across the past five years, China's life sciences sector has undergone major structural changes such as the quick emergence of start-ups, a reverse brain drains of talents into the field, successful listings of start-ups in the capital market, and the entrance of products into the international market. These factors seep into the global life sciences sector, gradually exerting meaningful influences. Investments in this sector will be rewarding both financially and socially if one takes advantage of China's development and closely follows China-related companies (regardless of the nationality of the company founders) that have an international vision.

Many life sciences practitioners outside of China have little understanding of the sector's development in China. Through a systematic review on recent dynamics in China, the author hopes to deepen the understanding among various stakeholders globally, promoting cross-border collaborations.

This chapter consists of four parts: 1) reasons for the abovementioned structural changes, 2) progressive results from international collaborations, 3) the realistic gap between China-related companies and global industry leaders, and 4) profound factors shaping the industry in decades.

Six key factors have prompted profound changes in China's life sciences:

i.   **Economic foundation:** from the past experiences, when a major economy reached the benchmark of US$10,000 GDP per capita, society usually paid more attention to social welfare and paid more on expensive and innovative medicines. China reached that milestone in 2020.[326]

ii. **Regulation:** a series of new laws and regulations related to healthcare reform, medicines and MedTech spur innovation.

iii. **Payment:** The reform of the medical insurance policy benefits the public, encourages innovation, and provides affordable products more accessible to the general public. The country's government is usually the largest healthcare purchaser in that market.

iv. **Globalization:** China's participation in the International Council for Harmonization of Technical Requirements for Pharmaceuticals for Human Use (ICH)[327] has brought great challenges along with ample opportunities to the industry.

v. **Talents:** Due to the rising trend of anti-China sentiment and policies, many Chinese scientists previously based in the U.S. choose to return to China where it may be easier to raise funds, start entrepreneurship and seek for meaningful career opportunities that achieve individual goals.

vi. **Capital:** The introduction of Chapter 18A to the main board on the Hong Kong Stock Exchange and establishment of Shanghai Science and Technology Innovation Board (STAR Market) on Shanghai Stock Exchange have attracted tremendous capital into the life sciences industry.

Driven by the strong support of the capital market and international talents, China's life sciences sector has been developing rapidly. This can be evidenced by the facts that some leading companies have begun to license innovative technologies and products to renowned Multinational Corporations (MNCs). Moreover, a group of start-ups have implemented the international strategy of conducting concurrent clinical trials in at least two key global markets, namely the U.S. and China.

---

326 http://www.gov.cn/xinwen/2021-02/28/content_5589379.htm#1
327 https://www.ich.org/

2. PART ONE

1) Economic foundation and strength are prerequisites for the development of life sciences.

In global context, the Chinese economy is becoming increasingly important. In the past decade, China's GDP has grown from RMB54 trillion to RMB114 trillion to account for 18.5% of the world economy, up by 7.2%. China remains the world's second largest economy, and its per capita GDP has risen from RMB39,800 to RMB81,000.[328] It ranks first in the world in terms of grain output, and it has ensured food and energy security for 1.4 billion people. China's manufacturing sector is the largest in the world, as it is the largest trading partner with 120 countries.[329] China's life expectancy has reached 78.2 years, its per capita disposable annual income has risen from RMB16,500 to RMB35,100. Its basic medical insurance covers 95% of the population.

China accomplished the task of "eradicating poverty" by the end of 2020. This is the largest battle against poverty not only in the Chinese history, but also in human history. Since 2014, all 832 counties designated as poverty-stricken, where resided close to 100 million poor rural residents, have been lifted out of poverty within a time span of seven years. Among them, more than 96 million have been relocated from inhospitable areas. They account for half of the country's total land area, reducing China's poverty incidence rate from 10.2% to 0.6%.[330] The significant improvement of public services such as education, healthcare and housing in these counties precisely addressed people's unmet needs. These populations are the new wave of drivers for the China national healthcare system.

With a large population base of 1.4 billion, steady and sustainable economic development, increasing disposable income, an exacerbating aging population and large unmet clinical needs, China's healthcare market has enormous potential. These fundamental factors all shape China as the fastest growing region in the world.

---

328 https://www.mfa.gov.cn/eng/zxxx_662805/202210/t20221025_10791908.html

329 https://www.wilsoncenter.org/blog-post/china-top-trading-partner-more-120-countries

330 https://www.chinadaily.com.cn/a/202101/25/WS600e2858a31024ad0baa4cd6.html

2) Regulatory reforms greatly foster innovation and internationalization.

Life sciences are unique realms in the sense that government regulation is very stringent around the world. There is a close correlation between government regulations and local industry development. Since 2015, the China State Council and the National Medical Products Administration (NMPA)[331] have implemented policies and welcomed Request for Comments (RFCs) to address various issues in the drug registration process and to explore cutting-edge therapeutic modalities. The Center for Drug Evaluation (CDE) of the NMPA has expanded its review channels, recruited more reviewers, strengthened the management of review programs, and improved the efficiency of drug applications. Presently, the serious backlogging of applications related to drug registration has been largely resolved.

In 2018, the "Technical Guiding Principles for Accepting Data from Overseas Clinical Trials of Pharmaceutical Products" was published in response to the growing trend of simultaneous R&Ds of pharmaceutical products both domestically and internationally, speeding up the listing process in China. In August 2019, the Drug Administration Law[332] of the People's Republic of China[333] received its first major revision, signifying the first comprehensive amendment since its first pass at the Sixth National People's Congress in 1984. This amendment reflects the summation of China's drug management experiences and the convergence of China's supervision and management standards with that of the international community, especially of the high-income countries. Examples include the clarification of the Marketing Authorization

---

331 http://english.nmpa.gov.cn/

332 http://www.npc.gov.cn/englishnpc/c23934/202012/3c19c24f9ca04d1ba0678c6f8f8 a4a8a.shtml

333 Since 1984, the Drug Administration Law of the People's Republic of China was first adopted at the Sixth National People's Congress, revised for the first time in 2001, and then revised twice in 2013 and 2015.

Holder (MAH) system[334] and the implementation of the clinical trial record system.

Continuous reforms by the NMPA have greatly enhanced the efficiency for innovative drugs and devices being marketed in China, this is vital for industry innovation. In 2016, the average time for new drugs to be marketed in China was eight years longer than the European and the U.S. markets; in 2019, the average marketing time was shortened down to five years,[335] with individual breakthrough innovative drugs being approved in less than a year. These figures demonstrate China' determination in aligning its own regulation system with the world's leading ones.

The revised "Administrative Measures for Drug Registration" enacted in 2020 follows four programs for accelerating the review and approval of New Drug Applications (NDA). They are namely Breakthrough Therapy Designation (BTD), Conditional Approval (CA), Priority Review (PR) and Special Approval (SA). Additionally, the "Measures for the Administration of Drug Registration" drew on approval experience in Europe and the U.S. and saw improvements.

Breakthrough Therapy Designation (BTD):[336] For innovative or modified drugs that are used during clinical trials for the prevention and treatment of diseases that seriously endanger life or seriously affect quality of life; and for which there is no effective means of prevention and treatment; or for which there is sufficient evidence of clear clinical advantages over existing treatment options. Under this procedure, the reviewers communicate closely with the applicants in the early clinical stage to speed up drug development and review.

Conditional Approval (CA): Applicable during drug clinical trials, including 1) drugs for the treatment of serious life-threatening diseases for which no effective

---

334 Refers to the mechanism by which drug R&D and/or manufacturing companies and other parties individually or jointly apply for drug marketing authorization and obtain marketing authorization approval, and such drug marketing authorization holders assume primary responsibility for drug quality throughout its life cycle. Under this system, the holder of the listing license and the holder of the production license can be the same entity or two independent entities.

335 https://link.springer.com/article/10.1007/s43441-022-00472-3

336 http://english.nmpa.gov.cn/2020-07/07/c_538688.htm

treatment is currently available, and where clinical trial data of drugs confirm the efficacy and predict for a positive clinical value, 2) drugs in urgent demand by public healthcare, and clinical data of drugs confirm and predict the efficacy and clinical value, 3) vaccines urgently needed in response to major public health emergencies or other vaccines that the National Health Commission determines as urgently needed, provided that assessed benefits outweigh risks. For drugs approved via this channel, alternative or intermediate care sites may be used as the basis for submitting marketing applications to shorten marketing time. Upon receiving marketing approval, the applicant must complete the clinical trials and provide supplemental application materials within a time limit set by term conditions. If the applicant fails to complete the application within the time limit without acceptable reasons, the NMPA will cancel the certificate of registration of the product.

Priority Review (PR): Applicable during drug marketing authorization, such as 1) urgently needed drugs in short supply, innovative drugs and improved new drugs for the prevention and treatment of major infectious diseases and rare diseases, 2) new medicine modalities for children corresponding to their physiological characteristics, 3) vaccines urgently needed for disease prevention and control and innovative vaccines, 4) drugs included in the breakthrough therapy designation, 5) drugs that received conditional approval, 6) drugs receiving priority review and approvals by the NMPA directly. For drugs included in priority review, the Center for Drug Evaluation will give priority to allocating resources for review as well as shortening the time limit for target review.

Special Approval (SA): If the threat of public health emergencies arises, or after its occurrence, the NMPA may decide in accordance with the law to implement special approval for preventative and treatment drugs to respond to these public health emergencies. Drugs receiving special approval are only distributed within a certain scope and time according to the specific needs for disease prevention and control.

These four accelerated approval procedures reflect China's determination to learn from advanced procedures worldwide and further promote innovation. This is compared to the four expedited approval procedures by the U.S. FDA and the EMA, namely fast track designation, breakthrough therapy designation, accelerated approval designation and priority review.

A research paper "Trends and Characteristics of New Drug Approvals in China, 2011-21" summarizes the outcomes of these regulation reforms: the New Drug Approval time is significantly shortened from the pre-reform time. The newly instituted expedited regulatory pathways are taking effect. More imported drugs are entering China, with less leg time of global first launch.[337] More importantly, we have seen the first global launch of innovation drugs happening in China.

3) The frequent updates of China's medical insurance formulary benefits innovation.

In major countries, the governments are often the largest customer of national medical and health products and services. Their strong purchasing power and market influence are mainly reflected in the form of reimbursement formularies or catalogues. Between 2009 and 2017, the Chinese medical insurance formulary has yet been updated, signifying that innovative drugs newly approved for marketing during this period could not be reimbursed through the national medical insurance system, in turns patients shoulder the total cost of treatments. This negatively impacts the willingness of companies to innovate, and hampers progress of introducing innovative products to market. Since 2017, the National Reimbursement Drug List (NRDL) has been updated four times, with the most recent one in 2023.

Systematic updates on the NRDL including innovative products into the reimbursement catalogue not only benefit the health care of Chinese citizens, but also enable companies to reap proper rewards by investing in innovation.

Volume-based procurement program has lowered drug prices. This presents both opportunities and challenges for the development of innovative drugs. In 2019, the National Healthcare Security Administration published their opinions on the management of current drug prices, emphasizing on volume-based procurement and pricing strategies which reduced the average price of enlisted drugs by about 50%. Under the measure of centralized procurement of medicines, the magnitude of drug price reduction is relatively large. Generic drugs with a wider range of suppliers' choices are further impacted due to fierce competition and

---

337 https://link.springer.com/article/10.1007/s43441-022-00472-3

weak bargaining power. This greatly limits a company's possibility to make huge profit from generic drugs.

Meanwhile, as innovative drugs are included in the NRDL, their sales volume upon entering the market is guaranteed, which is conducive to investment returns and encourages companies to increase their innovation efforts. To be cautious, popular therapeutic areas and mechanisms of action are exceedingly overwhelming. For example, up to July 2022, eight PD-1 immunotherapy cancer drugs from Chinese companies have been launched, with more still in the clinical stage or awaiting marketing approval. Innovative drugs in the same class face strong competition, resulting in limited bargaining power. However, if drugs prices are set too low, their generated revenues will not cover their R&D costs, eventually dampening the enthusiasm of companies to engage in innovations. Faced with opportunities and challenges, innovative companies can attempt to expand into areas with less competition, develop their own innovative R&D pipelines, enhance their own bargaining power, and strive for a reasonable return on investment in the domestic market. China-based companies can also actively explore the international market by conducting clinical trials in other countries and selling products to earn incomes as another means to achieve investment returns. However, it is easier said than done.

4) The NMPA of China joined the International Council for Harmonization of Technical Requirements for Pharmaceuticals for Human Use (ICH) as a new regulatory member.

While the entrance to the ICH[338] is a positive measure to promote China's integration with the global market, Chinese companies also face unavoidable global competition.

The ICH was first initiated by the U.S., EU, and Japan, it is composed of drug regulatory bodies, pharmaceutical companies, and management agencies. Since its inception in 1990, more and more countries and regions joined in as its influence gradually extended. It has grown into an organization with 20 members

---

338 https://www.ich.org/

and 35 observers. The members of ICH represent countries and regions with the highest number of global sales and drug use, including China, the U.S., Japan, Canada, South Korea, Switzerland, and Brazil. The main goal of establishing the ICH is to build a standardized drug registration procedure to harmonize new drug declaration processes and reduce duplicate testing and declaration arises when the same drug is marketed in different regions of the world. This encourages listings of drugs and avoids unnecessary waste of resources.

The ICH is an agency that promotes global mutual recognition and understanding of new drug R&D. Member countries and regions commit to implementing the principles and guidelines set by the ICH within their jurisdictions, including Good Clinical Practice (GCP), Good Manufacturing Practice (GMP), stability testing and the use of international standards encouraged by the ICH according to each member's circumstances, such as requirements on drug safety and efficacy. The most observable impact of implementing ICH's international standards is mutual recognition and comparison of data between different countries and regions, especially clinical data and manufacturing data, thereby reducing the entry barrier of drugs among different countries while speeding up the process. It is worth noting that although the ICH promotes mutual recognition of new drug R&D data, the decision on approving a drug for marketing lays in the hands of drug regulatory agencies from each country or region.

China and Brazil are among the few developing markets within the ICH member countries, with the others being established pharmaceutical powerhouses, such as the U.S., the EU[339] and Japan. Chinese companies do not have a competitive edge, and they must recognize the R&D data by other member countries. This spells an accelerated approval time for foreign drugs to enter the Chinese market. Although joining the ICH has shaken China's pharmaceutical industry in the short term, this courageous move will benefit the industry's progress and internationalization in the long term. Moreover, China's accession to the ICH is conditional, providing a buffer period for Chinese regulators and the industry to adapt. In the integration process, the Chinese drug regulation agency will have to modify policies, systems, regulations and refine regulatory requirements to

---

339 Most of the European markets are from Germany, France, Spain, the U.K. and Italy.

enhance its capacity and efficiency. Systematic improvements concerning clinical trial design, execution, and manufacturing are mandatory for Chinese companies to achieve higher standards. China's participation in international multi-center clinical projects has become more frequent after joining the ICH. Simultaneously, the number of registered and/or listed new drugs is on the climb, benefitting the global CRO industry (please refer to Chapter 12 for details).

Presently, the economic situation between various countries in the world is complicated. The intensification of geopolitical conflicts as well as the prevalence of extreme nationalism and racism will have an impact on international cooperation and the normal operation of ICH. China's access to ICH is likewise to China's access to the World Trade Organization (WTO) in 2001. If globalization can progress smoothly, it is very likely for China to soon contribute innovative medicines that are of low cost and high quality to both high and middle-low-income countries, benefitting the whole humanity.

5) Chinese scientists have made outstanding contributions to promoting the development of the global life sciences industry, and many have returned to China to realize their entrepreneurial dreams.

Talents are crucially prominent in the discovery and development of life sciences. Over the past century, talented Chinese students and scholars have gone overseas to study and work. From 1949 to 1978, they were mainly from Taiwan and Hong Kong. The respectful and diligent tradition of the Chinese nation enabled some of them to become leaders in the life sciences research, such as Dr. Fu-Kuen Lin, an important contributor of Epogen®. Others have found huge success in the drug industry, such as Allen Chao, the founder of Watson Pharmaceuticals, who was born in Shanghai then moved to Taiwan during to Chinese Civil War.[340] Since China and the U.S. established diplomatic relationship on January 1, 1979, many students have left China to study in the developed countries such as the U.S., the U.K., Germany, etc.

The economic gap between China and these countries was considerably large

---

340 https://www.britannica.com/event/Chinese-Civil-War

then. Many Chinese students worked diligently in laboratories which did not appeal to the locals due to the repetitive and boring job nature. To survive, many students chose careers such as biology and computer science that made it relatively easier to be accepted into institutions and obtain local residence status. 30 years later, biology has evolved into life sciences and technology, while computer science has evolved into Telecommunications, Media, and Technology (TMT), or information technologies. At present, Chinese scientists can be found in almost every world-leading laboratory, research institutes and companies globally, with many playing core roles within the team. They have made outstanding contributions to the discovery and development of the life sciences and technology sector but are hardly recognized.

As China's economic growth and living standards have improved significantly over the past decade, many overseas Chinese have returned to live and work. Some knowledgeable and experienced Chinese scientists living abroad have acted as bonds in bridging China with foreign countries; some have chosen to return to their hometown and started businesses, spurring rapid development of biotechnology start-ups; some scientists who started their business overseas and proceeded with expansion in China. The founders and chief scientists mentioned in Chapter 7 and Appendix 1 are typical examples. These linkages benefit China, the U.S., EU, and the entire world.

Unfortunately, geopolitical tensions in the recent years have had a negative impact. For example, During Trump Administration, China Initiative was launched in November 2018, with the purpose to prosecute perceived Chinese espionage. This is the first country-specific initiative in Justice Department history of the U.S.[341] The announcement was followed by months of confrontational rhetoric by Trump and his administration officials who portrayed China as a threat requiring a "whole-of-society" response and casted all Chinese students in American universities as potential spies. Under China Initiative, the FBI initiated thousands of investigations, yet setbacks prompted criticism of the program being racially biased, inconsistent and FBI misconducts. The Department of Justice announced the end of the program on February 23, 2022.

However, the damages are imposed not just to the U.S., but also to China and the

---

341 https://www.technologyreview.com/tag/china-initiative/

humanity. One of the foundations which shaped the U.S. as the most powerful country in the past century is its ability to attract worldwide talents, such as German talents after World War Two, the Soviet Union talents after its collapse, and Chinese talents since diplomatic relationship established between two countries in 1979. The major appeal for these talents is the American Dream, in which personal freedom and justice system are essential parts of it.

According to an advocacy group, the prosecutions contributed to worsening U.S.-China tensions and 71% rise in incidents of violence against Asian Americans from 2019 to 2020. A poll by the Committee of 100[342] and the University of Arizona in summer 2021 found that four out of ten scientists of Chinese descent had recently considered leaving out of the U.S. out of fear of government surveillance. Asian American advocacy group described the China Initiative as a new chapter in Asian American history, stretching back to Chinese Exclusion Act[343] and the internment of Japanese Americans during World War Two. In *Nature*[344] dated March 10, 2022, Mr. Gang Chen, a victim of China Initiative and a Mechanical Engineer at the Massachusetts Institute of Technology in Cambridge, shared that "the chilling effect will have a long-lasting damage to the U.S. higher education and American's ability to attract and retain world talents unless the government acknowledges its own wrongdoings".

By contrast, the Chinese government adopts an open and friendly approach to attract foreign talents (regardless of their origin, country or race) and capital on favorable terms. Numerous China-originated scientists and entrepreneurs working abroad inevitably chose to return due to the relative ease with which they could secure venture capital, garner support from local governments, and list their companies on the Hong Kong and Shanghai stock exchanges. They can pursue their dreams as entrepreneurs and recognize their meaning in life in this manner, making meaningful contributions to society.

---

342 https://www.committee100.org/

343 https://www.archives.gov/milestone-documents/chinese-exclusion-act

344 https://www.nature.com/articles/d41586-022-00555-z

6) Large capital injection into China's life sciences sectors. The establishment of Shanghai Science and Technology Innovation Board and the activation of Hong Kong Chapter 18A listing guidelines make the investment loop completed.

Life sciences companies require financial support at all stages of discovery and development, either from private or public capital markets, or from joint strategic partners. Even though there is no universal consensus on data and numbers, international industry statistics manifest that from 2009 to 2018, it took about ten years for an innovative drug to enter the commercial market starting from early drug discovery, drug development to clinical trials. The average R&D cost was more than US$1.3 billion. Drug development costs are largely dependent on the corresponding therapeutic areas and indications of the medicine. The median R&D cost of drugs for neurological diseases are US$770 million, and that of antitumor and immunomodulatory are around US$2.77 billion. The success rate from early drug discovery to regulatory approval is less than 0.01%. If only considering candidate drugs that successfully enter to clinical phase I, less than 10% pass the final review and enter the market.

The former editor-in-chief of the NEJM and author of the book titled *Truth about the Drug Companies: How They Deceive Us and What to Do about it* presented another perspective and reviewed on these analysis and numbers.

During the R&D stage, companies lack stable income. Hence, feasibility of debt financing is low, thereby posing a serious challenge for a continuous, long-term inflow of capital. Equity fundraising is naturally the best solution. In the first eight months of 2020, the world raised at least US$87 billion in life sciences alone, US$13.25 billion of which was raised through IPO fundraising and US$37.72 billion was through follow-up financing or borrowing. Global market sentiment remains bullish in the healthcare sector.

China's rapid growth in life sciences financing is remarkable: the opening of Chapter 18A of the Hong Kong Stock Exchange and Shanghai Science and Technology Innovation Board (STAR Market) attracts close attention and active participation from Chinese financial institutions and foreign investment institutions. With a market value of over US$140 billion, China's life sciences market is the second largest in the world after the U.S. market.

A major Chinese financial group named China Renaissance[345] published 2020 Global Medical and Life Sciences Report, which summarized the following numbers: Private Equity (PE) financing, Merges and Acquisitions (M&A) transactions, and Initial Public Offering (IPO) in China's healthcare industry exceeded US$45 billion in 2020.[346] 1) There were 243 private financing transactions in the fields of pharmaceutical and biotechnology sectors; the total financing amount exceeded US$10.7 billion; there were 15 transactions related to M&A, involving approximately US$800 million; in terms of IPO, more than 50 companies went public, resulting in a total financing amount that exceeded US$14.7 billion. 2) In the field of medical devices, the total financing amount of private financing transactions exceeded US$2.4 billion; the total financing of M&A transactions turned out to be US$360 million; and IPO financing exceeded US$2.2 billion. 3) In the field of In Vitro Diagnostics (IVD), private equity financing exceeded US$4 billion; M&A transactions amounted to approximately US$500 million; IPO financing exceeded US$1.3 billion.

Hong Kong Stock Exchange Chapter 18A

In February 2018, Hong Kong Exchanges and Clearing Market (HKEX)[347] published its consultation conclusions on the listing rules of pre-revenue biotech companies in Hong Kong, heralding a new era for the Hong Kong capital market.[348] The new Chapter 18A permits the listing of pre-revenue biotech companies on HKEX, subject to certain investor protection safeguards that sought to ensure only biotech companies at a relatively late stage of development could go public. Shares of companies listed under Chapter 18A are denoted by a "-B" suffix.

Since the listing reform of the HKEX in 2018, Hong Kong has become the largest life sciences financing center in Asia. As of June 30, 2021, 67 healthcare companies were listed on the HKEX, raising a total of HK$209 billion. Among

---

345 https://chinarenaissance.com/m/aboutUs

346 https://finance.sina.com.cn/stock/relnews/hk/2021-02-10/doc-ikftpnny6131990. shtml

347 https://www.hkex.com.hk/?sc_lang=en

348 https://www.skadden.com/insights/publications/2022/06/quarterly-insights/2021-report-of-hong-kong-listed-biotech-companies

them, 33 were pre-revenue biotech companies listed through Chapter 18A, raising HK$87 billion.[349] BeiGene, Innovent, and Junshi Biosciences were pre-revenue at the time of listing under Chapter 18A, and they have seen considerable operating incomes to date, hence their "-B" suffix was removed.

HKEX's biotech initiative has gathered momentum over the last four years: five listings in 2018, nine listings in 2019, 14 listings in 2020, and 20 listings in 2021, totaling 48 companies. Among them, 17 are headquartered in Shanghai, nine in Suzhou, eight in Beijing and six in Hangzhou. Particularly, among the nationality of board members, 51% are China nationals, and 27% are U.S. nationals, this exemplifies the unique nature of life sciences sector.

Shanghai Science and Technology Innovation Board

The Science and Technology Innovation Board (STAR Market) of the Shanghai Stock Exchange[350] in China was initiated in 2019 and is independent from the Main Board. This Innovation Board details specific requirements for listing companies to "adapt to the frontiers of global technologies, focus on areas with great economic potential, and address major national needs", "support applicants that adopt national strategies, possess key core technologies, bring outstanding technological innovations, and has a production and operation model founded on key core technologies that is reflected by a stable business model, high market recognition, positive social images and strong growth potential."[351] The Innovation Board includes highly technical enterprises, provides capital services to innovative businesses in fields such as biomedicine, biotechnology, new energy, and new materials.

In 2020, 45 companies in the healthcare related industry were listed on A-shares, raising about RMB65.3 billion, of which 30 companies were listed on the Science and Technology Innovation Board, raising approximately RMB49 billion. Regarding the number of companies listed and amount of funds raised, the

---

349 https://www.hkex.com.hk/Join-Our-Market/IPO/Listing-with-HKEX/HKEX-in-Biotech?sc_lang=en. Global Markets Asia Timezoon HKEX, 2021. HEWX in Biotech Issue No.6.

350 http://star.sse.com.cn/en/

351 http://english.sse.com.cn/start/rules/sse/public/c/4938263.pdf

STAR Market is an attractive listing market for non-profitable life sciences and technology companies.

Twin cities of China: Hong Kong and Shanghai

The reform of the HKEX in 2018 allowed pre-revenue companies to be listed, attracting outstanding biotech and life sciences companies to list in Hong Kong. The Shanghai Stock Exchange followed suit in 2019 with the establishment of the Science and Technology Innovation Board to encourage yet-profitable biotech and life sciences companies to list. The two exchanges have simultaneously paved the path for innovation companies to go public at ease, and each has their own unique features, therefore, they act in form of cooperation over competition.

The shareholders' structures and bases, preferences and product market for each company are different. While some shareholders prefer to list in Hong Kong, others have their eyes on Shanghai. There have been successful cases of dual listing in Hong Kong and Shanghai. These two listings present a more complementary and cooperative landscape, rather than competition.

Hong Kong has the advantage of being the connector of Mainland China and overseas markets, and at the geographic center of Asia, four hours flights to all the major capitals of Asian countries. While Shanghai is in the heart of the industrial hub and close to the Chinese market.

3. PART TWO

1) Through decades consistent efforts, China has become one of worldwide innovation powerhouses, with the humanity in mind to help its own people and globally.

According to the *Nature* Index in 2019, China ranks the second to the U.S. among the top ten countries in terms of high-quality scientific and research journals related to natural science published. China's academic contribution increased by 15.4% compared to the previous year.[352] On August 9, 2022, The

---

352 https://www.nature.com/nature-index/news-blog/the-ten-leading-countries-in-natural-sciences-research-nature-index-annual-tables-twenty-twenty

Japan Ministry's National Institute of Science and Technology Policy released a report citing that China leads in both the number of scientific research papers as well as most cited papers.[353] The report compiles the data from research-analytics company Clarivate.[354] The figures represent 2019 levels, based on the annual average between 2018 and 2020, to account for the fluctuations in publication numbers.

In *Science*, one article analyzed various methods and concluded that China rises to first place in most cited papers, however the U.S. is still ahead in scientific prowess.[355] This trend reflects China's accentuation in the value of scientific research through its support and investments. Although the development process will be fraught with twists and turns, steady progress is all that matters in the long run.

Recently, a report released by the *U.S. News & World Report*[356] ranked 2,000 schools from more than 90 countries. For the first time, China surpassed the U.S. in term of numbers of universities making this list, specifically 338 from China, 280 from the U.S., and Japan made the third with 105 universities on this ranking. However, the U.S. universities most appear on the top half the ranking.[357] the U.S. and the U.K. occupied the top ten spots.

World Intellectual Property Organization (WIPO) [358] has identified the top 100 most vibrant clusters of science and technology worldwide. Its methodology includes inventors listed in patent applications under WIPO's Patent Cooperation Treaty (PCT), spanning the years 2014 and 2018. Authors listed in Web of Science's Science Citation Index Expanded (SCIE) and covering the same period. The geocoding of inventor and author addressed and the use of density-based spatial clustering of applications with noise algorithm to the geocoded inventor

---

353 https://asia.nikkei.com/Business/Science/China-tops-U.S.-in-quantity-and-quality-of-scientific-papers

354 https://clarivate.com/

355 https://www.science.org/content/article/china-rises-first-place-most-cited-papers

356 https://www.usnews.com/education/best-global-universities/china

357 https://www.marketwatch.com/story/for-the-first-time-china-outnumbers-the-u-s-on-this-ranking-of-the-worlds-best-universities-11666729011

358 https://www.wipo.int/edocs/pubdocs/en/wipo_pub_gii_2020-chapter2.pdf

and author points. The top 100 clusters are spread out in 26 countries. The U.S. accounts for 25 clusters, while China accounts for 17 clusters. The Shenzhen-Hong Kong-Guangzhou cluster[359] is ranked second, only behind Tokyo-Yokohama Cluster.

Most importantly, as the author went through the missions and visions of these leading China-based life sciences companies in Chapter 7, majority of the founders are determined to help middle-low-income countries and uphold humanity's needs in mind.

2) The rise of China's life sciences in global Business Developments domain.

China has gradually involved in global Business Development (BD) over the past decade with significant progress. The core value of life sciences companies, which involve medicines, MedTech and therapies, is manifested in product pipelines. Companies around the world face the common challenge of developing innovative products. This challenge is accomplishable only through either in-house Research and Development (R&D) or business development pathways. In-house R&D has become a bottleneck due to the very lengthy R&D period, extremely high cost and low success rate. Even worse, many innovative drugs approved by the regulatory authorities do not reach estimated peak sales, as pointed out by one of the L.E.K. analysis.[360] Transactions between established global pharmas that started from chemical drugs and biotech start-ups have grown rapidly. Business development is an essential part of their strategy to enrich pipelines and product portfolio, alongside in-house R&D.

Business Development (BD) in China's pharmaceutical sector originated from Multinational Corporations more than a decade ago. The value of business development was only recognized after the urgent need for innovation and improvements in the life sciences ecosystem. However, the meaning of the term "Business Development" varies by different understandings.

---

359 The GBA area

360 https://www.lek.com/insights/ei/biopharma-launch-trends-lessons-learned-leks-launch-monitor

In view of the profound changes over the past ten years in China, the author, as one of the earliest professionals in BD, believes that the purpose of business development is to complement a company's in-house R&D, by means of enriching the number of product pipelines, or value through license-in, license-out, partnership, investment and other methods to ultimately enhance the market value of the company, and reach companies' mission. The company CEO must put business development as a priority, as it often involves a relatively large transaction amount or an important partner. Additionally, a successful BD project requires a high degree of cooperation from all parties, as well as strong execution capability and teamwork spirit.

When valuing license-in and license-out projects, some key elements include down payments, milestone payments, profit sharing and aggregate amount. Down payment is a significant metric, some companies only announced the lump-sum of the transaction while omitting the down payment amount. Another key metric is whether the company is receiving milestone payments on time.

According to statistics from the big data service platform PharmCube, the transaction value of China's innovative drug license out reached US$17.4 billion in 2022, the highest in history, an increase of 22.8% over 2021. The number of transactions reached 48, compared to 42 in 2021.

4. PART THREE

1) Scale gap between China-related[361] life sciences companies and global players.

When we look at the worldwide leading companies, they can be broadly categorized into three groups. First, some of them have more diversified business portfolios. For example, the U.S.-based J&J is involved in the pharmaceutical in both chemical and biopharmaceutical, MedTech, and consumer healthcare businesses, while the Swiss-based Roche is involved in both pharmaceutical and diagnostics businesses. Second, some companies, during the COVID-19

---

361 China related: market is primarily in China. However, the owners do not have to be Chinese by legal or by race.

pandemic, are tied to pandemic-related products, and generally saw improvement in sales and ranking. Third, some companies are facing more patent cliff threats from their flagship products in upcoming years, hence there has been a trend of increasing R&D spending to develop new products to cover potential sales loss from patent expiration.

There are a few rankings suggested by various agencies, and sometimes numbers cited do not echo with one another, for example: one ranking from Fiercepharma,[362] one ranking by Pharmaceutical Executive,[363] one ranking by PharmaBoardroom,[364] and Nature Reviews Drug Discovery.[365] They are all good references; readers can go through the details in each article to better understand this industry's complexity. Here are some observations and insights that author would like to pinpoint:

i.   Life is full of uncertainties and great surprises. This once-in-a-century pandemic has brought unexpected changes to the industry, articulated by Pfizer's return to number one due to sale of its mRNA vaccines and COVID-19 pill Paxlovid®, with US$72 billion in contrast to the company's 2020 revenue of US$41.9 billion. In addition, all COVID-19-Related diagnostic reagent and protective equipment companies' business boomed.

ii. Breakthrough innovations make industry paradigm shift. Originally intended for use in cancer immunotherapy, the mRNA technology has been recognized as a breakthrough technology for novel vaccine development route owing to the outbreak of COVID-19 pandemic. It has, without notice, shaken the rankings of established global life sciences industry, with Moderna and BioNTech at their heights, climbing up the top 20 MNCs ladder by market capitalization. mRNA technology broke the time record of discovery, development, manufacturing, and distribution vaccines on the global scale. More importantly, mRNA technology has revolutionized our understanding of the vaccine sector and caused vaccine industry paradigm shift.

iii. Business foundation is built on a strong and innovative pipeline. Swiss-based

362 https://www.fiercepharma.com/special-reports/top-20-pharma-companies-2021-revenue

363 https://www.pharmexec.com/view/2022-pharm-exec-top-50-companies

364 https://pharmaboardroom.com/articles/top-10-global-pharma-companies-2021/

365 https://www.nature.com/articles/d41573-022-00047-9

giant Roche is a great example. The 2020 sales of Roche Pharmaceuticals declined comparably to 2019, mainly due to the worse-than-expected sales of its three long-term leading drugs: Herceptin[®],[366] Avastin[® 367] and Rituxan[® 368] following the flooding of biosimilars into the market. However, its innovation is so strong that the lion's share of growth came from a new wave of products, namely, Tecentriq[®] which saw a 55% increase in sales in 2020 compared to 2019, and several more indications for the drug have been approved by the U.S. FDA. Multiple Sclerosis medication Ocrevus[®],[369] hemophilia drug Hemlibra[® 370]. The U.S. FDA further approved three drugs by Roche in 2020, including Gavreto[® 371] for cancer treatment, Evrysdi[® 372] for the treatment of spinal muscular atrophy and Enspryng[® 373] for the treatment of neuromyelitis optica spectrum disorder. Notably, Roche owns the world's industry leading IVD business, positioning the company to an unshakable status in the field of cancer precision therapy.

iv. M&A is the most effective method to expand global market share. M&A led to AbbVie's 2020 sale rise by 38% compared to that in 2019 and Bristol-Myers Squibb's rise by 63% in the same period. AbbVie acquired Allergan for US$63 billion in May 2020, moving AbbVie higher on the ranking, while Bristol-Myers Squibb acquired Celgene at the end of 2019, with their cancer drug Revlimid[®] bringing in US$12.1 billion in sales alone in 2020. However, the long-term benefits and growth after M&A remains to be seen.

v. There are currently no China-related companies on the global top 20 list. China is still in the early stages of innovative life sciences. Previous analysis shows that established global drug players have at least decades' experience accumulation, while biotech companies established leadership positions in the early paradigm development stage within their respective technological fields. Originating from capitalist countries, these MNCs have all benefited

---

366 https://www.herceptin.com/

367 https://www.avastin.com/patient/mcrc.html

368 https://www.rituxan.com/

369 https://www.ocrevus.com/

370 https://www.hemlibra.com/

371 https://www.gavreto.com/

372 https://www.evrysdi.com/

373 https://www.enspryng.com/

from globalization primarily through M&As. China will face a torturous pathway ahead, with further impediment from discrimination and anti-globalization.

2) Innovation gap between China-related life sciences companies and global players.

According to Boston Consulting Group,[374] the innovation of drugs and treatment modalities are classified into three respective groups: high innovation, medium innovation, and low innovation.

High innovation refers to the use of new drug targets, mechanism of actions, or novel technologies to develop new drugs and treatment therapies. Examples include Novartis's CAR–T therapy Kymriah®, and Moderna's mRNA vaccine Spikevax®.

Medium innovation refers to drug targets that have been verified, or the reliability of the technology has been proven. On this basis, rapid "me-too", technological improvements, molecular modification, and the expansion of new combination therapies emerge. Examples are Chinese biopharma's development of anti-PD-1/PD-L1 monoclonal antibodies.

Low innovation refers to new formulations, innovative drug delivery methods, reagents, biosimilars and generic chemical drugs etc.

At present, China-related companies cannot compete with industry global players in the fields of technological innovation, capital, and global operational capabilities. It is hardly seen for these companies to successfully develop new targets or novel technologies. However, some companies emphasize innovation, consequently, have achieved better results. Most of these companies focus on products in the Medium Innovation category, implementing "fast follow-up" strategy or obtaining the authorization of innovative overseas products that have better predicted clinical value. The R&D pipelines are more feasible and have lower investment risk.

---

374 BCG: China's rise in Pharmaceutical Innovation.

Innovations within China-related companies tend to target unmet domestic clinical diseases. Due to racial and lifestyle differences, the incidence rates for some diseases are different across China, the U.S. and Europe. China's vast 1.4 billion population by comparison also presents greater unmet clinical need, therefore some companies are more active in R&D activities related to indications unique to the Chinese patient population.

3) China-related life sciences sector on the global landscape.

IQVIA Institute for Human Data Science[375] independently published a detailed report on Global Trends in R&D in February 2022, as a public service, without any industry or government funding. Some key findings related to China are as follows: over 3,000 life sciences companies or organizations around the world are involved in research, and notably, 12% of the pipeline is currently held by companies headquartered in China, up from 4% five years ago. Life sciences deal transactions have shifted actively and geographically to include more companies in China and Asia-Pacific (APAC) countries, fewer Europe-based companies, while North American companies remain the largest number.

Emerging Biopharma companies (EBPs), defined as estimated expenditure on R&D less than US$200 million, and revenue less than US$500 million, are responsible for a record of 65% in the R&D pipeline, up from less than 50% in 2016, and one-third in 2001. These headquartered in China now account for 17% of the overall EBPs pipeline, up from 6% just five years ago.

Oncology is a good example to demonstrate both similarity and difference in China and other markets. Cancer treatments have been an essential part of global discovery and development in the past 20 years, and each global player has heavily invested in oncology pipelines. The driving factors to the growth of the oncology drug sector are increasing patient population, rise in clinical demand, favorable policies, and increased R&D spending. The growth of this market has, for a large part, been propelled by the emergence of targeted therapy.[376] The global oncology drug market saw huge growth, accounting for 8.1% and

---

375 https://www.iqvia.com/insights/the-iqvia-institute

376 https://www.cancer.gov/about-cancer/treatment/types/targeted-therapies

11.6% of the overall drug market in 2016 and 2020 respectively. In China, the oncology drug market accounted for 9.4% and 13.6% in the same period. Globally, the top ten tumors by patient population accounted for 69.6% of all new cases. They include prostate cancer, skin cancer and liver cancer which have a higher Compound Annual Growth Rate (CAGR) compared to other cancer types. However, cancer incidence rates in China are on the rise, with lung cancer, liver cancer, gastric cancer, colorectal cancer, and thyroid cancer ranking among the top five cancers, accounting for more than 50% of all new cases in China. Another key factor to the growth of the global oncology market is the increasing significance placed on immunotherapies, figures-wise, that is an upswing from US$93.7 billion in 2016 to US$150.3 billion in 2020. In China, the sales of oncology drugs have increased at a CAGR of 12.1% from 2016 to 2020, resulting in a market size of RMB197.5 billion.

China is a key global player in combination therapy, dual antibody therapy and the expansion of indications, for example, nasopharyngeal carcinoma and late-stage cancer stem cells, as well as pioneering in new targets and technologies, such as ADC, PROTAC, cell therapy, CAR-T therapies etc. This is also evident through the dramatic increase of first IND applications at an average annual growth rate of 32% between 2010 and 2020, totaling 1,636 innovative drugs that were submitted. The top three therapeutic areas that have been approved with IND application are oncology, infection, and endocrine disorders.

5. PART FOUR

Looking into the future, the following factors directly influence the structure of global industry, making impacts either negatively or positively.

1) Industry leading players have solid foundations of talents, technologies, brand recognition, and global experiences.

Development of the life sciences requires longstanding accumulation of technologies, talent pools, intellectual properties protection, global operational capabilities, heavy investment in manufacturing etc. The world's top 30 industry leaders can be broadly categorized into two natures: one is traditional, established, and global giants with long history, such as Merck founded in 1891, and Eli Lilly established in 1876 which started with chemical drugs, and gradually entered the biopharmaceutical, life sciences sectors. Another is companies such as Amgen founded in 1982, and Genentech founded in 1976, which accompanied the rise of the biotech industry, and have garnered several decades of experiences. However, China's innovative companies have only emerged in the past decade. Hence, there is a huge gap between them and the established as well as leading global players, in terms of product innovation, technological leadership, and global management standards. Regardless, the rising trend is unstoppable.

2) The global top life sciences leaders are all MNCs, which have benefited from globalization beginning in the 1980s.

They built up their global market position, via numerous M&As, and partnerships across continents. Among the top 30 MNCs worldwide, only two companies originated from Asia, namely Japan-based Takeda Pharmaceuticals and Astellas Pharmaceuticals. Both rose to prominence through continuous M&As of American and European companies. Takeda even employs a non-Japanese as group CEO. It is to a large extent, impossible for a China-based company to become a Multinational Corporation by solely relying on the China market. Unfortunately, geopolitical tensions have complicated cross-border M&As for Chinese companies. Normal business activities have been politicized, many cross-borders transactions are hampered, resulting in significant sufferings for international law firms, investing funds and investment banks.

3) The nature of capitalism has never changed and now the ugly truth of the system is slowly revealed.

The core ideology of capitalism is "Profit Maximization". A few prominent industry leaders, namely the founders of Johnson & Johnson, and Merck, strived to uphold the people-oriented credos, the true nature of business. These credos attracted and inspired worldwide talents to work for them. Unfortunately, many virtues in the industry have been disregarded over the past decade, as companies sacrifice morals in the face of capitalism or CEO's self-interest. John Bogle was the founder of the U.S.-based financial giant Vanguard Mutual Group and the creator of the first worldwide index mutual fund. He wrote a reflective book at his late age titled *Enough: True Measures of Money, Business and Life*, to share his views on the fall of morality of the Corporate American.

During Mr. Bill Cliton's presidency[377] from 1993 to 2001, the First Lady oversaw healthcare reform. However, 30 years have passed, and the U.S. has yet solved the universal healthcare coverage problem, even with the largest healthcare budget on earth. Many elderly people and low-income people have limited access to their needed medications due to the costs. Medications access is the basic human right.

4) Global North and Global South, is there fair play?

There is a huge gap between high-income and middle-low-income countries, in healthcare infrastructure, innovation, manufacturing, and distribution. The gap has increasingly widened. Coincidently, these high-income with relatively large population size countries, typically G7, were and have been colonial states. While middle-low-income countries were colonized in the past. The high-income countries often emphasize their technological advancements, hence they tend to ignore the economic damages brought along to the colonized regions or countries.

While the transactions over orphan drugs value at billions of dollars in the Global North, majority population in the Global South do NOT even have the access to basic medical remedies in many preventable and curable therapeutic diseases. The World Health Organization repeatedly mentions the lack of basic medications to prevent and cure many diseases in the low-income member states in its reports.

6. AUTHOR'S INSIGHTS

China is a middle-low-income country with 1.4 billion people (roughly 17.5% of the eight billion global population), 100 million of which is just lifted out of poverty. The principle of Chinese government's policy is to help its citizens live healthy and longer, which is a tremendous challenge, given its gigantic population size. Meanwhile, China has the second largest number of millionaires[378] behind

---

377 https://www.whitehouse.gov/about-the-white-house/presidents/william-j-clinton/

378 https://www.statista.com/topics/5788/millionaires-in-china/#dossierKeyfigures

the U.S. Moreover, China is also the home of the largest middle-income population in the world, approximately 700 million people.[379] Therefore, China is an extremely complicated market.

China is a country with over 5,000 years documented history and it has accumulated grand civilizations. Chinese philosophy believes in harmony and peace, not aggression and invasion as well as not going extremes but taking a balanced and compromised approach. Philosophy dictates thinking and thinking dictates behaviors. People must respect each other and respect different civilizations. This is the only way that eight billion people on earth survive in harmony.

China-related life sciences sector has been an important integrated part of global community. Its mass and quality manufacturing capabilities have helped people globally during this pandemic. Its success can certainly make a good example for the Global South developing counties. Equipped with fast-moving innovation, China-related life sciences companies will help not only its own people, but also the patients and people throughout the world.

---

379 https://www.statista.com/statistics/875874/middle-class-population-in-china/

Chapter 5

China Market Opportunities for International Pharmas

1. STRATEGIC OPPORTUNITIES IN CHINA

China's pharmaceutical market is characterized by its sheer size of the population and patient base, significant unmet clinical needs, as well as the rapidly improving regulatory and market access environment. These factors have long been the key drivers for international pharmaceutical companies who made their strategic decisions to enter China and invest in the Chinese market.

In 1981, Japan's Otsuka was the first international pharma to enter the People's Republic of China through a Joint Venture (JV) with the local government of Tianjin. This, together with the establishment of Sino-American Shanghai Squibb (SASS), Xi'an Janssen, and a few others, marked the start of a new era of the Chinese pharmaceutical industry. Over the past four decades, these international pharmas have invested over US$20 billion in the Chinese market,[380] contributing to the development of commercial infrastructure, manufacturing, and advanced R&D. These international pharmas have introduced more than 350 innovative medicines[381] for the benefit of Chinese patients, and trained hundreds of thousands of technical and commercial talents for the Chinese pharmas and biotech industry. Data published by IQVIA shows that as of 2021, there are hundreds of international pharmas operating in China, contributing to about 30% of the Chinese in-hospital pharmaceutical market.

- *In 2021, five out of the top ten pharmas by hospital sales are international companies, with AstraZeneca taking the top spot ahead of any other domestic or international peers. Others on the list are Pfizer (No. 4), Roche (No. 5), Bayer (No. 9), and Novartis (No. 10).*

---

380 Ministry of Commerce, Report on Foreign Investment in China

381 DXY Insight

- *AstraZeneca's Osimertinib (Tagrisso) for lung cancer attained the fastest New Drug Application (NDA) approval in the National Medical Products Administration (then China Food and Drug Administration)'s history, taking less than two months.*
- *Merck & Co./MSD's GARDASIL9 (9-valent HPV vaccine) received the fastest conditional approval in NMPA (then CFDA)'s history in just nine days on grounds of its significant efficacy breakthrough.*
- *Of the 59 innovative products that were granted with expedited reviews by the NMPA in 2021, 29 (49%) are from international pharmas.*

Over the past decade, as aforementioned in other chapters of this book, Chinese pharma companies have begun to accelerate their investments and R&D activities in innovative therapies, moving rapidly from generics to fast followers to the present positioning of leading global development in certain therapeutic areas and modalities. This, in parallel to the evolving policies, expedited regulatory pathways, expanded reimbursement coverage, centralized procurement and pricing pressures, has fundamentally changed the market environment and competitiveness for the international pharmas in China, posing challenges nonetheless presenting new strategic opportunities.

China provides not only a sizable and growing pharmaceutical market, but also strategic values for those companies who operate a global business. China has become an important source of innovation for the global pharmaceutical and biotech industry, generating first-in-class and best-in-class assets that represent significant global commercial opportunities. At the same time, it offers world-class clinical development capabilities and resources with a large patient population which is backed up by abundant fundings from both public and private institutions that place biotech and life sciences on the top of their investment priorities.

Despite the recent geopolitical tensions and market fluctuations, most Multinational Corporations (MNCs) pharmas remain committed to the Chinese market with continued presence and investment in the country. They continue to be a strong confidence in the future of the Chinese pharma market acting as a critical and integral part of the global industry.

"… Greater China is an important region for global pharmaceutical products broadly, and specifically for medicines that treat cardiovascular and metabolic diseases …"

- CEO, Arrowhead, April 2022[382]

"... The one thing I'll say about China is that, going forward, and given the fact that the country is now so open to innovation, we are now thinking about China as we think about any other country ..."

- President, Novartis, February 2022[383]

"... [China serves] not only as a market but very much so also as an innovation hub. That's also the reason why we are present in China across the full value chain, from research, development, manufacturing to distribution ..."

- CEO, Roche, February 2021[384]

"... Tremendous patient need and a fast-developing healthcare infrastructure make China a strategic priority. We are eager to not only expand late-stage therapies to the broader patient population there, but also to accelerate our clinical development efforts in Asia and better understand and address the needs of patients there ..."

- CEO, BridgeBio, August 2020[385]

2. MNC PHARMAS: ADAPTING TO NEW NORMAL

China's pharmaceutical market has certainly evolved significantly from what it was when the first MNCs came to China in the 1980s, and the speed of change has even accelerated in the past few years, which called for MNC pharma's bold transformations in their China strategies to adapt to this "new normal".

382 Global Genes, https://globalgenes.org/2022/04/25/arrowhead-and-vivo-capital-launch-joint-venture-in-china-to-develop-rnai-based-therapies/

383 Fierce Pharma, https://www.fiercepharma.com/pharma/astrazeneca-sounds-slowdown-alarm-jefferies-beats-85b-drum-chinas-branded-drug-market

384 Xinhua News, http://www.xinhuanet.com/english/2021-02/05/c_139722043.htm

385 BridgeBio, https://bridgebio.com/news/bridgebio-pharma-expands-reach-into-china-and-other-major-asian-markets-through-strategic-collaboration-with-perceptive-advisors-founded-company-lianbio/

1) Accelerated path to market

Over the past six to seven years, China's National Medical Products Administration (NMPA) made continuous efforts to standardize product registration processes and introduce expedited registration pathways for innovative therapies. China also joined the International Council for Harmonization of Technical Requirements for Pharmaceuticals for Human Use (ICH) in 2017, aiming to upgrade the drug regulatory system to international standards. As a result, new drug development and launch have been expedited with China's early involvement in International Multicenter Clinical Trials (IMCTs). This has led to more rigorous and globally recognized clinical trials, and the use of Chinese patient trial data as leverage to support global registrations.

In 2017, China's NMPA (then CFDA) only recorded 82 trials involved in IMCT. This number nearly tripled in 2021, among which Phase I / II trials more than quintupled, contributing to 37% of the 302 IMCTs recorded in that year. Over 80% of these IMCTs were carried out by international pharmas.

As a result, the lag between the first global launch (excluding China) and China's launch for innovative therapies is rapidly narrowing. In 2016, there were only four new international pharma drugs being approved in China, an average of 8.4 years after their first global launch. In 2021, NMPA approved 32 NDAs by international pharmas with an average of 5.7 years lag – the closest of which was Blueprint Medicines' Pralsetinib (Gavreto®), which was licensed to CStone and obtained approval in China only six months after its first ex-China approval by the U.S. FDA.

Table 1: Launch lag between China and global first launches (2016 vs. 2021)

2016: 5 products in total	Launch lag (years)
Sirturo (bedaquiline)	3.9
Prevnar13 (pneumococcal conjugate vaccine)	6.9
Cervarix (HPV vaccine)	8.8
Zavesca (miglustat)	14.0
Average lag (2016)	8.4
2021: 32 products in total	**Launch lag (years)**
Gavreto (pralsetinib)	0.5
Enspryng (satralizumab)	0.7
Qinlock (ripretinib)	0.8
Evrysdi (risdiplam)	0.8
...	...
Xenazine (tetrabenazine)	12.8
Average lag (2021)	5.7

Source: NMPA, the U.S. FDA, EMA, L.E.K. analysis

In addition, starting in 2020, within designated hospitals in several locations, namely Boao Lecheng International Medical Tourism Pilot Zone in Hainan Province and the Greater Bay Area in Guangdong Province, China has been allowing importation and clinical usage of innovative drugs and medical devices that have already been approved in a developed market but not yet approved domestically. Real-World Data (RWD) generated from these designated hospitals can be used for NMPA registrations in China. This created an opportunity for Chinese patients to access to innovative therapies from abroad much earlier than they would otherwise be able to. Almost all MNC pharmas have established "early access" task forces to fully leverage on this opportunity.

2) Faster to peak, faster to cliff

NRDL negotiations

In terms of pricing and reimbursement, China established the National Health Security Administration (NHSA) in 2018, consolidating all drug pricing, procurement, and reimbursement administration into one central government agency. Upon inception, the NHSA has initiated a series of drug pricing and reimbursement reforms that have profoundly changed the commercial lifecycle of pharmaceuticals and hence the pricing strategies of all pharma companies. For international pharmas, their newly approved innovative drugs are now eligible for annual negotiations to enter the National Reimbursement Drug List (NRDL) as early as the same year of receiving its NMPA approval, as opposed to having to wait for years for the next round of NRDL review in the pre-NHSA era.

In exchange, to list an innovative therapy on the NRDL, the NHSA is one of the toughest negotiators and demands a steep price cut, usually in the range of 50–60%. Each negotiated contract is valid for two years before a mandatory review for renewal, during which a further but more moderate price cut at around 10–20% is usually expected. Drugs negotiated onto the NRDL are eligible for approximately 70% reimbursement (i.e., the patient co-pays 30%). For patients, this means that their Out-of-Pocket (OOP) expenditure on the same therapy can be reduced by nearly 80–90%. As a result, prescription volume would significantly increase after NRDL listing, requesting the pharma company to invest heavily and quickly in commercialization efforts to secure this very steep ramp-up curve.

For international pharmas, listing on the NRDL through negotiation at low but acceptable prices remains their key strategic objective for most innovative therapies. For those whose products are already commercialized in the U.S., Europe, and other markets, the marginal costs of serving the Chinese market could justify the price compromises in exchange for significant volume upsides. The NHSA also provides the option of not formally disclosing the negotiation results to protect the pharmas from potential challenges from payors in other markets on international reference prices.

According to data published by NHSA, in the past five rounds of annual negotiations from 2017 to 2021, 140 imported drugs commercialized by international pharmas chose to cut prices for being listed on the NRDL, representing approximately 50% of all successful negotiations.

It is widely understood that there is a price ceiling of approximately RMB300,000 (or US$45,000, for the annual cost of the drug) for what the NRDL could accept. The government's rationale is that the NRDL should cover drugs that are, post-negotiation, affordable to ordinary Chinese families whose annual household disposable income, according to the data published by the National Statistics Bureau, was RMB92,000 (approx. US$13,500) in 2021. Therefore, ultra-high-price drugs/therapies such as CAR-T or those for rare diseases are yet to benefit from the NRDL. According to the statement by the NHSA in October 2020, it will aim to establish a "multi-layer co-funding" mechanism to support the payment for rare disease drugs, and that "the NHSA attaches great importance to medical security for patients with rare diseases, and constantly explores the establishment of drug security mechanism for rare diseases, including critical disease insurance, medical assistance, special funds, charity projects and commercial insurance".[386]

Volume-based procurement

While expanding spending on the reimbursement of innovative therapies, the NHSA also aims to save money on older and genericized drugs. In the words of many observers, this structural change in spending is "to vacate the cage for a new bird" and a critical piece of the jigsaw puzzle in China's healthcare and pharma market reform. Volume-Based Procurement (VBP) was first introduced in 2018 where originator and generic drugs with the same molecule name bid for a committed volume through the government's centralized procurement process. Incumbents are typically faced with a 60-80% price cut in exchange for committed volumes in the selected jurisdictions. Those giving up or losing the VBP bid are only eligible for a small fraction of the hospital prescription volumes. This mechanism is supported by a series of strict hospital prescription monitoring measures to ensure compliance to the commitments.

Between November 2018 and November 2021, six batches of national VBP were carried out, covering 234 varieties.[387] According to the NHSA, the savings of VBP on drug spending between 2019 and 2021 could reach RMB260 billion.

Apparently only a small number of international pharma products, mostly originators, were willing to offer such a large price cut required to win VBP, representing an average success rate of approximately 12% (compared to the

---

386 NHSA, http://www.nhsa.gov.cn/art/2020/10/13/art_26_3714.html

387 A variety is defined as a specific dosage form of a molecule (e.g., immediate-release oral form of rivaroxaban)

success rate of over 50% for domestic pharma products, mostly generics).[388] Those who put in aggressive bids to win expect volume gains to partially offset the price reduction, and their revenues would resume growth from a lower base after the "VBP reset". The majority of the international pharmas chose to walk away from VBP to maintain their high prices at cost of losing committed volumes in their core hospital markets.

"Off-Patent Originator" ("OPO") products had long been the "cash cow" for many international pharmas until the introduction of VBP. With continued investment in clinical education and branding, the majority of these OPO products were able to demand a much higher price than generics, but still maintained dominant market shares. For many, win or lose, VBP resulted in revenue avalanche although some were able to maintain or even increase sales volumes. They usually reduced sales and marketing investment in the hospital channel, shifted resources to market access and hospital listing efforts to minimize obstruction in the distribution pathway, and increased efforts in private hospitals, retail pharmacies, and e-commerce channels that are not subject to VBP procurement rules.

Shifting product lifecycle

The typical innovative drug product lifecycle in China has fundamentally shifted – the ramp up in the initial years after launch has accelerated as drugs now have much earlier access to the NRDL, and the post-LoE (Loss of Exclusivity) decline is likely to be much steeper as the launch of generics triggers VBP. For international pharmas, reconsidering their commercialization strategy in China and reshaping their go-to-market model have been on the top of their agenda.

---

388 Success rate is defined as number VBP winners divided by total number of VBP participants; data excludes Batch 6 for insulins where different rules were applied

Figure 1: Illustrative drug lifecycle shift in China (2000s vs. 2020s)

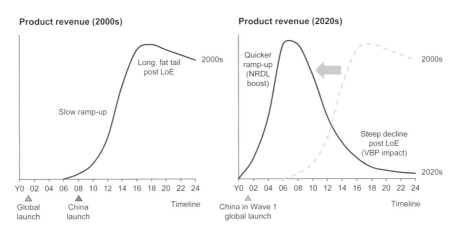

Source: L.E.K. analysis

3) Going digital

In the "pre-digital era", international pharmas helped shape China's pharmaceutical commercialization model with their "academic promotion" approach. Today, they are also pioneers in embarking on the digital journey.

The early movers are more focused on E-commerce, social media coverage, as well as online conferences and events. Fundamentally, like in any other country, and even more so in China, digital channels have become a critical means of accessing information. The gradual easing of governmental restrictions on online drug sales, increased scrutiny over sales rep visits to hospitals and physicians have been the important external forces that necessitated continued investments in these digital efforts. The rapid expansion of VBP has also driven the pharmas to significantly reduce commercialization investments and, as a result, turning to online and digital tools to maintain their reach to a broad customer base while controlling costs. Furthermore, the COVID-19 pandemic and the government's strict movement control policies have put a heavy stomp on the accelerator pedal, as patient access to hospitals and access to HCPs for pharma reps have become more challenging than ever.

According to a survey by Yibai (100 doc) in 2021 among oncology pharmas, over 80% of the international pharmas spent approximately 30% of their marketing budget on digital channels, whereas the majority of the Chinese oncology pharmas spent less than 20% on digital marketing.[389] WeChat is a critical tool for disseminating medical information to the target HCP audiences, through pharmas' own official accounts as well as third-party channels that publish proprietary articles, in many cases sponsored by pharma companies. Conferences and events are also moving online. This serves purposes of saving costs for the host, and significantly removing the constraint on the size of the audience, which is particularly helpful in reaching the large number of HCPs in lower tier markets, such as counties and community health centers, whom would otherwise be rarely invited to these events.

International pharmas are also working closely with the leading third-party digital health platforms such as JD Health and AliHealth, as well as internet hospitals in connecting the dots between diagnosis, treatment, and patient disease management. Leading MNC pharmas such as AstraZeneca, Novartis, and Sanofi have all established partnerships in China on this front, with dedicated internal digital or innovation teams steering the efforts, often times led by senior talents with extensive internet/digital experiences outside the pharma or healthcare industry. Certainly, a key challenge to overcome is payment, as the current reimbursement policies are still shy of providing full coverage for digital services.

In the 2022 APAC Hospital Priorities Survey by L.E.K. Consulting, one third of the 120 Chinese public and private hospitals surveyed are currently using some forms of digital tools, with the remainder either experimenting or exploring digital solutions. The importance of investing in digital health capabilities has risen significantly compared to a year ago, now ranked 4th among all strategic priorities of Chinese hospitals. We anticipate this trend to continue on a steep trajectory, and there will be tremendous opportunities for Chinese or international pharmaceutical companies to help shape and improve hospital and patient experience in the digital era.

---

389 100doc, Digital Marketing Insights of Oncology Pharmas, March 2021

Table 2: China hospital strategic priorities over the next three years –
ranking by importance

2022 rank	Top strategic priorities	2022	2021	Point change
#1	*Improving clinical outcomes*	*76%*	*53%*	*+23*
#2	*Standardization of clinical care protocol within and across hospitals*	*72%*	*53%*	*+19*
#3	*Improving healthcare worker safety*	*70%*	*48%*	*+22*
#4	*Investing in digital health capabilities*	*66%*	*39%*	*+27*
#5	*Investing in new IT systems*	*66%*	*55%*	*+11*
#6	*Reducing acquisition costs of capital equipment*	*63%*	*49%*	*+14*
#7	*Reducing costs of medical supplies*	*63%*	*52%*	*+11*
#8	*Improving labor efficiency/workflow optimization*	*58%*	*50%*	*+8*
#9	*Recovering from financial impact of COVID-19*	*58%*	*48%*	*+10*
#10	*Working with other sites of alternative care*	*58%*	*51%*	*+7*

Note: Survey question: How important are the following strategic priorities for your hospital over the next three years?

Source: L.E.K. 2021, 2022 APAC Hospital Priorities Surveys (senior management from 120 Chinese hospitals)

4) Sourcing innovation from China

China's innovation gaining global recognition

Another key mandate for many international pharmas is to scout for innovation originated in China. As local Chinese pharmas and biotech companies accelerate their innovation and R&D, they are quickly catching up and in some areas are on the cusp of parallel innovation to their counterparts in the developed markets. Over the past few years, many Chinese pharmas and biotech companies are enriching their pipelines from "China first" products to "global first" molecules. In 2021, according to the U.S. FDA records, a total of 26 drugs received Breakthrough, Fast-Track, or Orphan Drug designations, exemplifying the quality of innovations from China.

Figure 2: China innovation stages and timeline

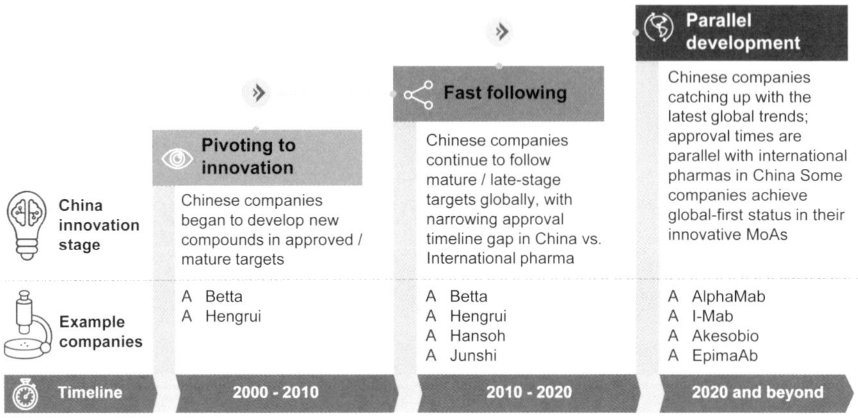

Source: L.E.K. analysis

Table 3: Example first-in-class* drugs under development in China (as of August 2022)

Company	Product	Therapeutic area	MoA	China clinical stage
Remegen	Telitacicept	Autoimmune	BLyS/APRIL fusion protein	Approval
Alphamab	KN046	Oncology	PD-L1/CTLA-4 bispecific antibody	Phase III
Ascletis	ASC40	Oncology	FASN Inhibitor	Phase III
Generon	F-652	Hepatitis	IL-22 agonist	Phase II
Junshi	JS-004	Oncology	BTLA4 antibody	Phase II
Jacobio	JAB-3068	Oncology	SHP2 inhibitor	Phase I/II
Fosun	ORIN1001	Oncology	IRE-1α inhibitor	Phase I

*Note: * First molecule globally within a specific Mechanism of Action*

Source: Pharmaprojects, NMPA/CDE, L.E.K. analysis

Many of these Chinese biotech companies have a clear ambition to become a full-fledge pharmaceutical company and commercialize these products in China on their own, but at the same time, opportunities outside of the Chinese market are becoming more strategically important, especially as the current NRDL negotiations expect low prices, which limits the revenue potential in China. However, only very few Chinese biotech companies have the confidence and appetite in setting up their own commercialization capabilities in the developed markets – this presents an opportunity for international pharmas to enrich their global portfolio with innovative assets originated from China to realize commercial value outside of China.

China-to-international deals

Both the volume and value of "China to international" licensing deals increased remarkably over the past two years. In 2021, about 45 deals were disclosed where a Chinese licensor licensed ex-China rights to an international licensee, totaling over US$10 billion, with an average deal size of over US$500 million.

Figure 3: China local to international licensing deals (2015-2021, number of deals)

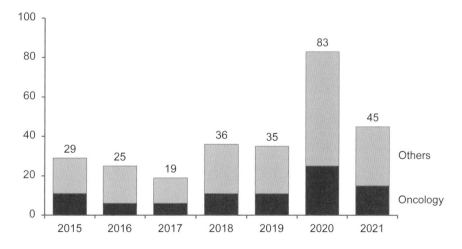

Source: Cortellis, L.E.K. analysis

Figure 4: Average size of China local to international licensing deals (2015-2021, US$million)

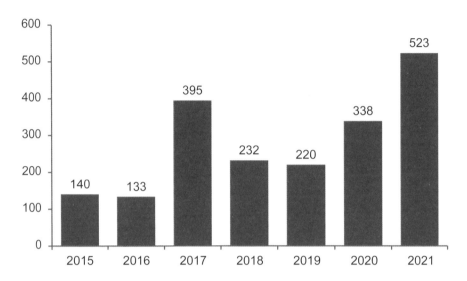

Note: Only includes deals with value announced

Source: Cortellis, L.E.K. analysis

Novartis, AbbVie, Lilly, and Seagen are among the international pharmas that have struck major deals, which undoubtedly continue to demonstrate global confidence in the high quality and strong commercial appeal of Chinese innovation. The Chinese government's efforts over the past decades in building and cultivating a healthy biotech innovation ecosystem are now bearing fruit. Nonetheless, international pharmas now view China as a powerhouse for supplying true innovative pipelines that they need to place heavy bids on, rather than the mere "me-too" followers.

Table 4: Top oncology out-licensing deals (>US$500 million) by Chinese pharmas (August 2020 – August 2022)

Date*	Licensor	Licensee	Product(s)	Deal size* (US$million)	Territory
Aug. 2022	Jemincare	Genentech	JMKX-002992	650	Global
Jul. 2022	CSPC	Elevation Oncology	SYSA-1801	1,245	Global excl. Greater China
Jun. 2022	Henlius	Organon	HLX-11, HLX-14	644	Global excl. Greater China
May 2022	Kelun	MSD	Undisclosed	1,363	Global excl. Greater China
May 2022	LaNova	Turning Point	LM-302	1,100	Global excl. Greater China and South Korea
Mar. 2022	Adagene	Sanofi	Masked monoclonal and bispecific antibodies	2,518	Global
Dec. 2021	BeiGene	Novartis	Ociperlimab	2,900	Canada, EU, UK, U.S., Japan and other six markets
Aug. 2021	RemeGen	Seagen	Disitamab vedotin	2,595	Global excl. Asia, plus Japan and Singapore
Jun. 2021	Allist	ArriVent	Alflutinib mesylate	805	Global excl. Greater China
Feb. 2021	Junshi	Coherus	JS-006, JS018-1, Toripalimab	1,110	Canada, U.S.
Jan. 2021	BeiGene	Novartis	Tislelizumab	2,200	Canada, EU, UK, U.S., Japan and other six markets
Nov. 2020	Henlius	Binacea	HLX-35	768	Global excl. Greater China
Oct. 2020	CStone	EQRx	CS-1003, Sugemalimab	1,300	Global excl. Greater China
Sep. 2020	I-Mab	AbbVie	Lemzoparlimab	1,940	Global excl. Greater China

*Note: * Including upfront and milestone payments*

Source: Cortellis, L.E.K. analysis

In 2021, more than 60% of the ~400 pharma collaborations in China were cross-border.[390] Beginning in late 2021 and continuing into 2022, the Chinese biotech market plunged amid ongoing concerns over geopolitical tensions, forced delisting from the U.S. stock exchanges, and slowdown in China's macroeconomic growth, casting shade on cross-border deal-making. Despite these volatilities, long-term confidence in China remains the mainstream view among investors, as analysts of major Wall Street banks continue to believe in the compelling investment values in China's biotech sector. In 2022, international pharmas have continued to invest in sourcing innovation from China, with Sanofi, Turning Point, Merck, and Elevation Oncology, among others, striking licensing deals over a billion U.S. dollars with Chinese innovators.

3. NEW ENTRANTS: OPTIONS AND TRADE-OFFS[391]

International pharmas have employed a range of options to enter China, but most companies, especially biotechs, take partnering into first consideration. The larger, established companies mostly invested in their own presence outright. Smaller firms might look to China only as a source of funding or incremental opportunity, and thus would choose to out-license their rights.

For those who are not yet in China, choosing the approach before discussing partnership strategy is a critical task.

The choice of entry approach goes beyond simply the right local partner company. An effective entry strategy should be geared around the pharma's overall strategic plan and commercial objectives. These objectives are unique for each firm and may change depending on specific internal objectives for China and more broadly for Asia, the firm's current stage of development, and the key decision-makers' willingness to invest financially and operationally.

Entry strategies can be chiefly grouped into four broad categories, each with its own advantages and challenges.

---

390 ChinaBio, State of China Life Science – 2021

391 *Adapted and updated from Heading East – Biopharma International Expansion to China and Asia*, L.E.K. Consulting, 2018

Figure 5: Options for China market entry

	Level of own control High → Low			
	Acquisition	**Greenfield**	**Joint Venture**	**Out-licensing**
	Own presence	*Own presence*	*Own presence*	*No presence*
Pros	· Immediate access to existing products, talents, and other local capabilities · Full control of business · Full revenue booking	· Full control of business · Full revenue booking · Build own brand, capability, and network · Can use support from service partners (e.g., CRO, CSO)	· Leverage partner resource to fill in the gap and save time · Shared investment, risks and upsides	· Good for company with limited local presence or strength · Low investment and easy recovery / upside · Low risk
Cons	· High upfront investment · Difficult to find right target · Risk in integration	· Need to ramp up on full set of capabilities / infrastructure at all fronts from scratch · Speed to launch may be slower given new to market	· Require time and effort to identify right partner and negotiate · Difficulty in JV set-up · Potential conflict of interest	· Limited control over product sales, brand, and marketing · Low profitability potential

Source: L.E.K. analysis

1) Acquisition

Acquisitions provide a jump-start into a new market, with already established infrastructures, supply chains, and ready commercial portfolios. This is in addition to, and can work in cooperation with, the acquiring firm's own pipelines. Italy's Menarini entered Asia through the acquisition of Invida in 2011, giving Menarini a commercial presence in 13 Asia-Pacific markets, including China, Australia, and major Southeast Asia countries such as Singapore and Malaysia, in a single purchase. Australia's CSL acquired Chinese plasma fractionator firm, Wuhan Ruide in 2017 in order to expand into the local market for plasma-derived products.

2) Greenfield

Starting a brand-new, startup business in China can produce a highly committed organic growth process. The level of upfront investment can be limited to supporting product registration via regulatory consultants and/or contract research organizations, and it does not require much direct physical infrastructure. Alternatively, this can start with initial setups and product registration preparation prior to making further decisions on acquisitions or joint ventures later on. This is similar to FibroGen's, Gilead's, Biogen's (all U.S. companies) and Taiho's (Japan) approaches to China. U.S. pharma Biohaven (now Pfizer) also established a new entity in China, Bioshin, to develop and commercialize its pipeline products in China and other Asia-Pacific markets.

3) Joint Venture

This is the most frequently considered option for biotech companies on the cusp of becoming international commercial operators. Firms seeking a joint venture have an interest in maintaining some level of their own presence in China yet are often daunted by the challenge of managing an operation on the opposite side of the globe with different cultural norms. A Joint Venture is a good option for executives who feel more comfortable having "locals" navigate the market. Joint Venture projects must navigate steep communication and cultural challenges while maintaining the integrity of both Chinese and international partners.

Kite (now Gilead) and Juno (now BMS) both opted for Joint Ventures in China, with Fosun in 2017 and WuXi AppTec in 2016 to develop and commercialize their CAR-T and other cell therapies. Both JVs had their first CAR-T product approved in China in 2021. More recently, Allogene formed a JV with Overland (backed by Hillhouse Capital) in 2020 for China and other Asian markets, and Arrowhead formed a JV (Visirna) with Vivo Capital in 2022 for the Greater China market. The participation of private equity and venture capital funds provides alternative source of funding and greater degree of managerial flexibility.

4) Out-licensing

The rise of out-licensing to China has been complemented and facilitated by the rise of biotech startups in China. Companies such as Everest, CStone, and CANbridge allow international firms to out-license, develop, and commercialize in China with limited direct presence. Smaller pharmas such as Puma, Mirati, Tesaro, and Blueprint have all granted companies with exclusive product rights in China in return for upfronts and milestones.

Table 5: Examples of in-licensed drugs approved by NMPA (non-exhaustive)

Product	Therapeutic area	China approval date	Licensor	Licensee
Ramucirumab	Oncology	Mar. 2022	Eli Lilly	Innovent
Ivosidenib	Oncology	Feb. 2022	Servier (Agios)	CStone
Dinutuximab beta	Oncology	Aug. 2021	EUSA	BeiGene
Carfilzomib	Oncology	Jul. 2021	Amgen	BeiGene
Avapritinib	Oncology	Mar. 2021	Blueprint	CStone
Pralsetinib	Oncology	Mar. 2021	Blueprint	CStone
Ripretinib	Oncology	Mar. 2021	Deciphera	ZAI Lab
Niraparib	Oncology	Dec. 2019	Tesaro	ZAI Lab

Source: NMPA, L.E.K. analysis

4. PARTNERSHIP CONSIDERATIONS[392]

Once international pharmas start down the path of partnership, selection criteria for suitable Chinese partners are mostly consistent with partner selection patterns in other regions, and do not necessarily differentiate between multinational/international pharmas in China versus domestic Chinese pharmas.

Key selection criteria include:

- Upfront financials: Willingness to supply capital is universal to biotech companies in the development stage. The injection of cash up front is often necessary for them to run late-stage trials, and additionally represents validation of the technology.
- Clinical trial competence: Given China's requirement of Phase III clinical trials for product registration, clinical trial competence and access to key opinion leaders are particularly important for innovative companies. This is also reflected in the desire for therapeutic area expertise.
- Commercial capabilities: Partners are expected to have demonstrated

---

392 *Adapted and updated from Heading East – Biopharma International Expansion to China and Asia*, L.E.K. Consulting, 2018

commercial expertise based on hospital coverage, market access, and market positioning. This means, for example, a larger company in China must have at least 1,000 large teaching systems (known as "Level 3A hospitals") out of the 20,000 hospitals nationwide in order to have a reasonable coverage.

- Intellectual Property (IP) protection: IP protection continues to be a key concern raised by international pharmas and is often a key selection criterion exclusive to emerging markets. Without enforceable and effective IP protection, pharmas would either choose not to consider China (or any other markets with under-developed IP protection system) or would retreat to partners that are considered "safer" from this perspective.

Over the past five years, international pharma out-licensing deals in China continued to grow at a 13% CAGR, reaching over 100 deals in 2020 and close to 90 in 2021. Among these, approximately 80% are licensed to a Chinese partner, the remaining 20% to international peers already operating in China. This ratio has remained largely stable over the years.

Figure 6: International pharma drug license-out deals in China (2016-2021, number of deals)

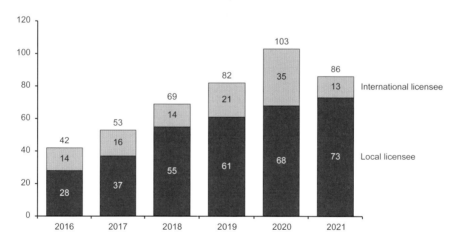

Source: Cortellis, L.E.K. analysis

There are vast differences in the perception of the different partner group types by nationality.

1) Local Chinese pharmas

Established Chinese pharma companies have been operating in the market for decades and have built up their extensive clinical, commercial, and regulatory experiences and networks. Many are transitioning from their traditional generics business to innovation, and from developing internal pipelines to actively seeking in-licensing opportunities. The decision-making process is usually efficient. The trade-off, in many cases, is potential concerns over their compliance (in regulatory, commercial, IP protection, etc.), especially for licensors less familiar with the Chinese market.

There is also a considerable number of newly established Chinese biotech companies focusing on innovation. In addition to developing their own pipelines, they are aggressively licensing international assets to jump-start their clinical development and commercial presence. They may not have much of an existing track record in successful registration or commercialization of innovative drugs as a company, but they are typically led by experienced industry veterans from established international or Chinese pharmas, and are backed by financial investors who provide the funding needed for clinical development and commercialization.

2) International pharmas

There are significant advantages associated with having international pharmas as partners in China as well, especially in terms of safety perceptions. The top reasons for partnering with an MNC are related to safety and risk reduction. Extensive global/regional experience and better IP protection are always favored, and strong corporate reputation and stringent compliance practices are also considered key merits. China-only or Asia-only development and commercialization deals are part of the global/regional pharmas' business development considerations, or even a key part of portfolio expansion in the region. However, the trade-off is that, depending on the organizational setup for their business development functions, transactions with MNC pharmas likely require decision-making at the regional and global level, potentially resulting in lengthier timelines and increased transaction costs. In most cases when considering China-only deals, MNC pharmas also have a much stronger preference for late-stage pipelines or commercialized products and are reluctant to put in major clinical development investments for China-only in-licensing deals.

5. CONCLUSION

The Chinese pharmaceutical market, at US$300 billion in size, is the world's second largest pharma market with the highest expected growth among major economies. Underlying drivers for healthcare demand, including the aging population, rising living standards, and improving healthcare infrastructure, will sustain strong growth.

For international pharma companies, China is too important to a market to neglect, for not only serving the unmet healthcare needs of the 1.4 billion population, but also participating in the increasingly important hub for global pharmaceutical, life sciences, and digital innovation. Understanding how to interpret policy directions and navigate through the complexities of this market is critical to seizing these opportunities.

The objectives of the policy makers and regulators in China are clear – they are making every effort to cultivate high-quality innovation and provide affordable healthcare to the world's largest population who are pursuing their happiness and wellbeing. The NMPA, among others, is probably one of the most open-minded Chinese government institutions that is working relentlessly to catch up with the highest global standards. In the Chinese pharmaceutical market, international companies are granted the same right of access, while the origin of innovation or location of production is never a limiting criterion for procurement decisions.

After all, China is a developing market, and participants should expect policies to keep evolving. Sometimes changes may seem abrupt, and regulations may appear vague, as policy makers persist in adapting to the rapidly evolving technologies and market dynamics, but their objectives have remained consistent. China is such a unique market that no other existing institutions can be replicated domestically. This is also the reason that "crossing the river by feeling the stone" has been and will continue to be probably the best approach to ensure continued advancement.

China's grand vision is to "build a community for mankind with a shared future" – this is a solemn commitment to openness and inclusiveness. The pharmaceutical industry, with both Chinese and international participants complementing each other, will contribute to and harvest from this journey.

Chapter *6*

China Capital Market for Biotech Investment

1. INTRODUCTION OF CHINA'S CAPITAL MARKET

China reopened its doors to foreigners in 1978, which allowed a number of companies to start trading securities and led to a surge in economic reform and continued business development. The 1980s saw the establishment of a socialist market economy which eventually led to the reopening of the Shanghai Stock Exchange (SSE) in 1990. At the same time, China opened a secondary exchange in Shenzhen (SZSE), aiming mainly at high-tech companies, and Small and Medium-sized Enterprises (SME). Both exchanges began operations in December 1990.

In November 2021, the third stock exchange in China opened in Beijing (BSE) with the objective to provide financing for innovative start-up companies. BSE acts as a new "Third Board," with the strategic goal of nurturing an array of SMEs specializing in niche sectors and fostering strong innovative capabilities, including medicine, mechanical equipment, new materials, information technology, etc.

Currently, a number of regional security exchanges also exist. However, they have only played a relatively minor role in China's overall stock market both in terms of total market capitalization and trading volume. We therefore focus on exclusive analysis of the two major exchanges: the Shanghai and Shenzhen stock exchanges.

Likewise to its economy, China's capital market has experienced fast growth over the past three decades. By market capitalization, China is now the second largest in the world. As of December 2021, both SSE and SZSE ranked among the top ten exchanges globally in terms of market cap.

Rank	Exchange	Country/region	Market cap (US$trillion)
1	New York Stock Exchange (NYSE)	U.S.	27.69
2	NASDAQ	U.S.	24.56
3	Shanghai Stock Exchange (SSE)	China	8.15
4	EURONEXT	Europe	7.33
5	Japan Stock Exchange (JPX)	Japan	6.54
6	Shenzhen Stock Exchange (SZSE)	China	6.22
7	Honk Kong Stock Exchange (SEHK)	Hong Kong	5.43
8	LSE Group	U.K. and Italy	3.8
9	National Stock Exchange (NSE)	India	3.55
10	Toronto Stock Exchange	Canada	3.26

Source: Trade Brains https://tradebrains.in/10-largest-stock-exchanges-in-the-world/

NASDAQ, NYSE, SSE, SEHK, and SZSE were the top five exchanges globally in terms of IPO fundraising in 2021.

	NASDAQ	NYSE	SSE	SEHK	SZSE
No. of shares listed in 2021	351	113	248	97	232
Fund raised in 2021 ($billion)	100	58	57	42	26
Ranking in 2021 by fund raised	1	2	3	4	5

2. CAPITAL MARKETS FUNCTIONALITY AND RESULTS

1) General functionality of China capital market: high risks & high rewards

Biotech, an industrial sector applying biology to develop products, is a key part of China's economic development strategy, as the country looks to become a global leader in emerging technologies.

China's leadership has designated biotech as a "strategic emerging industry" in the 14th Five Year Plan covering the years 2021-25. Between 2016 and 2020, the number of biotech science parks in China grew from about 400 to 600, reflecting the government's priorities to develop the sector.

Biotech companies often invest heavily in R&D, but the returns are uncertain, especially for start-up companies. They need significant capital to support daily operation and projects development for years before being able to generate income. In absence of some traditional basic financial data, including revenue, gross margin, fixed assets, etc., it is difficult for traditional fund providers such as banks to see the development prospects and technology risks of a project. Under the influence of these factors, biopharmaceutical companies receive less financing under the traditional credit model of banks. As a result, Biopharmaceutical companies mainly rely on private equity and IPOs for financing.

In April 2018, the HKEX added Chapter 18A "Biotechnology Companies" to the Main Board Listing Rules, allowing biotechnology companies without revenue and profitability to submit listing applications. In June 2019, the "Fifth Set of Listing Criteria" of the STAR Market of SSE provided new options for yet-profitable R&D companies to go public.

As of May 31, 2022, a total of 50 biotech companies have been listed on the Main Board of HKEX through Chapter 18A. As for SSE, as of May 31, 2022, there are a total of 16 biotech companies being listed on the STAR Market of SSE through applying the Fifth Set of Listing Criteria, and another 71 companies belonging to the biotech industry but did not apply the Fifth Set of Listing Criteria.

According to the *2021 China Biopharmaceutical Investment and Financing Blue Book*, issued by China Pharmaceutical Enterprises Association (the "Blue Book"), in 2021, a total of 89 China-based biotech companies completed IPO financing in China, Hong Kong(China), and the U.S. raising over RMB130 billion. Among which, 57 companies were A share listings, raising RMB84.3 billion (including 34 companies listed on the STAR market, raising RMB57.7 billion); 24 companies listed on SEHK, raising a total of HK$56 billion; and eight companies listed in the U.S., raising a total of approximately US$1.1 billion.

According to the *Blue Book*, a total of 588 China-based biotech companies have successfully raised funds through private equity, and the total disclosed financing amount exceeds RMB118.7 billion, of which 276 biotech R&D-focused companies have raised a total of RMB88.8 billion, accounting for 75% of the overall market financing amount. This shows that the field of new drug research and development has always been a key area of focus for investment institutions.

However, in recent days, investors' concern about the overall financial return has intensified, given that many pre-revenue biotech listed companies seem to fail to make profits after years of listing. From Figure 1, we have observed that, regardless of the A-share market or HKEX market, both biotech indices had negative percentage growth from 2021 to H1 2022, even lower than their respective overall stock market growth rate. This has shown that the returns of investment of these biotech companies have become more uncertain. The high valuation of pre-revenue biotech companies has been reset in response to such a trend. The recycling of funding to new biotech companies in HKEX and A-share markets has become more challenging in the near term.

Figure 1: A share & HKEX Market Accumulative Growth % (Jan. 2021 to Jun. 2022)

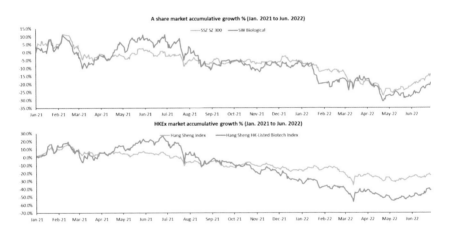

Source: Wind, Deloitte Research

2) Whether the funds are invested in breakthrough or best-in-class drugs

In recent years, China's biopharmaceutical industry has been strengthened by the rapid pace of development, both in terms of talent and products innovative capability. According to the Center for Drug Evaluation, the number of applications that required technology review of biologics has increased from 573 in 2017 to 1999 in 2021, with a CAGR of 36.7%. In addition, the IND and NDA applications of innovative biologics have increased from 74 and 2 in 2017 to 643 and 23 in 2021, respectively, with a CAGR of 84.2% and 81.0%, respectively. This has shown that the boost in biotech and biopharma companies in China, which is supported by the strong influx of investments.

- **Price cut negotiations from authorities become a norm, pushing pharma companies to develop novel drugs:**
  In recent years, we have witnessed rapid changes throughout the whole pharmaceutical industry in China, including the dynamic adjustment of the National Reimbursement Drug List (NRDL) and the implementation of Volume-Based Procurement (VBP). The time frame for the inclusion of novel products in NRDL has been shortened, which resulted in the fastening of the production expansion for pharma companies. It has also brought fiercer competition among fast-following products and encouraged pharma companies to devote more effort into developing first-in-class and best-in-class products. The VBP implementation has become another driver, pushing local pharma companies to develop novel drugs, particularly first-in-class and best-in-class drugs by reducing the economic value window for me-too, me-better, and fast-following products.

- **Stock markets, especially for STAR and HK Chapter 18A, have stricter scrutiny on the innovation character:**
  In H1 2021, we saw steady growth in the biotech sector of the A-share market, with a growth rate up to 11%. Similarly, the biotech sector of the HKEX market had a growth rate up to 27%. However, in H2 2021, the biotech stock market has shrunk significantly at a growth rate of -9% and -31% for the A-share biotech market and HKEX biotech market respectively. The impact has been further emphasized in H1 2022, with a growth rate of -27% and -56% for the A-share biotech market and HKEX biotech market, respectively. The main reason for such trend is the adjustment of the valuation of biotech IPOs, especially the increased focus on the "innovation" characteristics of the listing applicant.

- **VC/PE favor more on the innovative technologies and breakthrough therapies:**
  In 2021, there were a total of 474 fundraising events held in China, an increase from 364 in 2020. Traditional biological development is still taking the lead. What is notable are the fundraising events in Cell & Gene Therapy (CGT) field. Investment in this field has reached RMB5.7 billion in value and 33 in volume, a growth rate of 327% and 44%, respectively, in

2021. This has marked a shift of investors' focus from traditional biologic development to new generation therapy. Another notable field is the clinical outsourcing field (CRO, CMO, CDMO, etc.). In 2021, there were a total of 22 fundraising events held with a total deal value of RMB6.8 billion, a growth rate of 152.4% and 29.4%, respectively, from 2020. The rise of these two sectors has shown the popularity of the new generation therapy in the Chinese biotech capital market—from the increasing investments in drug developers and the clinical outsourcing service providers.

- **License-out deals focus on oncology, and almost half of the deals are novel drugs:**
Looking at licensing deals from another perspective, there are also interesting trends that we should pay attention to. In 2021, there were 53 licensing out deals, 25 of which were novel drugs. From the disease areas perspective, oncology still accounts for the largest proportion at around 80%. Viewing the disease map of the Chinese population, we believe that the oncology field will remain the hot area in both R&D and investment. In addition, given the aging population, there is a demand for metabolism and immune disease. Among the top 15 license-out deals by value, seven are for oncology disease, two for metabolism disease, and two for immune disease.

However, unlike in the U.S., Chinese biotech and biopharma fundraising still lacks strong support from the industrial specialized investment institutions. Therefore, it is critical for the Chinese biotech industry to assemble a professional investment team to better identify and evaluate innovative projects. In other words, investing in the right team with know-how and talents. In the long run, however, the Chinese biotech industry will gradually shift from pursuing short-term investment returns (fast-following, me-too, me-better products) to the long-term pipeline design for the deployment of a complex value proposition.

3. OUTLOOK

In general, we foresee two trends going forward in the biotech and biopharma industry investment landscape in China:

- **Shortening of the business cycle and reducing the economic value window: will capital markets lose attractiveness in favor of less 'volatile' investors**
With the rapid advancement of medical reforms, such as the dynamic

adjustment of the National Reimbursement Drugs Lists and the frequent tenders of volume-based procurement, the business cycle of an innovative product in China has been shortened significantly. Pricing pressure has already become a critical factor impacting the business plan of a new product launch in China. This will result in the reduction of the economic value of the product, and eventually causing investors to reduce or lose their interest in the investment in innovative biological products. Instead of investing in innovative biological products, investors may gradually shift to products that are less volatile, such as vaccines, medical devices, or chemical drugs.

- **With markets seeing access restrictions there will be a localization factor eventually (local money financing local innovation)**

Several restrictions have been released or announced in China in recent years against foreign investments, such as R&D activities related to Chinese human genetic resources have become harder to perform in China Free Trade Zone for foreign investors. In the future, local innovation will have to rely more on local funds. As mentioned, we expect to see more mature and professional local investment teams that are capable of making long-term investments in the biotech and biopharma sectors in China in the future. The government and investment institutions should cooperate more to better evaluate and inject funds into truly innovative projects in the biotech and biopharma industries.

- **Privatization of U.S.-listed biotech companies and their return to the HK Capital market**

In recent years, as the U.S.-China tension tightens, the privatization of U.S.-listed Chinese biotech companies and their return to the Hong Kong capital market has emerged. For instance, BeiGene and Zai Lab. BeiGene is the first biotech company listed on three major capital markets – NASDAQ, HKEX, and A-share; while Zai Lab was listed on NASDAQ in 2017 and then returned to HKEX in 2020. In addition, more Chinese companies, including biotech companies, have been warned to comply to the latest U.S. requirements or otherwise delist in the U.S., including BeiGene, Zai Lab, HUTCHMED, etc. As the Chinese biotech capital market gradually become more mature year by year, coupled with the de-globalization trend, we expect to see more U.S.-listed Chinese biotech companies flow back into China's capital market (HKEX and A-share) in the future.

- **The rising of medical equipment and other subsector themes**
  Apart from biotech, capital investment in medical equipment and other subsectors has also increased in recent years. As of 31 July 2022, the growth in average market cap of medical equipment and device companies listed on the HKEX and A-share market have achieved 725% and 167%, respectively. With the resetting of high valued biotech companies, some VC/PE have started to shift their investment to medical equipment and its subsectors as an alternative. Following the rising awareness of self-health management in China, the demand for medical equipment and health monitoring products is expected to grow further in the mid to long term, providing a new investment zone for LSHC investors.

Chapter *7*

China Unicorns and Beyond

The definition of unicorn in the technology investment realm stems from Aileen Lee in last decade.[393] It refers to private-held company with valuation at US$1 billion. The author further refines this investment unicorn concept: 1) only focusing on life sciences unicorns, 2) the valuation is US$1 billion or above, either private-held or public, 3) in leading position within its sector, 4) preferably less than ten years since inception.

The following are exemplars of China-related life sciences unicorns, readers can ponder and compare their growth strategies to those companies mentioned in part one of this book.

1. INNOCARE PHARMA (9969.HK)

With the core focus to provide worldwide patients with modern, innovative drugs in the battle against cancers and autoimmune disease, two highly motivated scientists Dr. Jasmine Cui and Prof. Yigong Shi[394] co-founded InnoCare in Beijing, China in 2015. Ms. Cui, the Chairwoman and CEO of the Company, was former CEO and CSO of BioDuro, a PPD company; former head of early development team, cardiovascular diseases at Merck U.S.; former fellow at the world-renowned Howard Hughes Medical Institute[395] and author of 50 plus papers on peer-reviewed journals. Prof. Shi is a globally acclaimed structural biologist, previously served as professor at Tsinghua University and Princeton University, now the president and founder of Westlake University, and an academician of the Chinese Academy of Sciences, the Honorary Foreign member, American Academy of Arts and Sciences. He is the author of 180 plus papers in peer-reviewed journals.

---

393 https://fortune.com/recommends/investing/what-is-a-unicorn-company/

394 https://en.westlake.edu.cn/faculty/yigong-shi.html

395 https://www.innocarepharma.com/en/about-us/our-team/

In March 2020, InnoCare was listed on the Hong Kong Stock Exchange (HKEX) and raised US$289 million with its initial public offering, reaching market cap of HK$11.2 billion on the debut day. It was oversubscribed over 300 times, including some very supportive cornerstone investors.[396] On September 21, 2022, InnoCare raised RMB2.92 billion (around US$412 million) in a second listing on Shanghai STAR Market.[397]

InnoCare's vision is to grow into a global pharmaceutical leader that develops and delivers innovative therapies for patients worldwide. Its lead asset, Orelabrutinib, one of Bruton's Tyrosine Kinase (BTK) inhibitor received approval in China in the short period of five years. This is a remarkable achievement as the average time for such a process takes at least ten years. Within the same therapeutic class, J&J's Ibrutinib (Imbruvica®) is among the global best-selling drugs.

Small molecule targeted oncology therapies are receiving more and more attention globally as they represent novel, safe and more effective, less side effects approaches to treat cancers, as compared to traditional chemotherapics. Additionally, small molecules are easy to manufacture and distribute. Another benefit for patients is to administrate it orally, much better than intravenously for large molecules.

InnoCare has a fully integrated innovation platform and competent in-house R&D capabilities for the discovery of drug candidates and identifying novel targets. Two state-of-the-art research facilities have been established, including an 8,300 m^2 laboratory in Beijing and a 3,350 m^2 laboratory in Nanjing.

It has established innovative pipeline with global competitiveness, core products include:

Orelabrutinib, a BTK inhibitor: The product has excellent target selectivity and favorable Pharmacokinetics (PK) and Pharmacodynamics (PD) profile that enables once-daily low-dosage administrations and improves target occupancy.

---

396 https://www.biospace.com/article/china-s-innocare-pharma-raises-289-million-in-ipo/

397 https://www.bioworld.com/articles/689915-innocare-raises-292b-in-shanghai-ipo-but-shares-fall-on-debut?v=preview

Its indications are Mantle Cell Lymphoma (MCL), and Chronic Lymphocytic Leukemia/Small Cell Leukemia (CLL/SLL). In 2021, a revenue of RMB241 million had been generated with 5,000 doctors being educated, covering over 1,000 hospitals in 200 plus cities. Later, this drug was successfully listed on the NRDL, generating RMB217 million revenue in the first half of 2022.

ICP-192: a clinical stage pan-GFGR inhibitor targeting multiple solid tumors. Currently undergoing Phase I/IIa study.

ICP-723: a second-generation small molecule pan-TRK inhibitor designed to treat patients with NTRK gene fusion-positive cancers. Clinical I clinical trial was carried out in China.

In 2021, Biogen obtained MS worldwide rights and certain autoimmune disease rights outside China.[398] Meanwhile, InnoCare retained oncology worldwide rights and certain autoimmune disease rights in Greater China. On September 22, 2022, InnoCare received an upfront payment of US$125 million, and the potential to receive milestone US$812.5 million and mid-teens royalty. In February 2023, Biogen notified InnoCare to terminate the signed deal, this news surprised the industry.[399]

From U.S.-based Incyte, InnoCare obtained the exclusive rights in Great China of Tafasitamab under the brand name Monjuvi®.[400] Monjuvi® in conjunction with lenalidomide is the first and only the U.S. FDA approved treatment for the second line DLBCL. This transaction solidified its long-term strategy in hematology. Its IND for bridging trial was accepted by China Center for Drug Evaluation (CDE).

---

398 https://investors.biogen.com/news-releases/news-release-details/biogen-and-innocare-announce-license-and-collaboration-agreement

399 https://endpts.com/biogen-ceo-says-company-lost-its-way-cuts-125m-ms-partnership-amid-declining-revenue/

400 https://www.thepharmaletter.com/article/incyte-out-licenses-tafasitamab-to-innocare-for-greater-china

2. LEGEND BIOTECH (LEGN.US)

Legend Biotech[401] was initially founded by GenScript as an internal venture research project. Eight years after inception, Legend has Biotech become a fully integrated leading global cell therapy company, operating in the U.S., China, and European Union (EU). Its pipeline programs cover both hematologic and solid tumors.

Legend Biotech completed its initial public offering in June 2020, raising US$487 million, the largest biotech raising of the year by then.[402] As of July 2022, Legend holds US$796 million in cash and cash equivalents.

In 2017 at Chicago ASCO meeting, Legend Biotech presented an excellent clinical trial result in China on R/R multiple myeloma with its leading CART product LCAR-B38M, immediately drawing an extremely high interest among leading pharmaceutical companies of the whole world.

In 2017, Legend Biotech signed the worldwide collaboration and licensing agreement for LCAR-B38M/JNJ-4528 with Janssen,[403] a leading global pharma group. This agreement sets an example of first 50/50% worldwide co-development, and co-commercialization between a China biotech company and a global pharma. In January 2018, Legend Bio received a down payment of US$350 million and as of July 2022, received a total of US$300 million milestone payments.

Multiple Myeloma, the third most common blood cancer, accounts for 18% of all hematologic cancers. There were 176,404 new cases worldwide in 2020, accounting for 1% of worldwide new cancer cases. In Legend Biotech's clinical trial CARTITUDE-1 study, the Objective Response Rate (ORR) is 97.9%, a potential best-in-class cell therapy.

On February 28, 2022, the U.S. FDA approved CARVYKTI® (brand name of

---

401 https://legendbiotech.com/

402 https://www.reuters.com/article/us-legend-biotech-ipo-idUKKBN23C2CP

403 https://www.jnj.com/media-center/press-releases/janssen-enters-worldwide-collaboration-and-license-agreement-with-chinese-company-legend-biotech-to-develop-investigational-car-t-anti-cancer-therapy

LCAR-B38M/JNJ-4528) for the treatment of adults with relapsed and refractory multiple myeloma, who have received four or more prior lines of therapy, including a proteasome inhibitor, an immunomodulatory agent, and an anti-CD38 monoclonal antibody. Legend Biotech's global partner, Jansen, has publicly stated that this product has the potential to save tens of thousands of lives and generate peak sales of US$5 billion per year. On May 26, CARVYKTI® was also granted conditional approval by the European Commission. On September 27, CARVYKTI® received approval from Japan's Ministry of Health, Labor, and Welfare.

3. ZAI LAB (9688.HK)

Founded in 2014, it is a fully integrated commercial-stage global biopharmaceutical company based in China and the U.S. The company's founder and CEO, Ms. Samantha Du,[404] received her Ph.D. in biochemistry from the University of Cincinnati before beginning her research career with Pfizer. Before founding Zai Lab, Dr. Du led healthcare investments at Sequoia Capital for two years.

Zai Lab has a dual listing on both NASDAQ and the HKEX, and its shares are included in the Shenzhen-Hong Kong Stock Connect Program[405] as well as the Shanghai-Hong Kong Stock Connect Program to provide additional opportunity for investors in mainland China to invest in the company. On September 20, 2017, Zai Lab announced its initial public offering of American Depository Shares (ADSs), raising approximately US$150 million. On September 28, 2020, Zai Lab set to net more than US$761 million form Hong Kong Stock Market listing.[406]

Zai Lab has a comprehensive understanding of the global industry, and it has set a very high standard on Business Development (BD) on the global level. Its unique business model is based on China patients' unmet medical needs and the resources limitation of some global middle size to small size biotech companies to

---

404 https://www.zailaboratory.com/leadership/samantha-du-ph-d/?t=executive-team

405 https://www.hkex.com.hk/Mutual-Market/Stock-Connect?sc_lang=en

406 https://endpts.com/zai-lab-hauls-in-761m-from-hong-kong-ipo-to-push-zejula-more-budding-candidates-in-china/

reach China market. Its high efficiency of execution on registration, marketing and sales to hospitals has demonstrated its competitiveness. It rapidly and purposely seized the once-in-a-generation opportunity to build Zai Lab into a biopharma leader, first in China, and then in the world. It only took Zai Lab eight years to build a portfolio with 28 products, including 11 that were developed internally with global rights, four from the market.

Zai Lab has a proven track record in assets selection capabilities. It has expanded its product pipeline to increase product candidates from four in 2015, to 28 in 2021, spanning across areas such as oncology, autoimmune disorders, infectious diseases, and neuroscience. 12 are in the late-stage development. Notable products include:

Zejula® **(Niraparib):** a potent and Small-Molecule Poly (ADP-Ribose) Polymerase 1/2 inhibitor taken once-daily. It belongs to a new class of small molecule inhibitors called PARP inhibitors. This drug was originally developed by Tesaro, which was later acquired by GSK in 2019.[407] In 2016, Zai Lab obtained an exclusive license from Tesaro[408] for the development of this drug in greater China. In addition to a US$15 million upfront and aggregate milestone fees up to US$39.5 million, Zai Lab is expected to pay loyalties in the range of middle to high teens on the net sales of the drug. It was first approved in March 2017 by the U.S. FDA for the maintenance treatment of adult patients with recurrent epithelial ovarian, fallopian tube or primary peritoneal cancer who exhibit a complete or partial response to platinum-based chemotherapy. In 2019, this product was approved in mainland China and commercially launched in 2020. It took Zai Lab less than 30 months from clinical trial initiation to get approval for its first product in mainland China.

Optune® **:** Tumor Treating Fields (TTFields) cancer treatment therapy that uses electric fields to disrupt cancer cell division process. In 2015, Optune® was approved by the U.S. FDA for the treatment of adult patients with newly diagnosed Glioblastoma (GBM) in combination with Temozolomide (TMZ). In September 2018, Zai Lab obtained an exclusive license agreement from

---

407 https://www.fiercepharma.com/pharma/checkered-path-a-replay-how-tesaro-got-its-5-1-billion-glaxosmithkline-buyout

408 https://www.reuters.com/article/idCNASC099MZ

Novocure[409] to commercialize this platform technology in Greater China. The agreement included an upfront payment of US$15 million, commercial milestone payments up to US$78 million, and tiered loyalty on the net sales. Zai Lab will purchase the licensed products exclusively from Novocure. In 2019, Optune® was approved in Hong Kong; in 2020, it was approved by NMPA, the first therapy for Glioblastoma in the past 15 years.

Qinlock® (Ripretinib): a dual-action switch-control tyrosine kinase inhibitor that regulates the activation loop and switch pocket of the kinase to broadly inhibit KIT and PDGFR mutant kinases. In June 2019, Zai Lab obtained the rights of Ripretinib from Deciphera. Deciphera[410] would receive an upfront cash payment of US$20 million, up to US$185 million in potential future milestones, and sales loyalties. It was approved by the U.S. FDA in May 2020 and by the NMPA in 2021 for the treatment of adult patients with advanced Gastrointestinal Stromal Tutors (GISTs). GISTs has a patient base of approximately 100,000 in China.

NUZYRA® (Omadacycline): a novel tetracycline-class antibacterial specifically designed to overcome tetracycline resistance and recover from various bacterial infections. It can be taken orally once daily or administered intravenously.

4. JUNSHI BIOSCIENCES (1877.HK)

With the mission "to provide patients with treatment options that work better and cost less", Junshi Biosciences was founded by Mr. Jun Xiong, President of Junshi Biosciences. It has been headquartered in Shanghai, China since 2012. Ten years later, with the strategy "In China, For Global",[411] Junshi Biosciences now operates in Suzhou and Shanghai, China, and San Francisco and Maryland, U.S.

Mr. Ning Li is the CEO and General Manager. Mr. Li obtained his bachelor's and master's degrees from Shanghai Medical College, Fudan University

---

409 https://www.novocure.com/novocure-and-zai-lab-announce-strategic-collaboration-with-a-license-agreement-for-tumor-treating-fields-in-greater-china/

410 https://investors.deciphera.com/news-releases/news-release-details/deciphera-pharmaceuticals-inc-and-zai-lab-limited-announce

411 https://www.junshipharma.com/en/about-us/

Shanghai, China, and his doctoral degree in preventive medicine from the University of Iowa, U.S. Before joining Junshi Biosciences, Li worked for U.S. FDA and French pharmaceutical giant Sanofi. Li has extensive experience and expertise in clinical research and medical product evaluation.

Junshi Biosciences has become an innovation-driven biopharmaceutical company dedicated to the discovery, development, and commercialization of innovative therapeutics. It has built a pipeline consisting of over 50 drug candidates, concentrating on five therapeutic areas: cancer, autoimmune, metabolic, neurological, and infectious diseases. Its innovative R&D ranges from monoclonal antibodies to the development of various modalities, including small molecules, ADCs, bi-specific antibodies, nucleic acid drugs, polypeptides, etc.

The company's financial foundation was solidified with a few important and strategic decisions. In 2015, Junshi Biosciences was listed on NEEQ in Shanghai. On December 24, 2018, the company was listed on the HKEX.[412] It raised HK$3.08 billion.[413] On 15th July, 2020, Junshi Biosciences was listed on the Shanghai STAR market, and raised up to nearly RMB4.84 billion.[414]

Its leading drug, Toripalimab, was the first China-made recombinant humanized anti-PD-1 monoclonal antibody for injection approved by China's NMPA, with five indications including malignant melanoma, urothelial cancer, gastric cancer, esophageal cancer, and Nasopharyngeal Cancer (NPC). Toripalimab was granted the "China Patent Gold Award", the highest recognition for domestic patents, and has been supported by two National Major Science and Technology Projects for "Major New Drugs Development". Its commercial team of over 1,100 members covers over 2,000 medical institutions and 4,000 retail pharmacies.

Toripalimab has been granted two Breakthrough Therapy Designations, one Fast Track Designation and five Orphan-drug Designations for the treatment of mucosal melanoma, NPC, soft tissue sarcoma, esophageal cancer, and small cell lung cancer.

---

412 https://www.reuters.com/article/shanghai-junshi-ipo-idUSL8N1YM1MY

413 https://www.dealstreetasia.com/stories/junshi-biosciences-ipo-195630

414 https://www.dealstreetasia.com/stories/junshi-star-market-ipo-197507

In 2022, JUNMAIKANG® (adalimumab), jointly developed with Mabwell Bioscience for the treatment of rheumatoid arthritis, ankylosing spondylitis, psoriasis, Crohn's disease, uveitis, polyarticular juvenile idiopathic arthritis, pediatric plaque psoriasis and pediatric Crohn's disease, received marketing approval from NMPA. JUNMAIKANG® also received support from the national "Major New Drug Development" project.

In the battle against the COVID-19 pandemic, Junshi Biosciences assumed the responsibility of a China based biopharmaceutical company in collaboration with partners to rapidly develop innovative drugs since 2020. Its neutralizing fully human monoclonal antibody JS016 (etesevimab) administered with bamlanivimab was granted Emergency Use Authorizations (EUA) in over 15 countries and regions worldwide in 2021. Aside from that, the company's novel oral nucleoside anti-SARS-CoV-2 agent, VV116, has been approved for the treatment of COVID-19 patients in China and Uzbekistan. The results of a Phase III clinical study evaluating the efficacy and safety of VV116 versus PAXLOVID® was published in *The New England Journal of Medicine*.

5. INNOVENT BIOLOGICS (1801.HK)

Founded in China in 2011, it is a biopharmaceutical company focusing on the developing, manufacture and commercialization of innovative medicines for the unmet medical need of cancers, metabolic diseases, and autoimmune diseases. The company's founder, Dr. Yu Dechao (Michael) [415] received his Ph.D. in Genetics from the Chinese Academy of Sciences, followed by his training and working in the U.S. Yu is currently the inventor and owner of more than 60 patents (38 from the U.S.). In October 2018, Innovent was listed on the HKEX, raised US$485 million. [416]

The company has exhibited remarkable performance since inception, up to December 30, 2022, they have eight products including five antibody medicines approved for commercialization, over 3,000 people sales team and RMB4.2 billion annual sales in 2021.

---

415 https://www.innoventbio.com/AboutUs/LeadershipTeam

416 https://www.ifre.com/story/1515639/asia-pacific-ipo-innovent-biologics-hk38bn-ipo-90cplvyclj

Superb global business development capabilities, both inbound and outbound make the company stand out. Innovent attracts reputable investing institutions from China, the U.S., and other Asian countries, such as SDIC, Fidelity, FMR, Temasek, etc. It has established various partnerships including collaborations with U.S. Eli Lilly[417] on the developing of three bispecific antibodies,[418] as well as strategic collaboration with EU Roche in 2020 for the clinical development and commercialization of several bispecific antibodies and cell therapies. It also assisted Eli Lilly on importation, marketing, distribution of three commercial products including Cyramaza® and Retsevmo®.[419]

Strong R&D capabilities are also appreciated such as its team of 1,577 people, pipelines consist of 36 products, including eight in commercialization, six in Phase III or pivotal clinical trials, RMB2.5 billion budget. Up to December 2022, TYVYT®[420] (sintilimab injection) was the only PD-1 inhibitor in China with five major indications (1L nsq NSCLC, 1L sq NSCLC, 1L HCC, 1L GC, 1L ESCC, and cHL) approved and included in China's NRDL. Consequently, Innovent is the front-runner in immuno-oncology treatment in China.

Cross-cultural and cross-board teams also make the company stand out from the crowd. Dr. Yong-Jun Liu was the global head of R&D of Sanofi prior to his current position as the president of Innovent. Both scientific and strategic committees consist of world-class professionals, located in Asia, U.S., and Europe.

6. WUXI BIOLOGICS (2269.HK)

With the mission "to accelerate and transform the discovery, development and manufacturing of biologics through a comprehensive open-access platform, enabling our global healthcare partners and benefiting patients worldwide",[421]

---

417 https://investor.lilly.com/news-releases/news-release-details/lilly-and-innovent-biologics-announce-strategic-alliance-bring

418 https://www.innoventbio.com/AboutUs/AwardsAndMilestones

419 https://www.sanofi.com/en/media-room/press-releases/2022/2022-08-04-15-30-00-2492626

420 https://investor.lilly.com/news-releases/news-release-details/lilly-and-innovent-announce-global-expansion-tyvyt-licensing

421 https://www.wuxibiologics.com/company/#Vision_Mission

WuXi Biologics was founded in Wuxi, China in 2010. Today, it is one of the global leaders in Contract Research, Development and Manufacturing Organization (CRDMO) focusing on biologics.

CEO Dr. Chris Chen[422] obtained a Ph.D. degree in chemical engineering from University of Delaware, B.S. from Tsinghua University Beijing. He has more than 20 years' experience in monoclonal antibodies, therapeutic proteins, and vaccines.

On June 13, 2017, WuXi Biologics[423] completed its initial public offering at the price of HK$20.60 per share for a total offering size of approximately HK$4 billion on the HKEX. It is one of the largest IPOs in the year 2017 globally. As of June 30, 2022, the group has approximately RMB9.9 billion available funds, total liability to equity ratio 33.8%, sufficient for capacity expansion.

As of 2022, WuXi Biologics has 17 sites globally, including ten in China, three in the U.S., one in Ireland, two in Germany and one in Singapore. It plans to spend US$1.4 billion over ten years to build a cutting-edge, fully integrated CRDMO center in Singapore to strengthen its global supply chain.[424] The group acts in Global Dual Sourcing strategy, makes heavy investments in U.S., EU, and China to meet the robust demands from the industry.

The largest market for the group is the North America, contributing 54% of the total revenue, the second market is China, contributing 25% of the total, the third market is EU, contributing 18% of the total. WuXi Biologics collaborate with all the top 20 pharma companies globally and 42 out of 50 of the largest pharma in China to diversify its customer base.

The state-of-the-art vaccines facility in Ireland of WuXi Vaccines, a subsidiary of the group, won the title of "Large Pharma Project of the Year". The Group has signed nine vaccine contracts and has help clients with three different modalities

---

422 https://www.wuxibiologics.com/leadership/

423 https://www.fiercebiotech.com/cro/wuxi-biologics-prices-share-at-top-end-aims-for-510m-ipo-bloomberg

424 https://www.biopharma-reporter.com/Article/2022/07/21/WuXi-Biologics-to-build-CRDMO-center-in-Singapore

of COVID-19 vaccines.

WuXi XDC is the integrated Antibody-drug Conjugate ("ADC") platform, which secured 60 ADC integrated projects globally, including two phase III projects. ADC is a new class of highly potent biologics. Compared to traditional chemotherapies and mAbs, ADCs show super efficacy, less toxicity, and a larger therapeutic window. The industry is optimistic that ADCs will shape the future of cancer treatment paradigms.

To help combat this pandemic, the Group enabled more than 35 COVID-19 projects and one of the COVID-19 neutralizing antibody products enabled by WuXi Biologics obtained Emergency Use Authorization by the U.S. FDA in 14 months.

7. BEIGENE (6160.HK)

With "cancer has no borders, neither do we"[425] in mind, Mr. John Oyler and Mr. Xiaodong Wang co-founded BeiGene in 2010 in Beijing.[426] Oyler, the Chairman and CEO of BeiGene, received his bachelor's degree in mechanical engineering from Massachusetts Institute of Technology, and MBA from Stanford University in the U.S. Wang is the Chairman of Scientific Advisory Board of BeiGene. In 2004, Wang became the member of the U.S. National Academy of Science, one of the highest honors available. He is also the founding director of the National Institute of Biological Science in Beijing, serving since 2003.

In 2016, Beijing-based oncology biotech BeiGene[427] priced its offer of 6.6 million American Depositary at US$24 each, in an initial public offering on the NASDAQ, shares closed 19.25% to US$28.62 and raised US$182 million. In 2018, BeiGene completed public offering on the HKEX and raised US$903 million.[428] On December 14, 2021, BeiGene announced pricing of its RMB22.2 billion (US$3.5 billion) initial public offering on the STAR market of

---

425 https://www.beigene.com/our-company-and-people/

426 https://www.beigene.com/our-company-and-people/leadership-and-board/

427 https://www.fiercepharma.com/financials/updated-beigene-comes-at-top-end-of-range-nasdaq-ipo-raising-158-4m

428 https://www.reuters.com/article/us-beigene-listing-idUSKBN1KN0E1

the Shanghai Stock Exchange,[429] the largest initial public offering by a biotech company in 2021 to date. Globally, BeiGene is the first biotech to be listed on all three capital markets: New York, Hong Kong, and Shanghai.

Being committed to advancing best-in-class or first-in-class clinical candidates, BeiGene's 800 scientists and 2,500 worldwide clinical professionals facilitate 90 ongoing or scheduled clinical trials for over 30 drug candidates. As of June 30, 2022, BeiGene has three approved medicines that were discovered and developed in own labs. BRUKINSA®, a small molecule inhibitor of Bruton's Tyrosine Kinase (BTK) for the treatment of various blood cancers, has been approved in over 50 markets, with additional filings pending or planned. Tislelizumab, an anti-PD-1 antibody immunotherapy for the treatment of various solid tumors and blood cancers; and Pamiparib, a selective small molecule inhibitor of PARP1 and PARP2 were both approved by NMPA in China.

In November 2019, a global biotech leader, Amgen,[430] acquired 20.5% stake in BeiGene for US$2.7 billion in cash, both parties reached a strategic cooperation in the field of global cancer. In January 2021, BeiGene entered into a collaboration and license agreement with Novartis,[431] a Swiss-based global oncology leader. Novartis obtained the rights to develop, manufacture, and commercialize Tislelizumab in the U.S., Canada, Mexico, member states of the European Union, United Kingdom, Norway, Switzerland, Iceland, Liechtenstein, Russia, and Japan, all called the Novartis territory. In December 2021, the collaboration was expanded with BeiGene's investigational TIGIT inhibitor Ociperlimab in the Novartis Territory. Novartis granted BeiGene the rights to market, promote and detail five approved Novartis oncology products, TAFINLAR®, MEKINIST®, VOTRIENT®, AFINITOR®, and ZYKADIA®, across regions of China referred to as "Broad Markets".

---

429 https://endpts.com/beigene-gets-the-ball-rolling-on-its-3rd-ipo-and-this-one-is-expected-to-fetch-3b/

430 https://www.amgen.com/newsroom/press-releases/2019/10/amgen-enters-into-strategic-collaboration-with-beigene-to-expand-oncology-presence-in-china

431 https://www.novartis.com/news/media-releases/novartis-strengthens-immunotherapy-pipeline-option-collaboration-and-license-agreement-beigene-tigit-inhibitor-ociperlimab

BeiGene believes that global clinical development capabilities are essential to succeed now and, in the future, therefore, it builds a size of 2,500 worldwide professionals in clinical development and medical affairs to develop product candidates largely without assistance of third-party Contract Research Organizations (CROs, please refer to Chapter 12 for details).

With over 3,100 commercial staff spread across China, BeiGene has a broad and deep sales and marketing coverage. Coupled with its China-inclusive clinical development capabilities conducted with global first-class quality standards, BeiGene can attract more in-licensing opportunities. Currently, BeiGene has the in-license rights for 13 approved medicines for the China market.

8. REMEGEN (9995.HK)

The Company was co-founded in 2008 by Mr. Weidong Wang and Dr. Jiangmen Fang,[432] in Yantai, China. Wang, Chairman of the Board, obtained his bachelor's degree in Chinese Medicine manufacturing at Harbin University of Commerce, later he made his fortune in traditional Chinese medicine business. Fang, the CEO and CSO, obtained his doctorate degree in Biology from Dalhousie University in Canada. He was a post-doctoral fellow focusing on cancer research at Harvard Medical School, Boston Children's Hospital from 1997 to 2000.

Through over ten years' efforts, RemeGen is now the leader in the ADCs in China. It has carried out fully integrated, end-to-end therapeutics development encompassing all biologic functionalities, including discovery, pre-clinical, process and quality development, clinical development, and manufacturing in compliance with global Good Manufacturing Practice (GMP), primarily targeting autoimmune diseases, oncology, and ophthalmic diseases.

On November 9, 2020, RemeGen was listed on the HKEX. Its IPO raised US$515 million, setting one of the highest records for a global biotech company IPO fundraising event.[433] On March 31, 2022, RemeGen was officially listed on the Science and Technology Innovation Board of the Shanghai Stock

---

432 http://www.remegen.com/?v=listing&cid=86#dsh

433 https://www.fiercebiotech.com/biotech/remegen-grabs-one-world-s-largest-ever-biotech-ipos

Exchange,[434] realizing the "A+H" dual listing plan.

RemeGen discovers and develops a robust product pipeline consisting of more than ten drug candidates, including Antibody Drug Conjugates (ADCs), fusion proteins, monoclonal antibodies, and dual-antibody drugs. Core products include:

Telitacicept (RC18): a proprietary novel TACI-Fc fusion protein for treating autoimmune diseases. It targets two cell-signaling molecules critical for B-lymphocyte development: B-Cell Lymphocyte Stimulator (BLyS), and A Proliferation Inducing Ligand (APRIL), which effectively reduce B-cell medicated autoimmune responses. In China, it was granted the Conditional Marketing Approval by the NMPA for the treatment of Systemic Lupus Erythematosus (SLE) on March 9, 2021, and it was included on the updated National Reimbursement Drug List (NRDL) in December 2021. This medication served 2,400 patients, 445 hospitals, 168 cities in 31 provinces across China since its approval in 2021. The company also launched a phase III clinical study of RC18 for the treatment of SLE in the U.S. in March 2022.

Disitamab Vedotin (RC48): its NDA for the treatment of Gastric Cancer (GC) was granted Priority Review by the China NMPA in August 2020, followed by Conditional Approval in June 2021. Its NDA for the treatment of Urothelial Cancer (UC) was granted Priority Review by the NMPA in September 2021, followed by Conditional Marketing Approval in December 2021. It is the first ADC drug developed in China to receive Breakthrough Designations in both the U.S. and China.

In August 2021, RemeGen entered into an exclusive worldwide agreement with Seagan,[435] a global leader in the ADCs. Seagan is granted to develop and commercialize disitamab vedotin in countries of the world other than Greater China and all other countries in Asia (excluding Japan and Singapore).

RC28: is an innovative fusion protein targeting both Vascular Endothelial

---

434 http://www.chinabiotoday.com/articles/remegen-410-million-shanghai-ipo

435 https://investor.seagen.com/press-releases/news-details/2021/Seagen-and-RemeGen-Announce-Exclusive-Worldwide-License-and-Co-Development-Agreement-for-Disitamab-Vedotin/default.aspx

Growth Factor (VEGF) and fibroblast growth factor (FGF), RemeGen is conducting clinical trials for several ophthalmic diseases, including wet Age-Related Macular Degeneration (wet AMD), Diabetic Macular Edema (DME), and Diabetic Retinopathy (DR).

9. SIRNAOMICS[436] (2557.HK)

Sirnaomics was founded in 2007 by Dr. Patrick Lu, who is also the President and CEO of the company. The company is headquartered in Maryland, the U.S., with operations in Boston, Suzhou, Guangzhou, and Hong Kong.

Sirnaomics is currently a clinical-stage RNAi therapeutic company that discovers and develops innovative drugs for indications with significant unmet medical needs. The company's mission is to become a fully integrated, and internationally recognized company, leveraging their profound experience in RNAi therapeutics and novel delivery platform technologies to rapidly discover, develop and, commercialize a portfolio of transformative therapeutics for patients suffering from a wide range of diseases. The company has demonstrated its leadership position in oncology application of the RNAi-based drugs.

Sirnaomics holds proprietary delivery platforms for RNA-based therapeutics which are the technological foundation of its pipeline. The company's Polypeptide Nanoparticle (PNP) formulation and the second generation of GalNAc (GaLAhead®) structure give unique strengths for innovative RNAi drug development. Sirnaomics aims to focus initially on oncology and fibrosis, then expand to anticoagulant therapies, cardiometabolic disease, complement mediated disease, viral infections and medical cosmetics.

Sirnaomics targets global market, with the current emphasis specifically on the U.S. and China owing to its strong and well-established R&D capabilities and manufacturing facilities in both countries. It is adopting a clinical development strategy to conduct clinical trials for its product candidates initially in the U.S. and then to extend those trials globally.

Sirnaomics is advancing a deep and broad portfolio of product candidates,

---

436 https://sirnaomics.com/

including its seven ongoing clinical trials in the U.S. with its three lead candidates, which are STP705, STP707, and STP122G. After positive clinical readouts STP705 from several clinical studies of Phase IIa and Phase IIb, involving non-melanoma skin cancer treatment, the company decided to speed up its late-stage clinical development effort for specifically treating skin Squamous Cell Carcinoma in situ (isSCC) and skin Basal Cell Carcinoma (BCC). STP707, a systemic delivered siRNA therapeutics gives a strong safety profile and clear therapeutic effect through a Phase I basket clinical study, based on this result and a preclinical validation, the company has decided to proceed with a combo therapeutics for treatment of liver cancer and pancreatic cancer, testing both STP707 and Immune Checkpoint Inhibitory (ICI) mAd synergistic efficacy. STP122G is a GalANc delivery system driven siRNA therapeutics with siRNA inhibitor targeting coagulation Factor XI and having demonstrated long-lasting (>28 weeks) target knockdown and therapeutic benefit with a non-human primate study. A Phase I clinical study is in progress.

Sirnaomics raised US$105 million in Series D funding in July 2021,[437] followed by Initial Public Offering on December 30, 2021 and raised US$50 million on HKEX.[438]

10. AIER EYE HOSPITAL GROUP (300015.CN)

Founded in 2003 by Bang Chen[439] and Li Li, in Changsha, China, it is a global leading ophthalmic medical group providing high-standard eye-care services for patients across Asia, Europe, and North America.

Chen said "First we are a hospital, and then an enterprise. We try to help all people, rich or poor, to enjoy healthcare." Since its inception, AIER has committed to its mission,

"Enabling everyone, whether rich or poor, has the right to eye health."

---

437 https://www.fiercebiotech.com/biotech/eschewing-ipo-for-now-sirnaomics-nabs-a-rare-series-e-worth-105m-for-its-next-gen-rna-work

438 https://www.bloomberg.com/news/articles/2021-12-19/biotech-firm-sirnaomics-targets-up-to-70-3m-in-hong-kong-ipo#xj4y7vzkg

439 https://www.forbes.com/companies/aier-eye-hospital-group/?sh=46192f5d1677

AIER has three listed companies, including AIER in Shenzhen, China; in Spain BME: CBAV;[440] and in Singapore SGX: 40T. The company has established over 700 ophthalmic hospitals and centers across the world, including 657 hospitals and centers in mainland China, seven in Hong Kong, one in the U.S., 94 in Europe, and 13 in Southeast Asia. In 2021, they performed over one million surgeries in mainland China and their worldwide medical service network covers approximately three billion patients. The company has a market cap of RMB235 billion as of February 2023.

AIER is the largest hospital chain in China. While domestic market is its core business, AIER takes parallel strategic approach, emphasis on exposure to global cutting-edge technologies and management concept as well as contributing to the evolution of China's ophthalmology market and medical care.

AIER put huge efforts in promoting teaching and learning, for instance: in 2013, AIER and Central South University jointly set up AIER School of Ophthalmology, CSU, to educate and train professionals with advanced degrees. Additionally, AIER works with Hubei University of Science and Technology to establish the AIER School of Ophthalmology & Optometry.

AIER founded Clinical College of Ophthalmology and Ophthalmic Research Institute in Wuhan University in 2019. Its comprehensive scientific research platform entails the construction of eight institutes, two stations, two bases, and three centers nationwide, forming a hierarchical chain with Shanghai positioned at the core.

On top of providing routine ophthalmology medical services such as diagnosis, treatment and medical optometry to patients, the company's main sources of revenue come from refractive surgery and cataract surgery, accounting for a total income increase from 18% to 21% in the past five years with tripled revenues.[441] As China's myopia population continues to grow, AIER has sped up the construction of county-level hospitals to cover more patients.

A case study provided by the International Finance Corporation (IFC), part

---

440 https://www.chinadaily.com.cn/business/2017-04/14/content_28929961.htm

441 https://equalocean.com/analysis/2020052214013

of World Bank Group, titled "Preventing Blindness in China" illustrates AIER develops efficient business model to promote quality eye care, and how IFC closely worked with AIER in both businesses and socially responsibilities.[442] AIER's successes should be studies not just in China, but also in other countries as well.

11. GENSCRIPT BIOTECH (1548.HK)

In 2002, with the mission of "Make People and Nature Healthier through Biotechnology", Dr. Fangliang Zhang and Dr. Luquan Wang co-founded GenScript Biotech[443] in a basement in New Jersey, the U.S. Later, Ms. Ye Wang joined the company as a co-founder. 20 years since inception, GenScript has become a global leader in gene synthesis with coverage in more than 100 countries. More importantly, it has developed into a platform-based biotech group with internal incubation capabilities and raised three life sciences unicorns.

In 2009, GenScript received venture capital investment from KPCB and TBIG. In December 2015, it was listed[444] on the HKEX, with China Resources Group being the sole cornerstone investment institution. On June 6, 2020, Legend Biotech, one of its subsidiaries, spun-out and listed on NASDAQ, with stock price rising more than 60% on the first trading day. The stock opened at US$37 per share, making a market capitalization of US$4.79 billion. It was one of the largest IPOs of biotech companies globally in 2020.

GenScript Biotech primarily operates R&D centers, manufacturing facilities, and operation centers in both China and the U.S. Moreover, it has established the Ireland R&D center for Legend Biotech, a Netherlands Logistics Center, as well as subsidiaries in Japan and Singapore, legal entities in Korea, the U.K. and Hong Kong(China). The company has more than 140 granted patents and more than 450 patent applications. For its non-cell therapy revenue, only one third was generated in China.

---

442 https://www.ifc.org/wps/wcm/connect/news_ext_content/ifc_external_corporate_site/news+and+events/news/health_aier_featurestory

443 https://www.genscript.com/overview.html?src=leftbar

444 https://www.genscript.com/Genscript-Corporation-Finishes-Year-with-Successful-Hong-Kong-IPO.html

GenScript Biotech Group has established four main platforms as follows. 1) A life-science services and products provider, under the brand GenScript, is a global leader in gene synthesis. It also provides DNA sequencing, oligonucleotide synthesis, peptide synthesis, protein production and antibody development for global research institutions and companies. GenScript built its competitiveness through providing quality, fast-delivery, and cost-effective services and products. Its services and products had been cited in over 65,600 international peer reviewed journal articles as of December 31, 2021, 2) Legend Biotech is a subsidiary focusing on the development of CAR-T therapy with a U.S. marketed and a potential best-in-class for Multiple Myeloma, 3) a biologics Contract Development and Manufacturing Organization (CDMO) platform, under PROBIO, provides a selection of products and services ranging from end-to-end cell and gene therapies and macromolecular drug discovery services to process development and GMP services for pharmaceutical, biotech, government, and academic clients around the world. After receiving funding from Hillhouse Capital[445] in May 2021, this business entered a rapid expansion phase, including an antibody drug process development and GMP manufacturing site in Nanjing, virus, and plasmid process development and GMP manufacturing site in Zhejiang. 4) Bestzyme, is currently among the top three industrial enzyme suppliers in China. With a production capacity of 150,000 tons of industrial enzymes annually for food and feed end processing users, it is capable of independently developing various types of enzymatic reagents by gene and protein engineering to produce engineered strains.

12.   WUXI APPTEC (2359.HK)[446]

In 2000, with the vision that "every drug can be made, and every disease can be treated", the visionary Dr. Ge Li registered WuXi PharmaTech[447] in the city of WuXi, Jiangsu, and operated in Shanghai, China. In 2008, WuXi PharmaTech acquired AppTec Laboratory Service, with locations in Minnesota, Pennsylvania and Georgia in the U.S. and renamed the company as "WuXi AppTec" since then.

---

445 http://www.chinabiotoday.com/articles/genscript-1-billion-hillhouse?

446 Statistics updated as of September 30, 2022

447 https://www.wuxiapptec.com/about/history

WuXi AppTec provides a broad portfolio of R&D and manufacturing services that enable the pharmaceutical and healthcare industry around the world to advance discoveries and deliver ground-breaking treatments to patients. Through its unique business models, WuXi AppTec's integrated, end-to-end services include chemistry drug Contract Research, Development and Manufacturing Organization (CRDMO), biology discovery, preclinical testing and clinical research services, and cell and gene therapies Contract Testing, Development and Manufacturing Organization (CTDMO).

Under the direction of Dr. Ge Li, the founder, Chairman and CEO of the company, WuXi AppTec has grown from a single laboratory of 7,000 square feet into a global enterprise with more than 45,000 employees including 42,000 scientists, and 32 R&D and manufacturing sites across Asia, Europe, and North America.

Beginning with synthetic chemistry, WuXi AppTec now owns five business segments: 1) WuXi Chemistry, the CRDMO integrated business model of which has proven to be very successful, acts as a funnel entrance for related downstream business units. Its small molecule drug discovery (R) services delivered over 370,000 synthesized compounds to the clients in the 12 months ended September 2022, and its development, and manufacturing service delivered total pipeline of 2,123 molecules, 2) WuXi Testing provides services related to Drug Metabolism and Pharmacokinetics (DMPK), toxicology and bioanalytical testing. Its Clinical CRO provided services to around 190 projects and enabling ten IND approvals in the first three quarters of 2022, and its SMO maintained number one leadership position in China with over 4,700 staffs in 150 cities and more than 1,000 hospitals, 3)WuXi Biology is the discovery biology enabling platform providing comprehensive biology services related to all stages and therapeutic areas of drug research and development, primarily in new modalities and large molecules, 4)WuXi ATU provides globally integrated CRTDMO services to cell and gene therapy products development, and 5)WuXi DDSU, the company's success-based drug discovery service unit which filed INDs on behalf of China-based customers.

WuXi AppTec continues to embrace cutting-edge innovations and enhance its capacity and capabilities. The company has established multiple research and manufacturing facilities globally for their CTDMO business involving cell and gene therapies. In China, following their first facility built in Huishan of WuXi

City, China, WuXi ATU built their second cell and gene therapy manufacturing facility in Lingang, Shanghai with a designed capacity of 21,500 square meters. In the U.S., as an expansion of WuXi ATU's existing Navy Yard Campus in Philadelphia, an additional state-of-the-art testing site was built in 2021, which includes 140,000 square feet laboratories.

In addition, WuXi AppTec keeps promoting interaction and collaboration within the global innovation ecosystem. Since 2013, the company has organized the WuXi Global Forum in San Francisco to bring together executives from pharma, partners from venture capitals, founders, and CEOs from emerging start-ups, and thought leaders and officials from regulatory agency around the world to exchange experience and address healthcare challenges for patients.

After being traded on the New York Stock Exchange under the ticker symbol "NYSE:WX" in 2007,[448] the company was privatized in 2015. In May 2018, WuXi AppTec was listed on Shanghai Stock Exchange[449] (stock code: 603259. CN). In December 2018, the company listed on the HKEX (stock code: 2359. HK).[450]

13. MICROPORT (0853.HK)

With the aspiration of "pushing boundaries so that patients everywhere can enjoy better and longer lives",[451] MicroPort[452] was founded in Shanghai in 1998. It is a global leading medical device group focusing on innovating, manufacturing, and marketing high-end medical devices. The founder and CEO, Mr. Zhaohua Chang[453] has over 30 years' experience in the medical device industry, and currently serves as a full-time professor at School of Medical Device, the University of Shanghai for Science and Technology. He completed his bachelor and master's degrees in China and received his doctoral degree in Biological

---

448 https://scrip.pharmaintelligence.informa.com/deals/200730763

449 https://www.fiercebiotech.com/cro/wuxi-apptec-gets-fast-tracked-approval-for-900m-plus-shanghai-ipo

450 https://www.reuters.com/article/us-wuxiapptec-listing-idUSKBN1O6098

451 https://microport.com/about-us/purpose-and-values

452 https://microport.com/about-us/history

453 https://microport.com/contact/nom-du-contact-en

Science from the State University of New York.

MicroPort takes full advantage of capital markets in both Hong Kong and Shanghai, to solidify its financial situation and build up brand recognition. On September 24, 2010, MicroPort Scientific (0853.HK) went public on HKEX.

On February 4, 2021, MicroPort CardioFlow Medtech Corporation[454] (2160.HK) was successfully listed on HKEX. The company raised HK$2.5 billion (US$324 million) by issuing 205.62 million shares at HK$12.2 per share. The stock opened at HK$21.5, 76% up from the offering price.

On November 2, 2021, Shanghai MicroPort Medbot., Ltd. (2252.HK) was listed on HKEX, raising HK$1.56 billion (US$201 million) at HK$43.2 per share.[455] On June 3, 2022, the company proposed a RMB2.8 billion (US$420 million) IPO on Shanghai STAR Market. [456]

On July 15, 2022, MicroPort NeuroTech Limited (2172.HK) was listed on HKEX. The offering raised net proceeds of HK$278 million. The public offering was oversubscribed by 45 times, at a valuation of HK$14.4 billion.[457]

On August 31, Shanghai MicroPort EP MedTech Co., Ltd. (688351.CN) was listed on the Sci-Tech Innovation Board of Shanghai Stock Exchange. It raised RMB1.17 billion (US$169.5 million). [458]

The Company rooted in China yet is with extensive global coverage. 1) The generated revenue in year 2021 was US$779 million among which 54% comes from outside China, 2) the group has a total of 8,010 employees across the globe,

---

454 https://www.bioworld.com/articles/503229-microports-spinoff-cardioflow-launches-324m-ipo-in-hong-kong?v=preview

455 https://www.bioworld.com/articles/512955-microport-medbot-raises-201m-in-ipo-shares-increase-6?v=preview

456 https://www.bioworld.com/articles/519433-microport-medbot-proposes-420m-ipo-on-shanghai-stock-exchange?v=preview

457 https://www.sidley.com/en/newslanding/newsannouncements/2022/07/sidley-represents-microport-neurotech-limited-in-successful-hong-kong-ipo

458 https://www.bioworld.com/articles/672666-microport-ep-raises-1695m-in-shanghai-ipo-shares-drop-in-debut?v=preview

of which 1,715 (21.4%) were overseas. The following are its core business lines:

Cardiovascular devices business: offering services and products for the treatment of coronary artery-related disease, including coronary stents and related delivery systems, balloon catheters and accessories. The global sales volume of MicroPort coronary stents amounted to 1.22 million units, with market share ranking the world's top two and China number one. This business has four drug eluting stents and four balloon products sold to over 36 countries and regions worldwide. It builds up headquarters for the Americans, and Southern California Innovation Center and Intelligent Manufacturing Base in the U.S. market.

Orthopedics devices business includes reconstructive joints, spine and trauma, and other professional implants and instruments. The Prime 3D printed acetabular cup system was approved for marketing and completed its first clinical implantation in the U.S. market. In China, its hip and joints products won bids in the state-organized Volume-Based Procurement, (VBP), which significantly increased market share and penetration rate.

CRM business: primarily includes pacemakers, defibrillators, and resynchronization therapy. Its implantable pacemakers Alizea®, and Borea® and SmartView Connect home monitor, all equipped with Bluetooth technology, have obtained the CE markings, and was launched in European market. In China, the "Rega series" pacemakers have accumulatively accomplished 10,000 implantations since its launch in 2018.

Neurovascular devices business: covering diseases such as hemorrhagic stroke, cerebral atherosclerotic stenosis, and acute ischemic stroke. The group has penetrated over 2,000 hospitals in China, including all top 100 hospitals ranked by the China National Stroke Center. It innovated the first and only intracranial stent graft for treating cerebral vessel diseases, Willis.

Heart Valve Business: the second generation of TAVI product Vita-Flow Liberty was approved by NMPA for marketing. It is a China-made electrical retrieval TAVI with global competitiveness.

Surgical robot business: A cutting-edge technology for the needs of minimal invasive surgery. The group is the only company in the worldwide robot industry that covers a portfolio of five specialties: laparoscopic, orthopedic, pan-vascular, natural orifice and percutaneous surgical procedures. Its flagship Toumai Laparoscopic Surgical Robot® was approved for marketing in 2022. It is the first four-arm laparoscopic robot approved for marketing introduced by a Chinese company.

14. MINDRAY (300760.CN)

In 1991, with mission to "advance medical technologies to make healthcare more accessible",[459] Mindray was established in Shenzhen, China. 30 years later, it has become a leading global provider of medical devices and solutions, and IT ecosystem solutions for both human and veterinary use. Mr. Xiting Li, now one of the most affluent Singaporeans, founded the company alongside with Hang Xu and Minghe Cheng. Li has actively made donations to help schools and people in need. For instance. on October 26, 2022, Li announced to donate RMB1 billion to his middle school back in his hometown. On June 12, 2022, he donated RMB106.8 million to the University of Science and Technology of China and established "Li Xiting Fund".[460]

In 1997, Mindray received the first round of investment from Walden International. In 2006, Mindray was listed on the New York Stock Exchange as the first Chinese medical device company and raised US$270 million. On the day of IPO, its stock opened at US$16, and closed at US$17.55 with a gain of 30%.[461] 10 years later, Mindray was delisted after completing its privatization.

In 2018, it was listed on the Growth Enterprise Market of the Shenzhen Stock Exchange, China, raising RMB6 billion (US$935 million). [462] As of February 2023, its market cap was approximately RMB400 billion.

Mindray firmly believes in "sharing medical innovations with the world". Today, with 14,000 employees, 52 subsidiaries in 30 countries, Mindray serves over 190

459 https://www.mindray.com/en/about-us/#mr--about us--purpose

460 https://www.mindray.com/en/about-us/social-responsibility/still-young-li-xiting-establishes-fund-for-university-of-science-and-technology-of-china/

461 https://www.marketwatch.com/story/mindray-medical-rallies-in-debut

462 https://www.caixinglobal.com/2018-05-30/medical-device-maker-looks-for-new-life-with-1-billion-ipo-101259716.html

countries and regions worldwide and generated US$3.9 billion revenue in 2021.

Innovation and development are rooted in Mindray's DNA. Starting from simple and single product to total healthcare solutions, Mindray has achieved several "the first in China",[463] such as: the first self-developed multi-parameter patient monitor, semi-automatic hematology analyzer, auto chemistry analyzer, digital ultrasound system, cart-based color Doppler ultra-sound system, biphasic defibrillator, ultra-high-speed auto chemistry analyzer, and more. In 2013, Mindray innovated the first anesthesia workstation with fully digital flowmeter in Asia. In 2015, it developed the world's first rotatable large-screen patient monitor, and in 2021, the world's first real-time visualized quantitative, non-invasive and fibrosis evaluation system.

Mindray has established and developed three core products lines: 1) Patient Monitoring & Life Support: offering a wide range of instruments for patient monitoring and life support as well as minimally invasive surgical products. 2) In-Vitro Diagnostic: namely analyzers for hematology, chemiluminescence immunoassay, biochemistry, coagulation, urine, microbiology diagnostic systems and related reagents and more. 3) Medical Imaging: providing hospitals, clinics, and imaging centers with various high-end and low-end ultrasound diagnostics systems, as well as digital x-ray imaging solutions to radiology departments and Intensive Care Units (ICU)s. Through a continuous high-end-oriented technology development approach, Mindray's ultrasound business surpassed similar imported brands.

Key drivers for Mindray to continue deliver performances include:

1) The new medical infrastructure constitution led by the expansion of large public hospitals enlarges China's medical device market. The COVID-19 pandemic pinpoints the weakness of healthcare infrastructure from the various levels of China. On October 27, 2021, the National Health Commission (NHC) issued the Work Plan for improving the comprehensive capacity of county hospitals under the "Thousand Counties Project (2021-2025)". At least 1,000 hospitals will advance to tertiary hospitals, so that they will play a central role fighting the common diseases on county level.

---

463 https://www.mindray.com/en/about-us/history

2) The promotion of China made products with high-quality with core technologies being accelerated. Aiming to ease the contradiction between the shortage of public medical insurance funding and people's pursuit for quality medical resources, Chinese government has launched various reforms, to shoulder the medical expenses for 1.4 billion people and reduce the social and economic burden of the society. China has made rapid developments in the past few decades, especially in economy, science, and technology. People no longer stick to the old assumption of "the imported products must be better than domestic products". Therefore, cost-effective and quality products usually win the contracts within hospitals, regardless of where and who made them.

3) EvaluateMedTech estimated the global medical device market was around US$500 billion in 2021. The CAGR of the sales value of global medical devices for 2020-2024 will be 5.6%. China has a huge population that is rapidly aging. Economic growth and the gradually improved healthcare system have already shaped China the second largest medical device market. Even as an industry leader, Mindray only has a low single-digit domestic market share. It still has huge growth space, both domestically and internationally.

During the COVID-19 pandemic, Mindray organized international academic and clinical exchanges, for Chinese doctors to share experiences in curbing the pandemic. These cross-border hospitals' clinical sharing to fight the common viruses and diseases demonstrated spirit and virtue of humanity. Mindray's ventilators, monitors and other anti-pandemic devices have appealed to a larger number of new customers worldwide.

PART 3

Stay Humble, Stay Foolish

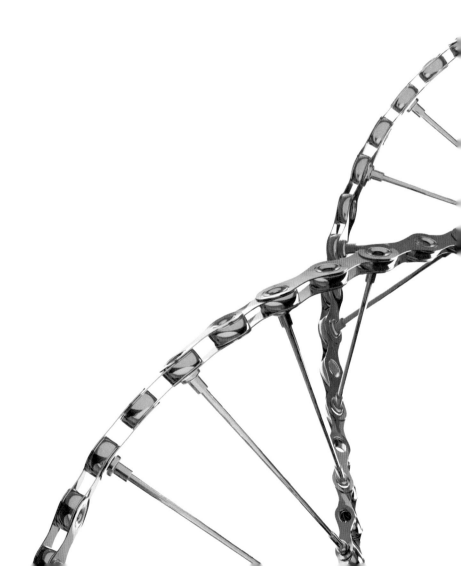

Chapter 8

Rare Diseases and Orphan Drugs

1. STATUS QUO OF GLOBAL MARKET

February 28, 2023, marks the 16th International Rare Disease Day.[464] The World Health Organization (WHO) defines rare diseases as the diseases which have an incidence rate of 0.065% to 0.1% of the total population. There are 6,000 to 8,000 rare diseases to date with 250 new diseases described annually, affecting up to 400 million patients and an estimated 6-8% of the human population. In the U.S. alone, there are approximately 30 million people suffering from a rare disease. 80% of rare diseases are genetic in origin, and about 50% or more impacts children.

Under the united efforts of government regulatory agencies, patient organizations, R&D centers, life sciences companies, as well as the advance in understanding of the life sciences, orphan drugs have become a research focus over the past decade. A paradigm shift favoring individualized medicines have also helped shape these rare diseases drugs that are used for diagnostic, therapeutic and preventative purposes. The number of orphan drugs approved by the U.S. FDA has been on the rise. According to the Pharmaceutical Research and Manufacturers of America (PhRMA) report on Rare Diseases, more than 600 medicines are approved in the U.S. for rare diseases, and currently, more than 700 medicines are in the development pipeline.[465] In 2020, there were 31 orphan drugs approved by the U.S. FDA, taking up 58.5% of all newly approved drugs that same year and marking a record high in ten years. Among these, 12 are first-in-class drugs. Again in 2021, based on Orphan Drug Report 2022 by Evaluate, over half of the U.S. FDA's approval were orphan drugs to treat rare disease. By 2026, orphan drugs will make up to a fifth of all prescription drugs

---

464 https://www.rarediseaseday.org/what-is-rare-disease-day/

465 https://phrma.org/resource-center/Topics/Medicines-in-Development/Medicines-in-Development-for-Rare-Diseases-2021-Report

sales, and almost a third of global drug pipeline's value.[466]

It is evident that orphan drugs are no longer "orphan" and rare disease are no longer "rare", this symbolizes an important milestone in the human history.

1) Challenges in combating rare diseases

Compared to common diseases, our current knowledge on rare diseases is even more confined, largely due to the nature, heterogeneity, progression of these diseases, and rarity itself. Even within a particular disease, there are subtypes and mutations, many are still unknown at present.

Up to date, humanity have developed many effective chemical drugs. Even so, many mechanisms of actions of these existing drugs remains unclear or to be defined. From a scientific perspective, researchers have named or characterized some rare diseases, but they may not know the cause or the potential causes of these diseases. Other challenges include identifying targets, developing biomarkers, designing animal models, working out complex pathways, coordinating global clinical trial centers, measuring endpoints and outcome, and convincing regulatory agencies, even securing payments.

2) Key factors in the development

The beginning of rare diseases and orphan drugs sector dates to the 1980s, with its total developmental history spanning only 40 years. The growth in this area is spurred by the following key factors.

Pivotal effect of laws and regulations

Pharmaceutical companies were initially reluctant to step into the sector of orphan drugs due to R&D difficulty and high costs, small target population and unlikely profitability. There were only around 30 rare disease drugs on the U.S. market before 1983. The subsequent enactment of the Orphan Drug

---

466 https://info.evaluate.com/rs/607-YGS-364/images/Evaluate%20Orphan%20 Drug%20Report.pdf

Act (ODA),[467] and implementation of the Orphan Drug Designation (ODD)[468] have heavily impacted this sector since then. The ODA defines rare diseases as any disease which 1) affects less than 200,000 American citizens, or 2) affects more than 200,000 American citizens and no alternative treatments exist, but expectation that sales of such drugs will be able to reimburse the cost of developing and commercializing the drug in the U.S. is unlikely.[469]

The U.S. FDA revised the orphan drug regulation in 1991, 1992, 2011 and 2013 respectively. This is accompanied by a series of beneficial policies, such as providing a potential seven years of market exclusivity after approval, accelerated review and approval, tax credits for qualified clinical trials, exemption from user fees. This can add up to a 50% reduction in R&D costs and greatly encourage developments in the orphan drug sector. As for 2021, 5,808 ODDs have been granted by the U.S. FDA and a further 952 approved under the ODA since its enactment 40 years ago. A series of innovative breakthrough technologies has been incorporated into the rare disease treatments, such as the RNAi and gene therapy. Consequently, these novel therapies have prolonged the lives of many patients.

There is no single and widely accepted definition for rare disease, it varies by region. For example, the European Union (EU) classifies rare diseases as life-threatening or chronically debilitating diseases which have a prevalence of 0.05%,[470] about 6,000 – 8,000 rare diseases affect roughly 30 million people in the EU.[471] There is no fixed definition in Japan,[472] and prevalence rate is higher than the 0.04%.[473] The definition for rare diseases in China is currently upheld in the form of the formulary "China Rare Diseases Definition and Research Report 2021", which is defined as any diseases with a prevalence or neonatal

---

467 https://www.fda.gov/industry/fdas-rare-disease-day/story-behind-orphan-drug-act

468 https://www.fda.gov/industry/medical-products-rare-diseases-and-conditions/designating-orphan-product-drugs-and-biological-products

469 https://www.cancer.gov/publications/dictionaries/cancer-terms/def/orphan-drug-designation

470 https://research-and-innovation.ec.europa.eu/research-area/health/rare-diseases_en

471 https://www.ncbi.nlm.nih.gov/pmc/articles/PMC3150005/

472 https://pharmaboardroom.com/legal-articles/orphan-drugs-rare-diseases-japan/

473 https://www.thelancet.com/action/showPdf?pii=S0140-6736%2808%2961393-8

morbidity of less than one in 10,000, or a total patient population that is less than 140,000.[474]

Historical pattern shows that rare diseases and orphan drugs rise with the economic strength

According to a report from Boston Consulting Group, whenever an economic body reaches the threshold of US$10,000 GDP per capita, its society begins to address high drug prices by means of legislation to benefit more rare disease patients. We have seen this correlation happened in the U.S., Russia, South Korean, Brazil and Mexico and other markets. China reached US$10,000 GDP per capita threshold in 2019 and US$12,000 in 2022. With its gigantic population base of 1.4 billion people, China will make impactful changes to the global life sciences.

The rapid growth of orphan drugs proves paradigm shift to individualized medicine

The 1980s to 1990s is the era of general medicines. Most of the patient population and research are associated with cardiovascular disease, hyperlipidemia, stomach disease, allergy, and depression. However, the prevalent problem was that these medicines did not work on everyone, even surprisingly, medication efficacy rates were often lower than 50% of treated population. Doctors adhered to the classic trial-and-error approach and prescribed drugs that had different mechanisms of actions to patients according to clinical guidelines and medication formularies.

Starting from the early millennium, new sciences and technologies emerged, such as targeted medicines used for cancer treatments, breakthrough in Next Generation Sequencing (NGS), early cancer screening, and applications of companion diagnostics. These technological advances instated the significance of precision medicine in cancer treatments, namely in the form of "genetic testing + *in vitro* diagnostics + targeted drugs". Cancer treatments are only the beginning, more diseases treatments will follow this form.

As human's understanding of diseases and biotechnologies deepens, the

---

474 https://www.ncbi.nlm.nih.gov/pmc/articles/PMC8898396/

classification of indications will branch out into finer sub-divisions, ultimately downplaying the concept of rare diseases and bringing us to the individualized medicine paradigm. For instance, the patient population in some rare diseases has already outnumbered that of certain cancer subtypes, such as Retinitis Pigmentosa vs. moderate to severe thalassemia.

The strategic role of orphan drugs spur higher stocks performance

In the beginning, pharmaceutical companies took advantage of the shorter R&D time and high approval rate related to the orphan drugs to initiate clinical trials and rapid launch. These companies maximized profits by gradually expanding indications. The orphan drug designation grants special legal protections, as evidenced by market exclusivity of seven years in the U.S. market and ten years in the EU market. Thus, filing for orphan drug designations has become a strategic action by MNCs to increase global sales. For example, the product with the highest number of approved orphan drug designations to date belongs to Avastin®, which has 11 orphan indications up to December 2020.[475]

Additionally, MNCs aggressively purchase assets related to rare diseases, such as commercially valuable products, technologies, or biotech start-ups. Evidently, orphan drugs sector carries strategic significance for these established MNCs to secure their leading market positions. These strategic moves show semblance to what happened in the cancer sector 20 years ago.

Moreover, independently listed life sciences companies focusing on orphan drugs have been seen higher above-the-industry-average returns. A report from Boston Consulting on rare disease in May 2021 demonstrated that from 2017 to 2020, the returns from listed rare diseases companies were four times higher than the average NASDAQ index.

3) Key players

In the last 40 years, pioneering biotech start-ups within the rare diseases realm have made significant contributions to humanity. Companies such as Vertex and

---

475 https://www.iqvia.com/insights/the-iqvia-institute/reports/orphan-drugs-in-the-united-states-rare-disease-innovation-and-cost-trends-through-2019

Alnylam operate independently on the market while others such as Genzyme[476] and Shire[477] were acquired by larger MNCs. Mergers and acquisitions are the consisting recipe in this sector. The following are examples that reflect the historical developments of rare diseases and orphan drugs.

Vertex[478] (VRTX.US)

The Billion-dollar Molecule[479] is one of the popular books to understand biotech industry. The book chronicles the legendary Joshua Boger's venture in creating the reputable orphan drug company, Vertex Pharmaceuticals, which he founded in Cambridge, Massachusetts, the U.S. in 1989. Vertex is among the top 30 global pharmaceutical companies by valuation. However, 95% of its sales is related to products in one single therapeutic area, cystic fibrosis.[480] Vertex is a successful exemplar that shows therapeutic and investment achievements in one single area.

Cystic Fibrosis (CF) is a genetic disorder that causes problems with breathing and digestion. There is no cure for cystic fibrosis, it is a rare and life-threatening disease. Globally, there are estimated 80,000 people affected, among which approximately 30,000 is in the U.S. CF mucus is so thick and sticky that causes airway blockages, easily infects the lungs, and hinders needed proteins reaching the intestines, which decreases the body's ability to absorb nutrients from food.

CF results from mutations in the Cystic Fibrosis Transmembrane Conductance Regulator (CFTR) gene, which carries the instructions for making the CFTR protein. Everyone has two copies of the CFTR gene, one inherited from the mother, another from the father. A CF patient has mutations in both copies of the CFTR gene.

The emergence of gene sequencing techniques confirms cystic fibrosis' etiology to be abnormalities in cellular ion transport. This gene has 2,000 mutation

---

476 Presently a subsidiary of Sanofi S.A.

477 Presently a subsidiary of Takeda Pharmaceutical Company

478 https://www.vrtx.com/

479 https://www.amazon.com/Billion-Dollar-Molecule-Companys-Perfect/dp/0671510576

480 https://www.nhs.uk/conditions/cystic-fibrosis/

permutations and 127 of them trigger abnormality. Thus, cystic fibrosis requires the use of combination therapy. Vertex's products continuously receive regulatory approvals, securing its existing leading position in this field.

In 2012, Ivacaftor, under the brand name Kalydeco[®] was approved in the U.S. as a CFTR potentiator for CF patients aged 6 and above, it was the first medicine to treat underlying cause of CF.[481] The modulator causes a synergistic effect through strengthening the gating flexibility of the CFTR protein at the cell surface. This compensates for the disabled CFTR gating capability in cystic fibrosis patients. Kalydeco[®] targets the g551d mutated gene which accounts for 4-5% of all CF cases. There are 4,900 patients worldwide taking Kalydeco[®]. At the annual cost of US$300,000 per patient, it is one of the most expensive drugs in the market and often leads to debates and criticism from patients' group and healthcare practitioners.[482]

In July 2015, the U.S. FDA approved Orkambi[®], the first medicine to treat the underlying cause of the CF patients aged 12 and above with two copies of the F508del mutation.[483] It is only indicated for these patients who are identified with a genetic test. Orkambi[®] is the combination of lumacaftor and ivacaftor, which is designed to increase the amount of mature protein at the cell surface by targeting processing and trafficking defect of F508del protein. In the U.S., the number of affected cystic fibrosis patients due to this mutation is around 8,000.

In February 2018, the U.S. FDA approved Symdeko[®] tablet, the combination of tezacaftor and ivacaftor, for the treatment of pediatric patients aged six years and older with CF who have certain genetic mutations.[484]

In October 2019, the U.S. FDA approved Trikafta[®], the first triple combination for the treatment of cystic fibrosis in patients aged 12 and above, with at least

---

481 https://investors.vrtx.com/news-releases/news-release-details/fda-approves-kalydecotm-ivacaftor-first-medicine-treat

482 https://www.heraldscotland.com/news/14386202.criticism-single-drug-accounts-85-rare-conditions-budget/

483 https://investors.vrtx.com/news-releases/news-release-details/fda-approves-orkambitm-lumacaftorivacaftor-first-medicine-treat

484 https://www.fda.gov/news-events/press-announcements/fda-expands-approval-treatment-cystic-fibrosis-include-patients-ages-6-and-older

one F508del mutation in the CFTR gene, which represents 90% of the CF population. The product consists of three active ingredients, elexacaftor, ivacaftor, and tezacaftor.[485] The U.S. FDA granted this application with Priority Review, in addition to Fast Track and Breakthrough Therapy Designation.

Joshua Boger is considered as a pioneer in the field of structure-based rational design. He combined computational science and organic chemistry principles to understand diseases on a fundamental level, allowing him to design drugs atomically. This structure-based rational drug design was widely adopted in the pharmaceutical industry and changed the way that drug discovery occurred.

Vertex began establishing other innovative technology platforms. For instance, in June 2019, the company signed a prepayment sum of US$245 million dollars to Exonics Therapeutics in exchange for their gene editing technology and intellectual property in Duchenne Muscular Dystrophy and other neuromuscular diseases.[486] Three months later, Vertex announced the acquisition of Semma Therapeutics for US$95 million dollars which signaled their participation in developing treatments for type one diabetes using stem cell therapies.[487]

Genzyme[488] and Sanofi

Genzyme was founded by Sheridan Snyder and George Whitesides in 1981, in Cambridge, Massachusetts, the U.S. Henry Blair, the scientific founder, initiated the plan of producing modified enzymes used in clinical trial testing for the National Institute of Health (NIH). With the help of venture funding, Genzyme started acquisition in the U.S. and U.K. markets.

In 1983, the Dutch-born Henri Termeer joined and re-directed the company's focus from diagnostic enzymes to modified enzymes used for human therapeutics. Termeer became the company's CEO in 1985, and he took the company public

---

485 https://www.fda.gov/news-events/press-announcements/fda-approves-new-breakthrough-therapy-cystic-fibrosis

486 https://www.pharmaceutical-technology.com/news/vertex-buys-exonics-therapeutics/

487 https://www.fiercebiotech.com/biotech/vertex-plunks-down-950m-for-stem-cell-player-semma-therapeutics

488 https://www.forbes.com/companies/genzyme/?sh=5ca1a4194a13

in 1986. During his 28 years at Genzyme, he built it into a global Future 500 company, with US$4 billion in annual revenue. A book titled *Conscience and Courage*[489] illustrates his tenure as the long-term CEO and his role in the U.S. biotech industry, as well as his impact in global rare diseases and orphan drugs sector. He is renowned as one of the most influential figures on the global biotech stage. Most importantly, his protégés spread across the globe and offer a helping hand to those patients in need.

Gaucher disease is genetic, rare, possible lethal characterized by the accumulation of lipids owing to malfunctions of enzymes responsible for breaking them down. Without proper treatment, lipids will accumulate in the bone marrow, liver, and spleen. This causes the enlargement of certain organs that leads to severe pain, in worst cases, death. The disease is very difficult to diagnose because there are many different symptoms. Currently, there is no cure, yet treatments help alleviate symptoms.[490]

Ceredase® received the U.S. FDA approval in 1991, as the first drug to effectively treat Gaucher disease in human history. It makes use of the Enzyme Replacement Therapy (ERT), which replaces the missing enzyme in patients with a modified version of the enzyme. Before ERT, the treatment for Gaucher disease was very limited, such as spleen removal and bone marrow transplants, which are ineffective, and sometimes high-risk procedures.[491]

The annual treatment cost was approximately US$250,000 to US$300,000, depending on patients' weight, marking injectable Ceredase® as the most expensive drug at that time. Henri persuaded insurance companies and the government to accept this hefty pricing to make sure that the patients had the ability to pay long-term. At the same time, Genzyme continually earned profit and operated smoothly. Genzyme also discovered and developed Cerezyme®, an injectable in 1994,[492] Cerdelga®, hard capsules in 2014 for the treatment of

---

489 https://www.amazon.com/Conscience-Courage-Visionary-Pioneered-Industry/dp/1621823709

490 https://www.hopkinsmedicine.org/health/conditions-and-diseases/gaucher-disease

491 https://www.gaucherdisease.org/blog/25th-anniversary-fda-approval-ert/

492 https://www.thepharmaletter.com/article/cerezyme-approved-in-usa

Gaucher disease,[493] securing its position as a global leader in this sector.

Being socially responsible, Genzyme made great contributions to the Massachusetts biotechnology community, and the U.S. Biotechnology Industry Organization (BIO) under Henri's leadership. In 2011, Genzyme was acquired by the French giant Sanofi at a share price of US$74, totaling US$20.1 billion in cash.[494]

Sanofi affixed its leadership role in the rare diseases and orphan drugs sector through a series of mergers and acquisitions. They include buying out Genzyme for US$20.1 billion; Belgian Biotech Ablynx for €3.9 billion and acquiring Cablivi®,[495] the first therapy specifically indicated, in combination with plasma exchange and immunosuppressive therapy, for the treatment of adult patients with acquired Thrombotic Thrombocytopenic Purpura (aTTP), a rare blood-clotting disease;[496] Biogen's spun-out Bioverativ for US$11.6 billion, which focused on hemophilia.[497]

Shire Pharmaceuticals and Takeda[498]

Shire was founded in the U.K. in 1986 by five entrepreneurs. Later in 2008, Shire relocated its tax domicile to Dublin, Ireland, in reaction to the new U.K. taxation measures on royalties of patents.

During its early era, Shire primarily developed calcium supplements for osteoporosis patients. Later, it built its leadership position in the Attention Deficit Hyperactivity Disorder (ADHD) therapeutic area, through a series of

---

493 https://www.reuters.com/article/us-u-s-health-gaucher-sanofi-idINKBN0GJ26G20140819

494 https://www.fiercepharma.com/pharma/sanofi-aventis-completes-acquisition-of-genzyme-corporation

495 https://www.fda.gov/news-events/press-announcements/fda-approves-first-therapy-treatment-adult-patients-rare-blood-clotting-disorder

496 https://www.fiercebiotech.com/biotech/sanofi-inks-eu3-9b-ablynx-buyout-to-pip-novo-m-a-fight

497 https://www.fiercepharma.com/pharma/sanofi-snaps-up-biogen-s-spun-out-bioverativ-11-6b-deal

498 https://www.takeda.com/

mergers and acquisitions. 1) During the 1990s, their products Adderall XR®
and Adderall® achieved outstanding sales performance in the U.S. market. 2) To
tackle the impending patent cliff of Adderall®, Shire launched the long-acting
drug Mydayis®. The drug duration of Adderall® was 12 hours. In comparison,
Mydayis® lasted up to 16 hours, and only required a single administration during
each morning.[499] 3) In 2007, the U.S. FDA approved Vyvanse® in children aged 6
to 12, and in 2008, approved it as the first and only once-daily prodrug stimulant
to treat ADHD in adults which are more long-acting than all its predecessors.[500]

Shire's official venture in the realm of rare diseases began in 2016, where they
bought out Baxalta for US$32 billion, transforming into a global giant.[501] This
merger gave them solid grounds across multiple categories, such as rare diseases,
hematologic diseases, immune diseases, and tumors in over 100 countries.

In September 2014, Shire reached a US$56.5 million settlement with the U.S.
Department of Justice for the False Claim Act allegations related to ADHD and
ulcerative colitis medications.[502] In January 2017, Shire settled at US$350 million
for the same allegation related to product Dermagraft®, a bio-engineered human
skin substitute for the treatment of diabetic foot ulcers.[503]

Shire was eventually acquired by Takeda Pharmaceuticals based in Japan,
paving path in areas including rare blood diseases, rare metabolic diseases,
and the nervous system. This transaction was the deal of the year 2018 in
the pharmaceutical industry in terms of the transaction amount, which was
equivalent to cash-and-stock bid worth US$64 billion.[504] There are currently over

499 https://www.fiercepharma.com/marketing/shire-launches-new-adhd-drug-mydayis-
as-it-weighs-a-neuroscience-exit

500 https://www.nbcnews.com/health/health-news/fda-approves-new-harder-abuse-
adhd-pill-flna1c9469833

501 https://www.theguardian.com/business/2016/jan/11/shire-clinches-32bn-takeover-
of-baxalta

502 https://www.justice.gov/opa/pr/shire-pharmaceuticals-llc-pay-565-million-resolve-
false-claims-act-allegations-relating-drug

503 https://www.justice.gov/opa/pr/shire-plc-subsidiaries-pay-350-million-settle-false-
claims-act-allegations

504 https://www.fiercepharma.com/pharma/shire-takeda-agree-to-preliminary-deal-
and-analysts-agree-other-bidders-aren-t-coming

40 undergoing clinical trials around the world, 50% of which are designated as orphan drugs, based on Takeda's portfolio.

Spark Therapeutics[505] and Roche

Spark Therapeutics was founded in Philadelphia in 2013 by two female scientists, Jean Bennett and Kathy High.[506] The initial funding was neither from venture capital firms nor from the pharmaceutical industry, but from the Children's Hospital of Philadelphia.

The company was listed on NASDAQ in 2015, raising US$161 million.[507] In December 2017, Luxturna® was approved in the U.S. to treat retinal dystrophy caused by biallelic RPE65 mutations, a rare inherited retinal disease.[508] This denotes Luxturna® as the world's first gene therapy targeting at single gene diseases. Treatment cost per eye is US$425,000, totaling to US$850,000 per patient.[509] Unlike other drugs which require repeated administration, patients only need to use gene therapy once in a lifetime due to its nature. To assist patients' payment, Spark explored innovative payment options, namely "pay-for-performance" programs. Patients will get a refund if they are not fully responded to gene therapy.

The Swiss giant, Roche Pharmaceuticals, acquired Spark Therapeutics for US$4.3 billion in March 2019 to get into gene therapy and enhance its hemophilia area.[510] According to Roche's portfolio, ten out of 82 (12%) of their clinical pipelines in 2017 were rare disease drugs. The percentage increased steadily to 13% in 2018 and 16% in 2020. Roche became a spearhead in the rare diseases and orphan drugs sector through both internal R&D and M&A.

---

505 https://sparktx.com/

506 https://www.nature.com/articles/d41573-021-00033-7

507 https://www.fiercebiotech.com/r-d/spark-nails-a-161m-ipo-to-fund-its-breakthrough-gene-therapy

508 https://www.fda.gov/news-events/press-announcements/fda-approves-novel-gene-therapy-treat-patients-rare-form-inherited-vision-loss

509 https://www.fiercepharma.com/pharma/spark-prices-gene-therapy-luxturna-at-850k-grabbing-top-spot-pharma-s-costliest-drugs

510 https://www.fiercepharma.com/pharma/roche-bulks-up-gene-therapy-and-hemophilia-4-3b-spark-buyout

Alexion Pharmaceutical[511] and AstraZeneca

Alexion was founded in New Haven, Connecticut in 1992, by Steven Squinto and Leonard Bell, a physician. Later, Alexion moved and headquartered in Boston, Massachusetts, the U.S. During its early days, Alexion lacked funding and it almost went bankrupt. It went initial public offering in the stock market in 1996, raising US$18 million.[512]

Alexion was saved miraculously by Eculizumab, under the brand name Soliris®, which was the first medication treating Paroxysmal Nocturnal Hemoglobinuria (PNH) and it was approved by the U.S. FDA in 2007.[513] PNH is characterized by the destruction of red blood cells that leads to severe anemia, and it is incurable. Approximately one in every three patients die within the first five years. Fortunately, clinical data manifested that Soliris® can greatly extend the life expectancy of patients. In 2011, Soliris® was approved for the treatment of atypical Hemolytic Uremic Syndrome (aHUS), a severe rare kidney disease.[514] In 2017, the U.S. FDA approved it for the treatment of adult patients with generalized Myasthenia Gravis (gMG).[515] With the price tag of over US$470,000 per year, Soliris® is one of the most expensive drugs worldwide.[516] This high price tag created arguments and controversy: critics proposed that much of the research for the development originated from publicly funded universities and there are no reason to charge this hefty amount. In 2020, Soliris® generated an annual revenue of US$4 billion, a true blockbuster drug.

Asfotase alfa, under the brand name Strensiq®, was acquired from Montreal-

---

511 https://alexion.com/

512 https://www.bioworld.com/articles/354990-alexion-pharmaceuticals-raises-18m-in-ipo-of-2-2m-shares?v=preview

513 https://media.alexion.com/news-releases/news-release-details/fda-approves-alexions-soliristm-all-patients-pnh

514 https://www.prnewswire.com/news-releases/fda-approves-soliris-for-rare-pediatric-blood-disorder-130421238.html

515 https://www.fiercepharma.com/pharma/alexion-s-soliris-wins-1b-myasthenia-gravis-approval-broader-than-expected-label

516 https://www.fiercepharma.com/pharma/alexion-s-soliris-wins-1b-myasthenia-gravis-approval-broader-than-expected-label

based Enobia Pharma at the transaction cost of US$1.08 billion in 2011.[517] In 2015, Asfotase alfa received the U.S. FDA approval to treat the highly rare inherited metabolic disease Hypophosphatasia (HPP).[518] Multiple body systems in these patients are seriously affected, giving rise to life-threatening complications. The disease has a very low prevalence rate globally of less than 20 patients in every 1,000,000 population.

Sebelipase alfa, under the brand name Kanuma® is an enzyme replacement therapy used for the treatment of Lysosomal Acid Lipase Deficiency (LAL-D), which is an inherited metabolic disease primarily caused by genetic mutation. The EMA fast-tracked its approval in August 2015 and the U.S. FDA followed suit by granting the drug a Breakthrough Therapy Designation, Orphan Drug Designation, and the Priority Review Designation. It was formally approved in December 2015.[519] In June 2015, Alexion Pharmaceuticals acquired Synageva Biopharma in a cash-and-stock deal of US$8.4 billion.[520] Alexion Pharmaceuticals was eventually acquired by AstraZeneca for US$39 billion in December 2020.[521]

Alnylam Pharmaceuticals (ALNY.US)[522]

Alnylam was founded in Cambridge, Massachusetts, the U.S. in 2002 by five scientists and inventors. It is the world's leading pioneer in the RNA interference (RNAi) field and set up abundant product pipelines related to rare disease therapies. The company listed on NASDAQ in 2004, raising US$30.2 million.[523] In 2016, Alnylam was included in *Forbes* as one of the 100 most innovative growth companies.

---

517 https://www.fiercebiotech.com/biotech/alexion-to-acquire-enobia-pharma-corp-and-first-potential-treatment-for-patients

518 https://www.fiercepharma.com/marketing/fda-approves-strensiq%E2%84%A2-asfotase-alfa-for-treatment-of-patients-perinatal-infantile-and

519 https://fda.report/media/96970/FDA-Update--FDA-approves-first-drug-to-treat-rare-enzyme-disorder-in-infants--children.pdf

520 https://www.genengnews.com/news/alexion-to-acquire-synageva-for-8-4-billion/

521 https://www.fiercepharma.com/pharma/astrazeneca-closes-mega-39b-alexion-buyout-despite-antitrust-fears-making-a-splash-rare

522 https://www.alnylam.com/

523 https://scrip.pharmaintelligence.informa.com/deals/200430188

The founding CEO, John Maraganore, reflected his 19-year journey with Alnylam. He guided Alnylam from a tiny start-up into a global mature company with over 1,600 employees in 20 countries and marked products.[524]

This remarkable and innovative RNAi therapeutic company has made the following achievements. In 2018, Onpattro®[525] (Patisiran) was approved by the U.S. FDA as the first-of-its kind targeted RNA-based therapy for the treatment of a rare nerve disease.[526] In 2019, Givlaari®[527] (Givosiran) was approved by the U.S. FDA as the first-in-class medication for the treatment of adults with acute hepatic porphyria, a genetic disorder.[528] In 2020, Oxlumo®[529] (Lumasiran) was approved by the U.S. FDA as the first treatment for Primary Hyperoxaluria Type 1 (PH1).[530]

2. STATUS QUO IN CHINA

China's rare diseases and orphan drugs sector is still in its early phase. Three major challenges stem from patients, doctors, and payments. This is evidenced through missed patient diagnosis, widespread misdiagnosis, lack of specialized doctors, drug shortage, high drug prices and difficult reimbursement. Similarly, other developed countries faced these challenges before. China will learn from their experiences and try to avoid proven mistakes.

The important role of the government is paramount. After all, laws and regulations reinforcement facilitate the economic development of a nation. Therefore, it is no surprise that policy support drives the development of the rare diseases and orphan drugs.

---

524 https://www.nature.com/articles/s41587-022-01304-3

525 https://www.onpattro.com/

526 https://www.fda.gov/news-events/press-announcements/fda-approves-first-its-kind-targeted-rna-based-therapy-treat-rare-disease

527 https://www.givlaari.com/

528 https://www.fda.gov/news-events/press-announcements/fda-approves-first-treatment-inherited-rare-disease

529 https://www.oxlumo.com/

530 https://www.fda.gov/news-events/press-announcements/fda-approves-first-drug-treat-rare-metabolic-disorder

From China's perspective, rare diseases not only pose a medical problem, but also a social problem. These diseases seem to only concern a relatively small fraction of China's population, but there are a chain of problems concerning medical treatment, rehabilitation, education, employability, and societal inclusion that are of great disconcert. It is only when they are solved for good that China can embody the idea of "Common Prosperity". Every single penny that is invested into the field of rare diseases helps facilitate improvements in the medicines and sciences. In the fullness of time, this benefits everyone.

1) The reality of rare disease diagnosis in China

Rare diseases involve multiple disciplines. Due to its complex pathology and low instances of cases, research is sparse. Resources for diagnostic technologies and treatments are limited, which leads to missed diagnosis and misdiagnosis. Clinical doctors have low awareness towards rare diseases. According to a survey by the China Rare Disease Association, 70% of medical professionals think they do not understand rare diseases fully. Most rare diseases can only be precisely diagnosed by multidisciplinary and interprofessional clinical experts as well as medical geneticists.

Approximately 80% of rare diseases is caused by genetics. Hence, they can be diagnosed via genetic testing. However, doctors with the necessary diagnostic skillsets and tools are relatively congregated in reputable hospitals in big cities. For many clinicians in third or fourth-tier cities, it is very difficult to diagnose rare diseases due to a lack of relative professional knowledge, clinical experience, and technical facilities. It has become a norm for rare disease patients to travel to cross-province hospitals to receive proper treatment in China.

2) Market size

The "The First Formulary of Rare Diseases" documents 121 rare diseases, 86 of which are treatable worldwide. Drugs for 77 of them are accessible in China, while the remaining nine reflects a challenge of no domestic treatments available. After Medicare negotiations in 2021, 58 drugs have been included into the national healthcare insurance, covering 29 rare diseases. Among the published 121 rare diseases in China, the patient population size for the top ten of them exceeds 100,000. This includes idiopathic pulmonary fibrosis, multiple sclerosis, and early onset Parkinson's disease. However, if applying the broader definition of rare diseases in the U.S. and EU (with over 6,000), then the prevalence of rare diseases in China could amount to 100 million. This is an astonishing number.

An investigation by the China Alliance for Rare Disease (CARD)[531] looked at 33 rare disease subsets, each having a patient sample size of approximately 20,000. It is revealed that nearly 60% of all rare disease patients aged under 20, with the age of onset for many being early infancy. In contrast, patients aged 60 plus make up less than 3% of the whole patient population. This indicates that if society pays close attention to developing treatments for rare diseases, the lives of many patients can be effectively and significantly lengthened. A good example is cystic fibrosis, where infant patients were traditionally expected not surviving past the age of one. Following the introduction of therapeutic drugs, the average life expectancy notably rises to 37 years. Likewise, the life expectancy of hemophilia patients can be extended from 30 to 68 years.

3) Policy support

The collaborative effort of the Chinese government, patient organizations, hospitals and pharmaceutical companies have greatly advanced development within the Chinese rare disease and orphan drug sector. This is reflected in the issue of Formulary for Rare Diseases. In May 2018, the National Health Commission (NHC) took the initiative to push "The First Formulary of Rare Diseases" and continuously refreshed it for more than two years. Subsequently, "Notice on the Registration of Diagnosis" and "Treatment Information for Rare Disease Cases" were published in October 2019. "Notice About the registration of rare disease pathological and diagnosis information" was also published a month later along with initial planning of developing an information system regarding rare disease diagnosis and treatment. In March 2020, the policy of guaranteeing medication coverage for rare diseases was incorporated into "Recommendations on Consolidating the Reform for the Medical Insurance System". Of the 68 approved orphan drugs to date, 46 have been included in the National Medical Insurance Directory which covers 23 therapeutic indications.

The Chinese government views the rare disease and orphan drugs sector as an

---

531 https://www.thepharmaletter.com/article/china-alliance-for-rare-diseases-launches-in-beijing

important steppingstone to achieving poverty alleviation and social harmony. This is shown by the legislation of multiple regulations concerning finance, taxation, and medical insurance to encourage cooperation between pharmaceutical companies, hospitals, and non-profit patient organizations.

The Center for Drug Evaluation (CDE) of NMPA has announced three lists of new overseas drugs that are urgently needed for clinical use. The listed drugs undergo a Priority Approval process and are marketed much faster.

In 2013, the State Department approved the establishment of Hainan Bo'ao Lecheng International Medical Tourism Pilot Zone[532] to provide chartered medical treatment, research, operations, and preferential policies for international medical exchanges. The pilot zone allows the innovative drugs, MedTech, and high-quality medical consumables to be used directly in clinical settings without the need to go through the application approval process with the NMPA.

4) Payment issues

According to Boston Consulting Group, China's basic medical expense in 2020 is RMB2.1 trillion. Drugs occupy RMB800 billion, or 39%. Assuming the growth of drug expenses is 6.5%, the total cost of drugs covered in the basic medical insurance will amount to RMB1.5 trillion. If the expense of rare diseases and orphan drugs is calculated as per 1.5 - 3% of the total cost, China roughly needs RMB20 billion to RMB40 billion in budget to guarantee basic coverage of rare diseases and orphan drugs.

At national level, the authority includes rare disease drugs into national formulary through negotiations. The national medical insurance formulary directly guarantees the availability of medicines for patients with rare diseases. The medical insurance policy is a drug purchasing strategy that "exchanges price for volume", allowing expensive rare disease medications to reach more accessible price levels in China. The annual treatment fee for high-value drugs included in the medical insurance are all less than RMB300,000.

The National Medical Insurance Bureau reviews drug candidates in strict

---

532 http://en.lecityhn.com/

accordance with the basic medical insurance, including the definite curative effect of the rare disease drug and whether it is affordable by the medical insurance fund. The most expensive examples are Biogen's Nosinagen Sodium Injection[533] and Agalsidase Alfa Injection for the treatment of Fabry disease.[534]

5) Key companies

Ascentage Pharma[535] (6855.HK)

The company was founded in SuZhou, China, in 2009, by Prof. Dajun Yang and others. It is a company with a global vision, engaged in novel therapies for cancers, age-related diseases, and Chronic Hepatitis B (CHB). The company was listed on the Hong Kong Stock Exchange in October 2019 and raised US$53 million.

As the founder of Ascentage Pharma, Yang focuses on cancer research and cell apoptosis mechanisms, and has been researching innovative drugs for 30 years. Yang is also a professor at the Sun Yat-sen University Cancer Center, China, and the Director of the Drug R&D Specialty Committee of China Pharmaceutical Innovation and Research Development Association. Another founder, Dr. Shaomeng Wang, was appointed as a tenured professor at the University of Michigan in 2001 and the editor-in-chief of *American Journal of Medicinal Chemistry* in 2011 (renewed in 2015).

Ascentage Pharma is the only life sciences company in the world that targets all three known classes of key apoptosis regulators in the clinical stages.

Its lead product, Olverembatinib is the first and only China-approved third generation BCR-ABL inhibitor. Olverembatinib was granted Priority Review and Breakthrough Therapy Designation (BTD), by the Center for Drug Evaluation (CDE) of China National Medical Products Administration (NMPA). On November 25, 2021, Olverembatinib was approved in China for the treatment

---

533 https://www.echemi.com/cms/622183.html

534 https://fabry-institute.com/disease-management/enzyme-replacement-therapy/agalsidase-alfa

535 https://ascentage.com/

of adult patients with Tyrosine Kinase Inhibitor (TKI) resistant Chronic-Phase Chronic Myeloid Leukemia (CML-CP) or Accelerated-Phase CML (CML-AP) harboring the T315I mutation. In January 2023, Olverembatinib has been included into the China 2022 National Reimbursement Drug List (NRDL). Additionally, it was granted four Orphan Drug Designations (ODDs) and one Fast Track Designation (FTD) by the U.S. FDA and one Orphan Designation (OD) by the European Commission (EC).

To date, Ascentage Pharma has received 16 orphan drug designations and one fast track designation from the U.S., and one orphan designation from EC for four drug candidates.

CANbridge Pharma[536] (1228.HK)

The company was founded in Beijing, China in 2012 by Dr. James Xue, who was the first Country Manager of Genzyme China. Xue is a protégé of the legendary Henri Termeer, a pioneer in the global orphan drug sector; and also the vice-chairman of China Orphan Drugs Alliance. The company focuses on the development and commercialization of products targeting rare diseases to address unmet medical needs. CANbridge was listed on the Hong Kong Stock Exchange in December 2021 and raised US$88 million.[537]

As of 2022, the company's pipeline consists of 14 drug assets, most of which have validated or semi-validated mechanisms of action. Among these, Hunterase® (CAN101) received marketing approval for Hunter Syndrome in China in September 2020, the first Enzyme Replacement Therapy (ERT) approved in China. Hunter Syndrome is a genetic, rare, life-threatening disorder, in which the human body cannot properly digest sugar molecules in the body. These molecules built up in the organs and tissues and cause physical, mental, and life-threatening damages.[538] This disorder affects roughly 8,000 people in China. Globally, there are only two ERTs approved for Hunter Syndrome.

---

536 https://www.canbridgepharma.com/

537 https://www.bioworld.com/articles/514174-canbridge-raises-774m-with-hong-kong-ipo?v=preview

538 https://my.clevelandclinic.org/health/diseases/17932-hunter-syndrome

CAN bridge is also developing therapeutics to treat other lysosomal storage disorders, complement-mediated diseases (rare life-threatening auto-immune disorders) and the rare brain cancer, glioblastoma. In addition, the CANbridge Next-Generation Innovation and Process Development Facility, in Burlington, Mass, is developing novel gene therapy products for the potential treatment of treat rare neuromuscular diseases with few medical options and the lysosomal storage disorders, Pompe and Fabry diseases.

Chapter 9

Viruses and Vaccines

In January 2020, the once-in-a-century COVID-19 broke out on a global scale. The last outbreak of a similar magnitude was the Great Influenza in 1918[539] in the U.S. military camps during the First World War. The COVID-19 pandemic constitutes one of the most serious global public safety crises in modern human history, with profound implications for geopolitics, lifestyles, work styles, racism, nationalism, and global life sciences.

A paradigm shift is once again happening due to the rapid emergence of breakthrough mRNA technology in the vaccine sector. Upon observing the actions that major countries have taken against this pandemic, as well as various opinions around the globe, the author laments that even though huge technology advances have been made over the past century, the dark sides of human nature persist, and human civilization has not advanced as much as we assumed.

1. INTRODUCTION

Before delving into this investment sector, it is essential to have a basic understanding on viruses and vaccines. This helps to steer clear of false information spread by some social media and unscrupulous politicians, which purposely attempts to seek attention. This topic is the most controversial and debatable among all the medication therapies; therefore, its analysis must be based on facts and data.

Viruses are infectious agents that can only be observed under a microscope.[540]

---

539 John M. Barry, *The Great Influenza: The Story of the Deadliest Pandemic in History*, Penguin Books.
Jeremy Brown, *Influenza: The Hundred Year Hunt to Cure the Deadliest Disease in History*, Atria Books

540 Definition from Oxford Advanced Learner's English Chinese Dictionary, 9th Edition: a living thing, too small to be seen without a microscope, that causes infectious diseases in people, animals, and plants.

They can infect humans, animals, and plants. Viruses cannot replicate independently and require the presence of a host cell to do so.[541] The term Virus may have originated from the French scientist Louis Pasteur[542] to name pathogenic microorganisms. Since then, microorganisms are categorized into bacteria and viruses. Viruses are so tiny that their existence had not been well understood until the advent of electron microscope in 1940.

The British physician and scientist Edward Jenner[543] pioneered the concept of vaccination and was called the father of immunology. He cultivated cowpox vaccines[544] that enabled humans to defeat smallpox.[545]

The multitude of differences between vaccines and drugs are worth noting, name a few: 1) Most of the preventative vaccines profit from large government orders, thus limiting the number of products that doctors and patients can choose from. 2) Most vaccinations given to healthy infants and young children are mandatory as part of the public health precautions. 3) Due to the nature of infectious diseases, governments have greater influence on vaccinations. Therefore, bureaucratic decision-making (independent of the scientific community) will impact the level of public vaccine deployment and coverage rate. 4) Therapeutic vaccines and preventative vaccines are distinctly different in terms of R&D, sales channels, marketing, and distribution.

Vaccines can be categorized into antiviral vaccines and antibacterial vaccines. In the 1930s, smallpox and rabies were the only two antiviral vaccines used globally. The development of virology lagged bacteriology, especially in vaccine

---

541 Jean Francois Saluzzo, *La saga des Vaccins: Contre Les Virus*

542 https://www.pasteur.fr/en/institut-pasteur/history

543 https://historyofvaccines.org/history/edward-jenner-frs-frcpe/overview

544 Vaccinia virus is a virus that can cause mild cowpox in cattle. If a person is infected with the virus, they will only experience mild discomfort and develop resistance to the vaccinia virus. Since vaccinia virus has the same antigenic properties as the variola virus that causes human smallpox disease, humans can acquire immunity against variola virus after taking the vaccinia vaccine.

545 Smallpox is a severe infectious disease caused by the smallpox virus. Infected people develop papules on the skin, which then turn into blisters and pustules. The smallpox virus, which can be contracted through droplets and direct contact, is highly contagious and killed 150 million people in Europe in the 18th century.

development, as the cultivation of viruses was more difficult. There were many antibacterial vaccines at that time, such as typhoid vaccine (1896), cholera vaccine (1896), plague vaccine (1897), diphtheria vaccine (1923), tetanus vaccine (1927), tuberculosis vaccine (1927) and pertussis vaccine (1926). Since the 1950s, advancements in cell culture technology spurred the leap-forward development of virology and shaped the antiviral vaccine industry. During the era of molecular biology in the 1970s, humans observed that viruses can frequently mutate during reproduction and evolve rapidly. Their mutation frequency increases when the virus cross species barriers. Conversely, bacteria are more stable.

In the beginning, viral vaccines are further categorized into live-attenuated vaccines and inactivated vaccines. In live-attenuated vaccines, the virulence of a pathogen is reduced but is kept viable and replicates in the human body, stimulating a strong and long-lasting immune response. The use of such technology helps prevent many diseases, such as yellow fever, measles, chicken pox, oral polio, Japanese encephalitis, etc. In inactivated vaccines, pathogenic microorganisms are neutralized by chemical or heating methods to destroy their ability to replicate inside the human body. Such vaccines include rabies vaccine, influenza vaccine, hepatitis A vaccine, injectable polio vaccine, etc. While the increased stability of inactivated vaccines allows easier storage and transportation, and a relatively easier manufacturing process, they stimulate a weaker immune response and multiple dozes of vaccinations are required to maintain a protective immunity.

Today, more technology platforms have been developed, such as viral vector vaccines, Messenger RNA (mRNA) vaccines.[546]

2. THE INDUSTRY HISTORY

The modern vaccine industry has evolved over the past 40 years. In the late 1980s, the vaccine industry was marginalized. Vaccines were regarded as humanitarian goods, and they were supplied by independent vaccine manufacturers in many countries. As a result, private organizations were rarely involved. Subsequent changes have had a profound impact on the vaccine sectors, leading to a paradigm shift:

---

546 https://www.pfizer.com/news/articles/understanding_six_types_of_vaccine_
    technologies

The dissolution of the Soviet Union and globalization: Due to the sudden political and economic changes in 1991, former Soviet Union member countries no longer prioritized private vaccine development and turned to purchasing high-quality and cheap vaccines in the international market. This provided great business opportunities for Western pharmas in the NATO countries.

The pneumococcal conjugate vaccine Prevenar®,[547] first approved on February 24, 2010, achieved unprecedented market success upon its launching and became a blockbuster with annual sales exceeding US$1 billion. Pharma executives started to realize the lucrative potential of vaccine products.

People gradually understood the direct relationship between healthcare and economic development. The Gates Foundation[548] has made outstanding contributions and helped many developing countries by generously donating vaccines with the aim of improving public health and economic development. Consequently, the Foundation played an active role into the growth of vaccine industry.

Due to the scarcity and monopoly of vaccines, vaccine prices began to climb and made the industry profitable. Multinational Corporations (MNC) began acquiring vaccine laboratories and manufacturing facilities globally. However, some mergers were not successful, and they subsequently exited this sector. For example, in 2006, Swiss-based Novartis acquired the California-based Chiron, then the second largest flu vaccine provider and the fifth largest vaccine business in the world, at the cost of US$7.5 billion. It built a vaccine division[549] and later sold its entire vaccine business (except for flu vaccines) to U.K.-based GSK in 2014.[550]

As of 2020, the global vaccine sector was dominated by four MNCs, which are GlaxoSmithKline (U.K.), Merck & Co. (U.S.), Sanofi (France) and Pfizer (U.S.),

---

547 https://www.drugs.com/history/prevnar-13.html

548 https://www.gatesfoundation.org/

549 https://www.sfgate.com/business/article/Novartis-to-buy-Chiron-Swiss-pharmaceutical-2598690.php

550 https://www.fiercepharma.com/vaccines/novartis-bids-farewell-to-vaccines-7-1b-sale-to-gsk

each with a history traced back over 100 years. The size of the vaccine industry is approximately US$38 billion, accounting for 4% of the global life sciences sector in 2019. These four companies, the author named as the Big Four, capture 90% of the global vaccine market revenue. Vaccine companies in developing countries such as China, India and Russia primarily target at their domestic markets. Concurrently, there is a huge gap between vaccine companies in developing countries and the Big Four MNCs in terms of innovation and products diversity. The Big Four have well-grounded global business strategies and deep market penetration in developing countries through cooperation, joint ventures, and direct production. For example, Merck partners with Zhifei Biological[551] to distribute its vaccines in China; GlaxoSmithKline has a joint venture company for vaccines in China; while Sanofi vaccines[552] has manufacturing facilities in the U.S. France, China, and Mexico.

3. DEVELOPMENT TRENDS IN VACCINES DURING THIS PERIOD

i.   From single to combination vaccines: Combination vaccines vastly reduce the number of vaccinations that infants must take. This simplifies vaccination plans and effectively increases the market penetration rate of the product.

ii. From univalent to polyvalent vaccines: Due to the technological advancement in safety, production and immunogenicity in the biotechnology industry, multivalent vaccines are the focus of global vaccine development. The number of polyvalent vaccine products dramatically increased after 2020, as represented by pneumonia vaccines. Streptococcus pneumoniae contains more than 90 subtypes, and ten-valent vaccines have a higher serotype coverage than heptavalent vaccines. The present coverage rate of pneumonia vaccine is less than 50%, spelling a large room of growth in the market.

iii. New vaccine types have replaced older ones following technological advancement. For examples, GSK's second-generation shingles vaccine Shingrix[®553] is far superior in safety compared to the previous generation.

---

551 http://en.zhifeishengwu.com/

552 https://www.sanofi.com/en/science-and-innovation/partnering/areas-of-interests/
    china-and-emerging-markets

553 https://www.cdc.gov/vaccines/vpd/shingles/public/shingrix/index.html

Dynavax's Heplisav-B[554] is the first U.S. FDA-approved Hepatitis B vaccine in 25 years,[555] which uses a novel adjuvant that enhances protection and reduces the number of doses.

iv. Cancer vaccines have become a R&D priority in various companies. Dendreon Company (U.S.) developed Provenge®, the world's first prostate cancer therapeutic vaccine. This was a milestone event as the vaccine shifted from defensive to more therapeutic orientation. In 2020, real-world data by The American Society of Clinical Oncology (ASCO) showed that incorporating Provenge® to any course of a conventional oral drug regimen reduces mortality by 45% and increased overall survival timespan by 14.5 months.

4. IN 2020, THE OUTBURST OF THE COVID-19 PANDEMIC FORMED THE TIPPING POINT[556] OF PARADIGM SHIFT AND HAS UNPREDICTABLE COMPLICATIONS:

i. **Coronavirus Stigma** is taking place with extreme nationalism and racism against Asians running rampant everywhere, as stated by *Nature* editorial. As countries struggle to control the spread of virus, some irresponsible politicians, and public figures, such as Donald Trump in the U.S. Brazilian lawmaker Bolsonaro, the son of Brazilian president, and some politicians in the U.K. persisted with using outdated scripts to blame China.[557] History has repeatedly taught us that pandemics lead to communities being stigmatized. The rising hate crime against Asian Americans has surged and real. [558] [559] The fueling racism against Asians, especially Chinese people, has nullified decades of efforts to promote diversity in university campus and international research mobility. One study from Stanford Center on China's

---

554 https://www.dynavax.com/product/heplisav-b/

555 https://www.contagionlive.com/view/heplisavb-approved-by-fda

556 Gladwell, Malcolm, 1963-. The Tipping Point: How Little Things Can Make a Big Difference. Boston: Back Bay Books, 2002.

557 https://www.nature.com/articles/d41586-020-01009-0

558 https://www.theguardian.com/society/2022/apr/23/asian-american-fighting-rising-hate-crime

559 http://www.chinadaily.com.cn/a/202301/17/WS63c5e36fa31057c47eba9f4a.html

Economy and Institutions shows that anti-China sentiment on Twitter accelerated dramatically since the viral outbreak.[560] This is very unfortunate as the potentially highly negative U.S. foreign policies towards China will only hurt both countries, and the globe.

ii. **Politics** severely interfered in the anti-pandemic decision-making process by disregarding scientific evidence and using the internet to incite hatred and populism for their own political votes. This puts extraordinary strain on the global battle against the COVID-19 pandemic and at the same time symbolizes regression in human civilization. Donald Trump, made a negative example, and *Nature* published an article on October 7, 2020, titled "How Trump damaged science – and why it could take decades to recover". However, Trump was not alone, his view was quite popular not just in the U.S. but also in some other countries. Three global leading scientific journals, namely *The Lancet, New England Journal of Medicine (NEJM)* and *Nature* do not usually publicly express their views on political figures, and they all condemned Trump for his action during this COVID-19 pandemic, especially *NEJM*, which avoided politics in the past 208 years, made its first condemnation. Science must prevail over political agenda and personal interests.

iii. **Global Inequities (GI)** in vaccine access is sadly the rule rather than the exception globally, as the Director-General of the World Health Organization emphasized in the 2022 Global Vaccine Market Report.[561] For example, Human Papillomavirus (HPV) for cervical cancer, while it is saving lives in 83% of high-income countries, it is only introduced in 41% of the low-income countries. It is common to see that middle-income countries pay as much as, sometimes more than wealthy countries for several products. In fact, diseases with low commercial value remained neglected and faced sub-optimal investments with very few in the development pipeline. However, these diseases primarily occur in low-income countries, particularly in the African, Eastern Mediterranean, and South-East Asian regions. Inequitable distribution, although not unique to COVID-19 vaccines, was a moral and global security failure issue with negative consequences. For example, the

---

560 https://sccei.fsi.stanford.edu/china-briefs/impact-covid-19-american-attitudes-toward-china-0

561 https://www.who.int/publications/m/item/global-vaccine-market-report-2022

African region represents one fifth (20%) of the global population, but only received 3% of all the COVID-19 vaccine doses by 2021.

iv. **Global supply chain reset:** During the pandemic, vaccines, testing reagents, Personal Protective Equipment (PPE), etc. are beginning to be regarded as national strategic materials while related industries are seen as national strategic sectors. As countries are leaning towards a global supply chain reset and doubling down on domestic manufacturing, global isolationism is emerging. The widening division between high-income countries and low-income countries will make global citizens suffer even more.

v. **Established players and new entrants:** During the pandemic, the Big Four vaccine leaders have not made breakthrough in technologies. However, great efforts and credit should be given to Pfizer for its global large-scale manufacturing and rapid distribution to save lives. Pfizer cooperated with Germany-based BioNTech.[562] Merck & Co. gave up on the development plan of two candidate vaccines,[563] while R&D cooperation between GlaxoSmithKline and Sanofi has not been very impressive.[564] To everyone's surprise, Moderna (U.S.)[565] and BioNTech (Germany)[566] rose among the ranks. Their mRNA products were the first ones approved for use by the U.S. FDA. Within three years of listing on the NASDAQ, they were among the top 30 biotech companies in the world by market capitalization. It is also worth noting that these two companies initially focused on cancer treatment.[567]

vi. **Market size:** The World Health Organization (WHO) estimates that the 2021 global vaccine market supplied approximately 16 billion vaccine doses (up from 5.8 billion in 2019), with a value of US$141 billion (up from US$38

562 https://www.fda.gov/emergency-preparedness-and-response/coronavirus-disease-2019-covid-19/pfizer-biontech-covid-19-vaccines

563 https://www.fiercepharma.com/pharma/merck-after-canning-covid-19-vaccine-programs-talks-to-help-shot-production

564 https://www.fiercepharma.com/pharma/sanofi-and-gsk-crash-covid-19-vaccine-late-world-first-nod-next-gen-booster-vidprevtyn-beta

565 https://www.modernatx.com/

566 https://www.biontech.com/int/en/home.html

567 https://www.cancer.gov/news-events/cancer-currents-blog/2022/mrna-vaccines-to-treat-cancer

billion in 2019).[568] The global vaccine market has made another paradigm shift.

vii. **Lesson learnt:** The legendary Bill Gates wrote a popular book *How to prevent the next pandemic?*[569] We must be soberly aware that due to the huge impact of climate change on our living environment, large-scale infectious disease outbreaks will only become more probable and frequent. Theoretically, if any outbreak happens in a forest on any continent, the virus can reach New York, London, Beijing, and Tokyo within 24 hours.[570] Moreover, no one is immune to the new outbreak regardless of origin, race, class or country. Therefore, global cooperation is a must to tackle this crisis. If governments do not see the world as a Community of Shared Future for Humankind but a Zero-Sum Game, then humans will lose this battle against virus. Consequently, everyone on this planet will suffer from this, and exceptionalism does not exist in this context.

5. GLOBAL INDUSTRY LEADERS

1) GlaxoSmithKline[571] (GSK.US)

GSK has been a leader in the vaccine business for decades. Today, the company has around 30 vaccines approved for marketing, which are used for the prevention of 21 diseases. Over one billion doses of vaccines are supplied each year. GSK's vaccine R&D center is based in Belgium, and its manufacturing facilities are in France, Germany, and Hungary. In 2014, GSK acquired Novartis' global vaccine business (excluding its flu vaccines sector) for a payment of US$5.25 billion, and up to US$1.8 billion in milestones to enrich its product portfolio, especially Bexsero® for meningitis B.[572] The great efforts in meningitis vaccines, influenza vaccines, recombinant herpes zoster vaccines, hepatitis vaccines, and

---

568 https://www.paho.org/en/news/9-11-2022-who-releases-first-data-global-vaccine-market-covid-19

569 https://www.gatesnotes.com/How-to-Prevent-the-Next-Pandemic

570 https://www.amazon.com/Hot-Zone-Terrifying-Story-Origins/dp/0385479565

571 https://www.gsk.com/en-gb/

572 https://www.fiercepharma.com/vaccines/novartis-bids-farewell-to-vaccines-7-1b-sale-to-gsk

10-valent pneumonia vaccines made GSK an outstanding global player. The annual sales of each of these products exceed US$500 million. On October 20, 2017, the recombinant shingles vaccine Shingrix® was approved by the U.S. FDA for the prevention of shingles.[573] It is a new generation of recombinant protein vaccines that can prevent more than 90% of the complications of shingles and postherpetic neuralgia.

In 2020, Shingrix® sales were GBP1.99 billion. Moreover, GSK has an extensive R&D pipeline, one-third of their vaccine products address diseases prevalent in developing countries, including HIV, tuberculosis, and malaria which are the three major infectious diseases highlighted by the World Health Organization. Additionally, vaccines with great commercial value, such as COPD vaccine and Respiratory Syncytial Virus (RSV) preventive vaccine are also in its pipeline.

According to the World Health Organization, malaria is a life-threatening disease caused by parasites that are transmitted to people through the bites of infected Anopheles mosquitoes. In 2021, there were estimated 247 million malaria cases, and caused 619,000 malaria death worldwide. The African region accounted for 95% of malaria cases, and 96% of malaria death. Children under five years old accounted for 80% of all the death in the region in 2021. Malaria is preventable and curable.[574] [575] [576] GSK developed Mosquirix®, the first vaccine approved for malaria, a parasitic disease, which was considered one of the ten Breakthrough Technologies 2022 by *MIT Technology Review*.[577] [578]

2) Merck & Co. (MRK.US)

Also known as Merck Sharp & Dohme outside of the U.S. and Canada, the company

573 https://www.drugs.com/history/shingrix.html

574 https://www.who.int/news-room/fact-sheets/detail/malaria

575 https://www.who.int/news/item/06-10-2021-who-recommends-groundbreaking-malaria-vaccine-for-children-at-risk

576 https://www.hsph.harvard.edu/news/features/is-new-malaria-vaccine-world-changing-maybe/

577 https://www.reuters.com/business/healthcare-pharmaceuticals/why-worlds-first-malaria-shot-wont-reach-millions-children-who-need-it-2022-07-13/

578 https://www.technologyreview.com/2022/02/23/1044969/malaria-vaccine/

was established as an American affiliate of the Germany Merck in 1891.[579] Since 1960, the company has developed and produced more than 40 vaccines, including measles vaccine, hepatitis B vaccine, chickenpox vaccine, HPV vaccine, etc.

Chronic hepatitis B and C cause 80% of all liver cancer worldwide, which is the second most common cause of cancer death. The hepatitis B virus was discovered by Dr. Baruch Blumberg in 1965, which made him the winner of the 1976 Nobel Prize.[580] Drs Blumberg and Millman discovered the first hepatitis B vaccine in 1975, which was the heat-treated form of the virus.

In 1981, Merck developed and got the U.S. FDA approval for the world's first plasma-derived hepatitis B vaccine for human use, under the brand name Heptavax®.[581] This inactivated type of vaccine involved the collection of blood from hepatitis B virus-infected donors, followed by multiple procedures to make the final product. The use of this vaccine was discontinued in 1990.

The blockbuster Gardasil® was initially approved for medical use in the U.S. in 2006 for females aged 9 to 26. In 2007, the Advisory Committee on Immunization Practices (ACIP) recommended Gardasil® for routine vaccination for girls aged 11 and 12. In August 2009, Gardasil® was recommended for both males and females before reaching adolescence and the beginning of sexual activities.[582] On December 10, 2014, one landmark vaccine, the nine-valent HPV recombinant vaccine Gardasil® was approved in the U.S. market for the prevention of certain diseases caused by nine types of Human Papillomavirus (HPV) to be used in females aged 9 to 26, and males aged 9 to 15. Gardasil 9® is administered as three separate shots, with an initial dose followed by additional shots given two and six months later. Clinical studies showed it prevents approximately 90% of cervical, vulvar, vaginal, and anal cancers.[583] For males, Gardasil® provides protection against genital warts, anal warts, and anal cancer.

---

579 https://businessplus.ie/industry-type/health-pharma/merck/

580 https://www.nobelprize.org/prizes/medicine/1976/blumberg/biographical/

581 https://www.hepb.org/prevention-and-diagnosis/vaccination/history-of-hepatitis-b-vaccine/

582 https://www.cdc.gov/mmwr/preview/mmwrhtml/mm5920a5.htm

583 https://www.esmo.org/oncology-news/archive/fda-approves-gardasil-9-for-prevention-of-certain-cancers-caused-by-five-additional-types-of-hpv

In 2020, HPV vaccine sales were US$3.9 billion; chickenpox vaccine Varivax®
sales were US$1.9 billion; and the 23-valent pneumococcal vaccine Pneumovax
23® sales were US$1.1 billion, they are all blockbusters. Gardasil® ranks number
to on the top selling vaccines ranking.

3) Sanofi (SNY.US)

Originated from France, Sanofi Pasteur[584] is a vaccine company under the Sanofi
Group. Its history traces back to 1885, when Louis Pasteur[585] developed the
rabies vaccine.[586] His great contribution in vaccination, microbial fermentation
and pasteurization made Louis Pasteur the honor of "father of microbiology".

Sanofi has an extensive product pipeline with more than 20 types of viral
and bacterial vaccines, including chickenpox, cholera, diphtheria, hepatitis A,
hepatitis B, Japanese encephalitis, pneumonia, tetanus, and more.

Their prominent vaccines include Pentacel®,[587] a pentavalent vaccine, which is
a combination vaccine indicated for active immunization against diphtheria,
tetanus, pertussis, poliomyelitis, and invasive disease due to Haemophiles
influenzae type B in children from six weeks to four years of age.

Influenza vaccines Fluzone® is an inactivated influenza virus indicated for active
immunization against influenza disease in people of six months of age and
older.[588] Flublok®[589] is the next generation recombinant Hemagglutinin (rHA)
vaccine produced in insert cell culture using the baculovirus expression system, as
an alternative to the current egg-based Trivalent Inactivated Influenza Vaccine
(TIV). [590]

---

584 https://www.sanofi.com/en/your-health/vaccines

585 https://www.britannica.com/biography/Louis-Pasteur

586 The Vaccine Research Institute founded by Louis Pasteur in 1888 was the predecessor
      of the company, which was renamed Sanofi Pasteur in 2004 through a series of
      mergers.

587 https://www.fda.gov/vaccines-blood-biologics/vaccines/pentacel

588 https://www.drugs.com/history/fluzone-quadrivalent.html

589 https://www.sanofiflu.com/flublok-quadrivalent-influenza-vaccine/

590 https://pubmed.ncbi.nlm.nih.gov/19297194/

Sanofi has the leading global flu vaccine market share, and its annual sales hit €2.6 billion in 2021.[591] [592] Sanofi owns two out of the five top selling vaccines.[593]

4) Pfizer[594] (PFE.US)

Pfizer Pharmaceuticals was established in 1849 in Brooklyn, New York, the U.S.. Pfizer made several acquisitions to get into the vaccine business, including the 13-valent pneumonia vaccine Prevnar® from Wyeth (U.S.) in 2009,[595] the vaccine business of Baxter (U.S.) in 2014,[596] and two vaccines from GSK (U.K.) in 2015.[597]

Pneumonia is a form of acute respiratory infection that is mostly caused by viruses and bacteria. It can cause moderate to life-threating illness in people of all ages. It is the leading cause of infectious death in children worldwide. Pneumonia killed more than 800,000 children under the age of five in 2017, accounting for 15% of all deaths of children under five years old. Pneumococcus is one of the most important pathogens of pneumonia, and is the main pathogen causing otitis media, meningitis, and bacteremia. Vaccines can help prevent pneumonia. Pfizer's vaccine revenue predominately comes from Prevnar®, which has been the only vaccine product among the top ten pharma products sold globally, and the bestselling vaccine.[598]

591 https://www.fiercepharma.com/vaccines/top-5-vaccines-by-2020-0

592 https://www.biopharma-reporter.com/Article/2022/08/11/sanofi-predicts-pivot-to-high-value-flu-vaccines-will-drive-another-year-of-record-sales

593 https://www.statista.com/statistics/314566/leading-global-vaccine-products-by-revenue/

594 https://www.pfizer.com/

595 https://www.theguardian.com/business/2009/jan/26/pfizer-pharmaceuticals

596 https://www.fiercepharma.com/vaccines/pfizer-completes-acquisition-of-baxter-s-marketed-vaccines-0

597 https://www.reuters.com/article/us-gsk-pfizer-vaccines-idUSKBN0P219820150622

598 https://www.statista.com/statistics/314566/leading-global-vaccine-products-by-revenue/

5) Summary

Big Four and investment opportunities

The Big Four vaccine leaders have a long history in the field, accompanying and spearheading their discovery and development. Firstly, their products are well-established in the global market and are highly recognized by doctors, patients, and healthcare professionals worldwide. Secondly, their pipelines considers both preventative vaccines and therapeutic vaccines, covering both high-income and low-income country markets. Furthermore, these companies have created strong entry barriers for new entrants through both in-house R&D and M&A. Their competitive advantages in accumulated talents, experiences and technologies will last for some time. Due to the above reasons, competition is fierce for any newcomers in the vaccine business. The author believes that investment opportunities in the field of human vaccines boils down to innovative technological breakthroughs, such as messenger RNA (mRNA) technology or the China market which has great potential.

Monopoly and supply concentration

The Big Four enjoyed blockbuster global sales and rising stocks prices for human papillomavirus, pneumococcal conjugate, measles, mumps, and rubella combination vaccines, which are used in more than 100 countries. These products are mainly produced by one to two companies, which benefit from over 80% of market share globally in the specific therapeutic areas.[599]

This monopoly scenario creates healthcare threats and potential supply disruptions not just to low-income countries, but also to high-income countries. For instance, in October 2004, news released by the U.S. public health officials shocked the entire nation, it stated that there would be a dearth of influenza vaccines on the brink of the winter flu season. A day before that announcement, the U.K. Medicines and Healthcare Products Regulatory Agency (MHRA) informed California-based Chiron Biotech of the safety concerns of its entire production facility in Liverpool, the U.K. and suspended its license. This resulted in a huge shortage of flu vaccines in the U.S. as Chiron Biotech was expected to

---

599 https://www.who.int/publications/m/item/global-vaccine-market-report-2022

supply almost half of 100 million doses.[600] [601] As a consequence, many elderlies could not receive flu vaccination for that winter.

6. THE RISE OF MRNA

Nature's featured article "The Tangled History of MRNA Vaccines" in September 2021[602] describes the development history of mRNA breakthrough technology. The important message delivered is that "hundreds of scientists had worked on mRNA vaccines for decades before the coronavirus pandemic brought a breakthrough." The pandemic has accented the value of mRNA and changed the world and the vaccine sector (please refer to Chapter 3 for details).

In 2005, the Hungarian-born scientists who immigrated to the U.S., Katalin Kariko and Prof. Drew Weissman, co-invented the technology of modified-nucleoside mRNA to inhibit mRNA immunogenicity. They immediately filed for a patent and published their breakthrough research in *Immunity*, signaling the birth of mRNA therapy.

In 2010, Robert Langer, Derrick Rossi and Noubar Afeyan, the chief investment executive of the well-known Cambridge Venture Capital Group (Flagship Pioneering)[603] jointly established Moderna. In Germany, two Turkish-German scientists Sahin and Tureci founded BioNTech with venture capital funding to develop tumor vaccines using mRNA technology. Shortly after Moderna was established, the Gates Foundation invested in the mRNA vaccine program that is mainly used to treat diseases caused by Zika virus and HIV.

In January 2020, Chinese scientists released the genetic sequence of the new coronavirus,[604] prompting Moderna and BioNTech to start the development of mRNA vaccines. The vaccine is designed to encapsulate the mRNA encoding for

---

600 https://economictimes.indiatimes.com/us-faces-vaccine-shortage-as-uk-shuts-chiron-plant/printarticle/881666.cms

601 https://www.nature.com/news/2004/041004/full/news041004-8.html

602 https://www.nature.com/articles/d41586-021-02483-w

603 Previously Flagship Ventures.

604 https://www.science.org/content/article/chinese-researchers-reveal-draft-genome-virus-implicated-wuhan-pneumonia-outbreak

coronavirus dendritic protein inside liposomes. Following vaccine injection, body cells synthesize a large amount of the viral protein through the mRNA which induces immune recognition and immune memory of the coronavirus to ward off viral infection. On December 2, 2020, BioNTech's vaccine was approved in the U.K. as the world's first coronavirus vaccine,[605] and emergency use[606] rights were granted by the U.S. FDA on December 11.[607] Moderna's vaccine closely followed suit, receiving emergency use rights as a coronavirus vaccine on December 18, 2020.

1) BioNTech SE (BNTX.US)

Founded in 2008 and headquartered in Mainz, Germany, BioNTech focuses on the development of messenger ribonucleic acid (mRNA) personalized therapies for cancer, infectious diseases, and rare diseases. A book *The Vaccine: Inside the Race to Conquer the COVID-19 Pandemic* by Joe Miller illustrates the early years of the company and how it successfully developed the first vaccine to use mRNA technology for human use. The couple scientists were very fortunate to secure a large amount of funding from the deep-pocketed and science-driven Strungmann family. This allowed them to focus on scientific discovery and development rather than fund-raising.

On October 10, 2019, BioNTech was listed on the NASDAQ at US$15 per share and raised US$150 million at the valuation of US$3.4 billion.[608] The company's main products include COMIRNATY®, the first mRNA coronavirus vaccine approved in the U.S. and Europe. BioNTech co-developed with Pfizer in the U.S. in 2020. In Greater China, BioNTech has a partnership agreement with Fosun Pharma. Its market capitalization reached over US$90 billion at the highest in 2021.[609]

---

605 https://www.nature.com/articles/d41586-020-03441-8

606 https://www.fda.gov/emergency-preparedness-and-response/mcm-legal-regulatory-and-policy-framework/emergency-use-authorization

607 https://www.fda.gov/news-events/press-announcements/fda-approves-first-covid-19-vaccine

608 https://www.reuters.com/article/us-biontech-ipo-idUSKBN1WO29B

609 https://www.macrotrends.net/stocks/charts/BNTX/biontech-se/market-cap

BNT122, an experimental mRNA cancer vaccine targeting personalized neoantigens, is in Phase II trials for the combinatory use of Keytruda® to treat melanoma. The company has also cooperated with Pfizer and the Bill Gates Foundation in the U.S. market to develop vaccines against other infections such as influenza, HIV, and tuberculosis.

2) Moderna (MRNA.US)

Moderna was founded and headquartered in Cambridge, Massachusetts, the U.S. in 2010. Its primary focus is cancer immunotherapy which includes mRNA-based drug discovery, drug development and vaccine technology.

On December 8, 2018, Moderna was listed on the NASDAQ at the IPO price of US$23 per share, and valuation of US$7.32 billion.[610] It raised US$604 million.

In July 2021, Moderna hit the market capitalization of US$100 billion, matching with the established pharma giant GSK.[611] It joined the S&P 500 index.

The company's core products include mRNA-1273, an mRNA coronavirus vaccine approved by the U.S. FDA for emergency use and is the company's first approved vaccine. mRNA-1647 is an investigational mRNA vaccine against Cytomegalovirus (CMV)[612] in Phase II clinical trials.

3) Basic information

For readers to better understand vaccines and make sound judgements, it is worth noting the following facts:

Vaccine products may have different efficacies because their technology platforms are different, hence it is only reasonable to compare products with the same technology platform. This is challenging since it is difficult to carry out a

---

610 https://www.reuters.com/article/moderna-ipo-idUSL4N1YC3NK

611 https://www.fiercebiotech.com/biotech/a-tale-two-bio-cities-moderna-tops-100b-valuation-matching-glaxosmithkline

612 Congenital CMV infection occurs in 1 in 150 infants worldwide and is the leading infectious cause of birth defects.

comparative clinical test between two vaccine products.

The practical significance of competent clinical trials is attributable to the openness and transparency of its data and results. Vaccine-related rumors are often meaningless and taken out of context, which only cause public unrest and distrust in science. Moreover, it is important to note that most of the clinical trials are sponsored by vaccine companies.

mRNA is a breakthrough technology. It takes time to find out its long-term clinical side effects and requires observation and documentation. History repeatedly reminds us not too optimistic.

The stability of mRNA is a major concern as it needs to be stored at very low temperatures (-20 degrees Celsius) for several months. Temperature monitoring during cold chain transportation is difficult even for the developed markets like the U.S., Japan. Currently, most refrigerated medicines can be stored at two to eight degrees Celsius. Achieving and maintaining ultra-low temperatures during cold chain transportation and storage is a significant challenge for developing country markets.

The unit price of an mRNA vaccine is around US$20–30. It is relatively affordable in high income economies but is very costly to most middle-lower income economies.

7. CHINA'S VACCINE SECTOR

China is the first country to use artificial immunization methods to prevent infectious diseases, and invented the technique of growing pox to prevent smallpox as early as the 10th century AD.[613] In 1978, China participated in the Expanded Program on Immunization (EPI) initiated by the World Health Organization (WHO) and strengthened organizational development, cold-chain constriction, and target management and planning implementation. Today, China is one of a few countries globally to solve its entire immunization programs by relying in its own capacity.[614]

---

613 https://www.atlantis-press.com/proceedings/icfied-22/125971843
614 https://www.ncbi.nlm.nih.gov/pmc/articles/PMC8903904/

Based on the Regulation on the Management of Vaccine Circulation and Use, vaccines in China are primarily split into two categories: National Immunization Program (NIP), also known as A-class program; and non-NIP vaccines, also known as B-class program. The NIP vaccines are provided free of charge to all the citizens, currently preventing 14 to 15 infectious diseases, such as Hepatitis B, MMR and DPT vaccines. Local government can add vaccines according to local regulations. The profit margin for this category is very thin, therefore, these vaccines are mostly made by large state-owned companies, roughly constituting 70–80% of market share. For the non-NIP category vaccines, such as Anthrax, Cholera, Rabies, Hib and PCV13 vaccines, citizens pay for themselves voluntarily. These vaccines are more expensive, and the competitions are very fierce. This market segment is dominated by private enterprises and multinationals (MNC) in China, with roughly 70% of MNCs taking up the largest market share by value. Additionally, the third vaccine program is for large-scale national emergency such as COVID-19 outbreak.

The market share of NIP gradually decreased from 80% in 2016 to 54% in 2022, while the vaccination rate is over 90%. The population in China started to shrink for the first time in the past 60 years.[615] Therefore, this market will remain stable. The non-NIP market rose from 20% to 46% during the same period. With the release of multiple polyvalent vaccines, and cervical cancer, pneumonia, and influenza vaccines, this segment will remain at a high growth rate.

1) Facts and data

i. The size of China's vaccine market in 2019 was approximately RMB42.5 billion.

i. Imported vaccines from MNCs accounted for six among the top ten vaccines sold in China.

iii. The concentration of China's domestic vaccine market is very low, considering the only company with more than 10% of market share is China National Biotech Group Company Limited.[616] Moreover, 19 of the 29

---

615 https://www.npr.org/2023/01/17/1149455643/for-the-first-time-in-over-60-years-chinas-population-fell-by-almost-a-million

616 https://www.bloomberg.com/profile/company/CNBTCZ:HK

vaccine companies only had one vaccine in the market for sale.

iv. Most vaccine companies started out as distribution agents, and they have weak R&D experience.

v. The market Compounded Annual Growth Rate (CAGR) from 2016 to 2020 is 35%.

vi. The number of clinical trials for vaccines has increased dramatically, from 22 trials in 2015 to 72 trials in 2021.

vii. In 2019, the number of vaccines exported from China is only one twentieth of that from India. China vaccines export lagged not only developed countries such as France, the U.S., and the U.K. but also developing countries such as India, Korea, and Indonesia.

2) Recent development

Like other sectors, the vaccine sector is another example of the latest development of China's life sciences industry in the past few years. Moreover, COVID-19 becomes a catalyst to move Chinese vaccine sector to the next paradigm.

i. **Regulation:** The "Vaccine Administration Law of the People's Republic of China",[617] which has been implemented since December 1, 2019, systemically regulates vaccine discovery, development, manufacture, distribution, and supervision to boost innovation. This is the first law specifically established for vaccines globally.[618] Moreover, the continuous and timely updates and revision of laws and regulations provide more guidance.

ii. **Capital market (both public and private funding):** Firstly, several Chinese vaccine companies have made improvements in product innovation, market share and market capitalization. The pandemic outbreak has placed the vaccine sector under the spotlight. Several listed vaccine companies have reached market capitalization the RMB100 billion at their heights, including Zhifei Bio (300122.CN), Walwax Bio (300142.CN), Biokangtai (300601.CN), CanSinoBIO (688185.CN), Wantai Biopharm (603392.CN). It is important to note that the market value of these companies is amplified in the rapid development Chinese market. Secondly, private equity and venture funds

---

617 http://www.npc.gov.cn/englishnpc/c23934/202012/0b1fd779c29e49bd99eb0e65b6 6aa783.shtml

618 https://www.ncbi.nlm.nih.gov/pmc/articles/PMC8903904/

have poured capitals in vaccine start-ups with new technologies potentials. Both the number of transactions and the deal sizes increased dramatically. For example, StemiRNA[619] raised US$200 million to develop COVID-19 vaccine candidate in June 2021.[620]

iii. **Innovation drive:** established Chinese vaccine companies realized that if they do not innovate, they will fall behind. Therefore, they are more actively participated in forging partnership and investing in start-ups, both in and out of China.

iv. **Export and donation:** Sinovac vaccines and Sinopharm vaccines have been included on the vaccine emergency use list by WHO.[621] China's foreign aid and vaccine exports exceed those of other countries combined, mainly to middle and low-income countries. As of August 2022, China has supplied more than 2.2 billion doses to more than 120 countries and international organizations. Chinese companies launched joint ventures and transferred vaccine-making technologies to over 20 countries, resulting in annual production of over one billion doses.[622] For example, a new vaccine manufacturing facility is under progress near Abu Dhabi.[623]

3) Listed leading vaccines companies:

CanSino Biologics[624] (6185.HK)

CanSino was founded in Tianjing, China by Xuefeng Yu, Tao Zhu, Dongxu Qiu and Huihua Mao, in 2009. CanSino also developed Ebola vaccine and received its approval in 2017 in China.[625] On March 28, 2019, CanSino debuted on the Hong Kong Stock Exchange, being the first vaccine company under the

619 https://www.stemirna.com/en/index.aspx

620 https://www.reuters.com/business/healthcare-pharmaceuticals/chinas-stemirna-raises-about-200-mln-fund-covid-19-vaccine-development-2021-06-03/

621 https://www.who.int/emergencies/diseases/novel-coronavirus-2019/covid-19-vaccines

622 https://www.chinadaily.com.cn/a/202208/26/WS63079f1ea310fd2b29e7449a.html

623 https://en.ndrc.gov.cn/news/mediarusources/202207/t20220729_1332323.html

624 https://www.cansinotech.com/

625 https://www.fiercepharma.com/vaccines/china-approves-self-developed-ebola-vaccine-from-2014-outbreak-virus-type

exchange's pre-revenue rules. Its shares raised 58%.[626] On August 13, 2020, CanSino listed on the STAR market of Shanghai Stock Exchange, making it the first dual listing vaccine company in China.[627]

The World Health Organization (WHO) granted an Emergency Use Listing (EUL) for CanSino recombinant novel COVID-19 vaccine, under the brand name Convidecia®. It is an engineered vaccine with the replication-defective adenovirus type five vector that expresses the spike S protein of the SARS-CoV-2 virus.[628] Its manufacturing takes place in China, Malaysia, Mexico, and Pakistan under the partnership of joint ventures.

In September 2022, the National Medical Products Administration of China (NMPA) granted Convidecia Air® the Emergency Use Authorization as a booster dose. This is the world's first inhaled COVID-19 vaccine approved for human use. On October 25, Shanghai was the first city to initiate this booster vaccination for adults aged 18 and above, who have received two shots of inactivated vaccines or one shot of Convidecia®.[629] Convidecia Air® is the partnership formed between Ireland-based Aerogen, which provides drug delivery technology, and CanSino.

Sinovac Biotech[630] (SVA.US)

Sinovac was founded in Beijing in 2001 and listed on NASDAQ in 2003. Its product pipelines include Hepatitis A vaccine, flu vaccine, varicella vaccine, poliomyelitis vaccine, etc. Its lead product, under the brand name CoronaVac®, is an inactivated virus COVID-19 vaccine. It is used in various countries and regions worldwide. On June 1, 2021, the WHO validated the vaccine for emergency use.[631] On 26th July, 2021, UNICEF signed a supply agreement with

626 http://www.chinabiotoday.com/articles/cansino-climbs-58-percent

627 https://www.lillyasiaventures.com/blog/cansinobio-s-successful-listing-on-star-market-makes-it-the-initial-dual

628 https://www.pharmaceutical-technology.com/news/who-eul-cansinobio-vaccine/

629 https://www.reuters.com/world/china/cansinos-inhaled-covid-19-vaccine-gets-emergency-use-approval-china-2022-09-04/

630 http://www.sinovac.com/index.php?lang=en

631 https://www.who.int/news/item/01-06-2021-who-validates-sinovac-covid-19-vaccine-for-emergency-use-and-issues-interim-policy-recommendations

Sinovac for the supply of up to 200 million doses of COVID-19 vaccines.[632] Sinovac also set up joint ventures in Indonesia[633] and invested in Pakistan.[634]

8. AUTHOR'S INSIGHTS:

1) Paradigm shift

The innovative breakthrough messenger RNA technology used in this once-in-a-century pandemic has reshaped the global vaccine market. Firstly, the global vaccine market was estimated US$141 billion by 2021,[635] over three times value of the pre-pandemic 2019. Secondly, the new entrants, namely Moderna and BioNTech, emerged as mRNA global players, both are ranked as the global top 10 vaccines companies. Thirdly, the secondary vaccine players, which usually served their domestic markets, such as China, Russia, and India, started to export to other markets. Fourthly, middle-lower income countries with sufficient population scale built their own vaccine manufacture facilities and distribution infrastructure, such as Indonesia, Egypt, Pakistan and more, as vaccine became a strategic sector, and they realize they could not rely on other's mercy.

2) Global inequalities

Life is the most basic form of human rights, while actions are the touchstone of people's beliefs. However, some rich countries pre-ordered and piled up far more vaccines than they need,[636] [637] while many other countries do not have enough. Those rich countries do not allow vaccines to be exported, while only allow exports to so-called Friends and Allies through government approval. They do

632 https://www.unicef.org/press-releases/unicef-signs-supply-agreement-sinovac-covid-19-vaccine

633 https://asia.nikkei.com/Spotlight/Coronavirus/Indonesia-teams-with-China-s-Sinovac-for-COVID-vaccine

634 https://tribune.com.pk/story/2384355/sinovac-global-to-invest-200m-in-punjab

635 https://www.who.int/news/item/09-11-2022-who-releases-first-data-on-global-vaccine-market-since-covid-19

636 https://www.cbc.ca/news/health/extra-vaccines-donation-pledge-1.6288998

637 https://www.ctvnews.ca/health/coronavirus/more-than-20-million-covid-19-vaccine-doses-now-stockpiled-in-canadian-freezers-1.5542930

not keep promises made in official government donation announcements to help low-income countries.

3) Patents and intellectual property

It is a widely acceptable concept that patents and intellectual property protect and drive innovations. Meanwhile, there are numerous facts to demonstrate that MNCs and their related stakeholders take advantage of this and abuse the existing system. They use it as a weapon to maximize profits. This hurts the patients or people who need medications the most. The latest example is that Moderna sued Pfizer over patent infringement,[638] [639] [640] then Pfizer and BioNTech sued back.[641]

For this COVID-19 pandemic, as stated in the WHO 2022 global vaccine report,[642] "access to life-saving innovations such as vaccines were not available to all who need them in a timely and equitable manner, including because of intellectual property monopolies."

The U.S. is the only worldwide major market without medical products price limitation, and MNCs and law firms tend to enjoy legal allegations and lawsuits. The result is clear that nearly 30 million people are still not covered by health insurance and do not have timely access to medical needs.[643] There must be a better way.

638 https://hbr.org/2022/09/moderna-v-pfizer-what-the-patent-infringement-suit-means-for-biotech

639 https://www.bbc.com/news/health-62691102

640 https://www.npr.org/sections/health-shots/2022/08/26/1119608060/moderna-sues-pfizer-over-covid-19-vaccine-patents

641 https://www.fiercepharma.com/pharma/moderna-vs-pfizer-lawsuit-heats-pfizer-and-biontech-clap-back-countersuit

642 Page 17

643 https://www.pgpf.org/blog/2022/11/nearly-30-million-americans-have-no-health-insurance

4) Arrogance and ignorance

The present global crisis is a major challenge for human beings as a race. Due to the nature of the virus and environmental destruction by humans, similar outbreaks are expected to occur more frequently. Viruses are human's real enemy, but the untrust of each other will only doom the outcome of our fight against viruses.

Chapter *10*

Vision Health[644]

Mankind seeks light by nature and builds civilizations upon it. Everyone experiences vision health problems in their lifetime: during different life stages from new-born, child, middle-aged to old-aged, people will encounter certain degree of various eye problems. More importantly, vision is the most dominant sense for mankind, playing a vital role in our lives. Vision health has a deep impact on our happiness, personal lives, financial outcomes, as well as social relations. Therefore, investing in vision health is not only for financial returns, but also for the unlimited benefits to humanity, and ultimately the civilization.

1. GLOBAL VISION HEALTH

1) Facts

The eye captures electromagnetic waves within a certain wavelength range (optical range) in the external environment through the peripheral sensory organs. The waves are then encoded, processed, and analyzed by certain parts of the central nervous system to give the organisms a sense of vision. As humans receive at least 80% of all external stimuli and information through the visual system, the eyes are the most important sensory organs.

There are at least 32 regions in the cerebral cortex[645] of humans and primates involved in visual information processing. Humans engage and interpret the world through vision and cognition.

Prevalence of treating visual disorders

Eye diseases are much more common than people think. According to the

---

644 Some people use the words "eye care". It is interchangeable with "vision health" in this context.

645 Occupies more than half of the cerebral cortex.

World Report on Vision published in October 2019 by the WHO,[646] among the global population of 7.8 billion: 1) Vision impairment poses an enormous global financial burden, the annual global costs of productivity losses associated are estimated to be US$411 billion. 2) The leading causes of vision impairment and blindness are refractive errors and cataracts. 3) At least 2.2 billion people have a near or distance vision impairment. Among them, at least one billion of these vision impairment cases could have been prevented and yet addressed. 4) There are 2.6 billion people suffer from myopic refractive error, which 312 million of whom aged under 19; 1.8 billion people suffer from presbyopia; 76 million people aged between 40 and 80 have glaucoma; 196 million people worldwide have Age-related Macular Degeneration (AMD);146 million people have diabetic retinopathy; and 2.5 million people suffer from trachoma.[647]

Among the main causes of blindness, cataracts accounts for 39%, uncorrected refractive errors account for 18%, and glaucoma accounts for 10%. The WHO forecasts a continual rise in the number of people with myopia and high myopia, which is expected to reach 3.32 billion and 520 million respectively by 2030. The number of AMD and glaucoma patients will also reach 240 million and 95.4 million respectively by then. Ageing populations and lifestyle shifts contribute to the increasing number of eye disease patients. The severity of vision problems has been underestimated as scientists and investment fund managers have focused primarily on tackling cancer.

Solving visual problems narrows wealth gap globally

As of 2020, 1.1 billion people worldwide had untreated visual impairment. By 2050, the number is expected to increase to 1.8 billion, the vast majority of whom will be those who live in low and middle-income countries. It is worth emphasizing that more than 90% of vision loss cases can be prevented or treated with existing cost-effective interventions.

New estimates show that tackling preventable vision loss could bring global economic benefits of US$411 billion annually, help to achieve the UN's Sustainable Development Goals, reducing poverty and inequality, and improving

---

646 https://www.who.int/publications/i/item/9789241516570
647 Page 25 of the report

education and employment opportunities. Therefore, investment in vision health is a noble means to reshape social equity, improve human well-being, and enhance global economic benefits.

Limitations of existing treatment options

Traditional means of treating eye diseases are bound to ophthalmic medicines and surgeries. The active ingredients in eye drops are limited to antibiotics, anti-inflammatory drugs, artificial tears, and medications that target at hypertension and angiogenesis. Innovation in ophthalmic medicine has been slower than other therapeutic areas. Generally, the treatment of ocular surface diseases via eye drops containing small molecules that can easily permeate the cornea. Eye drops are portable, non-invasive, and relatively cheap. Due to recent advancement, antibody therapy, gene therapy and cell therapy are preferred to treat fundus diseases.

Ophthalmic diseases and systemic diseases share many similar receptors and enzyme targets. Therefore, repurposing approved systemic drugs to treat ocular diseases is an attractive low-risk strategy that quickly brings ophthalmic drugs to the market in a cost-effective manner. Physically, the eye has various anatomical barriers and a low blood supply compared to other body organs. Therefore, systemic treatments, which must be administered at high dose concentration, may increase the risk of side effects. Topically administered drugs are safer, with higher bioavailability and simpler routes of administration. There are relatively fewer independent industry leaders focusing on treating eye diseases. Examples include Alcon (ALC.US), Allergan, and Bausch & Lomb (BLCO.US) in the U.S. and Santen Pharmaceutical (4536.JP) in Japan.

Shortage of ophthalmologists, especially in middle-low-income countries

There are on average 81 ophthalmologists per one million people in the U.S. and Germany. In China, this number decreases to 21 ophthalmologists per one million people. The severe shortage of ophthalmologists poses a major challenge for countries such as China and India. Considering the possibility of the outbreak of future pandemics, it is worthwhile to invest in vision health projects, such as digital technologies, to adress the shortage of ophthalmologists.

2) The most common ocular diseases

Myopia

The prevalence of myopia in East Asia is approximately 50%, which far exceeds the world average and is still on the rise. In 2018, the prevalence of myopia among Chinese youths aged between six and 18 ranks first in the world, reaching 54%. This rate reaches as high as 81% among high school students. The size of high myopia population in China is around 40 million to 50 million. Clinical evidence data has sufficiently proved that prolonged high myopia will lead to glaucoma, retinal detachment, macular degeneration, cataracts, and fundus neovascularization, which are the major causes of blindness.

Current measures to prevent myopia are related to lifestyle changes. This includes increasing outdoor activities and reducing close focusing of the eyes with intense concentration for a long period of time.

People of all ages can wear framed glasses, but the outcome is poor. Contact lenses such as orthokeratology lenses and soft contact lenses are not recommended to patients aged between eight and 18. Surgical treatments are only available for patients over the age of 18.

Low-concentration atropine eye drops have been clinically proven to slow the progression of myopia. Since 1999, the Singapore National Eye Center (SNEC)[648] has conducted a series of studies for the treatment of myopia. Atropine eye drops at concentrations of 0.01%, 0.1% and 0.5% control the progression of myopia to some extent, but the 0.01% concentration carries less published side effects. Launched by the SNEC, Myopine[®649] has been used clinically for 15 years and used in many countries and regions in Asia and Europe. It is noteworthy that atropine sulphate is an old drug whose main dosage forms include tablets, injections, and eye drops. The drug is clinically used to treat toxic shock syndrome as well as organophosphorus pesticide poisoning. It is also used to dilate pupils

---

648 https://www.snec.com.sg/patient-care/specialties-and-services/clinics-centres/
      myopia-centre/patient-care

649 https://www.eyelens.sg/products/ophthalmology/myopine

and paralyze ciliary muscles in ophthalmic treatment.[650]

Orthokeratology lenses[651] are designed with an inverse geometric shape to the corneal surface. The lens implements a reasonable, adjustable, and reversible programmed reshaping of the cornea through mechanical and hydrodynamic forces. This causes the thinning of the corneal epithelial layer (~20μm) and thickening of the mid-peripheral area. The central stromal layer of the cornea also thickens, alongside thinning of the mid-peripheral stromal layer. These effects alter the refractive power of the cornea and correct vision. According to "The Guidelines for the Prevention and Control of Myopia" issued by the Chinese Health Commission, orthokeratology lenses are more effective in controlling myopia than traditional glasses.

Soft contact lenses are more commonly known as contact lenses. They exhibit special optical properties through their defocusing and aspheric designs. When worn on the corneal surface, the lenses alter the path of external light entering the eye, producing a clear vision and thereby controlling the progression of myopia. Due to their high safety and efficacy, the U.S. FDA has approved products related to soft contact lenses for the treatment of myopia.

Refractive surgery, including corneal refractive surgery and intraocular lens implantation, is the only option to restore vision without the use of glasses. However, this treatment requires doctors with extensive surgical experience and is expensive. There may also be corneal and intraocular structure damage and related complications, as well as myopia regression.

Cataracts

Cataracts are the leading cause of blindness worldwide. Cataracts are characterized by clouding of the lens for a variety of causes, which can affect the imaging quality and lead to visual impairment. Common causes are, for instances, ageing, heredity, trauma, medications, and poisoning. Although there are many causes of lens clouding, the primary cause is a disorder in the alignment

---

650 https://www.straitstimes.com/singapore/singapore-national-eye-centre-offers-new-eye-drops-for-kids-with-severe-myopia

651 https://www.aao.org/eye-health/glasses-contacts/what-is-orthokeratology

of lens cells. This results in an irreversible change in the refractive index of the lens.

According to statistics by the Ophthalmology Branch of the Chinese Medical Association, 80% of the Chinese population aged 60 to 89 are affected by cataracts and the prevalence is 90% for those aged 90 and above. However, the awareness of cataracts in China is relatively low. About 20 million people are blind due to cataracts. In the U.S., it causes 5% of all blindness. In some parts of Africa and South America, it even causes nearly 60% of all blindness.[652]

At present, the only effective treatment for cataracts is surgical implantation of an intraocular lens to replace the cloudy natural lens. There are several ophthalmic medical device companies in the world that produce intraocular lenses, such as Alcon (U.S.), Johnson & Johnson (U.S.), Bausch & Lomb (U.S.), Zeiss (Germany), HOYA (Japan), Ophtec[653] (the Netherlands), and Rayner (U.K.).[654] The first four companies together account for roughly 2/3 of the global market.

Glaucoma

Glaucoma refers to a group of eye diseases that damages the optic nerve which connects the eye to the brain, leading to visual impairment. The main risk factor is an elevated intraocular pressure, making glaucoma the second leading cause of blindness in the world after cataracts.

The anterior chamber angle of the eye drains the aqueous humor. However, it may be blocked by the peripheral iris. Depending on the blockage of the anterior chamber angle, glaucoma can be categorized into closed-angle and open-angle accordingly. In open-angle glaucoma, the anterior chamber angle remains open when the intraocular pressure increases, but the aqueous humor[655] does not drain normally. This results in a peak intraocular pressure that exceeds 21 mm Hg in 24 hours. On the other hand, patients with closed-angle glaucoma generally have anatomical abnormalities. The anterior chamber angle is mechanically

---

652 https://en.wikipedia.org/wiki/Cataract

653 https://www.ophtec.com/

654 https://rayner.com/

655 https://www.britannica.com/science/aqueous-humor

blocked by the surrounding iris tissue, resulting in obstruction of aqueous humor drainage, and increased intraocular pressure.

Medications, laser therapy and surgery can be used in combination to treat glaucoma. According to "Primary Open-Angle Glaucoma PPP"[656] published by the American Academy of Ophthalmology (AAO), therapeutic drugs are the most basic treatments to reduce intraocular pressure in open-angle glaucoma. The common classes include prostaglandin analogues, beta-adrenergic receptor antagonists, alpha-2-adrenergic agonists, miotic agents, etc. Among them, Prostaglandin derivatives are the drug of choice, achieving an effective blood pressure reduction range of 25% – 33%.

The main products of prostaglandin drugs include: Latanoprost, under the brand name Xalatan®,[657] originally developed by Pharmacia & Upjohn, now a part of Pfizer. Xalatan® was the first of the new class medication called Prostaglandin Analogue (PGA). Compared to other medications back then, it gave superior safety, efficacy, and convenience of dosing. It was launched in the U.S. in 1996, and in EU and the U.K. in 1997 for the second line treatment of glaucoma.[658] It was the top-selling glaucoma medication since its inception and marked the milestone as the first blockbuster drug in the ophthalmology. After reviewed a five-year safety drug data, the U.S. FDA approved it as the first line treatment of open-angle glaucoma or ocular hypertensin, along with EU and Japan in 2002.[659] In 2011, its generics became available, one of these generics made by Greenstone, generic division of Pfizer, in the same manufacturing facility as Xalatan®. Some experts argued the generics were good for cost and medication compliance, as it was a major issue even in the high-income country, like the U.S.[660]

Other medications in PGA category include Travoprost under the brand name

---

656 https://www.aao.org/education/preferred-practice-pattern/primary-open-angle-glaucoma-ppp

657 https://www.xalatan.com/

658 https://www.thepharmaletter.com/article/eu-approval-for-xalatan?print=1

659 https://www.healio.com/news/ophthalmology/20120331/xalatan-receives-approval-as-first-line-treatment

660 https://glaucomatoday.com/articles/2011-june/xalatan-goes-generic-a-landmark-event-in-glaucoma

Travatan® among others by Alcon. It is highly selective and potent, a full agonist at the prostaglandin receptor.[661] Bimatoprost, under the brand name Lumigan® among others, developed by Allergan. It can be used alone, or with a beta blocker, such as Timolol. One interesting indication is that Lumigan® is also used to increase the length of the eye lashes. Tafluprost, under the brand name Taflotan® by Santen Pharmaceuticals, Zioptan® by Merck in the U.S., and Saflutan® by Mundipharma in Australia.

Laser technologies are widely used in glaucoma treatments. Examples include Selective Laser Trabeculoplasty (SLT), Laser Peripheral Iridotomy (LPI), Argon Laser Trabeculoplasty (ALT), and the innovative Direct Selective Laser Trabeculoplasty (DSLT) developed by the Israel-based Belkin Vision.[662] The American Academy of Ophthalmology (AAO) glaucoma treatment guidelines recommend SLT as a first-choice method for the initial treatment of open-angle glaucoma, or as an adjuvant treatment when the type of drug and dosage need to be reduced afterwards. Both SLT and DSLT can effectively reduce intraocular pressure and is repeatable.

Anti-glaucoma surgery: The purpose of Microinvasive Glaucoma Surgery (MIGS) is to reduce damage to the ocular surface and postoperative scar formation in the filtering bleb following conventional trabeculectomy. As a safer, more convenient, and repeatable alternative, MIGS is favorable as an anti-glaucoma surgery.

Corneal blindness

Corneal blindness is the third leading cause of blindness worldwide. The cornea, as the outermost refractive layer, is extremely vulnerable to various external injuries that may result in corneal blindness. Current treatment method requires corneal transplantation. Every year, there are 1.5 million to 2 million cases of corneal blindness occurring worldwide. More overwhelmingly, the total number of patients with bilateral corneal blindness is about 12.7 million. In China alone, there are approximately 2.99 million patients who have monocular corneal blindness and 440,000 with binocular corneal blindness.

---

661 https://www.ophthalmologytimes.com/view/travoprost-approved-first-line-iop-therapy
662 https://belkin-vision.com/

The global shortage of donor corneas is a serious bottleneck for corneal transplantation. Only 185,000 corneal transplants are performed worldwide every year, or one in every 70 patients in queue for corneal transplants. Moreover, some patients experience transplant rejection and complex inflammatory reactions after surgery and need a second transplantation. The small number of donors, the lack of physicians capable of carrying out surgeries, and the long surgical training period all severely limit the progress of corneal transplantation.

Fortunately, some technologies rapidly emerged over the past two decades, including lamellar keratoplasty, endothelial keratoplasty and limbal stem cell transplantation. Artificial cornea is an alternative option to restore vision.

Israel-based Eye Yon Medical innovates a corneal artificial endothelial layer under the brand name Endo Art®, which is the first synthetic implant to treat corneal oedema, saving vision and restoring function by creating a new type of corneal availability.[663] It is CE-marked, and approved in Israel and India, and is currently in clinical trial in China and the U.S. Eye Yon obtained Breakthrough Designation from both the U.S. FDA and China NMPA.

Choroidal and retinal neovascularization disorder

Retinal vessels and choroidal capillaries undergo germination, migration, proliferation, matrix remodeling and other processes under the stimulation of various pathological factors. This leads to choroidal and retinal neovascularization disorders, which are caused by the production of a new capillary bed. The capillary bed is prone to rupture and bleeding due to the subdevelopment of the vessel wall and fragility of the vessels. Consequently, hyperplasia can occur and form scars that eventually lead to irreversible blindness, as is commonly seen in wet Age-Related Macular Degeneration (AMD), Diabetic Macular Degeneration Edema (DME), Retinal Vein Occlusion (RVO), and Pathological Myopia (PM).

The macula contains 90% of the visual photoreceptor cells, and therefore any irreversible lesion in the macula may cause blindness. The objective in treating choroidal and retinal neovascularization disorders is to inhibit angiogenesis and eliminate bleeding, edema, and exudate to preserve and improve patients'

---

663 https://eye-yon.com/

vision to the greatest extent. Drugs, lasers, and surgeries are the main treatment pathways.

In the past two decades, neovascularization treatments have been developed rapidly. The use of anti-Vascular Endothelial Growth Factor (VEGF) drugs has been supported by a considerable sum of clinical evidence. Anti-VEGF drugs currently in clinical use include Ranibizumab developed by Genentech, marketed by them in the U.S., and by Novartis in other countries under the brand name Lucentis®. It was approved in the U.S. in June 2006. Aflibercept under the brand name Eylea®, was developed by Regeneron Pharmaceuticals in the U.S. and co-developed with Germany-based Bayer in other countries.[664] It was first approved in the U.S. in November 2011.[665][666]

Conbercept under the brand name Lumitin®, was developed by Chengdu Kanghong based in Sichuan, China. In 2012, the drug was included on the World Health Organization's Drug Information, 67th list of Recommended International Non-proprietary Names. It received marketing approval from the then China SFDA in 2013 for the treatment of AMD, and in 2014 for the treatment of wAMD in China.

Dry Eye Syndrome

Dry Eye Syndrome (DES), also known as Kerato-Conjunctivitis Sicca (KCS), refers to a chronic ocular surface disease caused by a variety of factors. As the tear quality, quantity and dynamics become abnormal, the tear film becomes unstable, and the ocular surface microenvironment becomes unbalanced. This is accompanied by ocular surface inflammation, tissue damage and neurological abnormalities that cause various eye discomforts and/or visual dysfunctions. The global prevalence of Dry Eye Syndrome varies between 5.5% and 33.7%, with an average of 20%, with Asia ranking on the top.

---

664 https://newsroom.regeneron.com/news-releases/news-release-details/regeneron-and-bayer-announce-approval-eylear-aflibercept

665 https://www.webmd.com/eye-health/macular-degeneration/news/20111118/macular-degeneration-drug-eylea-approved

666 https://www.fiercebiotech.com/biotech/regeneron-announces-fda-approval-of-eylea%E2%84%A2-aflibercept-injection-for-treatment-of-wet-age

The main treatment pathways for dry eye syndrome are categorized into drug and non-drug therapy. Drugs can be chosen based on criteria such as patients' etiology, degree of local lesions, systemic diseases, and more. These drugs function to lubricate the ocular surface or promote repairing, examples such as 1) artificial tears and promoting tear secretion, 2) anti-inflammatory drugs such as glucocorticoids and non-steroidal anti-inflammatory drugs, and 3) antibacterial drugs.

Non-drug therapies include physiotherapy, Intense Pulsed Light (IPL), thermal pulsation therapy, lacrimal surgery or punctal occlusion, therapeutic contact lenses, and if conventional treatments are not effective, surgeries are the only solutions.

Restasis® from Allergan[667] and Xiidra® from Novartis[668] are the two mostly used drugs in the world in this category, and they have been effective for moderate and severe dry eye syndrome.

Cyclosporine ophthalmic emulsion 0.05%, under the brand name Restasis®, was developed by Allergan, and approved by the U.S. FDA in 2003, as the first and only medication for dry eyes by then.[669] 20 years later, in February 2022, its first generic made by Mylan Pharmaceuticals, received the U.S. FDA approval.[670] The technological challenge with the drug is how to make an insoluble product cyclosporine at least partially soluble. The excipient was the key challenge to this development. Allergan adds castor oil, glycerin, and polysorbate 80 to present cyclosporine to the corneal epithelium. It took Allergan five years to get the excipient.[671] Later, AbbVie acquired Allergan in 2020.[672] The sale of Restasis® in

---

667 https://www.restasis.com/

668 https://eyewire.news/articles/novartis-completes-acquisition-of-xiidra-bolstering-ophthalmic-portfolio/?c4src=article:infinite-scroll

669 https://www.healio.com/news/optometry/20120225/fda-grants-approval-for-restasis

670 https://www.fda.gov/news-events/press-announcements/fda-approves-first-generic-restasis

671 https://www.eyeworld.org/2022/first-generic-cyclosporine-for-dry-eye/

672 https://news.abbvie.com/news/press-releases/abbvie-completes-transformative-acquisition-allergan.htm

2018 was US$1.2 billion in 2018, becoming a blockbuster drug.[673]

Lifitegrast ophthalmic solution 5%, under the brand name Xiidra®, was developed by Shire, and approved by the U.S. FDA in 2016,[674] the first and only prescription drug approved to treat both signs and symptoms of dry eye by inhibiting inflammation caused by the disease. Later, Takeda Pharmaceuticals acquired Shire in 2019. In May 2019, Novartis acquired Xiidra® from Takeda in a deal worth up to US$5.3 billion.[675] The sale of Xiidra® in 2018 was US$400 million. However, in June 2020, Novartis voluntarily withdraw an application for Xiidra® in Europe after the regulators had raised major objections. Critics questioned the value of this deal.

In China, Shenyang Xingqi Pharmaceutical (300573.CN) developed a cyclosporine eye drop which was approved by the NMPA in 2020, for the same indication.

2. CHINA VISION HEALTH

1) Hard facts

As of December 31, 2022, China's population is 1.4118 billion, dropped for the first time in 60 years. [676] No other region or country has as many eye-diseases patients as China. Firstly, China also has a large size of population with moderate to severe visual impairment or blindness, totaling 60 million people. Blindness and vision loss rank the second among all disability-causing health disorders. Secondly, about 20% of its population are aged 60 and above. Therefore, age-related eye diseases will emerge. For instance, cataracts affect 80% of those people aged between 60 and 89. Thirdly, the changes in living and lifestyles have worsened the situation as most of the population live on smart-phones and electronic gadgets. Fourthly, heavy schoolwork and highly competitive exam-

---

673 https://www.fiercepharma.com/marketing/novartis-seeing-no-hope-for-approval-pulls-takeda-bought-dry-eye-med-xiidra-europe

674 https://www.takeda.com/newsroom/shire-news-releases/2016/9pks5v/

675 https://eyewire.news/articles/novartis-completes-acquisition-of-xiidra-bolstering-ophthalmic-portfolio/?c4src=article:infinite-scroll

676 https://www.bbc.com/news/world-asia-china-64300190

based after-school study make China's children suffer one of the highest, if not the highest, myopia prevalence rates in the world.[677]   Fifthly, China is still very short of medical doctors, especially ophthalmologists. Among them, glaucoma specialists are extremely rare, only 500 in the whole China.

According to Frost & Sullivan Report, the prevalence of people with moderate visual impairment is rising at an alarming rate of up to 12.17% from 1990 to 2019, compared to the global average of 1.48%. The Disability-Adjusted Life Year (DALY) is a measure of the overall disease burden, represented by equivalent of one year of total health loss.[678] The "Current Status and Trend of the Burden of Eye Diseases in China over 30 Years"[679] report points out that the biggest contributor to China's 4.72 million DALY in 2019 is near-sightedness (32.4%), followed by phototaxis eye disease (26.9%) and cataracts (23.1%). The prevalence rates are 3.23% for moderate visual impairment, 0.33% for severe visual impairment and 0.61% for blindness, representing 45.92 million, 4.67 million and 8.69 million patients in China respectively.

2) A little comparison

Better still, the awareness of eye health in China is on the rise, it was the highest among China, Germany, Japan, Russia and the U.K. and the U.S. in 2020. Another example is that China took the WHO World Report on Vision very seriously, the National Prevention of Blindness Committee hosted the 2020 National Eye Health Meeting, incorporating the launch of this report in China.[680]

Between 2015 and 2021, the number of new ophthalmic drugs approved in the U.S. was much higher than that in China, with a total of 29 new ophthalmic drugs approved by the U.S. FDA, including 505b (1) and 505b (2) new drugs. In contrast, the China NMPA only approved seven new drugs, all of which were developed by MNCs and imported to China. These seven drugs include two new chemical drugs, two new biological drugs and three new chemically enhanced drugs.

---

677 https://eyesonchina.com/2020/11/eyes-diseases-in-china-the-problem-and-the-remedies/

678 https://www.who.int/data/gho/indicator-metadata-registry/imr-details/158

679 https://www.ncbi.nlm.nih.gov/pmc/articles/PMC8714487/

680 https://www.iapb.org/news/china-world-report-on-vision-launch/

During the same period, among the drugs approved and marketed in China, three are for the treatment of ocular hypertension or open-angle glaucoma, two are for the treatment of retinopathy (including DME, WAMD and RVO), one is for the treatment of dry eye, and one is for the treatment of the rare eye disease neurotrophic keratitis. The average time for a drug from submission of clinical application to final approval for marketing is six years. Approvals in the U.S. cover a wider range of indications. For example, in addition to common ophthalmic diseases, six additional drugs were included for the treatment of cystinosis, neuroretinitis,[681] Graves eye disease, hereditary retinal disease and neuromyelitis optica[682] alongside a first-in-class drug for ptosis.

It is expected that the number of clinical trials in China will increase in line with its global proportion. Between 2016 and 2020, the number of clinical trials related to the ophthalmology field in China was 180, representing approximately 14% of all clinical trials globally. Among them, retinopathy accounts for 41% of all clinical drugs in development, other main indications include optic nerve diseases 12%, ocular inflammation and infection 12% and dry eye syndrome 10%.

China has included various ophthalmic drugs in the national insurance formulary to provide a wide range of benefits for patients. These drugs, targeting at ocular inflammation and dry eye syndrome, have particularly eased the burden on patients.

3) Myopia crisis and China school reform

Myopia is a very serious healthcare problem in East and Southeast Asia. In these locations, 80% of secondary school students suffer from myopia, and 10-20% of them are highly myopic. High myopia may lead to irreversible vision impairment, even blindness. Myopia is not only a healthcare problem, but also a social-economic problem, resulting in worsening of quality of life in these patients and their families.

---

681 https://eyewiki.aao.org/Neuroretinitis

682 https://www.ninds.nih.gov/health-information/disorders/neuromyelitis-optica

Two major causal and modifiable risk factors for myopia have been identified,[683] namely educational pressures and outdoor time. It is an evidenced fact that there are fewer cases of myopia in children who get little or no schooling. In China, the competitions among students and schools are fierce, this phenomenon stems from the talents-selection process which has run for over thousands of years. The academically oriented streams began at a very early age and parents tend to use expensive and extensive private tutoring to boost children's competitiveness.

Much evidence has proven that children who spend more time outdoor are less prone from the onset of myopia. For instance, in a remote primary school in Yunnan province where they provide three hours of outdoor plays, no mobile phones, not iPads, no long-hour of screen sharing, children have much less chance of myopia.[684]

In 2012, Prof. Ling Li, a healthcare economist at the National Center for Economic Development, drafted a National Vision Care Report. The key part of this report is an analysis of economic costs of uncorrected myopia and presbyopia in China: the estimated cost of productivity was over 1% of China's GDP, while in terms of disability-adjusted life years amounted to nearly 2%. [685]

In 2018, Chinese President Jinping Xi again drew attention to the major impact of myopia on the health of children. This was followed by a document titled "Notice of Ministry of Education and 8 Other Departments on Issuing the Implementation Plan of Comprehensive Control of Myopia in Children and Adolescents", later followed by a document from State Council on "Opinions on Further Reducing the Burden of Student's Homework and Off-campus Training in Compulsory Education" in 2021. There is a consistent trend to reduce the schoolwork burden and improve several aspects of children's health, including myopia control, obesity, and mental health.

However, this seriously damaged those Hong Kong or Shanghai listed private

---

683 https://journals.lww.com/apjoo/Fulltext/2022/02000/China_Turns_to_School_Reform_to_Control_the_Myopia.6.aspx

684 https://www.chinadaily.com.cn/a/202209/20/WS6329cdf8a310fd2b29e78c1d.html

685 https://www.essilorseechange.com/new-study-reveals-critical-need-for-visual-health-solutions-in-china/

tutor education companies, which estimated value was at US$120 billion. The Western financial press speculated and questioned, many rumors raised.[686] [687] However, some criticized and doubted its effectiveness. At the same time, other problems may have emerged.[688] Regardless, the current talent-selection process and school system should undergo reform.

4) Why invest in this sector?

There are several driving forces within China's ophthalmic market:

i. **Population size:** When analyzing China-related issues, one should always consider its fundamental uniqueness - its gigantic population size remaining above 1.4 billion by 2035, and 1.3 billion by 2050. Moreover, people aged over 60 will exceed 30% by 2035.[689] Additionally, the decades-long one child policy was altered and replaced to encourage couples to have up to three children.

ii. **Huge unmet patient needs:** Lifestyle shifts, the indispensable use of electronic devices, such as smartphones and tablets, and an ageing population are all contributing to the soaring prevalence and incidence of eye diseases.

iii. **Government policy support:** A series of favorable policies have promoted the development of the ophthalmic industry. The "13th Five-Year National Eye Health Plan (2016–2020)" incorporated eye disease prevention and treatment models into the healthcare system. In January 2022, the National Health Committee (NHC) released the "14th Five-Year National Eye Health Plan (2021–2025)", proposing to further improve national eye health standards by quantifying goals within major diseases. For example, China promotes prevention and control of myopia as a part of national health policy.[690]

---

686 https://global.chinadaily.com.cn/a/201808/10/WS5b6cc2e1a310add14f384f48. html

687 https://www.china-briefing.com/news/china-bans-for-profit-tutoring-in-core-education-releases-guidelines-online-businesses/

688 https://www.theguardian.com/world/2021/aug/03/chinas-crackdown-on-tutoring-leaves-parents-with-new-problems

689 https://www.chinadaily.com.cn/a/202208/01/WS62e7f003a310fd2b29e6f97f.html

690 https://www.globaltimes.cn/page/202106/1225538.shtml

iv. **Strong capital flow:** This is strongly evidenced by the increasing numbers of large financing (both from private equity and venture capital), products licensing and strategic collaboration, initial public offerings.

v. **Innovation:** The emergence of novel technologies, such as new targeted drugs and gene therapies, facilitates the development of innovative drugs with lower drug toxicity, higher drug penetration, and longer ocular surface retention time. This establishes a trend to set up global multinational clinical trial centers. Additionally, MedTech start-ups are also very active.

vi. **Specialized eye hospitals and clinics:** These institutions play a critical role in China vision healthcare because they make patients more accessible to standardized services. The rise of chains on both national and regional level has increased penetration and coverage at county level,[691] and a few large ones even expanded their business across borders, such as AIER Group (300015.CN, please refer to Chapter 7 for details).

5) Leading Hong Kong listed companies:

OcuMension Therapeutics (1477.HK)[692]

Founded in 2017 and headquartered in Shanghai, China, this ophthalmic specialized company is dedicated to identifying, developing, and commercializing worldwide first-in-class and best-in-class eye medications to provide solutions for the huge unmet medical needs in China. It takes the pathways of in-licensing, commercial partnerships, as well as in-house research and development. On 10th July, 2020, OcuMension was listed on Hong Kong Stock Exchange, raised the US$184 million.[693] Morgan Stanley and Goldman Sachs were its joint sponsors.[694]

Its lead product, under the brand name Yutiq®, which was licensed in from U.S.-based Eyepoint Pharmaceuticals.[695] This drug was approved by Center for Drug

---

691 https://www.hevisiongroup.com/

692 https://www.barrons.com/market-data/stocks/1477/company-people?countrycode =hk&mod=quotes%2Cquotes

693 https://www.thepharmaletter.com/in-brief/brief-ocumension-ipo-raises-184-million

694 https://www1.hkexnews.hk/listedco/listconews/sehk/2020/0629/2020062900093. pdf

695 https://investors.eyepointpharma.com/news-releases/news-release-details/eyepoint- pharmaceuticals-and-ocumension-therapeutics-announce

Evaluation (CDE) of the National Medical Products Administration (NMPA) in April 2021, for chronic non-infectious uveitis.[696] It is a milestone of being the first medication approved, based on entirely real-world data in China. Yutiq® is a sustained-released, micro-insert fluocinolone acetonide intravitreal implant.[697] In August 2021, the company entered into an asset purchase agreement with Novartis for Emadine® and Betoptic-S® in China market at a deal valuated at US$35 million.[698]

Airdoc Technology (2251.HK)[699]

Airdoc is an AI-based medical device company with a platform of AI-empowered retina-based deep learning algorithms. The company is based in China and is expanding its business in the Southeast Asia.

Airdoc was founded in Beijing on September 9, 2015 by CEO Mr. Dalei Zhang who has accumulated over 12 years of robust experiences in the management of high-tech companies and accumulated technological knowledge in the R&D of AI technologies including Sina Technology, PPLive and Macintosh Business Unit of Microsoft.

Harnessing over ten plus millions of annotated retinal images, Airdoc provides software for diagnosis and health assessment on a real-time basis. The company has received Class III medical device certificate of Diabetic Retinopathy from China FDA (NMPA) in 2020, and expected to receive another Class III medical device certificate for multiple diseases including Hypertensive Retinopathy, Retinal Vein Occlusion and Age-Related Macular Degeneration (AMD) in 2023. Additionally, Airdoc received CE and the U.S. FDA approvals for fundus cameral as a medical device in 2021 and 2022. The software diagnoses and detects health risks for over 55 types of lesions and diseases.

In 2021, the company has conducted over 4.9 million cases via SaMDs and

696 https://www.healio.com/news/ophthalmology/20220623/yutiq-approved-in-china-for-chronic-noninfectious-uveitis

697 https://www.fiercepharma.com/pharma/first-china-approves-eye-implant-based-solely-real-world-data

698 http://www.chinabiotoday.com/articles/ocumension-35-million-novartis

699 https://www.airdoc.com/

health risk assessment. On November 5, 2021, Airdoc was listed on the Hong Kong Stock Exchange, and raised approximately HK$1.67 billion. UBS and CITIC securities were the joint sponsor.[700]

C-MER Eye Care Holding Limited (3309.HK)[701]

C-MER is the leading ophthalmology services provider in Hong Kong and the Great Bay Area, which is headquartered in Hong Kong, with a nationwide physical eye hospital network covering Beijing, Shanghai, Guangzhou, and Shenzhen, and with a broad and growing hospital service network in the Greater Bay Area. Dr. Shun Chiu Lam is the founder, chairman and CEO of C-MER. The Group has more than 60 medical facilities in Hong Kong and Mainland China, including nine eye hospitals are in the mainland China. The Group has expanded into other medical services, including dentistry, oncology, family medicine, etc. It aims to become a destination for Hong Kong quality comprehensive specialty medical service to its patients in the Greater Bay Area.

Lam is the former President of the Asia-Pacific Academy of Ophthalmology (APAO)[702] and the Asia-Pacific Vitreo-Retina Society (APVRS), and the Editor-in-Chief of the Asia-Pacific Journal of Ophthalmology (APJO), on the global prestigious "Top 100 Power List"[703] of The Ophthalmologist in 2014, 2016, 2018, 2020 and 2022. Lam is passionate about eliminating cataract blindness in China and he has been instrumental in establishing two charity projects, "Lifeline Express" and "Project Vision".[704]

On January15, 2018, C-Mer completed its IPO on Hong Kong Stock Exchange and raised HK$571 million. China Merchants Securities was its sole sponsor. The publicly offered shares were more than 1,500 times oversubscribed.[705]

---

700 https://www1.hkexnews.hk/listedco/listconews/sehk/2021/1026/2021102600003. pdf

701 https://cmereye.com/

702 https://apaophth.org/

703 https://theophthalmologist.com/power-list

704 https://theophthalmologist.com/power-list/2018/18-dennis-lam

705 https://www.wsgr.com/en/insights/c-mer-eye-care-holdings-completes-ipo-and-listing-on-the-hong-kong-stock-exchange.html

3. AUTHOR'S INSIGHTS

The author evaluated vision health investment projects based on availability, accessibility, and affordability. This means that technological innovation, product accessibility, medical care and affordability for patients are key metrics. Above all, the people are the center of care, and a cost-effective, value-based, and clinical effective system must be implemented.

Innovations in vision health are multidisciplinary and complex, spanning multiple disciplines such as mechanics, electronics, physics, optics, bioengineering, materials, molecular biology, and more. It also involves exploration of neuroscience and cognition. Moreover, digital treatments and wearable devices in recent years have also broadened applications of vision therapy technology.

The author sees investment potentials in three areas which are more likely for future unicorns to surface, include gene therapy, artificial intelligence, and digital eye care.

1) Gene therapy

Gene therapy refers to a technique of introducing foreign DNA constructs into host cells to treat a medical condition.[706] [707] The eye is a suitable target organ for gene therapy for the following reasons. Retinal nerve cells are non-renewable tissue. Eyes are immune to most immune responses from the host due to the naturally occurring blood-ocular barrier. Furthermore, the small size of the eyeball makes it highly fit for gene therapy. Retinal cells can continually turn out transgene products and have low volumes of distribution. Both factors can affect the transfection efficiency and thus enhance the clinical success rate.

Spark Therapeutics developed the first approved ophthalmic gene therapy product, Luxturna®.[708] The drug was approved by the U.S. FDA in December

---

706 https://www.ncbi.nlm.nih.gov/pmc/articles/PMC4329713/

707 https://www.fda.gov/vaccines-blood-biologics/cellular-gene-therapy-products/what-gene-therapy

708 https://retinahistory.asrs.org/milestones-developments/the-history-and-development-of-luxturna-gene-therapy

2017 for the treatment of retinal dysfunction associated with RPE65 gene mutation, mainly for diseases such as Leber Congenital Amaurosis (LCA).[709] This is a scientific milestone in retina treatment, and it revolutionizes the industry by proving the concept of gene therapy into reality. The challenge of this gene therapy is how to deliver transgene in vivo safely and effectively as well as how to work closely with regulatory agencies for approvals. An article written by the innovators "Development of Luxturna® Gene Therapy" is worthy of reading.[710]

2) Artificial intelligence

Fundus photography can interpret various fundus diseases, indicating not only changes in the fundus, but also the disease progression throughout the whole body. Artificial Intelligence (AI) can analyze massive amounts of data to help physicians identify disease patterns and clinical features, predict disease progression, provide guidance for clinical treatment, and optimize treatment operations.

As of June 2021, the U.S. FDA and China NMPA have each approved two AI companies in the ophthalmology sector for the diagnosis and screening of diabetic retinopathy. Although the companies are still exploring and building their business models, the industry has great expectations of enriching the vision health through AI. Among them, the Hong Kong listed Airdoc Technology (2251. HK) is an example.

3) Digital vision health

COVID-19 has put pressure on the vision health industry. From China, the U.S. to Europe, a considerable number of optometry clinics and optical stores have closed or restricted their operations during the peak of the pandemic owing to social distancing regulations. Existing medical care from internet hospitals revolves around outpatient diversion, preliminary inquiry, and circulation of prescription drugs. However, core procedures such as face-to-face doctor

---

709 https://eyewiki.aao.org/Leber_Congenital_Amaurosis

710 https://retinahistory.asrs.org/milestones-developments/the-history-and-development-of-luxturna-gene-therapy

consultations, medical examinations, hospitalization, surgery, treatment and monitoring still need to be executed in hospitals or clinics settings.

Vision health is both medical and consumerist in nature. Aside from medical standards, patients also demand convenient and pleasurable treatment processes and experiences. Since optometry primarily consists of optical and imaging processes, more and more examinations and treatments are being digitalized. As the consequences, business processes and patient-doctor relationships can be re-established via digitalization and provide patients with better services that meet the general expectation of medical quality.

Chapter **11**

Precision Cancer Medicine

1. BACKGROUND

According to the World Health Organization (WHO), cancer is a leading cause of death worldwide, accounting for nearly ten million deaths in 2020, which is equivalent to nearly one in six deaths globally. The most common cancers by incidence include breast, lung, colon, and rectum and prostate cancers. However, in 2020, the five leading cancers death were lung, colorectal, liver, stomach and breast cancers, accounted for over five million deaths in the same year. Many cancers can be cured if detected early and treated early.[711] There were 135 million cancer patients worldwide in 2020. Asian patients accounted for approximately 48.8%, with about 32 million in China alone. In 2020, there were three million deaths related to various cancers in China.[712]

Cancer is a generic term, also referred as malignant tumors, and neoplasms. Cancers are the results of interaction between genetic mutation factors and external factors, such as physical, chemical, and biological carcinogens. The incidence of cancer rises dramatically with age.

Cancer mortality is reduced if detected and treated early. There are two components of early detection: early diagnosis and early screening. Early diagnosis of symptomatic cancers is relevant in most cancers. It consists of three components, which are awareness to symptoms; access to clinical evaluation and diagnosis services; and timely referrals to treatment services. Early screening aims to identify individuals with findings suggestive of a specific cancer or pre-cancer before they have developed symptoms. Screenings are effective for some cancers, are far more complex than early diagnosis as they require specialized technologies and equipment. Depending on the type of cancer, screening and early diagnosis can increase survival rates by five to seven times, which is a boon for patients and their families. Meanwhile, early cancer screening can significantly reduce society's

---

711 https://www.who.int/news-room/fact-sheets/detail/cancer

712 https://gco.iarc.fr/today/data/factsheets/populations/160-china-fact-sheets.pdf

overall healthcare expenditure.

Precision cancer medicine includes companion diagnostics, prognostic management, and disease monitoring, along with treatments. The emergence of the breakthrough innovative technology Next-Generation Sequencing (NGS), also known as High-throughput Sequencing or Massive Parallel Sequencing, has significantly reduced the cost of large-scale sequencing and enabled the large-scale application of liquid biopsy, tissue biopsy, and other precision medicine. This makes precision cancer treatment possible.

The Human Genome Project[713] (HGP) is an international collaboration that successfully determines, stores, and renders publicly available sequence of almost all the genetic content of the chromosomes of the human organism, also known as human genome. HGP operated from 1990 to 2013, provided basic information of the three-billion-unit sequence of human genomic DNA in 2003, at the cost of half billion U.S. dollars to publish the first map.[714] On March 31, 2022, on *Science* magazine, global researchers announced the completion sequence of a human genome.[715] This is a remarkable and jubilant achievement for humanity.

The significance of Human Genome Project is that it accelerates the understanding of human biology and improved the practice of medicine, which symbolizes the beginning of Precision Medicine Era.

The cost of genome sequencing dropped to about US$10 million by 2007. At present, it is US$600[716] and it is predicted to drop further to US$100 by 2024. Consequently, humanity has entered the era of whole genome sequencing. U.S.-based Illumina[717] is the leader in next-generation sequencing, along with Swiss-based Roche Diagnostics, and China-based BGI.[718]

Traditional cancer diagnostic techniques use medical imaging tests, tumor marker

---

713 https://www.genome.gov/human-genome-project

714 https://www.britannica.com/event/Human-Genome-Project

715 https://www.science.org/doi/10.1126/science.abj6987

716 As of December 2020, please refer to Novaseq 6000.

717 https://www.illumina.com/

718 https://www.bgi.com/global

tests and tissue biopsies. Medical imaging is a non-invasive technology that views images of internal body tissues. The main detection methods include Computed Tomography (CT), Magnetic Resonance Imaging (MRI), X-ray, ultrasound imaging, and so forth. Medical imaging has been the major means for cancer detection and diagnosis. However, the imaging detection time is relatively long, and there are relatively high cost and requirements for equipment, facilities, and doctors, rendering its challenge to be used for large-scale screening. Protein tumor markers are a set of proteins confirmed by clinical studies, which are highly related to the emergence of malignant tumors. Common protein tumor markers include, among others, Carcinoembryonic Antigen (CEA) and Alpha-Fetoprotein (AFP). However, tumor markers give a poor prediction of cancer and are prone to give rise to false negative results. Tissue biopsy involves extraction of sample cells or tissues from the human body through medical devices for pathological examination, including gastroscopic examination, colonoscopy examination, etc. Although tissue biopsies carry high accuracy, they have disadvantages of being particularly invasive, cumbersome detecting procedures and low patient willingness. Moreover, tissue biopsies are not feasible in some organs such as lung.

2. LIQUID BIOPSY

Liquid biopsy is an emerging non-invasive detection method by extracting nonsolid tissue samples in the human body for detection. This mainly includes the collection and testing of blood, urine, saliva, other body fluids and faeces. Since the 1990s, with the discovery of circulating free DNA within blood plasma, breakthroughs in NGS and improvements in sample collection techniques, the commercialization of liquid biopsy has accelerated, and has mainly been used in areas such as reproductive health, genetic disease testing and transplantation rejection monitoring. Prof Yuk Ming Lo and his team from the Chinese University of Hong Kong achieved the milestone of detecting fetal cfDNA for the first time across the globe. Liquid biopsy was listed by the *MIT Technology Review* magazine, as one of the top ten Breakthrough Innovative Technologies in 2015,[719] emphasizing that Lo's breakthrough technology led to safer and simpler methods to test Down syndrome.

---

719 https://www.technologyreview.com/technology/liquid-biopsy/

Liquid biopsy technology mainly uses circulating tumor DNA (ctDNA) or circulating cell-free DNA (ccfDNA) in detection. Circulating tumor DNA refers to cell-free DNA released from cancer cells and tumors that may carry specific mutations. Circulating Tumor Cells (CTCs) are a common type of liquid biopsy sample. The classification and identification of circulating tumor cells can be used for prognostic diagnosis and detection of drug resistance. The technology of liquid biopsies in the U.S. and Europe started relatively early. Even so, the U.S. FDA has only approved six liquid biopsy products analyzing ctDNA over the past two decades, for example, CellSearch® liquid biopsy detection system incorporating CTC technology route in 2004 and Guardant360® incorporating ctDNA technology route in 2020. CellSearch® can identify circulating tumor cells from blood samples with 99% accuracy and only requires 7.5 mL of whole blood per sample. The system was approved by the U.S. FDA for the prediction of metastatic breast cancer in 2004, for the prediction of colorectal cancer in 2007,[720] and for the prognosis detection and survival assessment of prostate cancer in 2008.[721] In 2012, it was approved by the China NMPA for the evaluation of metastatic breast cancer.[722]

The global liquid biopsy market size was valued at US$11.3 billion in 2019 and is expected to reach US$24 billion by 2023.[723] Compared with traditional tissue biopsy, liquid biopsy has the advantages of being safer, non-invasive, repeatable, and can be monitored in real time. Liquid biopsy is the technological backbone of precision cancer medicine and enables disease diagnosis, molecular typing and classification, discovery of drug resistance mechanisms as well as detection of curative effects. Liquid biopsy has been widely used in companion diagnosis, minimal residual disease detection and early screening, covering the whole cycle of cancer diagnosis and treatment, in turns generating both clinical and commercial value. The following three areas have attracted attention in investments in the sector of life sciences and technology.

---

720 https://www.fiercebiotech.com/biotech/fda-clears-advanced-test-for-monitoring-metastatic-colorectal-cancer

721 https://johnsonandjohnson.gcs-web.com/news-releases/news-release-details/fda-clears-cellsearchtm-circulating-tumor-cell-test/

722 https://www.fiercepharma.com/pharma/cellsearch%C2%AE-liquid-biopsy-approved-for-breast-cancer-patients-china

723 Estimated according to BCC Research and LEK Consulting.

i. **Companion Diagnosis:** Liquid biopsy companion diagnostics based on NGS technology can perform comprehensive genomic testing for cancer. Targeted antibodies and immunotherapies can be matched with the specific molecular characteristics of cancer patients to improve the therapeutic effect. The traditional classification of cancer is primarily based on the location of tumor, while the current method is based on varying genetic mutations. Moreover, multiple mutation types can arise from the same cancer and doctors can select different targeting and immunotherapy methods accordingly. Targeted therapy for cancer has become one of the main methods of precision cancer medicine.

ii. **Minimal Residual Disease (MRD) Detection:** Upon reaching remission in a cancer treatment, high-throughput testing can be used to detect minimal residual disease that is otherwise difficult to be detected by conventional methods. This is mainly used to prevent cancer recurrence after surgery.

iii. **Early Screening:** Early screening and detection of cancer is the most effective way to reduce the clinical and economic burden of cancer treatment. Providing early cancer screening for high-risk groups can effectively improve patients' survival rate and quality of life and at the same time reduce mortality and incidence. For example, with active treatment, the five-year survival rate for stage 1 colorectal cancer is higher than 90%. While the five-year survival rate for stage 4 colorectal cancer is less than 10%.

3. LEADING U.S.- BASED COMPANIES

1) Exact Sciences (EXAS.US)[724]

Exact Sciences, now headquartered in Wisconsin, was founded in 1995 by Stanley Lapidus and Anthony Shuber. Exact Sciences was listed on NASDAQ on January 31, 2001.[725] Its main products include Cologuard® for colorectal cancer screening; and Oncotype Dx® Breast, Prostate and Colon for prognostic testing. In clinical development, the company collaborates with the reputable Mayo

---

724 https://www.exactsciences.com/

725 https://www.wsj.com/articles/SB980965741744785503

Clinic,[726] the inventor of Cologuard and with Pfizer in marketing and sales.[727] Cologuard® was approved by the U.S. FDA in August 2014,[728] making it the first and only marketed molecular diagnostic product for early colorectal cancer screening.

Colorectal cancer is the second biggest cancer killer in the U.S., causing 9% of all cancer deaths, according to the National Cancer Institute. More than 150,000 new cases are diagnosed each year.[729]

In 2019, Exact Sciences acquired Genomic Health and added Oncotype Dx® to their product line, expanding its market to European countries.[730] This transaction valuated at US$2.8 billion, creating a global leading cancer diagnostics company. On Oct. 27, 2020, Exact Sciences paid up to US$2.15 billion in stock and cash for the privately held Thrive Earlier Detection, which has developed blood screening test to detect numerous cancers at early stage.[731] Thrive's main product is called CancerSeek®, based on technology developed at Johns Hopkins University.

The screening technology of Cologuard® has multiple innovations, including fecal DNA isolation, fecal DNA stabilization, DNA biomarker detection, hemoglobin biomarker stabilization and advanced mathematical algorithms. The multi-label method is a distinguishing feature of the technology platform developed by Exact Sciences. The stool test has 90% sensitivity for stage 1 colon cancer, and 42%

---

726 World-renowned private non-profit medical institution. Founded by Dr. Mayo in Rochester, Minnesota in 1864, the Mayo Clinic is one of the world's most influential and representative medical institutions that is of the highest medical level. It is a leader in the field of medical research.

727 https://www.exactsciences.com/about/history

728 https://www.medscape.com/viewarticle/829757

729 https://www.barrons.com/articles/guardant-stock-colon-cancer-screen-51651588618?mod=Searchresults

730 https://investor.exactsciences.com/investor-relations/press-releases/press-release-details/2019/Exact-Sciences-Completes-Combination-with-Genomic-Health-Creating-Leading-Global-Cancer-Diagnostics-Company/default.aspx

731 https://www.fiercebiotech.com/medtech/exact-sciences-snaps-up-liquid-biopsy-company-thrive-2-15b-deal

sensitivity for precancer.[732]

Globally, there are 780,000 newly diagnosed cases of liver cancer every year, among which Hepatocellular Carcinoma (HCC) accounts for roughly 90%[733] of all primary liver cancers. Exact Sciences' HCC biopsy test, which is based on six biomarkers in blood, was awarded the Breakthrough Medical Device Certification by the U.S. FDA in 2019.[734]

Oncotype Dx® Breast assay[735] has been used widely to predict the recurrence risk of breast cancer after surgical resection. Based on the expression levels of 21 genes, the test calculates a risk recurrence score from 0 to 100. The Oncotype Dx® test has been endorsed by the American Society of Clinical Oncology (ASCO) and the National Comprehensive Cancer Network (NCCN).

2) Guardant Health (GH.US)[736]

Guardant Health, headquartered in California, is one of the leading companies in precision cancer medicine in the U.S. Since its inception in 2012, it has been highly sought after by various investment funds. On October 4, 2018, the company was listed on NASDAQ in the U.S., and its stocks rose by nearly 70% on the first day, raised US$238 million.[737]

---

732 https://www.barrons.com/articles/exact-sciences-stock-earnings-cancer-tests-51651066780?mod=Searchresults

733 Current diagnostic guidelines generally recommend that high-risk patient groups undergo ultrasonography every six months, in conjunction with alpha-fetoprotein (AFP) testing.

734 https://investor.exactsciences.com/investor-relations/press-releases/press-release-details/2019/Exact-Sciences-Presents-Data-On-Blood-Based-Test-For-Detection-Of-Hepatocellular-Carcinoma-Earns-FDA-Breakthrough-Device-Designation/default.aspx

735 https://www.cancer.gov/publications/dictionaries/cancer-terms/def/oncotype-dx-breast-cancer-assay

736 https://guardanthealth.com/

737 https://www.investors.com/news/technology/guardant-health-ipo/

The company's main product, the Guardant360® test,[738] mainly provides a comprehensive cancer genomic view for patients with intermediate-advanced stage cancer. Its Guardant Reveal™ is a revolutionary blood-only liquid biopsy test that detects circulating tumor DNA (ctDNA) for Minimal Residual Disease (MRD) assessment in early-stage colorectal, breast, and lung cancers.[739] On May 2, 2022, Guardant launched its first blood-based screening test for colon cancer, called Shield test. It requires a simple blood draw, can detect early-stage colon cancer with sensitivity of around 90% and detect precancerous adenomas with 20% sensitivity.[740]

Guardant Health simultaneously collaborates with biopharmaceutical companies or research institutions to provide retrospective sample studies, patient screening, clinical selection, and companion diagnostics for cancer drugs, speeding up clinical development and assisting in drug commercialization.

4. LEADING CHINA-BASED COMPANIES

According to the World Health Organization International Agency for Research on Cancer (IARC) and the National Cancer Center in China, in 2020, there were 4.569 million new cancer cases and three million cancer-related deaths in China, accounting for 24% of new cases and 30% death rate respectively around the world. The number of cancer patients and deaths in China are on the rise. Cancer is the leading cause of death in China. The main types of cancer include lung cancer, stomach cancer, bowel cancer, liver cancer, breast cancer, thyroid cancer, esophageal cancer, etc. The five-year survival rate of cancer patients in China is only about 39%, which is lower than the 68% in the U.S. This is mainly due to the limited opportunities of timely diagnosis and treatment, as about 60% of Chinese cancer patients are in the middle and late stages when cancers are discovered and diagnosed.

---

738 https://www.cancer.gov/news-events/cancer-currents-blog/2020/fda-guardant-360-foundation-one-cancer-liquid-biopsy

739 https://guardantreveal.com/

740 https://investors.guardanthealth.com/press-releases/press-releases/2022/Guardant-Health-Announces-Shield-Blood-Test-Available-in-US-to-Detect-Early-Signs-of-Colorectal-Cancer-in-Average-Risk-Adults/default.aspx

Compared with traditional chemotherapeutic methods, targeted therapy and immunotherapy have higher efficacy with less side effects. In 2019, targeted therapy and immunotherapy in China only accounted for about 27% of the revenue from various types of cancer treatment. China's NMPA has fastened the approval of innovative products from China and worldwide, especially for drugs and therapies with urgent clinical demand. Drugs with superior curative effects are also listed on the medical insurance reimbursement formulary, thus improving accessibility of these innovative products to physicians and patients.

Effective genotyping analysis of the patient's tumor is required for targeted therapy and immunotherapy. This accelerates the growth of products involving NGS companion diagnostic technology. In 2019, only 6% of advanced cancer patients and patients recommended for cancer genotyping testing in China used NGS cancer companion diagnostics, while this percentage was about 24% in developed countries such as the U.S. market.

1) New Horizon Health (6606.HK)[741]

New Horizon Health (NHH) was founded by three Peking University classmates Drs. Yiyou Chen, Yeqing Zhu and Ning Lv in 2015 and is headquartered in Hangzhou, China. The company's mission is to prevent and cure cancer through screening and early detection. It is the only liquid biopsy company with cancer screening approval by China's National Medical Products Administration (NMPA).

NHH is one of the first life sciences companies in China to develop non-invasive screening products for early cancer. Their core product ColoClear® builds on grounds of multi-target FIT-DNA technology and is used for screening of colorectal cancer. This product has obtained the Class III innovative medical device registration certificate from the NMPA and received the first and only early cancer screening approval from NMPA in November 2020. China has the highest incidence of colorectal cancer globally, with 120 million patients at high risk, ranking top two by incidence and top five in mortality rates. However, prompt detection and removal of precancerous lesions can significantly improve

---

741 https://www.barrons.com/market-data/stocks/6606/company-people?countrycode =hk

the five-year survival rate of patients by more than 90%. The traditional method for early screening of colorectal cancer is colonoscopy, but it has disadvantage of the poor accessibility and discomfort. NHH's early screening products are non-invasive and improve the penetration rate among high-risk patient groups of colorectal cancer, which are of great significance in clinical and public health realms by addressing unmet clinical needs.

The clinical validation of ColoClear®, known as Colorectal Cancer Early Screening in China (CLEAR-C), was initiated in September 2018, and lasted for 16 months. During the process, a total of 5,881 patients were enrolled and a prospective, large-scale, and multi-center registrational clinical trial as Clear-C was implemented. With the clinical "golden standard" of colonoscopy as benchmark, Clear-C conducted a head-to-head[742] comparative study between ColoClear® and FIT, a traditional clinical screening method for colorectal cancer. In September 2020, clinical trial results showed that ColoClear®'s detection sensitivity towards colorectal cancer reached 95.5%, much higher than the 69.8% of FIT. Its negative predictive value in colorectal cancer screening reached 99.6%, indicating extremely unlikely chances for missed diagnosis related to colorectal cancer and polyp.

NHH has advantages over time, clinical results and cost, compared with its potential competitors. Meanwhile, the company also owns the patent to their self-innovated DNA stabilizers, facilitating the transportation of faeces sample without refrigeration.

Since its establishment, NHH has been highly sought after by venture capitalists and leading international and Chinese investment institutions. The author's fund participated and co-led the company's financing round in June 2020. NHH was successfully listed on the Hong Kong Stock Exchange on February 18, 2021. The public offering was oversubscribed by 4,133 times and the closing price on its opening day was HK$84, which was 215% higher than its offer price.[743]

---

742 A head-to-head trial is a non-placebo-controlled trial where the test subject is compared against therapeutic drugs or treatment regimens that are already in clinical use as opposed to a standard of care.

743 https://www.nasdaq.com/articles/new-horizon-health-shares-surge-200-in-hong-kong-debut-2021-02-17

On January 18, 2022, NHH launched the first and only NMPA-approved H. Pylori self-test for gastric cancer prevention. In June 2022, CerviClear®, a self-sampling cervical cancer screening test utilizing urine or vaginal swab samples has started its prospective, large-scale and multi-center registrational clinical trial in China with 15,000 to 20,000 patients to be enrolled in three years.

NHH has developed STAR-seq® technology, a proprietary multi-omics platform to address the challenges of cancer screening beyond colorectal and cervical cancers. Leveraging on the STAR-seq® platform, LiverClear® is a blood-based liquid biopsy test designed for liver cancer screening in China and has been validated in difficult-to-detect patient cohort. LiveClear® released preclinical data in 2021 and demonstrated its ability to detect early-stage liver cancer at high accuracy. For pan-cancer screening, NHH has launched PANDA (Pan-Cancer Early Detection in China) Clinical Program targeting over 22 cancer types in collaboration with Beijing University Health Science Center with 50,000 participants to be enrolled in six years.

On February 17, 2023, NHH launches an international R&D center in Hong Kong Science Park, as the first step of global expansion.[744]

2) Burning Rock Biotech (BNR.US)[745]

Burning Rock Biotech (Burning Rock) was founded in 2014 and is headquartered in Guangzhou, China. It is the market leader in China's NGS companion diagnostics sector with the largest market share. Its lead product is a combination testing kit that identifies human gene mutations (EGFR/ALK/BRAF/KRAS), and it is used for non-small cell lung cancer genetic testing. This product obtained the Class III medical device certificate from the NMPA in July 2018, and is the first NGS kit approved in China. The company currently has three early-stage cancer screening products in clinical trials, targeting lung cancer, colorectal cancer, and liver cancer respectively.

---

744 https://www.scmp.com/business/china-business/article/3210476/hangzhou-based-cancer-screening-firm-new-horizon-health-opens-rd-centre-hong-kong-tech-hub-it-eyes

745 https://www.barrons.com/market-data/stocks/bnr?mod=searchresults_companyquotes&mod=searchbar

Burning Rock collaborates with more than 20 companies globally and adopts the simultaneous development and marketing model of "diagnostics plus therapeutic drugs" in the Chinese market. For example, Merck KGaA and Burning Rock announced a strategic partnership in Companion Diagnostics (CDx) development for the MET inhibitor Tepotinib in the mainland China market. Tepotinib is the first oral MET inhibitor to obtain regulatory approval in the world for the treatment of advanced Non-Small Cell Lung Cancer (NSCLC) harboring MET gene mutations, with its approval in Japan in March 2020.[746]

The company's laboratory has obtained technical audits from high-throughput sequencing laboratories in Guangdong Province, China, as well as laboratory qualifications from the CLIA[747] and CAP[748] in the U.S.

In May 2020, Burning Rock initiated 14,000 patients pan-cancer early detection study project called PREDICT, it is the first multiple cancers early detection study in China.

On January 3, 2023, Burning Rock received the U.S. FDA Breakthrough Device Designation for its OverC Multi-Cancer Detection Blood Test (esophageal, liver, lung, ovarian and pancreatic cancers.)[749]

Burning Rock attracted some reputable investment funds. On June 12, 2020, its NASDAQ IPO stock price surged nearly 50%, and the company raised about US$281.2 million through its IPO and a concurrent private placement.[750]

5. LEADING SINGAPORE-BASED COMPANY

The region of Southeast Asia has a growing population of over 660 million and

---

746 https://seekingalpha.com/news/3772250-merck-kgaa-burning-rock-collaborate-on-liquid-biopsy-based-cdx-development

747 https://www.cdc.gov/clia/index.html

748 https://www.cap.org/

749 https://seekingalpha.com/news/3921574-bnr-stock-gains-fda-breakthrough-device-designation-cancer-test

750 https://www.spglobal.com/marketintelligence/en/news-insights/latest-news-headlines/china-s-burning-rock-raises-281-2m-from-nasdaq-ipo-private-placement-59134528

is expected to become the fourth global largest economy by 2030, after the U.S., China, and EU. The World Health Organization (WHO) reported 1.09 million new cancer cases in Southeast Asia in 2020 and has projected the annual cancer number to increase by 65% to 1.80 million by 2040.

Singapore, with the highest per capital GDP (US$79,426 in 2022) and the most aged population among Southeast Asian countries (median age of 42.1, with 18.4% of Singapore population aged 65 and above in 2020), has led the region in scientific research and clinical translation in the domain of human health. Singapore's annual R&D budget remained constant at approximately 2% of GDP over the past few years, with the government dedicating over US$18.5 billion in public R&D funding in their latest Research, Innovation and Enterprise 2025 plan[751] Singapore is a leading hub for biomedical manufacturing, with eight of the world's top ten pharmaceutical companies establishing local facilities, manufacturing four of the top ten drugs by global revenue.[752] In Feb 2022, the Health Sciences Authority (HSA) of Singapore (U.S. FDA equivalent) became the first National Regulatory Authority (NRA) assessed by the WHO to achieve Maturity Level (ML) four for its advanced medicines regulatory system, further highlighting Singapore's quality and regulatory excellence in biomedicine. Singapore's growing biomedical ecosystem is supported by talents trained in two world class universities, namely the National University of Singapore and the Nanyang Technological University, as well as a globally renowned, mission-oriented research institution, the Agency for Science, Technology and Research (A*STAR). As a result, Singapore has seen a growing number of biomedical start-up companies in recent years, with a record of over US$600 million venture funds raised in 2021, up from just US$86 million in 2016.[753]

MiRXES[754]

Founded in 2014 by Prof. Heng-Phon Too, Drs. Lihan Zhou and Ruyang Zou, as a spin-off from the Singapore A*STAR, MiRXES has grown over the last eight

---

751 https://www.nrf.gov.sg/rie2025-plan/human-health-and-potential

752 https://www.edb.gov.sg/en/our-industries/pharmaceuticals-and-biotechnology.html

753 https://www.enterprisesg.gov.sg/media-centre/news/2021/december/local-biomedical-companies-raise-record-$820m-from-jan-to-sept-this-year

754 https://mirxes.com/about/#our_story

years to become a globally recognized leader in RNA technologies and a pioneer in liquid biopsy cancer early detection. Widely regarded as one of Singapore's most promising biotech companies, MiRXES has raised US$130 million from a diverse group of reputable healthcare specialists from the U.S., Singapore, and China, including their latest round of US$87 million fundraise in 2021.[755]

Since founding, MiRXES has pursued a product strategy distinct from most of the cancer early detection technology companies based in the U.S. and China. Instead of the centralized laboratory testing service strategy perfected by Exact Sciences, Guardant Health, and New Horizon Health, the MiRXES team is making cancer early detection tests accessible and scalable globally through localized and decentralized PCR tests. Their flagship product, GASTROClear®, the world's first molecular blood test for early detection of gastric cancer, is an In Vitro Diagnostic Multi-Variant Index Assay (IVDMIA) measuring 12 human circulating miRNAs associated with gastric cancer. GASTROClear® is manufactured as an IVD PCR test kit and sold to accredited PCR laboratories in multiple Asia-Pacific countries for localized testing of individuals at-risk of developing gastric cancer.

GASTROClear® is unique in several ways, it addresses a critical unmet need in the underserved market of gastric screening. Despite the relatively low incidence in North America and Western Europe, gastric cancer remains to be the fourth leading cause of cancer deaths worldwide and third in Asia, causing heavy clinical and economic burden in China (480,000 new cases in 2020), Japan (140,000 new cases), Korean and ASEAN countries. The current golden standard for gastric cancer screening is gastroscopy, which has been successfully implemented as national screening programs in Japan and Korea, saving countless lives in the past two decades. However, the approach requires heavy infrastructure investment and incurs high running cost, with modest compliance due to the invasive nature of the procedure, making it unrealistic for most other countries to adopt at scale. GASTROClear®, a simple blood test, serves as a viable alternative as a screening test to identify those high-risk individuals for follow-up with endoscopy.

GASTROClear® is a novel miRNA biomarker assay developed over seven years from 2012 to 2019 and is prospectively validated in a population cohort

---

755 https://www.a-star.edu.sg/

of 5,248 patients in Singapore. Benchmarked against gastroscopy and biopsy, GASTROClear® demonstrated 87.5% sensitivity for stage 1 gastric cancer and 60% sensitivity for stage 0 gastric cancer or high-grade dysplasia, achieving a high negative predictive value of 99.5% and a positive predictive value of 6.7%, a performance consistent with that of Cologuard for colorectal cancer screening and LDCT for lung cancer screening. GASTROClear® has since been approved by Singapore HSA as a class C medical device for early detection of gastric cancer in average risk population aged 40 and above.[756] GASTROClear® has been CE-marked, and is currently undergoing a large registration trial (n>10,000) in China, expected to complete in 2023.

Based on the same technology platform, MiRXES has recently reported preliminary data on their blood-based miRNA biomarker for early detection of colorectal cancer, demonstrating about 80% sensitivity with 90% specificity. MiRXES' maturing clinical pipeline also includes lung, liver, breast cancer and a multi-cancer multi-omic biomarker assay for nine high incidence and high mortality cancers.

MiRXES has grown from a three-men team in 2014 to an integrated R&D and commercialization operating globally in Singapore, China, U.S., and Japan, making it the first potential life sciences unicorn in Singapore and South East Asia. On May 27, 2022, it launched the first industry 4.0 in vitro diagnostic manufacturing facility in Southeast Asia to scale up production of miRNA-based cancer liquid biopsy test kits.[757]

---

756 https://www.straitstimes.com/singapore/blood-test-for-early-detection-of-gastric-cancer-being-evaluated-for-use-in-primary

757 https://www.straitstimes.com/business/companies-markets/biotech-firm-mirxes-opens-southeast-asias-first-industry-40-facility-in-singapore

PART 4

Looking into the Future

Chapter 12

Overview of the CROs and Pharma Services Sector

Contract Research Organizations (CROs) are service providers to the pharmaceutical, biotech, and medical devices industries, performing a variety of functions and roles to support the successful completion of Research and Development (R&D) activities. They are organizations that contractually assume one or more of a clinical trial sponsor's obligations. The roles performed by CROs span the entire pharma R&D cycle, from research on new drugs in the laboratory, lab and animal testing, clinical research (or testing drugs on people), supporting regulatory applications including New Drug Applications (NDAs) and all the way to conducting post-market safety monitoring studies.

The reader may be familiar with the concept behind the chart below, showing the R&D process for a successfully approved new drug. The process can take around 10 to 15 years and requires an average cost of US$2.6 billion (incorporating the costs of failures). Millions of compounds may be screened early in the R&D process. Furthermore, for every 5,000 compounds initially evaluated through laboratory and animal studies, only five enter human testing, and only one ends up being approved.[758] The overall probability of clinical success (the likelihood of a drug entering clinical testing eventually being approved) is estimated to be less than 12%.[759] This is an increasingly complex and highly expensive process for biopharma sponsors. This highlights the importance of having highly competent and experienced outsourcing partners along the way. CROs can thus be divided into early stage, or pre-clinical, and late-stage, or clinical CROs.

---

758 The Drug Development and Approval Process. FDA Review website. The Drug Development and Approval Process | FDAReview.org

759 *Biopharmaceutical Research & Development,* The Process Behind New Medicines. PhRMA. 2015.

The Drug Research and Development Process, and Associated CRO Services at Each Stage

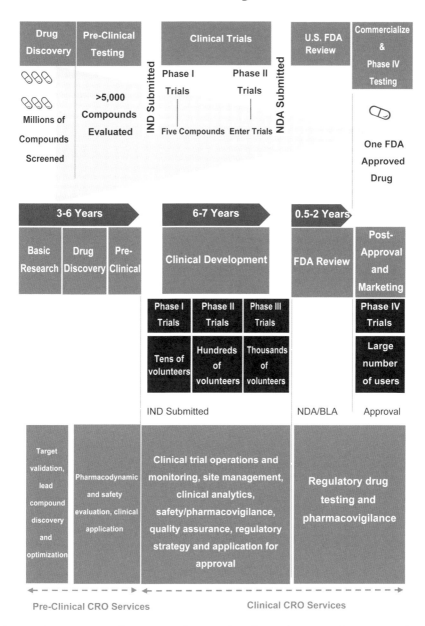

Source: the U.S. FDA, Pharmaceutical Research and Manufacturers of America, author's analysis.

The aggregation of all these efforts leads to a total global drug R&D expenditure of US$205 billion in 2020, some US$140 billion of which was used in the clinical phase.[760] The size of CRO market depends on the total available R&D spending and the degree to which biopharma companies outsource such activities to CROs (i.e., the "CRO penetration"). The global CRO market (or portion of R&D spending outsourced to CROs) was thus worth US$65 billion in 2020 (of which the clinical CRO was US$42 billion). While there are different estimates of the size of market, the clinical CRO market is generally estimated to be larger than the pre-clinical, which related to both the scale and cost of clinical development spending, as well as the fact that biopharma companies tend to keep certain aspects of pre-clinical work (such as early-stage research) in-house, which limits outsourcing potential. Overall, the growth of CRO industry is driven by two factors: i) the underlying growth in R&D spending, and ii) the percentage of R&D outsourcing. Since this book extensively covers some of the drivers behind R&D spending, we will spend more time on the drivers and historical dynamics behind outsourcing to CROs.

The birth of CRO industry in its current form can specifically be traced back to 1982,[761] when two newly formed companies in the U.S. started offering fee-for-service consultative data support for clinical trials as well as clinical trial monitoring services. One of these companies was Quintiles, which is now known as IQVIA (IQV.US). CROs expanded their reach from providing "spill-over capacity" to biotech and pharma companies to all aspects of clinical trials, including clinical trial planning, initiation and management, medical monitoring, collecting samples for laboratory analysis and conducting analysis as well as assisting with the preparation of reports and regulatory submissions. While in some cases, sponsors (especially larger pharmaceutical sponsors companies which have full in-house resources) may do an entire clinical trial by themselves, CROs have become an essential part of the clinical trial infrastructure. By 2020, about

---

760 Information provided by Frost & Sullivan, a global consulting firm. With a team of experts based in 45 global offices, Frost & Sullivan generate intelligence spanning 10 industries, 35 sectors, and 300 markets using a powerful understanding of how value chains operate on a global level.

761 Daniel A. Roberts, MD; Hagop M. Kantarjian, MD; and David P. Steensma, MD. *Contract Research Organizations in Oncology Clinical Research: Challenges and Opportunities.* American Cancer Society, 2016.

70% of clinical trials were conducted by sponsors with the help of CROs. The role of CROs has also become more significant as they are increasingly seen as long-term strategic partners by customers, rather than pay-per-service providers.

There are multiple fundamental reasons why institutions which have clinical trial needs or conduct other R&D activities ("sponsors") decide to work with a CRO:

i. **CROs provide sponsors with scalable and specialized capacity and help reduce cost.** CROs provides access to best-in-class resources without the costly investment required if the sponsor wanted to build such capabilities in-house. This is particularly relevant for biotech clients, when there is a lack of in-house resources and infrastructure necessity to conduct extensive development process internally. Meanwhile, in the case of big pharma companies, they may require flexible capacity to complement in-house resources. Given the increasing cost and complexity of development, customers can thus rely on CROs to optimize their cost structure, and effectively turn a fixed internal overhead cost into a variable cost.

ii. **CROs can be a highly effective and efficient partner.** As they concurrently run clinical trials for numerous clients, CROs accumulate highly specialized expertise and knowledge that can be relevant to the product or therapeutic area of focus. When it comes to global clinical trials, sponsors can also benefit from the CRO's understanding of different local regulatory requirements and standards of care, which allows them to operate effectively and consistently in all geographies. CROs can in some cases also offer dedicated and best-in-class technology to support clinical trial management and decision-making.

iii. **CROs allow sponsors to progress their R&D process more efficiently and shorten timelines.** According to the Tufts Center for the Study of Drug Development, R&D projects managed by CROs typically deliver shorter cycle times despite growing protocol complexity and expanding study scope. Specifically, a report published by the Tufts Center in 2019 highlighted that among other things, sponsors using CROs were able to speed up the study initiation or the time required to build and release a database.

iv. **CROs can act as an independent party.** CROs, with their strong experience and insight into different regulatory environments and local stakeholders, can provide additional third-party oversight and validation to the R&D effort.

There are two other growth drivers which are relevant to clinical outsourcing, and having inter-related aspects. They are i) globalization of clinical trials, with companies seeking approvals in multiple markets worldwide, and with Asia/China being an increasingly important site for drug development; and ii) strong innovation and funding momentum coming from emerging biopharma companies (some would also called as small and mid-sized biotech and pharma companies, or "SMid" segment). Regarding the first topic, the United States Food and Drug Administration (U.S. FDA) has recently reiterated the importance of Multi-Regional Clinical Trials (MRCTs), which represent "efficient" drug development. In the context of a recent AdCom decision, the U.S. FDA highlighted both the importance of switching from a local mindset to global mindset for efficient drug development and ensuring safe and effective drugs worldwide, but also the growing role of Asian and Chinese patient populations in such trials. While the contribution of such populations to oncology submissions to the U.S. FDA is still relatively small, it has been growing very rapidly.

Small and mid-sized biotech and pharma companies are developing an increasing proportion of novel therapeutics compared to the big pharmas, which often rely on acquisitions to grow their pipelines. In seeking to develop their products in several global markets, small and mid-sized biotech and pharma companies require support and a more customized approach from CRO partners. As a result, several CROs strategically focus on the emerging biopharma segment to generate above-market revenue growth. This segment's spending on R&D grew by more than three times the rate of total drug industry spending from 2001 to 2020.[762]

As the result of all these factors the CRO sector shows explosive growth. On the clinical development side, the size of global clinical CRO revenues grew from about US$2 billion in 1993[763] to what different publicly available sources now estimate to have reached anywhere from US$42 to US$55 billion in 2020.[764] In

762 *Tufts Center for the Study of Drug Development, Summary of Impact Report,* Volume 23, Number 4, July/August 2021.

763 Daniel A. Roberts, MD; Hagop M. Kantarjian, MD; and David P. Steensma, MD. *Contract Research Organizations in Oncology Clinical Research: Challenges and Opportunities.* American Cancer Society, 2016.

764 *Frost & Sullivan,* publicly available presentations from PPD and Medpace.

the pre-clinical space, the estimate of the size of the market ranges from US$9.5 billion to US$16 billion in 2020.[765]

The impressive growth of revenues in global CRO space also shown impressive development in terms of capital markets as well as strategic activity. As of 18th July, 2022, there was nearly US$80 billion in total market capitalization accounted for by five leading global CROs which are listed in the U.S., while five leading CROs have a combined market capitalization of US$89 billion in Hong Kong and Mainland China. Both the U.S. markets as well as China markets shown strong activity in the past five years, with large-scale IPOs for WuXi AppTec (2359.HK, 603259.CN), Pharmaron (3759.HK, 300759.CN), Tigermed (3347.HK, 300347.CN) and Joinn (6127.HK, 603127.CN) in Hong Kong and Mainland China in 2018-2021, and IPO for PPD in the U.S. in 2020, which was acquired by Thermo Fisher (TMO.US) in 2021.

---

765 According to the public disclosure of Inotiv, a pre-clinical CRO.

1. MARKET CAPITALIZATION OF CRO COMPANIES

	Ticker	Listing Venue	Market Cap ($000s)
WuXi AppTec（药明康德）	2359.HK/603259.CN	Hong Kong, Shanghai	54,267
Pharmaron（康龙化成）	3759.HK/300759.CN	Hong Kong, Shanghai	14,286
Tigermed（泰格医药）	3347.HK/300347.CN	Hong Kong, Shanghai	13,199
JOINN Laboratories（昭衍新药）	6127.HK/603127.CN	Hong Kong, Shanghai	6,518
Frontage Holdings（方达医药）	1521.HK	Hong Kong	867
HK/China-Listed Total			**89,137**
IQVIA	IQV.US	NYSE	40,292
ICON	ICLR.US	NASDAQ	16,619
Charles River	CRL.US	NYSE	10,801
Syneos	SYNH.US	NASDAQ	7,264
Medpace	MEDP.US	NASDAQ	4,899
US-Listed Total			**79,875**

Source: FactSet, market cap as of 18th July 2022. The list is based on the author's assessment of representative listed companies in the CRO sector and may not represent a fully exhaustive list.

This leads naturally into another trend, which has been the significant global M&A activity in this sector. From December 2020 to the end of 2021, the following transactions took place:

- **December 2020 – Syneos Health (SYNH.US) acquired Synteract, a clinical CRO focused on the emerging biopharma segment, for US$400 million.** The acquisition meant to enhance Syneos Health's position in the small to mid-sized customer category, especially pre-revenue companies, which is a rapidly growing space.
- **April 2021 – dMed Global, a full-service clinical CRO based in Shanghai, merged with Clinipace Incorporated, a full-service**

Clinical CRO with headquarters in North Carolina. This transaction creates a differentiated mid-sized CRO that rivals the leading global CROs in geographic scope, services and therapeutic expertise. The merged company would be focused on serving the needs of fast-moving emerging biopharma companies across all the key markets in the world. In October 2022, dMed-Clinipace announce a corporate name change to Caidya, reflecting the successful integration of the legacy brands after their merger in April 2021.

- **April 2021 – ERT, a global leader in clinical endpoint data solutions, merged with Bioclinica, a technological and scientific leader in clinical imaging.** The combination creates the global leader in clinical trial endpoint technology and leading partner to pharmaceutical and biotechnology companies, providing best-in-class technology, scientific and therapeutic expertise, and digital innovation. Both businesses were private equity owned before the merger. In November 2021, the combined company renamed as Clario.

- **July 2021 – ICON (ICLR.US) plc concluded the acquisition of PRA Health Sciences (PRAH.US) for a total of US$12 billion, at the time the largest M&A transaction in the history of the CRO sector.** The combined business will be number one or number two in key clinical market segments and have strategic partnerships with a majority of the top 20 biopharma companies. Based on pro forma 2020E revenues, the combined entity would jump ahead to become the number two global CRO after IQVIA, with nearly US$6 billion in revenue.

- **July 2021 – EQT Private Equity and Goldman Sachs Asset Management acquired Parexel, a global CRO, from Pamplona Capital Management for US$8.5 billion.** This transaction reflects that CROs are thematic focus for many private equity firms, particularly when they can acquire fast-growing assets.

- **December 2021 –Thermo Fisher Scientific Inc. (TMO.US), the world leader in life sciences tools and solutions, completed its acquisition of NASDAQ-listed PPD, Inc. (PPD.US), a leading global provider of clinical research services to the biopharma and biotech industry, for US$17.4 billion.** This transaction becomes the largest M&A transaction in the sector ever. The deal allows Thermo Fisher offer a comprehensive suite of world-class services across the clinical development spectrum – from scientific discovery, to assessing safety, efficacy, and health care outcomes, to managing clinical trial logistics, to the development and manufacturing of the drug product.

The strategic activity mentioned above highlights the increasing consolidation of the competitive landscape, which has historically been quite fragmented. In the clinical CRO space, the number of large and mega CROs, or companies with several billion U.S. dollars in revenue and whose typical customer focus is big pharma has been steadily decreasing because of M&A activity.

As it can be noticed in the chart below, the global landscape currently includes six large CROs (IQVIA, ICON/PRA, Covance, PPD, Syneos, Parexel), in addition to Medpace (MEDP-US) that has grown to over US$1 billion in revenue. If we assume that the total market is around US$50–60 billion in revenue, these seven companies represented half, or a bit more than half of the total market size (based on 2020 data). The percentage of the market being taken by the top clinical CROs has been constant in recent years, with the key change is the decreasing number of large CROs that account for this percentage–a few years ago one would have seen nine or ten CROs. The rest of the market is accounted for 10 to 15 mid-sized CROs, or companies with a revenue above US$100 million, who typically cater to biotech and small and mid-sized pharma clients–these include companies such as Worldwide Clinical Trials, Premier Research or Caidya (formerly dMed-Clinipace). There are also several hundred small or niche CROs that serve specific needs, but which are only able to operate in select regions and in certain capacities.

2. 2021 CLINICAL CRO REVENUE – LARGE CROs (US$ IN BILLIONS)

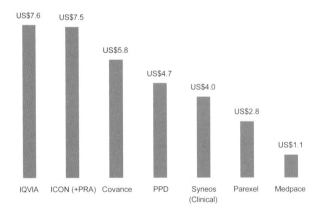

Source: Public company filings and presentations. Represents revenue in the most relevant segment. IQVIA revenue is IQVIA R&D Solutions revenue. Icon revenue is pro forma for PRA acquisition. Covance is now Labcorp Drug Development PPD and Parexel revenue

is for FY 2020. Parexel revenue is estimated based on latest publicly available data.

In the pre-clinical CRO space, the sector is generally regarded as less competitive compared to the clinical. Charles River Laboratiories (CRL.US) with US$2.9 billion in revenue in 2020 (US$3.5 billion in 2021) is a leading drug discovery, non-clinical development, and more recently a manufacturing company, followed by WuXi AppTec (2359.HK, 603259.CN) that had US$2.4 billion in revenues in 2020 (US$3.3 billion in 2021). Other players in the space include Envigo (now owned by Inotiv), as well as large CROs which have a pre-clinical offering, such as Covance (owned by LabCorp; LH.US) and PPD (now owned by Thermo Fisher, TMO.US), and many smaller niche players.

This chapter so far has focused mainly on CROs, which focus on the R&D stages of the of the biopharmaceutical value chain, but it is worth noting that the broader category of "pharma services" (companies which provide outsourced services to the pharma industry) also includes companies involved in activities such as manufacturing, drug distribution and marketing. In particular, Contract Manufacturing Organizations (CMOs) which focus on the manufacturing phase of the pharma value chain is a well-established sector that is often looked together with CROs by investors, who sometimes employ the term "CXO" to refer to both sectors. CMOs are companies that take a pre-formulated drug and manufacture it, whether pre-approval or for commercial production. Some CMOs also support the development stage of a drug, through services such as pre-formulation, formulation development, stability studies, method development, in addition to providing preclinical and Phase I clinical trial materials, late-stage clinical trial stage materials, registration batches, and commercial production. These are called Contract Development and Manufacturing Organizations (CDMOs). The figure below shows what services CMOs and CDMOS can offer at different points of pharma value cycle. Throughout the chapter, we will also touch upon other aspects of pharma services and outsourcing, particularly since certain Chinese companies became dominant players in those spaces at a global level.

3. THE RESEARCH AND DEVELOPMENT PROCESS AND CRO/CDMO SERVICES AT EACH STAGE

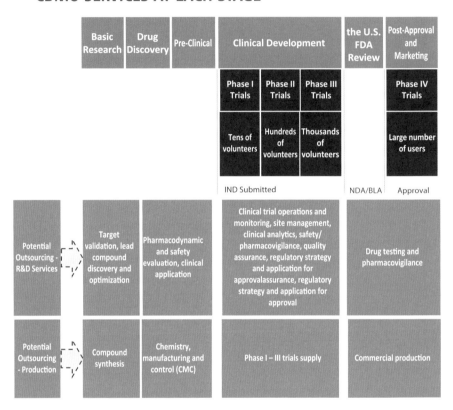

Source: the U.S. FDA, Pharmaceutical Research and Manufacturers of America, author's analysis.

With this global backdrop, we can now turn to the CRO sector in China. Historically, Chinese CRO companies focused on the earlier stages of the R&D process, where less global competition, and services could provided out of China for a global customer base, leveraging lower-cost yet highly qualified human resources in China. For example, WuXi Pharmatech's initial core focus was on discovery chemistry services in its China laboratories, consisting primarily of lead generation and lead optimization, and provided to the US-based customers. WuXi subsequently expanded its capabilities into the pre-clinical development, formulation and manufacturing areas, as well as eventually into clinical development capabilities, both organically as well as through acquisitions. Most notably, the AppTec acquisition in the U.S. in 2008 expanded the manufacturing services to include biologics-based manufacturing and testing, which ultimately resulted in the creation of what is now WuXi Biologics (2269.HK), a separate listed company, which is now one of the leading biologics CDMOs in the world.

Similarly, Pharmaron (3759.HK, 300759.CN) evolved from a pure laboratory chemistry service provider to have a more comprehensive R&D service platform which includes pre-clinical, clinical as well as manufacturing. Meanwhile, Joinn (6127.HK, 603127.CN) is a non-clinical CRO focused on drug safety assessment.

The significant industry reformation made in China since 2015 also provided accelerated momentum to the emerging clinical CRO segment, as clinical trial approvals were streamlined and the government started providing strong support for innovation. China's entry into the International Council for Harmonization of Technical Requirements for Pharmaceuticals for Human Use (ICH) as a new regulatory member in June 2017 was a significant event, which brought beneficial impact on the quality and scale of local drug development conducted by local innovators as well as foreign companies. As of 2015, the total size of the pre-clinical and discovery CRO sectors in China was similar to the size of the clinical CRO sector, both representing roughly US$1.3 billion.[766] With the industry reform to stimulate innovation in China, the clinical CRO space saw accelerated growth, and became the fastest growing segment, soon surpassing the pre-clinical and discovery CRO segments in terms of aggregate revenue. In 2020, the clinical CRO market in China reached US$3.8 billion, with the expectation that CAGR from 2020 to 2025 will around 26%, and with growing cross-border component. Tigermed, listed in Shenzhen and Hong Kong was the largest clinical CRO in China in terms of revenue in as of 2019, offering both clinical trial as well as clinical-related and laboratory services (through subsidiary Frontage Holdings, which is also a Hong Kong-listed company), while other rapidly growing players also emerged in the clinical CRO market.

As China biopharma continue their globalization strategy and willing to derive more value from the global rights for their first or best-in-class products (as evidenced by recent successful out-licensing deals to international biotech and pharma companies), the support of CRO partners will be essential. In particular,

---

766 Frost & Sullivan.

Chinese biopharma needs CRO partners who can operate under a global model, while having a strong understanding of the China market. The above-mentioned merger between dMed and Clinipace is a key showcase of this trend, with the merger creating a combined company with delivery capability in China as well as in the Americas, Europe and rest of Asia.

This market needs also evidenced by a rapid acceleration in the number of new MRCTs conducted in China, especially after 2017. The number reached 210 trials in 2020, having growth at 35% CAGR since 2015, when there were only 46 such trials. These trials are initiated and driven by both Chinese biotechs as well as by global sponsors who make China part of their studies. Recent the U.S. FDA positions on several products' approval applications also highlight the importance of conducting MRCTs as a way to support the U.S. FDA approvals in the future.

4. NEW MRCTs IN CHINA

(New MRCTs in China)

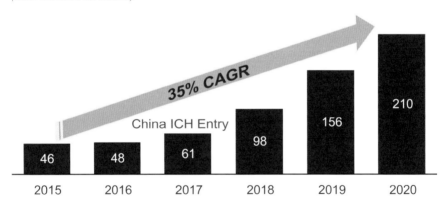

Source: Frost & Sullivan.

From a capital markets perspective, the CRO sector shown unprecedented value creation and growth in Mainland China and Hong Kong. Many of the above-mentioned companies are listed in Shanghai, Shenzhen and/or Hong Kong, and have conducted successful IPOs that attracted notable investor interest, including well-established global investors.

In December 2015, as WuXi PharmaTech was taken private from the U.S. in a US$3.3 billion transaction, the only other listed CRO in the China healthcare space was Tigermed, with a market capitalization of US$2.1 billion in China's domestic market. Six and a half years after, by mid July 2022, the sector had the earlier mentioned market capitalization of US$89 billion, composed of the Mainland China A-share and the Hong Kong market capitalizations of only five companies (hence only a 2.5 times increase in the number of listed companies), which represents a 16.5 times increase in the total market value of what investors would label as the CRO sector. While this is a staggering figure, it is also worth noting that the market capitalization of these companies was significantly higher in 2020 and first half of 2021.

The decrease in valuations since the second half of 2021 can generally be attributed to i) the overall market weakness in Greater China, partly due to regulatory risks that impacted a number of industries in China, and had a particular impact on share prices in offshore listing venues, and ii) broader macroeconomic concerns that intensified throughout 2022 such as inflation, supply chain issues, war in Ukraine, geopolitical concerns, which affected global capital markets. A wide variety of market participants expect a recovery and believe the market has reached the bottom, but the shape and timing for that recovery remains a matter of discussion. There is a consensus that the fundamentals and size of opportunity remain extremely attractive, and that the CRO and other pharma services players shall continue to benefit from secular growth trends in the global biopharma sector. For example, China is an increasingly important driver from many points of view, which will be further discussed below.

5. THE RISE OF THE CHINA-BASED CRO SECTOR FROM AN EQUITY CAPITAL MARKETS PERSPECTIVE

(Number of Companies)   *(Market Capitalization, US$billions)*

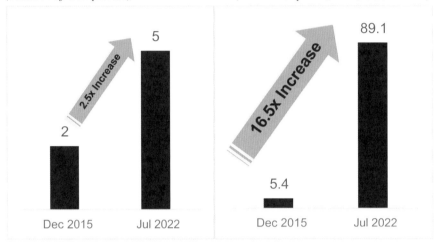

Source: FactSet, Press Releases. Latest market data as of 18ᵗʰ July, 2022, and reflects total for WuXi AppTec, Pharmaron, Tigermed, Joinn Laboratories and Frontage Holdings. The number of included companies represents the author's assessment of representative companies in the China CRO sector and may not represent a fully exhaustive list.

There are multiple drivers for the momentum in public market valuations. Some drivers are consistent with what global market investors have liked about this sector for many years. It is a high-growth segment with a high degree of defensibility and visibility. In serving a wide variety of clients, CROs are less vulnerable to binary risk compared to the usual biotech investment. The contract-based nature and backlog provide visibility into future revenue. The rise in biotech funding that reached all-time highs in 2020/2021 contributed to even stronger demand for CRO services.

Specific to China, CROs benefit from additional growth drivers. First, the rise of China as a clinical trial location helps speed up global drug development, given China's entry into the ICH, rapid regulatory reform and convergence with the rest of the world. China is also establishing itself as a location for effective early-stage R&D and source of innovation. Second, the rise of China biotech created a new client base with increasing access to funding, which will require high-quality services as well as support to globalize. All these factors contributed to China CROs having grown at a CAGR of approximately 30% over the past few years, all organic, while global peers have been growing at high single-digits to teens. As the sector becomes increasingly globalized and China becomes a more integral part of drug development, China-based CROs are also increasingly expanding overseas, through both M&A as well as organically.

The CDMO sector has also strong activity and interest, with the strong rise of WuXi Biologics in the biologics CDMO space. More recently, in December 2021, Asymchem (6821.HK, 002821.CN), a China-listed CDMO with number one position in China's commercial stage chemical drug CDMO market, and top five position globally in global drug substance CDMO market, conducted a successful Hong Kong dual listing, raising US$1.05 billion.

A few words on COVID-19, like other healthcare segments which rapidly adapted and responded to an unprecedented operating and economic environment, the clinical research industry also had to react accordingly to a world in which traditional, and in-person methods were no longer feasible, whether in terms of monitoring sites, or caring for clinical trial participants. The industry rapidly shifted to certain decentralized clinical trial methods, including greater use of remote monitoring, phone and video visits, and electronic forms. CROs build a level of knowledge in relation to do such work remotely and also adapted their processes and templates. It is interesting to note that many of these approaches had been around for several years, with the pandemic being a significant catalyst for adoption

While people concerned about the impact, market consensus seems to be that changes will ultimately be for the better. A late 2021 survey[767] found that 84% of respondents implemented new clinical trial approaches during the pandemic. Most importantly, the vast majority of respondents thought these had a positive overall impact, were more confident about the data generated from these new approaches and indicated that they would continue to use at least one of these new methods.

As a concluding note to this chapter, it is worth reminding readers that the newal

---

767 Clinical Trial Management in a Post-Pandemic World. October 2021. https://www. oracle.com/a/ocom/docs/industries/life-sciences/clinical-trial-management-post-covid.pdf

of developments in this chapter. The first modern clinical trial can be traced back to the 18th century, when James Lind evaluated six different treatments for scurvy in 12 patients onboard a naval ship called the HMS Salisbury. There were several other comparative studies in the 18th and 19th centuries. However, it was only the first half of the 20th century that saw the introduction of important concepts such as randomization and blinding, and only the second half of the 20th century that clearly established the randomized clinical trial as the preferred method in evaluating experimental drugs and medical interventions.[768] In the backdrop of late 20th century establishment of the modern clinical research paradigm, the CRO industry went from its beginnings in the 1980s to the current stage where CROs take US$70 billion of nearly US$200 billion in global R&D spending (based on figures in 2020). There has been rapid industry growth on the back of global drug innovation, unprecedented biopharma funding availability, regulatory reform and convergence in growth markets like China, and trials became increasingly complex. These trends resulted in hundreds of billions of dollars of value created in the public markets. Now is the best time to be in this sector, and the prospects of coming ten years are very exciting.

---

768 Lawrence M. Friedman, Curt D. Furbert, David L. DeMets, David M. Reboussin, Christopher B. Granger – *Fundamentals of Clinical Trials*, Firth Edition, Springer, 2015.

Chapter *13*

Oncolytic Virus (OV)

Cancer is one of the major challenges for global public health. There were approximately 19.23 million new cases diagnosed worldwide and 4.57 million cases in China.[769] Among those, solid tumors are majority, especially in China, that occupy 58.7% of all new−onset cancers.[770] Although treatments for solid tumors have ameliorated over the past decade, they are still unmet medical needs that are uncovered by current therapies due to low response rate, low efficacy, and serious adverse effects etc. Among numerous oncology treatments, chemotherapy has been broadly used in clinics and showed potent anti-tumor effect, but it results in serious adverse effects and unexpected adverse effects. For two decades, target-specific monoclonal antibody has been developed as anti-cancer agent and showed precise and specific tumor suppression, while it lost significant efficacy at late-stage disease and created resistance after multiple-cycle treatments. Lately, immunotherapy became highlight in oncology drug development and several immune checkpoint inhibitors were identified as anti-cancer candidates. The inhibition of PD-1/PD-L1 pathway showed an extremely promising and beneficial. However, PD-1/PD-L1 inhibitors lost long-term anti-cancer response although the biomarker expression of PD-1/PD-L1 existed, implying that tumor environment might develop novel inhibitory signal. To address these unmet medical needs and to overcome the shortcomings existing therapies, looking for novel treatments never cease. Recently, oncolytic virotherapy attracted lots of attention because of great effectiveness, barely adverse effects, and suitable combination. After first approval of oncolytic virus Oncorine® from Shanghai Sunway Biotech, there are two oncolytic viruses, Imlggic® (T-Vec) from Amgen and Delytact® from Daiichi Sankyo, approved in U.S. and Japan respetively. Oncorine® was approved by the Chinese State Food and Drug Administration

---

769 World Source: Globocan 2020, World Health Organization, International Agency for Research on Cancer. https://gco.iarc.fr/today/data/factsheets/populations/900-world-fact-sheet.pdf.

770 China Source: Globocan 2020, World Health Organization, International Agency for Research on Cancer. https://gco.iarc.fr/today/data/factsheets/populations/160-china-fact-sheet.pdf.

(now NMPA) in 2005, then used in combination with chemotherapy for the treatment of nasopharyngeal carcinoma; Amgen's Imlygic® was approved by the U.S. FDA in 2015 for the treatment of recurrent malignant melanoma that cannot be surgically removed; In June 2021, Daiichi Sankyo announced that it received conditional and time-limited approval from the Ministry of Health, Labour and Welfare for Delytact®, which is the first oncolytic virotherapy approved for the treatment of glioma in the world. OVs provide a breakthrough technology for cancer treatment and an opportunity to generate the unicorn life sciences companies.

Oncolytic Virus (OV) is defined as naturally occurring or genetically modified viruses that can selectively replicate in tumor cells. The difference in cellular metabolic environment between tumor cells and normal cells is leveraged by oncolytic viruses to maintain its function of selectivity, replication, and cytotoxicity only occurred in tumor cells. In the early 20th century, clinicians observed tumor shrinkage in cancer patients due to accidental viral infection and speculated that certain type of viruses would be a potential anti-cancer property since its preferential infection and killing. In the nearly 20 years after 1950, a large number of clinical trials emerged to use various wild-type viruses to treat tumors that marked the first attempt at oncolytic virotherapy. However, the individual spontaneous response by oncolytic virus treatment without statistic significancy was restricted to further development as anti-cancer agent. Till 1990s with completely understanding of molecular virology, genetic modification of viruses using molecular biology technology made the "dream comes true", which generated several druggable viruses with specific site deletions or insertions. For example, Herpes Simplex Virus-1 (HSV-1) based product HSV1716 from Virttu Biologics removed the neurovirulence factor ICP34.5, the gene has nerve cell tropism, to reduce neurotoxicity. Since the 21st century, new technology tools become popular and easy use, and many elements elucidated well to provide the platform for oncolytic virus drug development.

Upon viral genetic modification, oncolytic viruses are categorized into natural strain and artificial strain. Natural strain consists of wild-type viruses and naturally mutated viruses. Their virulence is difficult to control and the capability of tumor cell killing is limited. More important, natural virus strain is susceptible to activate the human immune system that initiates viral clearance pathway, compromising the antitumor effects. Artificial strain is able to overcome the shortcomings from natural strain with additional functionality by deletion of certain pathogenic genes, the insertion of exogenous therapeutic genes, and the introduction of new anti-cancer mechanisms. Most available oncolytic viruses are genetically modified to enhance tumor tropism and reduce virulence for non-neoplastic host cells.

Upon viral genetic characteristics, oncolytic viruses are also categorized into DNA virus and RNA virus. DNA oncolytic viruses include adenovirus, pox virus, herpes virus, etc., while RNA oncolytic viruses include reovirus, measles virus, Newcastle disease virus, etc. Both DNA viruses and RNA viruses used as an anti-cancer candidate directly or as a vector to reconstruct a novel anti-cancer candidate. Recently, various products, including adenovirus, herpes simplex virus, reovirus, coxsackie virus, vaccinia virus, retrovirus, and Newcastle disease virus, have been evaluated in clinical studies with promising anti-cancer properties.

Similar with other immunotherapies, oncolytic viruses have a multimodal mechanism of action which include three aspects:

i.   Oncolytic virus directly lyses tumor cell, defining as "direct killing". Upon oncolytic virus infects tumor cells, it can utilize cellular elements to initiate the process of viral DNA transcription and/or translation that facilitates virus replication and generates de novo[771] virus within tumor cells. Oncolytic viruses release and approach nearby unaffected tumor cells starting infection-replication process. Through the infect-replicate-reinfect cycles, oncolytic virus machinery lyses/destroys tumor cells directly that achieves the anti-cancer property.

ii. Oncolytic viruses indirectly induce anti-tumor effect, defining as "bystander effect". After oncolytic viruses infect tumor cells, human immunosurveillance system recognizes an intruder so that innate immune cells are recruited and activated. Following infection and replication, tumor cells lysed, and intracellular Tumor-Associated Antigens (TAA) are released, which are captured by Antigen-Presenting Cells (APCs) and delivered to Cytotoxic T Lymphocytes (CTLs). Upon receiving tumor antigen signals, CTLs are activated and released cytotoxic factors including interferon γ, perforin, granzyme B to enhance anti-tumor effect.

iii. Oncolytic viruses remodel tumor microenvironment enhancing lymphocyte infiltration. Firstly, tumor cells infected by oncolytic viruses may also

---

771 Biologically new or synthesis.

produce inflammatory factors e.g., IL-6, TNFα that induce tumor microenvironment inflammation. Secondly, infection of oncolytic viruses disrupts tumor microenvironment structure by degrading Matrix Metallo-Proteinase (MMP). Furthermore, oncolytic viruses modulate the signaling homeostasis by reversing perturb protein and suppressing tumor angiogenesis in tumor microenvironment. Therefore, oncolytic viruses can stimulate a proinflammatory environment by "cold tumor-to-hot tumor" switch and break down tumor resistant barriers, subsequently recruit and activate immune cells to counteract the immune evasiveness of cancers.

The advantages of oncolytic virus therapy are perceptive. Firstly, unlike other onco-therapies, oncolytic viruses show a broad-spectrum anti-tumor effect in many solid tumors including, but no limit to, melanoma, glioblastoma, breast cancer, ovarian cancer, non-small cell lung cancer, colon cancer, bladder cancer, head and neck cancer and prostate cancer. Secondly, Oncolytic viruses on human studies only have seen minor predicted adverse effects that mostly related to flu syndromes such as fever, fatigue, myalgia etc. Existing clinical data show that oncolytic virus therapy is generally safe compared to other immunotherapies. Simultaneously, through the genetic reengineering, the influence of oncolytic viruses on normal cells diminishes, improving its safety on clinical use. Thirdly, there are many transformation possibilities to oncolytic viruses that enhance tumor lysis and immune response. Introducing exogenous genes into oncolytic virus are common strategy to improve anti-cancer efficacy. For example, the U.S. FDA approval oncolytic virus T-Vec contains an affixed Granulocyte Macrophage Colony-Stimulating Factor (GM-CSF) that stimulate local immuno-response and recruit CTL into distant metastases lesion. T-Vec has exhibited remarkable success with up to a 15% complete regression in metastatic melanoma.[772] Fourthly, another feature of oncolytic viruses on oncologic care is as a therapeutic adjuvant. According to the principle of immuno-oncology therapeutic strategy, oncolytic viruses are feasible to combine with any oncotherapy agents, such as chemotherapy, targeted-specific drug, cellular therapy, and play a key role on combination treatment. Concomitant administration with other therapies has two primary aspects, which are augmenting other therapeutics and overcoming

---

772 Bammareddy, Praveen K., et al. Talimogene Laherparepvec (T-Vec) and Other Oncoytic Viruses for the Treatment of Melanoma. Amj Clin Dermatol.2017.18:1-15

primary resistance patterns.

Despite the prospects of oncolytic virotherapy, the technologies surrounding oncolytic virus therapy are still immature and there are challenges in terms of its application. Firstly, from present data, the efficacy of oncolytic virus therapy is relatively weak. The efficiency of tumor cell infection and replication is limited, and the sensitivity of oncolytic virus-induced tumor cell necrosis or programmed cell death needs improvement. Secondly, Oncolytic virus as a foreign pathogenic factor can be eliminated quickly by triggering an antiviral program in host immune system that attenuate viral loading into tumor. Thirdly, Oncolytic viruses are engineered for tumor tropism by deletion of virulence genes, which could impact its functionality in tumors. How to balance of selectivity and cytotoxicity should be considered and optimized during oncolytic virus drug development.

Local administration of oncolytic virotherapy into tumor is currently applied in clinics that could enable favorable pharmacokinetics and promising effect. The benefits of intra-tumoral injection include maximizing drug concentration at the target lesion, prolonging drug retained and limiting drug elimination. However, direct injection enables the prospect of delivering therapy via image guided, so far, the most resource-efficient modality localizing the target lesion, that create procedure difficulty and exclude uninjectable tumors. In the time of new and promising therapies, systemic administration[773] of oncolytic viruses will offer another avenue of hope for cancer patients. Still, there are many core challenges associated with systemic drug delivery, restricting tumor penetration, and affecting the therapeutic effect. For example, the concentration of oncolytic viruses in circulatory system is low due to great dilution, antibody neutralization, and immune elimination. Many biotech teams keep seeking better solution to the systemic administration of oncolytic virus. Enadenotucirev, an adenovirus-based recombinant oncolytic virus from PsiOxus Therapeutics, conducted phase I studies with intravenous administration in the U.S. and EU. PsiOxus has also collaborated with Bristol Myers Squibb (U.S.) to seek the anti-tumor efficacy of combination with Nivolumab on multiple solid tumors.

Another challenge for oncolytic viruses is manufacturing. As different oncolytic viruses have their own unique characteristics, the manufacturing process and

---

773 E.g., Intravenous therapy

scale up technologies must be specialized to each individual type. Optimization of culture conditions, improvement of virus yields and purity all must be addressed individually. For example, the manufacture of parvovirus H1 (H-1PV) uses suspension cells culturing in non-serum media, which increases virus yield and avoids employment of serum. However, its separation and purification process are more costly and time-consuming. And poxviruses commonly use adherent cell in manufacture process, which poses a huge challenge in terms of yield improvement. Furthermore, the harvest of virus from culturing cells plays another crucial step in manufacturing, which limits the virus yield generally. 1% of harvest rate increase means a lot for them. Therefore, companies need to focus on developing the appropriate manufacture procedure technology for each type of oncolytic virus.

Oncolytic virotherapy attracted wide attention and opened a prospective evolution in oncologic therapies. MNCs such as Amgen (U.S.) and Merck Sharp & Dohme (U.S.) put strategic imprints in this area in the past few years. In China, many companies also involved in oncolytic virus R&D, including ConVerd, Virogin, Binhui Biotech and ImmVira, that facilitate virus-related manufactory service provided by CDMO companies like OBiO Technology and Yuanxing Gene-tech. In addition, they were not only simple service but also the technique development cooperation on specific project.

Amgen, a flagship in biopharma, failed to meet its primary endpoint in the combination of T-Vec (OV) and KEYTRUDA® (PD-1) with a 692-patient phase III studies last year.[774] This was after its famed KEYNOTE-034 trials which historically increased Objective Response Rate (ORR), the Key Parameter of Immunotherapy, from 26% to 62% in 2017. However, VCN Biosciences announced the result of her six-year phase I clinical trials of adenovirus VCN-01 with intravenous injection on March 1, 2022, showing very excited data with an ORR of 50% against pancreatic cancer (deadliest carcinoma without any specific drug).[775] This orphan drug in EMA shines a light into the oncolytic virus field

---

774 ESMO report: http://dailyreporter.esmo.org/esmo-congress-2021/melanoma/the-role-of-t-vec-in-the-treatment-of-advanced-melanoma-just-a-matter-of-combinations

775 Garcia Carbonero Rocio, et al. "Pase I, multicenter, open-label study of intravenous VCN-01 oncolytic adenovirus with or without nab-pacilitaxel plus gemcitabine in patients with advanced solid tumors." Journal for immunotherapy of cancer10.3(2022). doi:10.1136/JITC-2021-003255

and we all look forward to the next phase II multi-center trials.

Faith in OV remains strong, but the path needs to be revisited. OV biotech companies differ the strategy from each other, so the time and data will reveal the coming stage. It will not take too long.

Progress in clinical trials of oncolytic virotherapies shows majority of candidates are in the pre-clinical and early clinical stages, with only a handful of products in the late clinical stage and already on the market. There is no "blockbuster drug" on the market yet, with the T-Vec's sales worldwide around US$70 million per year. But Frost & Sullivan expected the consecutive annual increase by 100% from 2023 to 2025.[776]

In the author's view, oncolytic virotherapy is still on an early stage of development, with both opportunities and challenges. Construction of armed virus and global patents is the starting line, and CMC (production or manufacturing) serves as the base for the preclinical stage. Finally, the "combo" therapeutic strategies with significant efficacy or breakthrough are the future of this field. Additionally, the technique and clinical collaboration between OV biotech companies and other anti-tumor partners may be the way to achieve the goal. We expect this promising therapy to play an important role in the treatment of solid tumors.

Below are examples of companies that the author and CRCP Fund has researched:

1.   US: CG ONCOLOGY

Founded in 2010 in California, the U.S., CG Oncology focuses on the development and translation of oncolytic virotherapy. Its core product CG0070 is an armed-adenovirus for non-muscle-invasive bladder cancer, and the stand-alone therapy developed into a global phase III clinical trial with significant clinical results. Meanwhile, the company also collaborated with both Merck Sharp & Dohme and Bristol Myers Squibb to use CG0070 in combination with KEYTRUDA® and OPDIVO® respectively for non-muscle-invasive bladder cancer. In March 2020, an agreement reached with Kissei Pharmaceutical in

---

776 Frost & Sullivan: China Oncolytic Virus Industry Development White Paper. 2021/09

Japan for CG0070: Kissei Pharmaceutical gains exclusive development and commercialization rights for CG0070 in Japan and other Asian countries, except China for a transaction value of up to US$140 million, plus royalties, including US$10 million upfront payment of licensing fee. Besides, another US$30 million in equity investment from Kissei is also made in this deal.[777]

2. CHINA

i. **Binhui Biologicals** is the only emerging OV biotech company which built its own CMC team and manufacture facilities at very beginning of enterprise establishment in China. Their unique HSV-2 product is now the project in advanced clinical stage, leading all other Chinese OV companies.

ii. **Virogin** featured in its TTDR backbone virus, developed multiple pipeline product. They initiated OV clinical trials in China, Australia, and the U.S., while they also stepped into the field of mRNA Vaccine with collaboration with China National Biotech Group (CNBG).

iii. **ImmVira** started with its HSV-1 project armed both cytokine and ICB, ahead of all the other OV biotech companies. They made a total amount of RMB1.15 billion deal for licensing its first product to Shanghai Pharma, which is also the very first licensing deal among Chinese OV companies. Recently, they even extended R&D to exosome vectors.

iv. **ConVerd** founded in 2012, developed multiple virus platforms including vaccinia virus, adenovirus and HSV for specific unmet clinical needs. The team focuses on their own systemic immuno-therapeutic theory and the combination therapy from the virus design and construction. Relatively, they filed more than 80 patent applications worldwide, which is likely to bring a prospective future to cancer therapy.

---

777 CG Oncology news release: https://www.cgoncology.com/news/press-release/032620/.

Chapter 14

Quantifying Circulatory miRNA for Disease Early Detection

1. INTRODUCTION TO miRNA BIOLOGY AND HISTORICAL MILESTONES

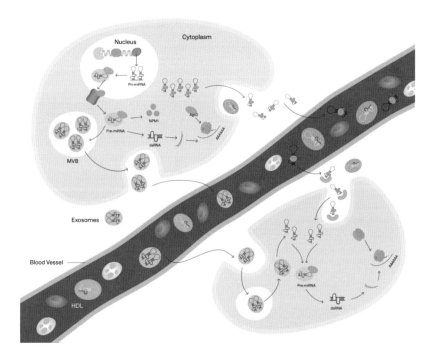

MicroRNAs (miRNAs) are short non-coding RNAs, approximately 16-22 nucleotides in length, discovered at the beginning of the 21st century. Over 48,000 miRNAs have been identified so far,[778] including 2654 miRNAs of human origin.[779] MiRNAs reduce the expression levels of target mRNAs by binding

---

778 miRBase release 22
779 Kozomara et al., 2019

to the three untranslated region, leading to cleavage of the mRNA, blocking its translation, or regulating its turnover.[780] A single miRNA may target several hundred different mRNAs. Over half of the human genes are predicted to be directly regulated by miRNAs.[781]

MiRNAs were discovered at the beginning of the 21st century and shown to play critical roles in both the development and disease pathogenesis. Over the past two decades, miRNAs being reported to have key regulatory roles in possibly every physiological and pathological aspect of biology. Dysfunctional expression of miRNAs is a feature of many pathological processes, including cancer, cardiovascular, metabolic, neuro-developmental, and autoimmune diseases.[782]

Insights into the functions of miRNAs in human development and diseases, especially in cancer, position miRNAs as attractive candidates for novel diagnostic and therapeutic approaches. MiRNA dysregulations are reported in all major human cancers, with growing evidence of their involvement in cancer hallmarks of proliferation, evasion of immunosurveillance, angiogenesis, activated invasion and metastasis, replicative immortality, resistance to cell death etc. Dynamic and real-time changes in miRNA expressions throughout different disease states have been observed. A multitude of studies examined the association between miRNAs expression and driver genetic alterations. Bjaanaes et al. identified 17 miRNAs differentially expressed between EGFR wild-type and EGFR-mutated lung adenocarcinomas, and three miRNAs differentially expressed between KRAS-mutated and KRAS-wild-type lung adenocarcinomas. Gasparini et al. found expression levels of miR-1253, miR-504, and miR-26a-5p could classify NSCLCs as rearranged-ALK, mutated EGFR, or mutated KRAS versus wild type. Recently, Kim et al. found that overexpression of miR-1343-3p and under-expression of miR-671-3p, miR-103a-3p, let-7e, and miR-342-3p to be distinctive features in the ALK-rearranged cases, compared to KRAS-mutated and EGFR-mutated cases.

Functional studies have confirmed that miRNA dysregulation is causal in many cases of cancer, with miRNAs act as tumor suppressors or oncogenes (oncomiRs). Several miRNA-targeted therapeutics reached clinical development, including a

---

780 Ameres and Zamore, 2013

781 Friedman et al., 2009

782 Rupaimoole and Slack, 2017

mimic of tumor suppressor miRNA miR-34, which reached phase I clinical trials for treating cancer, and antimiRs targeted at miR-122, which reached phase II trials for treating hepatitis.

While the majority of miRNAs found within the cells, a significant proportion of miRNAs also found in extracellular environments, including various biological fluids – known as circulating miRNAs.[783] The possibility of circulating miRNAs become easily accessible disease biomarkers for diagnosis and prognosis was brought up when miRNAs isolated from patient serum[784] and specific expression patterns observed across different groups of diseases.[785] Tumor-specific circulating miRNAs were discovered in patients with diffused large B-cell lymphoma; where elevated levels of miR21 correlated with improved relapse free survival. In an elegant study of a xenograft mouse prostate cancer model, tumor-derived miR629 and miR660 circulated in peripheral blood with 100% sensitivity and specificity. A myriad of subsequent studies further confirmed specific miRNA signatures in major cancers and many other types of human diseases,[786] and showed that such signatures can be measured in biofluids.[787] The increasing body of evidence led to the initiation of many clinical trials[788] as well as international efforts for characterization of circulating miRNA function and standardization of the miRNA analysis, such as Extracellular RNA Communication Consortium[789] and CANCER-ID.[790] Intriguingly, recent studies exemplified the possibility that tumor-derived miRNAs modulate non-tumor cells to the benefit of tumor.[791] The facts that miRNAs presented in various body fluids, are stable and may reflect the pathophysiologic condition of the tissue of origin brought them to attention as a new yet promising group of biomarkers, which could offer high clinical values for early disease detection, response to therapy, progression, and recurrence.

---

783 Pritchard et al., 2012a

784 Lawrie et al., 2008; Mitchell et al., 2008

785 Chen et al., 2008

786 Izzotti et al., 2016; Larrea et al., 2016; Matsuzaki and Ochiya, 2017

787 Godoy et al., 2018; Weber et al., 2010

788 Anfossi et al., 2018

789 ERCC: https://exrna.org/

790 https://www.cancerid.eu

791 Ruivo et al., 2017

2. THE ORIGIN, STABILITY, AND FUNCTIONS OF CIRCULATING miRNAs

The diagnostic and prognostic potential of circulating miRNAs as cancer biomarkers relies mainly on their high stability and resistance to storage handling. Unlike DNA and other RNA species, circulating miRNAs consistently remain stable even in severe conditions that would normally degrade most nucleic acids, such as boiling, very low or high pH levels, extended storage, repeated freeze–thaw cycles and fragmentation by chemical agents and enzymes.[792] Studies have demonstrated that miRNAs can be quantified in ten-year-old archived human serum and plasma, and detectable even in unrefrigerated dried serum blots.

This stability of circulating miRNAs triggered significant appeal from the field. Investigations subsequently showed that circulating miRNAs encapsulated inside extracellular vesicles of endocytic origin called exosomes or microvesicles (30–100 nm) or are bound by protein and lipoprotein complexes, thus protecting them from degradation even in harsh environment. Tumor-derived exosomes and associated miRNA signatures were reported in ovarian cancer patients. Such miRNA signatures correlated significantly with primary tumor-miRNA expression in cancer patients compared with benign cases and were not observed in healthy control subjects. Correlation of the circulating exosomal miRNA signatures and that in originating tumor cells was also found in lung adenocarcinoma, with a significant difference in exosomal miRNA levels between cancer patients and controls. Exosomal miRNAs may therefore provide clinically valuable information for the detection of human diseases. Several research groups have curated the expression of EV-associated biomarkers in various biospecimens across different diseases and organized the information in databases, such as EVmiRNA (miRNA-specific),[793] EVAtlas (ncRNA-specific)[794] and Vesiclepedia. These databases not only enable the generation of new hypothesis to identify

---

792 Chen et al., 2008; Gilad et al., 2008; Mitchell et al., 2008

793 Liu, T.; Zhang, Q.; Zhang, J.; Li, C.; Miao, Y.R.; Lei, Q.; Li, Q.; Guo, A.Y. EVmiRNA: *A database of miRNA profiling in extracellular vesicles. Nucleic Acids Res.* 2019, *47*, D89–D93.

794 Liu, C.J.; Xie, G.Y.; Miao, Y.R.; Xia, M.; Wang, Y.; Lei, Q.; Zhang, Q.; Guo, A.Y. EVAtlas: *A comprehensive database for ncRNA expression in human extracellular vesicles.* Nucleic Acids Res. 2022, *50*, D111–D117

actionable biological pathways that promote the disease state, but also facilitate the development of miRNA/ncRNA-based in vitro diagnostics.

Notably, growing evidence indicates packaging and release of circulating miRNA may occur non-randomly. Studies demonstrated nearly 30% of released miRNAs in vitro and in vivo do not reflect the expression profile found in donor cells, suggesting that specific miRNAs can be selectively retained intracellularly or released into extracellular space. Secretion of miRNAs by tumor cells may be associated with their ability to induce changes in the surrounding micro-environment for their own benefit and suppress immune surveillance.

3. THE PAST AND PRESENT OF miRNA DIAGNOSTICS

The unique biology and relatively high chemical stability of miRNAs in body Fluids and Formalin-Fixed Tissues (FFPE) has led to the development and commercialization of a number of miRNA diagnostic tests over the last decade.

The Rosetta Cancer Origin Test™ was the first miRNA-based test to receive Medicare coverage.[795] The assay utilized a microarray-based technology to measure 64 miRNAs from FFPE tissues, a signature that could identify 42 tumor types with a high concordance of 92% to final diagnosis achieved through more extensive clinical and pathological examinations. The test served as a useful tool for physicians to identify tumor origin in cancer of unknown primary and challenging metastatic cases. Based on similar approaches, this Israel headquartered and NASDAQ listed company Rosetta launched several others tissue miRNA tests including, 1) Rosetta Lung Cancer Test[TM], an eight-miRNA qPCR test which discriminates squamous cell cancers from adenocarcinomas for therapeutic guidance, 2) Rosetta Mesothelioma Test[TM], a three-miRNA qPCR test which distinguishes mesothelioma from carcinomas in the lung or pleura with high sensitivity, 3) Rosetta Kidney Cancer Test[TM], a 24-miR microarray based test which distinguishes between benign oncotytoma and malignant Renal Cell Carcinoma (RCC), and further sub-classified RCC into clear cells, papillary and chromophobe subtypes. The panel of tissue-based Rosetta tests led to significant interests from oncologists and achieved early success for miRNA-based diagnostics.

---

795 May 2012

The ThyraMIR® test, a ten-miRNA classifier for evaluating indeterminate thyroid nodules, was the second tissue-based miRNA test to receive Medicare reimbursement. First developed by Asuragen and subsequently commercialized by Interpace Biosciences, ThyraMIR® test achieved another milestone in 2020, when the Center for Medicare and Medicaid Services (CMS) increased the Medicare reimbursement for this miRNA classifier from approximately US$1,800 to US$3,000 reflecting a re-evaluation of the technical and clinical performance of the test relative to other molecular tests in the market. It should be noted that ThyraMIR® can be used in combination with a DNA mutational panel (ThyGeNEXT®). The latest studies have manifested the complementary information from miRNA markers and that of driver mutations such as BRAF, TERT, RET and RAS yielded a combined performance of 95% sensitivity and 90% specificity, significantly higher than competing technologies based on NGS alone. This is consistent with an increasing body of evidence highlighting the complementarity of biological information embedded in microRNA biomarkers to other types of analytes such as DNA, mRNA and proteins. For instance, in a recent comprehensive study involving 1,710 heart failures and control patients in Singapore and New Zealand, Wong et al found that the combination of eight-miRNA PCR panel with the protein marker NT-proBNP yielded almost perfect AUC of 0.97-0.99, a significant improvement over either type of markers alone. The miRNA panel was better in identifying the Heart Failure with preserved Ejection Fraction (HFpEF) subtype while NT-proBNP was superior in identifying the Heart Failure with Reduced Ejection (HFrEF) subtype. The authors concluded that combining the miRNA panel with the current clinical gold standard of NT-proBNP could improve the accuracy and specificity in identifying non-acute heart failure where clinical assessment and imaging may not be definitive, especially in HFpEF.[796]

For many types of cancer, there is currently a lack of early detection methods or screening tests, making the issue of early cancer detection a promising field for miRNA-based diagnostics. Based on the above-mentioned features of cancer cell and tissue-specific expression profiles and circulation in body fluids, miRNAs exhibit some characteristics for ideal biomarkers, significant efforts have been dedicated towards identifying circulating miRNA as biomarkers

---

796 JAmCollCardiol 2019; 73: 1300–13

suitable for screening and early detection of high incidence and high mortality cancers. Since 2014, large-scaled national programs were launched in the U.S., Singapore, Japan, and China with a combined research funding of more than US$300 million, significantly accelerating the discovery and translation of miRNA cancer biomarkers. In 2018, a seven-miRNA PCR test was approved by the China FDA (currently NPMA) as an adjunctive diagnostic test for detection of liver cancer, especially in high-risk patients with non-elevated AFP levels. In 2019, a 12-miRNA PCR test (GASTROClear®) became the first miRNA test to have undergone a large, prospective, multi-center screening trial involving 5,248 patients, and received regulatory approval in Singapore as a molecular screening test for the early detection of gastric cancer. This marks a significant milestone in the clinical translation of miRNA since its discovery in humans in 2000. The trial was among the largest for any molecular cancer screening tests in the last decade, with only two other approved molecular screening tests having undergone prospective trials at similar scale (Cologuard® by Exact Sciences, N=9,989, the U.S. FDA approved; and ColoClear® by New Horizon Health, N=5,881, China NMPA approved). Benchmarked against the clinical gold standard of gastroscopy and pathological examination, the 12-miRNA PCR test demonstrated an overall accuracy of 0.85 (AUC), a significant improvement over existing biomarkers such as Helicobacter pylori (HP, AUC=0.64) serology, serum pepsinogens (PGs, AUC=0.64), "ABC" method (AUC=0.65), Carcinoembryonic Antigen (CEA, AUC=0.58) and cancer antigen 19–9 (CA19-9, AUC=0.60). Most encouragingly, the 12-miRNA test demonstrated a sensitivity of 87.5% in detecting stage 1 gastric cancer and could even detect 60% of stage 0 gastric cancer or high-grade dysplasia. Cost-effectiveness analysis based on mass screening of Singaporean population demonstrated an incremental cost-effectiveness ratio (ICERs) of US$44,531/QALY, which is cost-effective in the local context, compared with the WHO-CHOICE threshold of approximately US$50,000/QALY. The cost-effectiveness of such a blood test is considerably better when compared to the ICERs of LDCT based lung cancer screening (US$75,000/QALY in the lowest risk decile to US$53,000/QALY in the highest risk decile based on the U.S. NLST study). Finally, in Oct 2020, the U.S. FDA granted Breakthrough Device designation to miRNA Sentinel™ PCC4 assay, a urine-based miRNA test to stratify patients into no evidence, low, intermediate, or high risk of prostate cancer to support early detection and more precise management of prostate cancer.

4. CHALLENGES IN TRANSLATING miRNA DISCOVERIES: A NEED FOR STANDARDIZATION

The translation of miRNA discoveries from bench-to-bedside has slowed, in part due to the differences in how clinical cohort studies were conducted. Variations in study design, selection of study participants, sample size, biospecimen type, isolation procedure, molecular profiling approach and data analytic used appear to be unavoidable at face value.[797] For example, the design of various clinical studies involving the same cancer type can vary dramatically, thereby making it extremely difficult for robust meta-analyses of existing datasets to generate useful insights to disease pathophysiology. We envisage that future studies involve the determination of the diagnostic accuracy of miRNA biomarkers can benefit from the use of several good study design elements, including consecutive enrollment of participants with uniform inclusion and exclusion criteria, blinded testing and interpretation, establishment of pre-specified thresholds, the use of one reference standard for all subjects and the application of relevant statistical analyses.

In addition, numerous clinical oncology studies have also confounded with many studies' participant-related variables such as age, race, ethnicity, gender, stage of cancer, cancer risk factors, comorbidities as well as concomitant medications. If these variables are left unchecked, it could deepen the existing data reproducibility crisis encountered by the biomedical community and diminish the clinical utility of any promising biomarker detection assays.

Although big data can be readily generated by the NGS, microarray and RT-qPCR approaches, data concordance for the same sample among these technology platforms remains to be poor. For instance, the human miRnome, reported by Next-Generation-Sequencing (NGS) to comprise of 2,654 human miRNAs, but only less than a third of them, the so-called "high confidence

---

797 Galvão-Lima, L.J.; Morais, A.H.; Valentim, R.A.; Barreto, E.J. miRNAs as biomarkers for early cancer detection and their application in the development of new diagnostic tools. *Biomed. Eng. Online* 2021, *20*, 21.; Singh, R.; Ramasubramanian, B.; Kanji, S.; Chakraborty, A.R.; Haque, S.J.; Chakravarti, *A. Circulating microRNAs in cancer: Hope or hype?* Cancer Lett. 2016, *381*, 113–121.; Witwer, K.W. *Circulating microRNA biomarker studies: Pitfalls and potential solutions*. Clin. Chem. 2015, *61*, 56–63.

miRNAs", can be cross-validated by other platforms.[798] The development of new bioinformatics algorithms can therefore help reduce or better still, eliminate false positives that have been incorrectly identified by the NGS approach.

To enable the bench-to-bedside translatability of experimental findings, standardization of the conduct of large multi-center prospective clinical studies, as well as pre-analytical preparation of clinical samples prior to storage in established biobanks are much needed. To enhance data reproducibility and translation of miRNA clinical assays, a national standard (SS656) was established in Singapore to guide the design, development, and performance evaluation of miRNA-based molecular diagnostic assays. This guide includes recommended standard operating procedures and reference materials that will help identify and correct pre-analytical variables, including sample handling from collection through transportation, processing, and storage. Furthermore, the development of specific reporting guidelines, such as consortium for randomized controlled studies, could also complement the SS656 standard by refining data reporting. This will undoubtedly help others better understand the study design and to assess the validity of findings.[799] Ongoing research that focuses on building an open access molecular atlas may also aid to deepen the understanding on the baseline expression pattern of miRNAs in various organs, tissues, and even distinct cell types, as well as documenting variations in miRNA expression that are associated with other physiological and pathological conditions, such organ-related injuries or inflammation after surgery.[800]

5. CONCLUSION AND OUTLOOK

The ability to detect and accurately measure disease-associated biomarkers, such as miRNAs, in liquid biopsy offers an unprecedented opportunity to achieve

798 Kozomara, A.; Birgaoanu, M.; Griffiths-Jones, S. miRBase: *From microRNA sequences to function*. Nucleic Acids Res. 2019, 47, D155–D162

799 Moher, D.; Hopewell, S.; Schulz, K.F.; Montori, V.; Gøtzsche, P.C.; Devereaux, P.J.; Elbourne, D.; Egger, M.; *Altman, D.G. CONSORT 2010 Explanation and Elaboration: Updated guidelines for reporting parallel group randomised trials. BMJ* 2010, *340*, c869.

800 Laterza, O.F.; Lim, L.; Garrett-Engele, P.W.; Vlasakova, K.; Muniappa, N.; Tanaka, W.K.; Johnson, J.M.; Sina, J.F.; Fare, T.L.; *Sistare, F.D. Plasma MicroRNAs as sensitive and specific biomarkers of tissue injury. Clin. Chem.* 2009, *55*, 1977–1983.

early disease detection and the delivery of precision preventive healthcare. The increasing body of clinical evidence gathered through large, prospective, multi-center clinical studies, as well as the regulatory approval and recognition both in Asia and the U.S. signify a wider recognition of the clinical value and utility of miRNA-based tests. Optimized pre-analytical sample handling and reliable analytics will be essential in ensuring clinically actionable results. Based on public information of various companies' miRNA pipeline, it is expected that a substantial number of tissue and biofluid-based miRNA tests will enter clinical practice both as Lab-Developed-Tests (LDT) and In Vitro Diagnostics (IVD), for applications both in cancer, cardiovascular and other chronic and acute diseases. With the advent of fully automated molecular testing platforms, or even Point-Of-Care-Testing (POCT) devices, precise quantification of miRNA expression will further promote preventive healthcare by generating, analyzing (by Artificial Intelligence-driven bioinformatics), collating (cloud-based health information system or electronic medical record) and returning actionable test results at primary care clinics or in the comfort of one's home (by using smart phones or wearables) in near real-time. Coupled with advanced imaging modalities and/or other standard-of-care assays, miRNA-powered multiomics cancer diagnostics are poised to shine in this golden era of precision medicine.

Chapter 15

3D Printed Pharmaceuticals

The concept of 3D printing (3DP) originated in the U.S. in the late 19th century with the development of photographic sculpture and geomorphic techniques. It did not take shape until the late 1980s when the Massachusetts Institute of Technology (MIT) developed it. 3D printing is based on a computer-aided design of a three-dimensional digital model, which is programmed to produce objects with a special shape or complex internal structure quickly and precisely through a "Layer by Layer" construction process of bondable materials such as metals, polymers and slurries.

1. OVERVIEW OF GLOBAL R&D AND MANUFACTURING OF PHARMACEUTICAL 3D PRINTING TECHNOLOGY

Pharmaceutical 3D printing is an emerging technological field in recent years. In June 1996, Professor Michael Cima of MIT first reported that Powder Binding (PB) 3D printing could be used in the field of pharmaceuticals. Since then, 3D printing has attracted a number of pharmaceutical companies and research institutes to explore this technology due to its advantages over traditional pharmaceutical technologies in terms of product design complexity, personalized drug delivery and on-demand manufacturing. The three main types of 3D printing technologies used in pharmaceutical manufacturing are Binder Jetting, Powder Bed Fusion and Material Extrusion.

Binder Jetting was one of the first 3D printing technologies to be applied to pharmaceuticals, most notably ZipDose®, developed by Aprecia. As one of the pioneers in the field of 3D printed pharmaceuticals, Aprecia was founded in 2003 in the U.S. and has been developing the mass-produced ZipDose® technology based on MIT's powder fusion 3D printing principles for nearly ten years. ZipDose® is used to prepare high-dose, fast-acting medications for central nervous system disorders. The adhesive-bonded tablets are porous and disintegrate quickly within seconds of contact with water, in turn assisting elderly patients and children with swallowing difficulties. On 31st July, 2015, Aprecia received the U.S. FDA approval for Spritam® (levetiracetam), the first 3D printed antiepileptic drug developed using ZipDose® technology. This marks the approval of 3D printing as an emerging pharmaceutical manufacturing technology by the U.S. regulatory authorities. However, Spritam® did not perform well in the market due to the high number of commercial competitors for the active pharmaceutical ingredient levetiracetam. Aprecia subsequently transformed into a pharmaceutical technology platform company based on its technological strengths, with a business model focused on the co-development and production of new drug products and global business partnerships with major multinational pharmaceutical and biotechnology companies.

Another type of 3D printing technology applied to the pharmaceutical sector is the powder bed melting technology represented by Selective Laser Sintering (SLS). Similar to the challenges of powder bonding, SLS requires pre-fabrication of the powder containing the drug and laser absorber, and post-powder removal and powder recovery. It does not offer much flexibility in the design of the internal structure of the drug dosage form, but it does allow some control of the drug release rate by adjusting the laser scanning speed to influence the print tightness of the tablet. The conventional SLS printing process of point-by-point melting and layer-by-layer stacking has limited the use of SLS in large-scale drug production, resulting in poor industrialization. Merck KGaA (Germany) has been experimenting with SLS technology for the development and production of drugs for clinical trials since 2020, and has entered a partnership with AMCM, a subsidiary of EOS (Germany), who is the world's largest manufacturer of selective laser sintering 3D printing equipment. Together, they plan to develop scale-up pharmaceutical SLS printing equipment for commercial production in the future.

Unlike the two powder-bed-based 3D printing technologies mentioned above, material extrusion 3D printing allows for layer-by-layer curing of drug-containing semi-solids by extruding them through an extrusion head. By controlling the precise movement of the print head or printing platform in all three dimensions, material extrusion technology allows for the construction of complex geometries and internal structures, thereby extrapolating to the controlled release of complex designed drugs. As one of the most popular material extrusion 3D printing technologies, Fused Deposition Modeling (FDM) is widely used in pharmaceutical 3D printing research due to its low equipment cost and operational flexibility. However, FDM technology and printers are not specifically developed to meet pharmaceutical requirements and regulations, and their application to pharmaceutical preparations has revealed a number of drawbacks, such as the need for prefabricated wire, low print accuracy (more than ±10% quality deviation), and difficulties in achieving scale and continuity of production. All these factors have prevented meaningful application of FDM technology to the development and commercial production of pharmaceutical products. It is more often used for personalized pharmaceutical manufacturing or as a tool to accelerate the early development of new drug products with drug release requirements. For example, Merck (U.S.) has chosen to use a combination of FDM printing and infusion to rapidly produce small batches of drug dosage forms with different release characteristics, as well as early clinical trials to identify prototype drug dosage forms with an ideal drug time-concentration profile. In the mid- to late-stage clinical and commercial production phases however, Merck continues to use traditional drug manufacturing technologies.

To expand on applying the principle of material extrusion to pharmaceutical manufacturing, Triastek, Inc. (China) and FabRx (U.K.) have developed the novel 3D printing technologies, Melt Extrusion Deposition™ (MED) and Direct Powder Extrusion™ (DPE) respectively. FabRx is a leader in pharmaceutical 3D printing, and they are one of the most active companies in this field and was founded in 2014 by two professors from University College London (UCL), Abdul Basit and Simon Gaisford. Since its inception, they have explored and researched several 3D printed drug technologies and have developed DPE™ technology to address the shortcomings of FDM, namely the pre-preparation of drug-containing wires. FabRx used powdered raw materials to reduce the constraints on material selection, thereby avoiding the need for a lengthy drug-containing wire prescription development process. DPE™ is suitable for the rapid and flexible preparation of multiple drug dosage forms in a personalized pharmaceutical setting and may also be applied in the future to accelerate the early development of pharmaceutical products. However, DPE™ does not address the shortcomings of FDM in terms of print accuracy, scalability, and continuous production.

The MED™ technology developed by Triastek was based on the characteristics of polymeric pharmaceutical adjuvants specific for pharmaceutical applications. Subsequently, all design and development of specialized 3D printing equipment are based on the MED™ process. Founded by Dr. Senping Cheng, a serial entrepreneur with experiences both in U.S. and China, and Dr. Xiaoling Li, a U.S.-based pharmaceutical expert and educator, Triastek has developed a proprietary 3D printing platform based on MED™ 3D printing technology for the entire pharmaceutical chain, from dosage form design and digital product development to intelligent pharmaceutical manufacturing.

MED 3D printing directly melts the powdered raw materials into a flowable semi-solid, and through a precise extrusion mechanism and accurate control of material temperature and pressure, the molten drug-containing material is extruded with high precision and printed in layers to produce a pre-designed three-dimensional structured pharmaceutical product. The process requires no wire preparation and no secondary heating. MED™ has an advantage over Direct Powder Extrusion™ (DPE), it uses a homogenous extrusion unit to efficiently mix, melt and deliver the API and auxiliary powders, offering the possibility of continuous feeding and printing. The unique precision extrusion unit enables high-precision printing with a tablet quality deviation of less than ±1%. Creative engineering designs such as multiple printing stations and print head arrays enable the use of multiple materials to build complex internal three-dimensional structures of drugs at will, as well as efficient, high-throughput production at scale. This enables it to become the most versatile and clinically useful 3D printed drug technology for solid dosage forms to date.

Such emerging technology revolutionizes the way traditional solids are developed and produced, as well as the way drugs are delivered in vivo. Through a unique three-dimensional structure design within the pharmaceutical dosage form, MED allows for precise programmatic control of the timing, site and rate of drug release, as well as flexible combinations of drug release characteristics. Practically, this means solving problems that cannot be addressed with existing formulation technologies and providing a rich range of product design tools to meet various clinical needs. The innovative "Formulation by Design (3DFbD®)" digital formulation development method has trivialized the traditional trial-and-error approach to formulation development, significantly improving the efficiency and success rate of new drug product development and reducing development time and costs. Notably, the continuous and digital MED 3D printed drug production line developed by Triastek is a continuous production process with real-time quality control through Process Analysis Technology (PAT), which is significantly better than traditional pharmaceutical production in terms of product quality and production cost. This digital pharmaceutical manufacturing technology will introduce new models to manage production and regulation.

In April 2020, MED 3D printing technology was accepted by the U.S. FDA's Emerging Technologies Team (ETT), which recognized it as a new means of producing solids with controlled release. The team appreciated this fully automated, integrated Process Analysis Technology (PAT) and feedback-controlled process innovation. In January 2021, T19, the first drug product developed by Triastek using MED 3D printing technology, received clinical approval Investigational New Drug (IND) from the U.S. FDA, making it the second 3D printed drug product in the world to submit an IND to the U.S. FDA and the first 3D printed drug product to enter the registration process in China. This is a major breakthrough for 3D printing technology in the global pharmaceutical manufacturing sector.

2. DEVELOPMENT TREND OF PHARMACEUTICAL 3D PRINTING

1) 3D printing of pharmaceuticals is set to become a hot topic in the pharmaceutical industry due to its fast, flexible, and precisely controlled release characteristics.

Over the years, leading companies in the field of pharmaceutical 3D printing have emerged. This technology offers significant technological advantages over traditional pharmaceutical processes in terms of pharmaceutical product design, accelerated drug development and advanced production manufacturing. As a result, the new players are on the path to regulatory registration through their products and will attract many traditional pharmaceutical companies to use such emerging technologies for drug development and production. Through technical collaborations with traditional pharmaceutical companies, pharmaceutical 3D printing companies are exploring additional R&D, production, and commercial applications, consequently accelerating the refinement and widespread use of new technologies.

2) 3D printing of drugs has shown great potential for both large-scale production and personalized drug use.

As personalized medicine requires breaking through greater regulatory barriers and potentially establishing new systems of commercial distribution of medicines, it is predicted that large-scale 3D printing of medicines will be the first to achieve commercial success. Regulatory authorities in Europe and the U.S. are working with pharmaceutical companies to explore guidelines for personalized medicines, helping new technologies to address the different clinical needs of patients due to their individual differences. While China and the U.S. have pioneered the scale-up of 3D printing for medicines, Europe is more active in the research and application of 3D printing for personalization of medicines. It is expected that the commercialization of 3D printed drugs will take place in these major drug market countries.

3) Pharmaceutical 3D printing will become an important advanced technology for the development and production of future solid dosage forms and product updates.

Solid-state pharmaceuticals have been produced for over 100 years and have a global market size of hundreds of billions of U.S. dollars. Compared to other industries such as semiconductors and automobiles, the pharmaceutical industry is relatively slow to innovate and iterate due to stringent regulations and the challenges of new technology development. Pharmaceutical 3D printing is one of the most promising technologies that can be seen to transform the manufacturing of pharmaceuticals. In 2017, the U.S. FDA issued industry guidance to facilitate the use of emerging technologies in pharmaceutical manufacturing, of which 3D printing and continuous manufacturing are key strategic directions.

4) 3D printing of medicines is a core technology for smart pharmaceutical manufacturing and will propel the pharmaceutical industry into a new era of intelligent pharma.

Pharmaceutical 3D printing is a digital production technology based on computer modelling, which forms the basis for the digital production of medicines. Through the design of pharmaceutical 3D printing equipment and production lines, other advanced informative technologies such as Big Data, Artificial Intelligence (AI), the Internet of Things (IoT) and sophisticated in-line physical and chemical detection technologies can be used in the production process and quality management of pharmaceuticals. Many of the production and inspection processes have been designed unmanned by integration of robots. At the same time, data-based central control systems can be used to monitor, feedback and manage digital production lines worldwide. The large amount of process and inspection data generated during the development and production of 3D printed drugs, combined with the models and algorithms developed in the technology platform, allows big data analytics and artificial intelligence technologies to be applied, fed back, and optimized throughout the process of 3D printed drug development and production, leading to intelligent pharma in the future.

PART 5

Hong Kong, a Rising Global Star in Life Sciences

Chapter 16

A Snapshot of Hong Kong's Life Sciences and Technology

Hong Kong is the Special Administrative Region[801] (SAR) of the People's Republic of China. As one of the global leading financial, and commercial centers, Hong Kong ranked the first in fund raised via Initial Public Offering (IPO) in six out of the past ten years, more than any other cities in the world. It also ranked second in life sciences IPO center, just after New York.

Along with Shanghai, Hong Kong is China's leading financial center as well as a commerce center trading with partners from Southeast Asia and others. Hong Kong's latest position in China's national development blueprint is to become a national innovation center.

Hong Kong's economy is well-known for its open markets, low tax rates, and limited government intervention, which combine to make it one of the freest economies across the globe.[802] Particularly, its tax system is simple, efficient, and straightforward: profit tax rate is at 8.25% for the first assessment HK\$2 million profits, and 16.5% for the remaining profits over. It also has neither sales tax nor capital gain tax.

Hong Kong began as a city with immigrants. Most of early habitants came from Guangdong province, China (pronounced as Canton), that is why local Hong Kong language is called Cantonese. Later, many moved in from Fujian province as well. During the World War II, there was a huge drop in the size of population as the Japanese defeated the British, who had occupied Hong Kong back then. The Japanese murdered many local Hong Kong people and forced them to leave, from 1941 to 1945, the population dwindled from 1.6 million to 600,000. A wave of people flooded in from the mainland China after the Chinese communist party retrieved authority in 1949 and during the Cultural Revolution.

---

801 https://www.investhk.gov.hk/

802 https://hongkongbusiness.hk/news/hk-still-worlds-freest-economy-fraser-institute

In 2022, Hong Kong population size was approximately 7.5 million, with four million workforces. Based on World Bank data, Hong Kong's GDP was approximately US$370 billion in 2021, likewise to Singapore, Malaysia, Philippines, and the per capita GDP around US$50,000.

Geographically, Hong Kong is the center of Asia. It takes four to five hours flight time to reach Beijing, Singapore, Tokyo, Seoul, Bangkok, Manila, the capitals of major Asian countries, accessing to 50% of the world population. Hong Kong consists of Hong Kong Island, Lantau Island, the Kowloon Peninsula, and the New Territories. It has long been a vibrant metropolis and a vital link between Mainland China and other parts of the world.

Hong Kong has built up a global competitive life sciences ecosystem, some of key elements are HKEX and its supporting services, professional incubation centers, the integration with the Greater Bay Area (GBA), world-class universities, active start-ups, and the links to other countries.

1. HKEX[803]

The author believes, for any company to claim itself as a global company, it must be listed in both New York and Hong Kong in the future.

In Hong Kong, almost all the global prestigious and reputable law firms, investment banks, and accounting and auditing firms have local offices to facilitate Initial Public Offering (IPO) listings and other services. Potential listing companies have a selection of services partners, both local and international, to fit their own needs. It is common that most companies work with more than one firm to handle various needs. Majority of professionals are proficient in English, Cantonese, and Mandarin; hence language barriers are minimized to do business.

In 2023, HKEX Chairwoman Laura Cha spoke at Davos that Asia must play a bigger role in international cooperation. Despite many uncertainties, the world's center of gravity continues to shift East with China as the focal point. As China's role in the global economy grows, so will Hong Kong's role as a super

---

803 https://www.hkex.com.hk/?sc_lang=zh-HK

connector.[804]

HKEX Chapter 18A,[805] which was initiated in 2018, is an important milestone for global life sciences industry, for the following reasons. Firstly, for China-based companies, this provides another listing alternative, besides New York. As the U.S.-China tension worsens, listing in Hong Kong appeals to many. Secondly, for China or Asia based investors, they can easily trade stocks and participate in local initial public offerings process. Better still, there is no 12-hour time difference. Thirdly, for other companies which plan to develop China or Asia markets, Hong Kong is clearly a better location. Fourthly, as the trust in U.S. dollar hegemony falls dramatically, there is an urgent need for replacements.

From 2018 to 2021, a total of 48 biotech companies have been listed in Hong Kong under the sections of Listing Rules 18A, raising a total of HK$112.6 billion. Moreover, as of December 2021, another 23 companies submitted forms and pending approval. In 2018, 2019, 2020 and 2021, there were 5, 9, 14 and 20 companies listed on Chapter 18A respectively, with annual fundraising of HK$18.5 billion, HK$16.1 billion, HK$40.4 billion and HK$37.7 billion respectively. The largest fund raised per company was HK$7.085 billion and the smallest was HK$479 million, with an average of HK$2.346 billion.

The total market capitalization of the 48 Chapter 18A biotech companies in Hong Kong stocks was HK$965 billion as of December 31, 2021, with great disparity between the biggest (BeiGene at HK$222.9 billion) and smallest (MedBot-B at HK$53.6 billion) companies.

Analysis of Chapter 18A-Listed Biotech Companies

As of December 31, 2021, among the 71 biotechnology companies (48 listed and 23 submitted for approval) with the "-B" suffix, their products layout corresponds to 30 pathogenic sites, including the liver, lung, stomach, blood vessels, lymph, chest, orthopedics, and other pathogenic sites, while the four companies which

---

804 https://www.hkexgroup.com/Media-Centre/Insight/Insight/2023/HKEX-Insight/Hong-Kong-Perspectives-Whats-Next?sc_lang=en

805 https://www.hkex.com.hk/-/media/HKEX-Market/Listing/Rules-and-Guidance/Listing-Rules-Contingency/Main-Board-Listing-Rules/Equity-Securities/chapter_18a.pdf?la=en

removed their "-B" suffix to cover a wider range of indications. Of the 47 companies focused on drug manufacturing, 31 have gone public, and 12 have filed applications, accounting for 66.2% of the total number of Chapter 18A companies. These companies primarily cover nine therapeutic areas: oncology, autoimmune diseases, ophthalmology, biologic vaccines, cellular therapies, diabetes, infectious diseases, respiratory diseases, and rare diseases.

There has also been increasing attention regarding MedTech and cutting-edge technologies. There were 20 companies in the MedTech track, with 12 listed and eight having filed applications. The overall total market value of the 12 listed companies is HK$137.05 billion, with an average market value of HK$11.42 billion. Among them, the vascular intervention field is the sub-sector with the largest number of layouts, with a total of 12 companies, including six listed companies covering indications that are mainly distributed between cardiac and vascular diseases. The global COVID-19 outbreak has accelerated the growth of the emerging healthcare sub-sector, with an increasing number of cutting-edge MedTech companies going public in Hong Kong, driven by key drivers such as surging demand for healthcare, increased perception of AI-enabled benefits, and favorable policies. The advanced technology track is currently dominated by the AI medical equipment sector, with the listing of Airdoc-B.

Companies that list via Chapter 18A have a shorter time between filing and issuance than other Main Board companies, with an average filing cycle of approximately 127 days.[806]

Furthermore, the 48 listed Chapter 18A companies raised 9.16% of the total funds raised by HKEX between the August 1, 2018[807] and December 31, 2021, equaling HK$103.7 billion.

From the perspective of issuance ratio, the issuance ratio of Chapter 18A companies is generally lower than the usual 25.00% issuance ratio of IPO. This is due to the lack of understanding of the life sciences and technology industry at the start of the Rule Chapter 18A issuance reform, as well as the tendency

---

806 Longest being Immunotech Biopharm-B (06978.HK) at 301 days and shortest being Ocumension-B (01477.HK) at 61 days.

807 Date of listing of the first biotechnology company on HKEX.

of Chapter 18A companies to undergo successive financings which resulted in a relatively fragmented shareholding structure. However, as the share price of companies surged over the years alongside deepened understanding of the industry by investors, there has been considerable changes to the issuance ratio, allocating more shares to cornerstone investors and anchor investors. In 2020, there was an explosive growth of Chapter 18A listed companies, with large amounts of retail and institutional money pouring in. This led to a 50:50 issuance ratio (50% cornerstone investors and 50% public offering) structure, which carried over to 2021.

2. GREATER BAY AREA[808]

The Guangdong-Hong Kong-Macao Greater Bay Area (GBA) includes nine cities in the Guangdong Province, China (Guangzhou, Shenzhen, Zhuhai, Foshan, Dongguan, Zhongshan, Jiangmen, Huizhou, and Zhaoqing), as well as two special administrative regions, Hong Kong, and Macau. The GBA covers an area of over 56,000 squares kilometers and resides approximately 70 million, (likewise to the U.K., Italy, and France), making it one of the most economically influential regions in China. The GDP of this region is about US$1.6 trillion, comparable to Australia or Spain.

This region is the youngest in China, attracting more talents, educated and affluent people. Its world-class network of high speedy trains, and highways make commute easily accessible. Some world-renowned companies, like BYD, Tencent, Ping An, are located in this region, they are also hubs to attract vehicles, information technology, financial companies.[809]

3. HEALTHCARE SYSTEM

Hong Kong residents enjoy one of the global longest life expectancies, if not

---

808 https://www.bayarea.gov.hk/en/home/index.html

809 https://www.mckinsey.com/cn/our-insights/perspectives-on-china-blog/the-rise-of-chinas-greater-bay-area

the longest.[810] [811] Hong Kong runs a very efficient dual-track healthcare system of both public and private. The public hospital sector provides over 90% of the medical services across seven geographical clusters, under the management of Hospital Authority.[812] The public system provides universal healthcare coverage for all residents, providing at least two languages in service. Up to 2020, there are 12 private hospitals, covering 10% of medical services. In 2018, Hong Kong was ranked the first for the most efficient healthcare system in the world by Bloomberg.[813] The regional-wide Electronic Health Record Sharing System (eHealth) offers a role-based access to control patient record and facilitates free-of-charge electronic heath record for all the members of the public.[814]

Four hospitals are accredited with phase I clinical trial by China NMPA. Its data are accepted by the U.S. FDA, EU and NMPA, the three major regulatory agencies worldwide.

810 https://www.oal.cuhk.edu.hk/cuhkenews_202101_life_expectancy/

811 https://edition.cnn.com/2018/03/02/health/hong-kong-world-longest-life-expectancy-longevity-intl/index.html

812 https://www.ha.org.hk/visitor/ha_index.asp

813 https://healthcareasiamagazine.com/healthcare/news/hong-kongs-healthcare-system-beats-singapore-worlds-most-efficient-bloomberg

814 https://www.gov.hk/en/residents/health/hosp/eHRSS.htm

4. HONG KONG SCIENCE AND TECHNOLOGY PARKS CORPORATION (HKSTP)[815]

Kao Kuen[816] *Conference Center, Hong Kong Science and Technology Park*

The Hong Kong Science and Technology Parks Corporation (HKSTP) was established in 2002 under the Hong Kong Special Administrative Region Government's Hong Kong Science and Technology Parks Corporation Ordinance (Chapter 565) to plan, develop, and sustain an economic ecosystem based on technological innovation, as well as to assist Hong Kong in its transformation into a technological innovation center and bolster Hong Kong's diverse economic development.

HKSTP is in Hong Kong's Pak Shek Kok district. It is approximately 22 hectares in size. It has developed into Hong Kong's largest R&D ecosystem. The technology companies in the park cover a broad range of disciplines, including biomedical, robotics, novel materials, precision engineering, communication technology, financial technology, green technology, artificial intelligence, and smart cities. As of March 2022, HKSTP attracted over 1,100 enterprises from 23 countries and regions. Around 18,000 work forces are employed at the park, including over 12,000 research and development professionals.

---

815 https://www.hkstp.org/
816 https://www.nobelprize.org/prizes/physics/2009/kao/facts/

During his two-day inspection tour of the Hong Kong's reunification with the motherland, President Xi visited HKSTP on June 30, 2022, which is the only company he visited during this tour. Xi expressed his appreciation to local scientific researchers and young entrepreneurs and encouraged HKSTP to continue its pivotal role in developing the SAR into an International Innovation and Technology Hub.[817] [818] This marks a historical moment for the park's development.[819]

HKSTP CEO Albert Wong believes the HKSTP will continue to drive the development of entrepreneurship and research in Hong Kong. Securing funding, from both public and private investment, would be critical in helping translate scientific achievements into commercial products and grow in the global market.

HKSTP maps out ambitious strategy to drive reindustrialization and develop a diverse plan to create opportunities for generations to come.

HKSTP has committed to enhancing and strengthening Hong Kong's innovation and technology ecosystem through a variety of actions: 1) established world-class offices and communal laboratories, as well as its own incubation and acceleration programs that nurture start-ups, 2) more than 770 businesses have graduated successfully from the entrepreneurial cultivation program, with more than 80% remaining in operation, 3) HKSTP Venture Fund invests in technology start-ups and assists park enterprises in developing relationships with other investors and investment institutions, more than HK$80 billion the park enterprises raised between 2018 and 2022, 4) continue to grow and cultivate the talent pool in Hong Kong and overseas, host an annual science park career fair to assist park enterprises in recruiting talent, and establish a talent pool network platform to assist park enterprises in disseminating recruitment information and soliciting resumes, 5) assist park businesses in attracting and retaining international talent, accommodation assistance plan has been developed to provide financial assistance.

---

817 https://www.chinadaily.com.cn/a/202207/04/WS62c229ada310fd2b29e6a15c.html

818 https://www.info.gov.hk/gia/general/202206/30/P2022063000874.htm

819 https://www.hkstp.org/media/sf4pxg0m/hkstpc-annual-report-2021-22-eng_wca.pdf

Within this vast platform, innovators, engineers, entrepreneurs, investors, and academic business partners work in close collaboration with government departments and regulatory agencies to address a range of technology innovation challenges.

5. HONG KONG CYBERPORT[820]

The Hong Kong Cyberport (Cyberport) is in the Southern District of Hong Kong Island. It is approximately 24 hectares in size, and it consists of four office buildings, a hotel, and a retail entertainment complex. It is managed by Hong Kong Cyberport Management Co. Ltd. wholly owned by the Hong Kong SAR Government.

Cyberport positions itself as a digital technology hub, thereby revitalizing Hong Kong (China) and the Asia-Pacific region's economies. Presently, Cyberport has attracted over 1,500 start-ups and technology firms, including six unicorns operating in a variety of sectors, including financial technology, smart life, e-sports, digital entertainment, cyber security technology, artificial intelligence, big data, and blockchain technology development.

Notably, Cyberport is home to the city's largest fin-tech ecosystem, with over 350 businesses spanning in personal finance, payment systems, and insurance technologies. Furthermore, Cyberport has attracted a sum of new venture capital and private equity funds to set up offices.

Cyberport is committed to cultivating technical talents, encouraging young entrepreneurship, replicating successful start-ups, and fostering a thriving innovation and technology ecosystem.

As of February 2022, Cyberport Incubation Program had incubated and funded over 1,000 technology start-ups since its inception in 2005. The Cyberport Macro Fund was launched in 2016 to support start-ups after seed money and around Series A.

---

820 https://www.cyberport.hk/en/

6. 2022 HONG KONG POLICY ADDRESS ON LIFE SCIENCES INDUSTRY

The Chief Executive's 2022 Policy Address was announced on October 19, 2022,[821] it revolves the goal of cultivating Hong Kong as a global leading innovation and technology hub, foregrounded life and health technology, artificial intelligence, advanced manufacturing, and data science as the key impetuses. Below summarizes the highlights with relevance to the development of Hong Kong's life sciences industry:

1) Better utilize fiscal reserve and government investments:

Introducing the Hong Kong Investment Corporation Limited and HK$30 billion Co-investment Fund to assist the growth of strategic industries. In parallel with HK$5 billion Strategic Tech Fund, Hong Kong Growth Portfolio, and the GBA Investment Fund, resources are systematically consolidated to streamline public investments and promote industries' development.

2) Reinforce the local Innovation and Technology (I&T) ecosystem from financial fundings, enterprises to infrastructure:

Implementing HK$10 billion "Research, Academic and Industry Sectors One plus Scheme" in 2023 to grow over 100 high-potential universities research teams into promising start-ups, this encourages the commercialisation of scientific research and development outcomes. With this funding, cross-sector collaboration between the realms of research, academia and industry is expected, motivating effective R&D outcomes transformation.

Attracting 100 plus competitive life and health technology, artificial intelligence, and data science companies to set up or expand in Hong Kong, which in turns brings along considerable investments and local job vacancies. With the newly established Office for Attracting Strategic Enterprises, the HKSAR government strives to appeal enterprises by allowing exceptional flexibility in facilitation

---

821 https://www.policyaddress.gov.hk/2022/public/pdf/policy/policy-full_en.pdf

measures and one stop services.

3) Improving technology talent admission scheme from December 28, 2022:[822]

The Scheme allows enterprises engaging in R&D in specific industries to admit professionals, such as biotechnology, quantum technology and microelectronics. The improvement further eases the recruitment process by lifting the local employment requirement, extending the quota validity period to two years, and expanding the coverage to more emerging technology areas.

4) Develop northern metropolis as the new "International I&T City":

With vision to construct an all-rounded metropolitan area emphasizing on the local I&T industry, this plan was first introduced in the The Northern Metropolis Development Strategy[823] in October 2021 in echo with the "Hong Kong 2030 Planning Vision and Strategy". The 30,000-hectare Metropolis lays across new towns in the Northern district such as Hung Shui Kiu, Ha Tsuen, Sheung Shui, Tin Shui Wai, Yuen Long, and nearby rural areas.

With its geographical proximity to Shenzhen, Qianhai and the Greater Bay Area, the Northern Metropolis opens possibility for cross-border co-operation, forming I&T cluster and synergy that is of tremendous competitive edge.

5) Improvements on current healthcare system:

Advancing the territory-wide Electronic Health Record Sharing System, eHealth.[824] As a systematic database with both public and private healthcare information, the industry sees great potential for eHealth as a sounded foundation for future precision medicine treatment.

---

822 https://www.itc.gov.hk/ch/fund_app/techtas/about_techtas.html

823 https://www.policyaddress.gov.hk/2021/eng/pdf/publications/Northern/Northern-Metropolis-Development-Strategy-Report.pdf

824 https://www.ehealth.gov.hk/en/whats-ehealth/our-team/background-and-way-forward/index.html

Promoting the role of Chinese medicine via Chinese Medicine Unit under the Health Bureau. In specific, increasing the annual government subsidy quota of Chinese Medicine outpatient service from 600,000 to 800,000, strengthening the Chinese Medicine services, and promoting the professional development of Chinese Medicine practitioners and drugs.

Widening the available supply of pharmaceutical products and medical devices by allowing National Medical Products Administration (NMPA) approved and Mainland-registered medical products that fulfilled requirements to be registered and commercialized in Hong Kong and allow more HK-registered products used in the GBA.

7. HONG KONG UNIVERSITIES AND LIFE SCIENCES INNOVATION

As rearticulated in previous chapters, a sustainable and prosperous life sciences industry is primarily determined by a sound and overarching ecosystem – from excellence in academic research capabilities, talents accumulation to supportive legislative infrastructure to sufficient capitals. Hong Kong's profound research talents, strong capabilities in scientific research, and world-renowned tertiary education have been widely recognized, the four local universities[825] below have expedited in the evolvement of the local life sciences realm.

1) The University of Hong Kong (HKU)

Founded in 1911 as the oldest tertiary education institution, HKU started with Arts, Engineering and Medicines as its first faculties, later expanded into Seven other disciplines such as HKU Business School, Dentistry, Science, and Law. Along with The Chinese University of Hong Kong, HKU is one of the only two with the faculty of medicine to train medical, pharmacy and healthcare practitioners and researchers. Its medical school was ranked the 13th by the Times in 2023 in the world.[826]

---

825 https://www.timeshighereducation.com/world-university-rankings/2023/world-ranking#!/page/1/length/25/sort_by/rank/sort_order/asc/cols/stats

826 https://www.med.hku.hk/en/news/press/20221025-the-world-university-rankings-2023

Researchers at HKU are famed for their continuous notable achievements in public health hazards. In face of Severe Acute Respiratory Syndrome (SARS) pandemic in March 2003, HKU is the first worldwide to announce its successful identification and isolation of the never-seen coronavirus SARS-CoV which was the causative agent of the disease.[827] This foregrounds its research into the current COVID-19 pandemic, with high-impact publications on leading scholarly journals.[828] [829]

In terms of innovation, the HKUMed Innovation Hubs (InnoHK@HKUMed) collaborates with global top institutions in the application of advanced technologies including genomics, and big data for further advancement in understanding and treatment for viruses and cancers. Five cross-disciplinary research laboratories are established under InnoHK@HKUMed, crossing disciplines such as oncology and immunology, translational stem cell biology, virology, vaccinology, and therapeutics.[830]

2) The Chinese University of Hong Kong (CUHK)

In 1963, CUHK was founded with Cantonese as its official teaching language, providing territory education for students from Hong Kong and Mainland China besides the only HKU then. Its Faculty of Medicine is highly reputed for the comprehensive programmes offered by 19 teaching schools and departments, namely Pharmacy, Clinical Oncology, Medicine and Therapeutics, Biomedical Sciences, and Nursing etc.[831]

Landmark discoveries from CUHK's researchers are innumerable, however, it is worth-noting that it is the only university in Hong Kong to be awarded with

---

827 "Severe Acute Respiratory Syndrome (SARS) – multi-country outbreak – Update 12". WHO. 2003-03-27.

828 Shuai, H., Chan, J.FW., Hu, B. *et al.* Attenuated replication and pathogenicity of SARS-CoV-2 B.1.1.529 Omicron. *Nature* 603, 693–699 (2022). https://doi.org/10.1038/s41586-022-04442-5

829 Du, Z., Wang, L., Pandey, A. *et al. Modeling comparative cost-effectiveness of SARS-CoV-2 vaccine dose fractionation in India. Nat Med* 28, 934–938 (2022).

830 https://www.med.hku.hk/en/research/innohk

831 https://www.cuhk.edu.hk/english/faculties/medicine.html

Nobel Prize, The Breakthrough Prize, Turing Award, Fields Medal and Veblen Prize. Its high-caliber research, to name a few, include the discovery of cell-free fetal DNA in maternal blood and development of non-invasive prenatal testing for Down syndrome,[832] as well as the application of MicroNeuro, a medical endoscopic robot for brain surgery with minimal invasion.[833]

CUHK also strives to actively transform high-potential R&D outcomes by its fellow researchers by establishing the Office of Research and Knowledge Transfer Services which assists in fundraising and intellectual properties [834] while the Office of Innovation and Enterprise takes responsibility for products' commercialization, and investment opportunities with both public and private strategic partners.[835]

3) The Hong Kong University of Science and Technology (HKUST)

As Hong Kong's third university, HKUST's proficient alumni are highly favoured among international employers, this is exemplified in its highest employment rate among Chinese universities for six consecutive years since 2018.[836] Housing schools of science, humanities and social sciences, engineering, as well as business and management, two of the latter is constantly ranked as one of the tops across the globe.

HKUST is unique for its Undergraduate Research Opportunities Program launched in 2005 with the aim to encourage undergraduates to explore academic research of their interests under professional supervision from faculty members. [837]

Considering its emphasis on material sciences, and engineering realms, HKUST introduced an extensive network of programmes and funding to

---

832 https://laskerfoundation.org/winners/noninvasive-prenatal-testing-using-fetal-dna/

833 https://www.cpr.cuhk.edu.hk/en/press/cuhk-scholar-jointly-awarded-first-bochk-science-and-technology-innovation-prize-in-artificial-intelligence-and-robotics/

834 https://www.orkts.cuhk.edu.hk/en/about/our-mission

835 http://www.oie.cuhk.edu.hk/

836 "Global University Employability Ranking 2018 results". *Times Higher Education.*

837 https://urop.hkust.edu.hk/

translate research outcomes: the Entrepreneurship Programme launched by the HKUST's subsidary, HKUST R&D Corporation Limited incubates start-ups founded by HKUST fellows. In parallel, the Bridge-Gap Fund assists with R&D transformation. In 2021, Seven internally incubated start-ups were shortlisted as "Unicorns HK 2021" by the Hong Kong X Foundation for Innovation and Technology[838] including 4Paradigm (Platform-centric AI solutions), SmartMore (Computer vision technology) and Googol Technology (Motion controls for manufacturing automation).[839] Until December 2022, nearly 2,000 IPs are active or in application.

4) The City University of Hong Kong (CityU)

Established in 1984, CityU offers a variety of programmes ranging from business, science, engineering, liberal arts and social sciences, law, creative media, and veterinary medicine. CityU ranked 1st in Hong Kong for the 5th consecutive year for the highest number of academic subjects (15 subjects in 2022) ranked in the world's top 50, according to Shanghai Rankings' Global Ranking of Academic Subjects list. It also ranked 1st in HK in Citations per Faculty in QS World University Rankings averaged over a five-year period from 2017–2021. Over 180 CityU faculty members (among the total of around 790) were listed among the top 2% of the world's most highly cited scientists, according to metrics compiled by Stanford University in 2022.

CityU actively advocates innovation and knowledge transfer, encouraging the transformation and application of outstanding research results of the University. National Academy of Inventors ranked CityU 29th in the world in 2021 among the top 100 universities granted US utility patents, placing the university No. 1 in Hong Kong for the 6th consecutive years. The number of awards that CityU won 22 awards at the Inventions Geneva Evaluation Days 2022, the highest number among local universities.

CityU has acted as a vital catalyst among local universities to incentivize faculty and students to transform their R&D outcomes into entrepreneurship. Acclaimed

---

838 News of Entrepreneurship Center (Dec 21, 2021): HK Unicorns 2021

839 https://seng.hkust.edu.hk/news/20220311/unicorns-spotlight-hi-tech-entrepreneurship

examples are Orbbec (688322.CN), a leading global provider of 3D sensing and artificial intelligence vision technology, and Prenetics (PRE.US), a technology driven life sciences company specializing in precision medicine and digital health, both are spinoff companies founded by CityU faculty and/or students.

Funded with HK$500 million, CityU's flagship innovation and entrepreneurship programme HK Tech 300[840] supports CityU students, alumni and other young people who aspire to start their own businesses. The four-phase program begins with a training programme and team formation, following by seed fund of HK$100,000, angel fund investment of up to HK$1 million, and co-investment with venture funds up to HK$10 million. HK Tech 300 has become a leading university-based entrepreneurship programme in Asia in terms of scale and investment. As of 2022, more than 400 project teams have each been awarded HK$100,000 Seed Fund in areas such as deep tech, information and communications technology, artificial intelligence, biotech, and health, as well as business and FinTech. In addition, over 90 start-ups have each been awarded up to HK$1 million each from the Angel Fund.

---

840 https://www.cityu.edu.hk/hktech300/about-hk-tech-300/about-programme

Chapter 17

HKEX Chapter 18A Listing

In comparison to many innovative technology sectors, biotechnology has gained considerable momentum in the last five years. The share of biopharmaceutical industry in the entire pharmaceutical market was expected to grow from 17% in 2008 to 30% in 2022, reaching to US$326 billion.[841] In the past, the support of the capital markets in the Greater China region to the biotechnology industry seriously lagged, and the difficulty in raising capital has significantly impacted the development of the local biotechnology industry. These shortcomings were not resolved prior to the listing mechanism reforms for biotech companies implemented by The Stock Exchange of Hong Kong Limited (HKEX) in 2018 and the launch of the Shanghai Stock Exchange Science and Technology Innovation Board (SSE STAR Market) in 2019. This chapter provides a concise overview of the financing cycle for biotech companies and the new landscape of the capital market thereafter.

The biotech industry is characterized by a long investment cycle, with bio-innovative drugs typically taking around 8 to 15 years from conception to launch. There is a high level of risk and uncertainty at each stage, as evidenced by the less than 10% success rate in Phase I clinical trials, as well as the often failure in Phase III clinical trials completion for Research and Development (R&D) of most biopharmaceutical projects could not successfully complete Phase III clinical trials. The industry is typically "asset-light", with a focus on talents and R&D. Prior to the commercialization of products, majority of the assets are patents. In terms of indirect financing, bank financings are mostly offered to companies with physical collaterals and are thus often unable to support biotech companies at an early stage. As a result, biotech companies rely on direct financing for their external financing, chiefly from their own founders and private equity/venture capital funds before the eventual initial public offering of the companies.

---

841 EvaluatePharma (June 2022). *World Preview 2017, Outlook to 2022*. Available at: http://info.evaluategroup.com/rs/607-YGS-364/images/WP17.pdf.

The total investment from concept to successful R&D ranges from US$300 million to US$1 billion, and the monthly cash burn is also rather substantial. The first slice of investment is usually from the company's founders themselves who have a profound background in scientific research yet have limited capital of their own. Commonly, the Pre-A round financing is supported by the founders' acquaintances as well. However, for the company to survive and sustain organically, acquiring support from third-party investment institutions to complete the Series A round financing is of high importance. Biotech companies generally enter the capital market after completing Series B round to Series E round financing, depending on factors such as their specific segment, valuation, and capital market sentiment.

As the market continues to develop over time, major exchanges around the world have opened to welcome the listing of biotech companies. In recent years, the exchanges in Shanghai, Hong Kong (China) and NASDAQ in the U.S. have become the most important listing and financing centers for biotech companies due to their market depth and liquidity. NASDAQ in the U.S. is a pioneer with 171 biotech companies listed.[842] Hong Kong and Shanghai have also successfully attracted many biotech companies to list after reforming their listing regimes in 2018 and 2019 respectively.

In February 2018, HKEX launched a consultation paper to reform the listing of companies in the emerging and innovative sectors. This is the biggest reform since 1993 when the H-shares of companies incorporated in Mainland China were allowed to list in Hong Kong. One of the most significant breakthroughs in this reform is to allow biotech companies without any revenue to qualify for listing if they meet, among others, the following criteria:

i.   The biotech company must have at least one core pipeline product (small molecule drugs or biologics) which has completed Phase I clinical trials and received approval from the recognized drug regulatory authorities (such as the National Medical Products Administration of China, the U.S. FDA of

---

842 Research Report on HKEX website (May 2019). *Investment Benchmark for Asia's Biotechnology Sector: CES HK Biotechnology Index.* Available at: https://www. hkex.com.hk/-/media/HKEX-Market/News/Research-Reports/HKEx-Research-Papers/2019/CCEO_Biotech_201905_e.pdf?la=en.

the U.S., and the European Medicines Agency of the EU) to commence Phase II clinical trials; medical devices categorized as Class II or above; or other biotech products (subject to further refinement of the acceptance requirement by HKEX);

ii.   Market capitalization of at least HK$1.5 billion at the time of listing;

iii. Track record of at least two financial years prior to listing under substantially the same management;

iv.   Sufficient working capital to cover at least 125% of the total of corporate costs (including general, administrative, operating and production costs) and R&D costs, for the next 12 months;

v.   A significant investment (ranging from 1% to 5% of the issued share capital of the biotech company depending on its market capitalization at the time of listing) by at least one sophisticated investor, such as an established investment firm, at least six months prior to listing;

vi.   Listing capital raised is primarily used for R&D to bring the core products to commercialization.

Biotech companies, venture capital funds and mutual funds from Mainland China and across the globe have shown extensive support and constructive advice on this key initiative to reform the listing regime. The consultation was soon endorsed and approved by the market and was officially implemented on April 30, 2018. As Hong Kong's listing regime has always been a disclosure-based nature, nine biotech companies have successfully passed the hearing and listed on HKEX in the nine months from the implementation, raising a total of HK$26.8 billion. From the implementation to June 30, 2022, 49 pre-revenue biotech companies have been listed and have raised HK$128 billion, covering different segments of the biotech industry such as biopharmaceuticals, medical devices, and R&D contract outsourcing services. With biotech companies becoming more and more accustomed to get dual-listed in two places, including simultaneous listing in Hong Kong and Mainland China, as well as in Hong Kong and the U.S., we can expect simultaneous listing in three venues to take place soon. With a well-established issuance mechanism and market depth, Hong Kong (China) has become the second largest capital raising hub for biotech companies worldwide in two years' time shortly after the implementation of the new regime.

In Mainland China, the consultation paper on the Establishment of a Science and Technology Innovation Board on the Shanghai Stock Exchange and Trial Registration System was launched in January 2019, leading to a shift in the IPO system to a registration system in Mainland China. The new system focuses on technology and innovation enterprises that serve national strategies, make breakthroughs in key core technologies, and have high market recognition. There are five routes to listing:

i.   Expected market capitalization of not less than RMB1 billion, positive profits for the last two years and cumulative profits of not less than RMB50 million, or an expected market capitalization of not less than RMB1 billion, positive net worth and operating revenue of not less than RMB100 million for the most recent year.

ii. Expected market capitalization of not less than RMB1.5 billion, operating revenue of not less than RMB200 million in the most recent year, and the ratio of accumulated R&D investment to the accumulated operating revenue in the most recent three years of not less than 15%.

ii. Expected market capitalization of not less than RMB2 billion, operating revenue of not less than RMB300 million in the most recent year and cumulative net cash flow from operating activities of not less than RMB300 million for the most recent three years.

iv. Expected market capitalization of not less than RMB3 billion and the operating revenue of not less than RMB300 million in the most recent year.

v.   Expected market capitalization of not less than RMB4 billion, with principal business or product approved by the relevant state authorities, large market potential, and milestones already achieved. Pharmaceutical companies must have at least one of their core products approved for Phase II clinical trials, and other companies that satisfy the corporate positioning requirement must have a distinct technological advantage and satisfy relevant requirements.

The HKEX's listing reform has opened the capital market to more biotech companies. In addition to IPO, the entire biotech investment and financing ecosystem in China has become much more active. There are increasing number of market participants in every sector of the ecosystem, including emergence of more biotech companies, venture capital and private equity funds in the early, growth and late stages, various types of investment funds at IPOs, and refinancing or placing of issued shares after listing. The technological innovation from biotech companies, coupled with the boost from the capital market, creates a tremendous impetus to drive business growth. Many newly listed biotech companies have invested the funds raised in R&D and product commercialization and have resulted in significant progress in global patent portfolio development.

Following the implementation of the biotech listing regime, China Exchanges Services Company Limited launched the CES HK Biotechnology Index in November 2018 to track shares of biotech companies listed on Hong Kong's Main Board. Subsequently in December 2019, Hang Seng Hong Kong-Listed Biotech Index was launched in Hong Kong. In August 2020, the Hang Seng Composite Industry Index allowed the inclusion of biotech companies listed under Chapter 18A. In December 2020, the Shenzhen Stock Exchange and the Shanghai Stock Exchange announced that eight Hong Kong-listed biotech companies would be included in the Hong Kong Stock Connect. In the U.S. where biotech development made an earlier start, market indices that track the biotech sector are well covered by NASDAQ[843] and S&P.[844] In terms of index funds, there are six biotech index funds in Mainland China, of which four track the Mainland China A-share biotech index and two track the US biotech index.

The interconnection of the Mainland China investors has become an important feature for Hong Kong to attract biotech companies to list in Hong Kong. It is widely believed that more biotech companies will be included under the Shanghai-Hong Kong Stock Connect mechanism, allowing Mainland investors to invest in Hong Kong listed biotech companies, and for international investors (including Hong Kong investors) to invest biotech companies listed in Shanghai. The interconnection of the three stock exchanges in Shanghai, Hong Kong and Shenzhen has greatly expanded the entire investor base. In the future, if the primary market (i.e. IPO connect) is further liberalized, it will be another major breakthrough in this common market.

Another new development in Hong Kong is the introduction of Special Purpose Acquisition Company (SPAC) IPO in January 2022. As of March 17, 2022, 10 SPAC applications have been filed with HKEX with the first SPAC listed on March 18, 2022. SPAC IPO allows promoters to raise funding of at least HK$1 billion for future acquisition of investment targets (via a process called De-SPAC). It is exciting to note that some SPAC applications have their investment theme focusing on biotech and healthcare sectors. We believe SPAC could be a complementary and alternative route for fundraising by biotech companies.

---

843 Includes 221 stocks

844 Includes 119 stocks

The total market capitalization of companies in the medical and healthcare sector listed in China is approximately US$1.5 trillion,[845] compared to the US$5.5 trillion in the U.S., there is still significant room for growth considering China's population is four times of the U.S. We believe Hong Kong and Shanghai will remain as key global centers for healthcare and biotech industries. The revolutionary breakthrough in the system and the improvement of the biotech investment ecosystem have opened a great new chapter for biotech companies. We believe this is just a prelude to a new chapter of success for biotech companies as the biotech industry continues to grow and the financial markets continue to develop. The fundraising and investment infrastructure will continue to prosper.

With more institutional funds, professional investors and research analysts joining the ecosystem, there is a shift in investors' valuation of biotech companies, paying more attention to the intangible assets of biotech companies such as patents, inventions and R&D investments, and future profitability has also become increasingly important.

---

845 Includes Mainland China and Hong Kong

Chapter 18

Valuations on Life Sciences Projects

Innovative drug development, the most central aspect of the pharmaceutical industry, is a time-consuming, expensive, and extremely risky process. In the U.S., it takes an average of 10 to 15 years and more than US$2.5 billion to develop an innovative drug from compound or biomarker discovery to the U.S. FDA approval, and that's assuming the R&D process goes relatively well at each stage of development. Most pipeline drugs will not make it to market due to clinical trial failure. The biopharmaceutical sector has long been sought after by investors as the entire process of innovative drug development requires a significant investment of time and money and is subject to great uncertainty; at the same time, success at each stage can lead to a surge in market value for innovative drug companies, creating significant investment opportunities.

1. Methodology

For pharmaceutical companies with mature products, comprehensive pipeline portfolio, and well-established sales channels, such as global pharmaceutical giants, a relatively simple PE valuation approach can be used to evaluate the value of the target company. For biotechnology companies that currently have no revenue and whose value is derived entirely from their pipeline, they need to use a risk-adjusted DCF (rDCF) approach to value their business based on their target indications epidemiology and other characteristics, taking into account the efficacy of their products and the competitive landscape, and to forecast the sales of their pipeline after approval. According to DCF valuation theory, a company's value is equivalent to its expected cash flows discounted by the company's cost of capital. It is necessary to forecast the balance sheet and profit and loss account for a sufficiently long period of time, and to forecast the company's future profit and loss account, balance sheet, and cash flow statement through an in-depth analysis of the clinical result and design of the pipeline products, industry's development characteristics, the competitive landscape and the company's competitive advantages.

The rDCF valuation method for innovative pharmaceutical companies is currently the most used methodology in the industry and involves the following key parameters:

- Probability of Success (POS)
- Patient pool
- Penetration rate
- Product pricing
- Patents and exclusivity

The model based on these key assumptions is also known as the 5P valuation model and is a special form of rDCF in the field of innovative biotech companies. The model can be analyzed in three main stages.

The first stage focuses on the time and cost of R&D investment, negative cash flow and the risk of product failure, and requires a focus on the Probability of Success (POS).

The second stage focuses on the period between product approval and patent expiry. The focus of this stage is on sales revenue of the pipeline product, which needs to be measured based on the epidemiology analysis and treatment pathway of its target indications to determine the upper limit of product revenue. Pricing is particularly important during this phase and is influenced by the competitive landscape and health insurance coverage assumptions. Finally, the penetration rate can be measured based on changes in pricing and the underlying economic context of the country or region in which the target drug is marketed.

The third stage measures the sustainable growth stage after patent expiry, which considers the reduction in peak sales from the launch of a biosimilar or generic drug, the centralized purchasing policy (for products expect to launch in China), and the subsequent stabilization of the growth process.

The valuation of each product of an innovative company requires an analysis of each different indication for each product, as well as detailed consideration of the unmet medical needs of the indication, to arrive at a relatively accurate value for the product. Our analysis of the five assumptions in the 5P valuation model requires the following considerations:

i. **Probability of Success (POS):** POS is always the most impactful parameter on valuation, its calculation is based directly on the clinical data of the drug itself. Investors need to consult, where possible, the clinical results of the target drug or its clinical data published at academic conferences. It is efficient to reference data from "Clinical Development Success Rates 2006-2015" published by Biomedtracker and Amplion particularly for drugs that has no available clinical data of current clinical stage. However, as the success rates in this paper are historical averages based on the accumulation of historical clinical status, it is easy for investors to be concerned about the success rates of potentially high-quality drugs, so academic research on the relevant mechanisms or targets is also necessary to avoid misjudging preclinical products.

ii. **Patient pool:** The majority of indications' epidemiology data can be obtained from the WHO or GHDX databases. In the case of patient pool calculations, the focus is on the analysis of treatment pathways, which requires detailed knowledge of the U.S. FDA and NCCN treatment guidelines, extensive interviews with physicians to understand real-world drug use practices and, in particular, detailed knowledge of how off-label indications are used in order to obtain an accurate patient base. To determine the upper limit of the patient base simply from epidemiological data would result in an overestimation of future expectations for the product and lead investors to misjudge the true valuation of the company.

iii. **Penetration rate:** Two factors are generally taken into account when considering product penetration rate. Firstly, the performance of marketed products with similar indications or similar mechanisms in the past. Secondly, competition from products currently under clinical development stage needs to be considered. If there are multiple products with similar mechanisms or generics on the market, this will significantly impact the price and penetration rate of the product.

iv. **Product pricing:** Traditional pricing model are straightforward. However, the current focus of biotechnology companies on oncology drugs makes drug pricing model of these products relatively complicated. As oncology drugs are currently used mainly for patients with advanced tumors, many of which have a survival period of less than one year, the traditional annual costing model is not applicable to oncology drugs. The use of PFS data from clinical trials, based on oncology drug unit prices, has become the main pricing logic for the valuation of oncology indication products. At the same time, the potential national medical insurance coverage or Volume-Based Procurement (VBP) of the target drugs, particularly in the Chinese market, also have a significant impact on pricing, and the current national medical insurance coverage for comparable drugs and the reduction in price after inclusion in health insurance provide a more reasonable frame of reference.

v. **Patents and exclusivity:** For drugs under development, investors need to consult professional IP lawyers to conduct a detailed investigation into the patent situation. This is an essential step as patent conflicts can directly lead to difficulties in market entry and may even face lawsuit from competitors, which will directly affect the value of the product as measured by all the above parameters.

The rDCF-based 5P valuation methodology can be used to provide a scientific valuation not only for innovative biopharmaceutical companies, but also for innovative medical device consumables companies. There are only some differences in details such as difficulty in marketing strategy, approval process and patent issues.

2. Case study

1) Case study one: Burning Rock Biotech Limited (BNR.US)

The core focus of Burning Rock Biotech lies within the field of precision diagnosis of tumors and early screening. Its products are mainly genetic sequencing kits which are medical devices. However, its valuation logic is very similar to that of innovative drugs, starting from the tumor patient population, and through the combing of the targeted treatment population and target research. By extension, they needed to inspect their drug pipelines and gauge the future demand of precision gene therapy, to obtain the value of their precision diagnosis related products. Other valuation methods include PS valuation based on peak sales, event driven NCF valuation for CROs, CMOs or vaccine companies, etc., which are not discussed here.

The valuation of biotechnology companies is not simply a numbers game. Even if a relatively reasonable valuation model is developed through rDCF, we need to consider non-quantitative indicators such as the company's management team, team of scientists, technology platform and R&D mindset. The region in which the product is intended to be launched is also important to consider, as there are significant differences in speed of approval, pricing, and affordability in different market environments. Even blockbuster drugs' that have seen success in one country may not necessarily do well in another due to regional differences, as the historical struggles of Humira® and Revlimid® in the Chinese market so warn us. At the same time, changes in approval policies and the outcome of yearly national health insurance negotiations have had a significant impact on the valuation of many biotechnology companies over the past two years, and the potential for volume-based procurement is an unavoidable topic, even for biologics.

2) Case study two: Cansino Biologics Inc. (6185.HK)

The founding team of CanSino Biologics are all former leading scientists from leading four MNCs in vaccine industry with extensive theoretical knowledge and practical experience in vaccine development. In 2017, the company received new drug approval for its Ebola vaccine Ad5-EBOV. As one of the first few biopharmaceutical companies to go public under HKEX's Chapter 18A, CanSino Biologics was keen to gain quick access to the capital market. However, investors' suspicion of Chinese vaccine companies was at its highest point when the Changchun Changsheng Bio-Technology vaccine scandal broke out in late 2017. During first roadshow, CanSino Biologics faced a huge challenge from institutional investors, delaying the entire listing process. Only OrbiMed and Lilly Asia (LAV) believed in the CanSino's experienced management team, becoming the only cornerstone investors focus on pharmaceutical area. In the face of volatile market sentiment, world-class investors saw the potential of a quality Chinese biotechnology company in the face of the overall enterprise value of CanSino Biologics, and the outbreak led investors to further discover the value of the company. As the only Chinese vaccine company on the Hong Kong stock market, CanSino Biologics market capitalization topped HK$100 billion. At the time of its listing in the Hong Kong stock market, it was only valued at around HK$4.5 billion. In terms of the valuation of the company itself, CanSino Biologics was only procured by the state during the early stages of its IPO due to surging emergency demands for the Ebola vaccine and the quadrivalent conjugate influenza vaccine, two relatively late-stage products. However, early investors were attracted to the background of CanSino Biologics' senior management team and the four core vaccine platforms built on its technological capabilities, which they placed a premium on these technological platforms. The value of its technology platforms was later validated by the rapid and successful development of a new adenovirus-loaded COVID-19 vaccine after the outbreak.

This begs the question whether pipeline-based rDCF valuation models are still the right way to value technology platform driven biotechnology companies. How can technology platforms be fairly valued?

3) Case study three: Sirnaomics Ltd. (2577.HK)

Sirnaomics is the first clinical-stage RNA therapeutics company to have a strong presence in both China and the U.S. In addition, Sirnaomics is the first company to achieve positive Phase II, a clinical outcomes in oncology for an RNAi therapeutics for its core product, STP705, which demonstrated efficacy and safety in an oncology Phase I/II clinical trial for non-melanoma skin cancer. Sirnaomics has since further advanced STP705 in clinical trials for other cancers and dermatological indications including a Phase IIb clinical trial for Squamous Cell Carcinoma in situ (isSCC), a Phase II clinical trial for the treatment of skin Basal Cell Carcinoma (BCC), a Phase II clinical trial for the treatment of keloid and a Phase I/II clinical trial for the treatment of Hypertrophic Scar (HTS), and a Phase I clinical trial using STP705 for treatment of liver cancer.

In addition to 19 RNAi therapeutics pipelines target oncology, fibrosis, medical aesthetics, antiviral medicine, and for other indications potentially treatable with GalNAc-siRNA conjugates, Sirnaomics also developed three proprietary delivery platforms for the administration of RNA-based therapeutics. The Polypeptide Nanoparticle (PNP) delivery platform is optimizable for local or systemic administration of RNAi therapeutics and targets beyond liver hepatocyte cells. The GalNAc-based delivery platforms are developed for systemic administration and liver-targeting RNAi therapeutics, and the Polypeptide Lipid Nanoparticle (PLNP) delivery platform is useful for the administration of mRNA vaccines and therapeutics. When considering the valuation of Sirnaomics, the value of its PNP delivery platform is quite crucial. RNA therapeutics have radically changed the global pharmaceutical market during COVID-19 pandemic. In addition to the clinical trials launched by Sirnaomics, we have to further evaluate the potential of developing other products, such as mRNA vaccines, or the possibility of licensing out its PNP platform to help other pharmaceutical companies to development RNA related therapeutical drugs.

Chapter 19

Legal Due Diligence of Biotechnology Companies before Investment

"Due diligence" refers to the careful investigation and analysis of the target company (including its business, assets, operations, financial and legal relationships, etc.) during the process of M&A and investment for the purposes of understanding the target company, identifying the risks involved, reasonably assessing the strengths, weaknesses and valuation of the target company, which will form the basis for determining whether to complete the transaction and how to proceed with the negotiation. If the target company is a biotechnology company, due diligence on its core products and technologies is of paramount importance. This article discusses the Intellectual Property ("IP") legal issues regarding investing in biotechnology companies, the content of due diligence and the issues that require special attention, with a focus on matters involving proprietary technology.

1. IP-RELATED RISK FACTORS

1) Ownership-related risks

The investor needs to ascertain whether the target company owns the relevant IP rights, for example whether target company is the patent owner. If the inventor of the relevant patent is an employee of the company, it must be established whether the employee is conducting the research and development as an employee of the company. If there are other co-owners of the patent, the legal relationship between the target company and the other co-owners must also be clarified.

2) Infringement risks

If the target company's technologies or products infringe the rights of any third party, the infringed party has the right to bring a claim against the target company, which may result in the target company being involved in endless litigation, incurring substantial losses and debts, or even facing closure. On the other hand, if the target company's products or technologies are substantially infringed by other third parties, the target company may incur substantial costs to defend its rights and may create uncertainty about the target company's business and prospect.

3) License-related risks

In addition to conducting their own research and development, some biotechnology companies also license in products or technologies from third parties. Changes in the shareholding of the target company (in particular the controlling interest) may trigger termination of the license under the relevant license agreement.

Initiating Legal Due Diligence on the Intellectual Property

In general, full legal due diligence will be conducted once a non-binding term sheet has been signed between the investor and the target company.

The investor must have a thorough understanding of the IP rights of the target company. There are registered IP rights (e.g. patents and trademarks) and unregistered IP rights (e.g. copyright and confidential information). While registered IP rights can be investigated through public searches, unregistered IP rights can only be investigated through looking into information provided by the target company. In any event, the investor will need to request the target company to provide a list of its owned, licensed-in, and licensed-out IP rights.

4) Three key areas of IP due diligence:

Confirmation of rights

The investor must verify the ownership and status of the IP rights owned and licensed by the target company. As mentioned above, the investor should request the target company to provide a list of its owned, licensed-in and licensed-out IP rights, based on which the investor should investigate into the ownership of the target company's patents and patent applications, including whether the ownership is in dispute, whether there are encumbrances (e.g. as security), etc. The investor should also conduct searches on public records to verify ownership and confirm payment of all the required fees, and review the chain of title and licenses.

Scoping

As the economic value of IP rights depends on the exclusivity of the rights, an investor would need to analyze the scope, validity, duration of exclusivity and enforceability of the IP rights.

The investor should review the strength of protection of the target company's patents and patent applications, including the global patent family, the type of patent protection, the duration of legal status protection, and the completeness of the patent portfolio. The investor should also prioritize specific IP assets based on their importance to the target company's business plan and make a judgment on the likelihood and timing of any challenge of its market exclusivity by me-too or copycat products after the commercialization stage. The investor should also develop a strategy to search for existing technologies worldwide for the business partners' patents and patent applications, and to compare and analyze the existing technologies identified with the target company's patents and patent applications. In addition, the investor is suggested to analyze and evaluate the global patent application history file to assess the validity of the patents and patent applications, the licensing prospects, the scope of protection that can be granted and the duration of protection, etc.

Mine removal

The investor is required to conduct a Freedom to Operate (FTO) procedure on the target company's products and processes to assess whether the manufacture, use, sale, license or import of the target company's products would infringe any third-party patents or other IP rights, in order to identify potential risks of infringement of third party's IP rights by the target company's products and processes.

Furthermore, the investor should read the technical materials provided by the target company, understand the target company's current products and processes, and interview the target company if necessary and develop an FTO search strategy based on the investor's knowledge of the technology. The investor should conduct a search for prior patents by others to identify potential blocking patents and to compare and analyze the target company's products and processes with blocking patents.

If a risky blocking patent is identified in the FTO investigation, the investor should investigate the validity of the blocking patent, develop a search strategy, conduct a search for existing technology worldwide for the blocking patent, conduct a comparison and analysis of the existing technology from the search with the blocking patent, and analyze and file a patent evaluation application history. On this basis, the validity of the blocking patent is assessed, and a determination is made as to whether the stability of the blocking patent will prevent the manufacture, use, sale, licensing or importation of the target company's products.

2. COMMON KEY IP-RELATED ISSUES THAT COULD BE IDENTIFIED DURING THE DUE DILIGENCE EXERCISE

Whilst each deal is different, set out below are the key IP-related issues that could commonly be identified during the due diligence exercise.

1) Ownership

One of the most common issues identified during due diligence process is the lack of imperfect ownership of the key IP assets of the target company. Examples include title of the IP rights acquired from a third party has not been updated for the new owner, the target company does not own the rights to, or all of the rights to, certain IP rights, the IP rights are jointly owned by the target company and a third party. The potential investor would need to require the target company to have all the required IP rights be properly assigned to the target company as a condition precedent to completion of the investment.

2) Missing the deadline of paying maintenance fee and/or annuities

The target company might have missed the due date of maintenance fees and/or annuities.

3) Scope of the parent and its coverage

The due diligence exercise may reveal that patent claims of the target company do not cover the key commercialized products that they were initially intended to cover or may be designed around easily by a competitor with the aim of evading coverage. This may be resulted from the negotiation between the patent office and the patent owner during the application process. In certain cases, the claims of the registered patent could be directed to a product envisioned early in the development cycle, instead of to the final commercialized product.

For IP rights that are in the prosecution process, the claims could be very broad to get the widest possible coverage. But it is common that the claims be narrowed at the request of the examiners. As such, it may be hard to determine with certainty the potential patent coverage if the application process is still at its early stage. Potential investors are thus reminded to be cautious in this connection during the due diligence exercise.

4) Assignment and change of control Issues

Certain IP license agreement contains prohibition or restriction (e.g. cannot assign to a competitor of the licensor, or prior approval would need to be obtained) on assignment of the IP rights. Some license agreements may deem a change in control of the target company as an assignment, and would automatically terminate the license or give the right of the licensor to terminate the license agreement, in case of a non-permitted assignment. This issue may not be that relevant in case of a financial investment of minority stake in a biotech company, but potential investors would still need to check the original license agreement.

5) Rights of the government

If any research and development exercise is funded by a government body (either entirely or partially), as a condition, it may have certain level of rights over the IP or the invention.

3. ADDRESSING THE ISSUES IDENTIFIED AND POSSIBLE SOLUTIONS

To address the issues identified and to mitigate the risks to the investor, the investment agreement should contain tailor-made representations and warranties, undertakings, and indemnification provisions.

The representations and warranties to be made by the target and the controlling shareholder should include matters like the definition of IP and the target company's ownership, whether there is any infringement of its IP by any third party and the target company has infringed any third parties' IP and no IP relating to conduct of the business of the target company is missing. Also, in case there is any ownership issue of the IPs, as abovementioned, the investor should typically request remedial actions to be taken as conditions precedent to closing, for example, the relevant IPs to be properly assigned to the target, and outstanding maintenance fee, or annuities to be paid before closing of the investment.

The investment agreement should include a schedule to set out all IP rights relating to the business of the target company, including the IP rights owned by the target company, licensed from and licensed to third parties. There should be a representation that the target company owns all of the rights of such IPs.

In addition, the investor should ask for a representation from the target company that there have not been any claims by any third party, and there is no outstanding or is threatened claims against the target company on the validity, enforceability, use or ownership of the IP rights.

Moreover, to ensure that the target company continues to own the IP rights until closing, the investor would need a representation that the target company maintained the IP rights up to closing.

Furthermore, the investor would request for indemnification for breaches of representations and warranties by the target company or controlling shareholder, and any IP claims by third party.

Despite the above measures, the investment agreement is normally heavily negotiated. The target company or controlling shareholder would try to limit their liabilities by cutting down the representations and warranties with regards to the above matters, and adding qualifying language and exceptions. Also, the target company or controlling shareholder would try to limit the scope and survival period of the indemnification. They may propose a cap, thresholds and/

or time limit for total and each indemnification claim. The final result would depend on the respective bargaining power of the target company or controlling shareholder on one side and the investor on the other.

4. CONCLUSION

The results of due diligence can affect the fundamentals of the project which is whether or not to complete the investment and thus an early understanding of the risks involved will increase the bargaining power of the investor. If problems are identified early, the investor will have more time to negotiate and resolve them.

The above only discusses some basic principles of conducting IP legal due diligence. Each investment project involves different objectives, time and costs, and investors should engage experienced lawyers to determine the scope and depth of due diligence and to formulate the most appropriate course of action together, taking into account the actual needs of the project.

Note: The above is only a summary of general legal principles and does not constitute any formal legal advice. Readers should seek professional legal advice in light of their individual circumstances if they are in any doubt.

PART 6

Appendix

Chinese Life Sciences Pioneers

1. FOREWORD

China is an innovative nation. Cambridge University Press published a serial book titled *Science and Civilisation in China*,[846] documenting in detail the achievements of its people. This ongoing series was initiated and edited by the well-respected British historian, Joseph Needham. The series was on the Modern Library Board's 100 Best Non-fiction books of the 20th century. Needham's work was the first of its kind to praise scientific contributions and provided their history and connection to global knowledge in contrast to euro-centric historiography.

By asking his grand question "Why did modern science not develop in China, and why China was technologically superior to the West prior to the 16th Century?" Needham is the key person to stimulate the reorganization of multicultural roots to modern science.

Another short version of popular book titled *The Genius of China* by Robert Temple,[847] is also a good start to know more about the Chinese civilization.

One of the Chinese philosophies is to be HUMBLE, not to promote or market oneself. Moreover, Chinese tend towards collectivism instead of individualism, meaning they usually contribute their achievements to teamwork, not the Principal Investigator (PI). However, the rewarding system dominating scientific community today is to reward individuals. Therefore, Chinese scientists seldom receive the international recognition they deserve.

The following Chinese key figures are, among the many more, who have made

---

846 "Science and Civilization in China" is a set of works on the history of science and technology in China compiled by Dr. Joseph Needham of the Needham Institute and international scholars.

847 https://www.amazon.com/Genius-China-Science-Discovery-Invention/dp/1594772177

great contributions to humanity.

2. YOUYOU TU – ARTEMISININ

Malaria is a life-threatening disease caused by parasites that are transmitted to people through the bites of infected female anopheles. There are five parasites that cause malaria in humans, and two of these species pose the greatest threat. Based on data released by the WHO, in 2020, nearly half of the world's population were at the risk of malaria.[848] Most cases and deaths occur in the sub-Saharan Africa region. However, malaria also exists in Southeast Asian, Western Pacific, and the U.S. regions.

Malaria has likely infected humans for more than 5,000 years. The first written reference to the periodic fevers of malaria traces back to 2,700 BC in China. Significant scientific studies began in the 1880s, when Scottish physician, Ronald Ross proved that malaria is a parasitic disease spread via mosquito bites. He won the 1902 Nobel Prize for his work.[849] Charles Laveran, a French military medical doctor, played an important role in the enquiry on the relationships between Anopheles and malaria. He won the 1907 Nobel Prize for this discovery.[850]

Severe cases can lead to severe anemia, respiratory distress, coma, and even death. Malaria is a preventable and treatable disease. Early diagnosis and treatment of malaria reduce disease and prevent death. Before artemisinin, the commonly used drug was chloroquine, but repetitive use led to drug resistance in malaria parasites, severely compromising its therapeutic effects.

Since the advent of artemisinin, the number of global deaths caused by malaria has dropped by 38%, and the incidence rate has also dropped by more than 50% in 48 countries. The mechanism of action of artemisinin differs from chloroquine and gives fewer side effects. Moreover, it targets a wider range of malaria parasites, including those that have developed chloroquine drug resistance.

Since the beginning of the 21st century, Artemisinin Combination Therapy (ACT)

---

848 https://www.who.int/health-topics/malaria#tab=tab_1

849 https://www.nobelprize.org/prizes/medicine/1902/summary/

850 https://www.nobelprize.org/prizes/medicine/1907/laveran/biographical/

has been listed by the WHO as the preferred antimalarial treatment.[851] This medication saved millions of lives, especially in the low-income countries. The global market size of ACT in 2017 was US$360 million, and it is expected to reach nearly US$700 million in 2025, with a compound annual growth rate of 8.7%.

Tu is the first Chinese Nobel laureate in physiology or medicine, and the first female citizen of the People's Republic of China to receive a Nobel Prize in any category. She is also the first Chinese person to receive the Lasker Award.[852] She shared the 2015 Nobel Prize with William Campbell and Satoshi Omura, "for her discovery of novel therapy against malaria".[853] However, Tu refused to take all the credit, but instead praised all her colleagues and Chinese herbal medicine. This is a typical traditional Chinese intellectual moral.

Tu and her team investigated Chinese ancient texts and folk remedies for possible malaria remedies. She narrowed down to a few promising candidates from over 2,000 recipes. The breakthrough in the discovery of Qinghaosu, later called artemisinin, was made in 1971. Qinghao stood out because it was mentioned as a treatment for the malarias hallmark symptom, intermittent fever, in the 1,600-year-old Chinese medicine book. More importantly, Tu also found the way to extract the active ingredient from Qinghao natural leaves.[854] [855]

The clinical value of artemisinin extends beyond malaria treatment. Tu and team are currently carrying out clinical trials for dihydroartemisinic tablets targeting systemic and discoid systemic lupus erythematosus, an autoimmune disease that causes widespread inflammation in tissue and leads to death in severe cases.

3. DAVID T WONG — PROZAC®

Born in Hong Kong, David Wong is one of the contributors to Prozac®, a drug

---

851 https://apps.who.int/iris/bitstream/handle/10665/274362/WHO-CDS-GMP-2018.18-eng.pdf

852 https://laskerfoundation.org/winners/artemisinin-therapy-for-malaria/

853 https://www.nobelprize.org/prizes/medicine/2015/tu/facts/

854 https://sitn.hms.harvard.edu/flash/2020/youyou-tu-an-exceptional-nobel-laureate/

855 https://www.ncbi.nlm.nih.gov/pmc/articles/PMC4731589/

deemed as "the medicine of the century" by the *Fortune* magazine.

Depression is a common mental illness that impacts estimated 5% of population worldwide.[856] Prolonged moderate or severe depression negatively impacts the daily lives of patients. Severe cases can lead to suicidal actions, yearly there are estimated one million depression related suicide deaths.

Traditional antidepressants mainly consisted of Tricyclic Antidepressants (TCAs) and Monoamine Oxidase Inhibitors (MAOIs). However, these medications have many side effects as well as drug interactions with food.

Wong discovered the regulatory effect that Serotonin (5-HT) has on the human central nervous system in moderating emotions. He joined the team of Ray Fuller and Bryan Molloy in Eli Lilly to develop the next generation of antidepressants, namely Selective Serotonin Reuptake Inhibitors (SSRIs). SSRIs outshined their two predecessors, namely TCAs and MAOIs, with superior safety, longer half-life, and stronger efficacy. Upon its marketing approval, Prozac quickly became the most used antidepressant in clinical settings across the EU and the U.S.

Since its inception in 1987, Prozac® has been sold in more than 100 countries and dosed to more than 40 million patients. It became a blockbuster drug, with peak sales reaching US$2.3 billion before its patent expiration in 2001. It was tied to one third of Eli Lilly's total sales at that time. *San Jose Mercury News* voted Prozac® as one of the most paramount technological innovations of the 20th century, and *Time* magazine interpreted its huge market potential as "a license to print money."

4. FU-KUEN LIN – EPOGEN®

Erythropoietin (EPO) is a hormone naturally secreted by the human kidneys to stimulate red blood cell regeneration, playing a key role in regulating the normal functioning of tissues and organs.

Reduction in EPO is usually observed in patients with chronic renal failure or those having undergone chemotherapy, causing severe anemia. There were no

---

856 https://www.who.int/news-room/fact-sheets/detail/depression

effective treatments for renal anemia. Typically, patients were subjected to blood transfusion or male hormone therapy once every two to three weeks.[857] This was proven to be unsustainable and ineffective due to the increased risk of infection and possible impairment of liver function in male hormone therapies.

Born in Keelung, Taiwan, Lin moved to the U.S. to study fungi physiology, and he obtained the doctorate in plant pathology in 1971. Lin joined Amgen in 1981 as a research scientist, and he was involved in the EPO project from the start. In 1983, Lin and team successfully developed the gene code for EPO.

In 1989, the first Erythropoiesis-Stimulating Agent (ESA) recombinant human erythropoietin was approved by the U.S. FDA, under the generic name Epoetin Alpha, and brand name Epogen®. It was the first blockbuster drug for Amgen and its sales peaked at US$12.6 billion in 2006, bringing a tremendous success. Lin received numerous global awards for his contribution.

5. PATRICK SOON-SHIONG – ABRAXANE®

Soon-Shiong is a Chinese-South African transplant surgeon, and later immigrated to the U.S. Additionally, he is a billionaire businessman, scientist, and media tycoon and philanthropist. Soon-Shiong was amongst the first billionaires in response to Bill Gate's and Warren Buffet's "Giving Pledge" call.[858]

He was born in South Africa to the Chinese parents who fled from China during the Japanese invasion in the World War Two.

Soon-Shiong joined the University of California in Los Angeles (UCLA) Medical School in 1983 and served on faculty until 1991 as a transplant surgeon. He conducted the first whole pancreas transplant done at UCLA.

Soon-Shiong purchased Fujisawa, a generic injectable drug company and used its revenue to develop Abraxane®. He invented Nanoparticle albumin bound

---

857 Testosterone promotes erythropoietin production and enhances bone marrow hematopoiesis.

858 In 2010, investor legend Warren Buffet and Microsoft founder Bill Gates announced the "Giving Pledge" call, calling for billionaires to donate at least half of their net worth either pre or postmortem.

(Nab) technology, which processes paclitaxel and human serum albumin into nanoparticles by high-pressure vibration technology. This breakthrough dosage formation technology promotes drug penetration of tumor cells and increases the drug's therapeutic effect.

Paclitaxel was one of the most effective chemotherapeutic drugs ever developed. It is active against a wild range of cancers, such as lung, ovarian, and breast cancers. Paclitaxel is isolated from the bark of Pacific Yew, which is natural and rare. Due to its low water solubility, it is formulated in a mixture of Cremophor EL and dehydrated ethanol in 50:50 by volume, under the brand name Taxol®, making it one of the most expensive cancer drugs back then. However, Taxol® has some very severe side effects due to this mixture. This resulted in a 2–4% chance of causing severe allergic reactions, which necessitated the injection of anti-allergic drugs such as corticosteroids or antihistamines into patients before usage.

The encapsulation of paclitaxel in bio-degradable and non-toxic nano-delivery systems can protect the drug from degradation during the blood circulation, and protecting the body from side effects, resulting in better pharmacokinetics outcomes and more patient compliance.

Soon-Shiong used this innovative nanoparticle delivery system and developed a new drug under the brand name Abraxane®, that was approved by the U.S. FDA for the treatment of metastatic breast cancer in February 2005. Additionally, it was approved as a first-line treatment of metastatic non-small cell lung cancer, in combination with gemcitabine as a first-line treatment of metastatic pancreatic cancer. Due to its superior safety and efficacy over Taxol®, Abraxane® has been favored by doctors and patients after its approval. In 2010, Celgene paid a cash and stock deal valued at US$3 billion to acquire Abraxis BioScience, maker of Abraxane®.[859] This deal made Soon-Shiong one of the richest medical doctors in the U.S.

Together with his wife, the couple founded the Chan Soon-Shiong Family Foundation. The family donate US$100 million for the reopening of the Martin

---

859 https://www.fiercepharma.com/pharma/celgene-completes-acquisition-of-abraxis

Luther King Hospital to provide medical services for low-income families.[860] [861] At the same time, they also established the National Medical Integration Alliance to promote the implementation of public electronic medical records.

6. DAVID HO – COCKTAIL THERAPY[862]

Acquired Immunodeficiency Syndrome (AIDS) is a serious infectious disease caused by the Human Immunodeficiency Virus (HIV). It attacks the human immune system, increasing the risk of developing opportunistic infections and tumors, and has an extremely high mortality rate.

HIV continues to be a major global public health issue, having claimed 40.1 million lives so far. In 2021, 650,000 people died from HIV-related causes and 1.5 million people suffered from HIV.[863] There is no cure for HIV infection. However, with increasing access to prevention, diagnosis, treatment and care, HIV infections have become a manageable chronic condition.

When AIDS was first discovered, the medical community had very little knowledge about it, and there was no effective treatment strategy. Although single-drug or dual-drug antiviral therapy can prolong the survival period of patients, the drug has limited efficacy and serious side effects which gave AIDS the notion of an incurable deadly disease.

It was not until the end of 1995 that protease inhibitors emerged, which formed the basis for Ho's discovery of "Highly Active Antiretroviral Therapy" (HAART), this recognized as the first-line treatment for AIDS.

HAART combines three or more antiviral drugs.[864] Each drug has a different

---

860 https://dailybruin.com/2009/11/05/billionaire-donate-100-million-reopening-martin-lu?cp=1

861 https://www.newyorker.com/magazine/2021/11/01/how-patrick-soon-shiong-made-his-fortune-before-buying-the-la-times

862 https://www.pbs.org/wgbh/pages/frontline/aids/interviews/ho.html

863 https://www.who.int/news-room/fact-sheets/detail/hiv-aids

864 Commonly used clinical anti-viral drugs include protease inhibitors, Nucleoside Reverse Transcriptase Inhibitors (NRTIs), Non-Nucleoside Reverse Transcriptase Inhibitors (NNRTIs).

mechanism of action or targets a different link in the HIV virus replication cycle, thereby maximally inhibiting the replication of the virus and avoiding drug resistance caused by a single drug. The widespread application of HAART has rapidly and dramatically reduced the mortality rate from 100% to 20%, prolonging the survival time of patients after infection. His championship for the combination anti-viral therapy instead of single therapy turns HIV from a deadly disease into a chronic disease.

In 1996, Ho was famed as Man of the Year by *Times* magazine, first time ever for a scientist since 1960.[865][866] In the same year, *Science* magazine appraised cocktail therapy as the lead in Top ten Most Influential Technology and Innovation Breakthroughs.

In 2002, Ho transferred the patent technology for vaccine manufacturing at his Aaron Diamond AIDS Research Center to China under a symbolic value of US$1 per year. He hopes to give back to the prevention and treatment efforts for AIDS in China.

In 2018, global market size for HIV viral drugs reached US$34 billion, with a speculative US$46.8 billion by 2023 given a compound annual growth rate of 6.0%.[867]

Ho was born in Taichung, Taiwan and moved to the U.S. at 6th grade. Ho has received numerous awards due to his remarkable scientific contributions. On January 8, 2001, he was presented with the Presidential Citizens Medal by U.S. President Clinton.[868]

Ho has published over 500 research papers as of February 2020, and he is the recipient of 14 honorary doctorates, including these from Columbia University and Tsinghua University.

---

865 https://content.time.com/time/specials/packages/article/0,28804, 2019712_ 2019703_ 2019666, 00.html

866 https://www.science.org/content/article/time-taps-aids-researcher-top-award

867 *Southwest Securities anti-HIV drug report*

868 https://www.rockefeller.edu/news/4205-rockefeller-and-aaron-diamond-researcher- david-d-ho-receives-presidential-citizens-medal/

7. YUK MING DENNIS LO – NON-INVASIVE PRENATAL DNA TESTING

Lo is currently the Associate Dean (Research) of the Faculty of Medicine of the Chinese University of Hong Kong, and President of the Hong Kong Academy of Sciences. His invention of Non-Invasive Prenatal DNA Testing (NIPT) technology was recognized by *MIT Technology Review*[869] as a part of the top ten innovative technologies in 2013. In the light of his research on NIPTs, Lo won the Life Sciences Award for the first Future Science Prize[870] in 2016 and was selected by *Nature Biotechnology*[871] as the Global top 20 Translational Researchers for five consecutive years (2016-2020). In 2005, He won the State Natural Science Award, the highest honor by the Chinese government. Recently in 2022, Lo received the prestigious Lasker-DeBakey Clinical Research Award.[872]

In 1997, his discovery of free-floating fetal DNA fragments in the peripheral blood of pregnant women laid an indispensable theoretical basis for the NIPT technology. The mechanism of action of NIPT uses high-throughput sequencing on collected blood samples from pregnant women to analyze the normalcy of fetal chromosomes and screens out aneuploidies associated with genetic diseases such as Down syndrome.[873] Traditional prenatal diagnosis was mainly based on serological screening and/or ultrasound examination. If a high-risk result is obtained, the case can only be confirmed by invasive methods such as amniocentesis. However, there are flaws in these methods such as insufficient detection rate of Down syndrome by serology being 70%, and a 0.3% risk of miscarriage in amniocentesis. In contrast, NIPT has a detection rate of more

---

869 Founded in 1899 in MIT, it is the world's oldest and most influential technology business magazine, with particularly emphasis on novel technologies and innovative businesses to highlight technological commercialization and capitalization.

870 Initiated by Hong Kong Future Science Award Foundation and co-organized by Beijing Huairou Future Forum Technology Development Center, the ceremony aims at acknowledging scientists with outstanding scientific and technological achievements in the Greater China region.

871 A subsidiary of Nature, it is an influential biotechnology magazine.

872 https://laskerfoundation.org/dennis-lo-circulating-dna-as-a-window-into-our-health/

873 Stems from chromosomal abnormalities, 60% of affected fetuses are aborted in early pregnancy, survivors are characterized by intellectual impairment, pronounced facial features, growth and development disorders and multiple deformities.

than 99% through blood sampling and is also safer and more effective. It is currently the preferred method for prenatal diagnosis in the world and is widely used in more than 90 countries, benefitting more than seven million pregnant women every year. The global NIPT market size in 2020 is US$3.48 billion, and is expected to reach US$13.16 billion in 2028, with a compound annual growth rate of 18%.[874]

In addition to Down syndrome, Lo and his team managed to fully decipher the full genome mapping in fetuses by analyzing trace amounts of DNA in maternal plasma, this allows the early detection for a wider variety of genetic diseases. The team is currently expanding the plasma DNA sequencing technology to cancer detection, with their intellectual properties underpinning a first multi-cancer early detection test.

8. LIEPING CHEN[875] —THE DISCOVERY OF THE PD-1/PD-L1 PATHWAY

Chen is an international leader in basic T cell biology and cancer immunotherapy. He has published over 370 peer-viewed research articles. His work in the discovery of the PD-1/PD-L1 pathway for cancer immunotherapy was cited as the number one breakthrough of the year by the *Science* magazine in 2013.

In the 1990s, he demonstrated for the first time that overexpression of molecules resembling the PD-L1 immunoglobin helps tumor cells evade immune responses. He later illustrated monoclonal antibodies as blockades to the combination of PD-1/PD-L1, effectively enhancing the body's anti-tumor ability.

PD-1 and PD-L1 changed the cancer immunotherapy, a paradigm shifts in the fight against cancer.[876] In the global top 20 drugs in 2022, Keytruda®(PD-1) from Merck was sold over US$20 billion and ranked number two, Opdivo®(PD-1) from BMS/ONO was sold over US$9 billion and ranked number 11th.

---

874 Fortune Business Insights

875 https://medicine.yale.edu/immuno/profile/lieping-chen/

876 https://www.nature.com/articles/d43747-021-00129-4

Chen was born in Fuzhou, China. He moved to the U.S. in 1986 to earn a doctorate degree. He has received numerous awards, including William B. Coley Award[877] in 2014, Warren Alpert Foundation Prize[878] in 2017, and the Giants of Cancer Care Award[879] in 2018. [880]

9. FENG ZHANG[881] – CRISPR-CAS9 GENETIC ENGINEERING

Zhang is currently the youngest Chinese tenured professor in the history of MIT. His most famous research work is the development and application of CRISPR-Cas system, which is one of the most popular emerging gene editing technologies. He was named as one of the top ten scientific figures of the year by *Nature* magazine in 2013 and won the Canada Gairdner Awards[882] in 2016.[883]

CRISPR-Cas is a prokaryotic immune system found in bacteria and archaea. Its mechanism of action utilizes CRISPR as a guide sequence which has been inserted with the DNA fragments of previously invading bacteriophages. In combination with CRISPR-associated Cas enzymes, the system cleaves gene sequences from similarly invading viruses. Zhang initiated the research of CRISPR-Cas9 and subsequently published his findings onto *Nature*. This proved the feasibility of incorporating CRISPR-Cas9 technologies in mammalian cell

877 Established in 1975, awarding ceremonies are held once per year and judged by Cancer Research Institute in New York. Outstanding scientists with major contributions in the fields of immunology and tumor immunology are rewarded. Many awardees of the William Colley Prize are Nobel Prize winners as well.

878 Founded in 1997 by entrepreneur and philanthropist Warren Alpert. In cooperation with Harvard Medical School, awards are given to scientists who have made outstanding contributions to the field of biomedicine by year.

879 A review committee comprised of 120 internationally recognized oncologists, doctors, and scientific researchers from 800 nominated cancer experts.

880 https://www.cancerresearch.org/blog/july-2018/former-cri-grantee-lieping-chen-giant-cancer-care

881 https://mcgovern.mit.edu/profile/feng-zhang/

882 Founded by the Gairdner Foundation of Canada in 1959, scientists who have made major discoveries and contributions in medicine are recognized. 80 of the 313 winners also won the Nobel Prize in Physiology or Medicine to date.

883 https://gairdner.org/2016-canada-gairdner-award-winners/

gene editing which has great prospects.

CRISPR-Cas technology has brought great societal benefits and contributes to several breakthroughs in healthcare applications such as the construction of aging models, editing of AIDS virus, and cleaving of hepatitis B virus, potentially giving rise to more effective therapies and drugs. Compared with previous gene editing technologies such as ZFNs and TALENs, the advantages of CRISPR-Cas technology are its simplicity, precision, low cost, and wide application range.

Today, one of Zhang's companies, Editas Medicine (EDIT.US), focuses on the development of drugs incorporating the CRISPR/Cas system to cover indications involving multiple genetic diseases, including eye disease, Duchenne muscular dystrophy and neurological diseases.

10. TAK WAH MAK
– THE DISCOVERY OF T-CELL RECEPTOR

Born in Hong Kong in 1946, Mak left for the U.S. for college and later conducted much of his research work in Canada.

As one of the most prominent pioneers of genetics of immunology and cancer, Mak's milestone identification of the cDNA and clone of encoding human T-cell receptor in 1983[884] has established a strong foundation for headway on T-cell biology, and CAR-T technologies. His subsequent discovery of the function of the immune checkpoint protein CTLA-4 in 1995 greatly contributes to immunotherapy and cancer treatment breakthroughs. Until present, Mak's work is applauded as the "Holy Grail of immunology",[885] laying grounds for 5,000 global laboratories.[886]

With the unique mission statements of being "connected through the science of

---

884 Yanagi, Y., Yoshikai, Y., Leggett, K. *et al.* A human T cell-specific cDNA clone encodes a protein having extensive homology to immunoglobulin chains. *Nature* 308, 145–149 (1984).

885 Williams, A. Immunology: The T-lymphocyte antigen receptor — elusive no more. *Nature* 308, 108–109 (1984).

886 https://cihr-irsc.gc.ca/e/51494.html

cellular metabolism, connected to patients, connected to one another (on personal level), and connected to partners and collaborators", Mak co-founded Agios Pharmaceuticals Inc. in Cambridge, Massachusetts in 2008 to develop therapies for genetically defined diseases.[887] In April 2017, under the anticipation for the U.S. FDA approval on its lead compound IDHIFA® (Enasidenib), the company raised US$250 million in a new stock offering.[888] Same year in August, IDHIFA®, was indeed the U.S. FDA-approved for acute myeloid leukemia merely after four years of clinic entrance. It was the first oral targeted therapy for patients who have few other treatment options.[889] In November 2019, the company went public on NASDAQ.[890]

Mak's achievements have been highly honored and awarded, to name a few: Gairdner Foundation International Award in 1989, Robert L. Noble Prize by the National Cancer Institute of Canada in 1996, Sloan Prize of the General Motors Cancer Foundation in 1996, the 2021 Szent-Gyorgyi Prize Award for Progress in Cancer Research. He was also selected to be in the book titled *A Cure Within – scientists unleashing the immune system to kill cancer*.

He also received recognition, such as being named as Officer of the Order of Canada, Foreign Associate of the National Academy of Sciences (U.S.), introduced to the Canadian Medical Hall of Fame. He continues to focus on underlying mechanisms of immune responses and tumorigenesis.

11. TINGDONG ZHANG, ZHENYI WANG, AND ZHU CHEN – THE USE OF ARSENIC FOR TREAT ACUTE PROMYELOCYTIC LEUKEMIA.

Zhang is well known for discovering the use of arsenic trioxide to treat Acute Promyelocytic Leukemia (APL). Wang performed the first successful therapy on APL patients using All-Trans Retinoic Acid (ATRA), which significantly

---

887 https://www.agios.com/about-us/

888 https://www.bizjournals.com/boston/news/2017/04/19/agios-bags-250m-in-offering-as-cancer-drug-speeds.html

889 https://www.businesswire.com/news/home/20170801006281/en/

890 https://www.nasdaq.com/press-release/agios-announces-pricing-of-%24256-million-public-offering-of-common-stock-2019-11-07

increased the survival rate of patients with APL. Chen made contributions to the identification of the molecular mechanisms of both ATRA and arsenic trioxide in APL. With their combined efforts, this therapy provides dramatic improvement in the five-year disease-free survival rate of APL patients, from 25% to 95%, which is regarded as a significant breakthrough in APL treatment.

The first paper was published by Zhang and his team in 1973, in the treatment of six cases of patients with chronic myeloid leukemia. His results were initially published in Chinese language journals. In the 1990s, he published in English, and his works became widely known after he co-authored with Zhu Chen, the president of the Shanghai Institute of Hematology. The discovery for arsenic as a cancer cure came from one of the Chinese medicine tenets "give poison to treat poison". An article in the *New York Times* on May 6, 2001 illustrated the story of Zhang's discovery and how the medicine was tried in the U.S. Now, the medicine is under the brand name Trisenox®.[891] Zhang was born in China and obtained a doctorate degree in Traditional Chinese Medicine. Zhang has received numerous awards for his discovery. One of these is 2020 Future Science Prize, the Life Sciences Prize.[892] [893]

Wang[894] and Chen have also received numerous awards for their contribution, including the 7th Szent-Gyorgyi Prize[895] for Progress in Cancer Research in 2012. Wang had never considered the option of patenting ATRA treatment because it could only increase the financial burdens of the patients.

12. ROGER YOUCHIEN TSIEN – THE DISCOVERY OF GFP

Tsien was born in a Chinese American family in New York. He went to Harvard

---

891 https://www.nytimes.com/2001/05/06/magazine/2-case-study-leukemia-location-harbin-china-chairman-mao-s-cure-for-cancer.html

892 http://www.futureprize.org/en/laureates/detail/42.html

893 https://www.nytimes.com/2002/07/15/science/sciencespecial/ancient-poison-modern-cure.html

894 https://www.ncbi.nlm.nih.gov/pmc/articles/PMC4875515/pdf/13238_2013_Article_3802.pdf

895 https://www.nfcr.org/research-programs/szent-gyorgyi-prize-for-progress-in-cancer-research/

University at the young age of 16. He traced his family ancestry to Hangzhou which has been one of the most prestigious and prominent families in China for over thousand years. His uncle, Hsue-Shen Tsien, was the architect of China national missile and space program. His father, uncles, and brothers all pursued studies at MIT.

In the 1980s, Tsien's development of novel calcium imaging techniques had already been widely recognized. Together with his team, Tsien created first-generation calcium indicators (quin-2, fura-2, indo-1, fluo-3, and others), their membrane permeable derivatives (acetoxymethyl [AM] ester forms) and caged calcium compounds.[896] He won the first prize in the nationwide Westinghouse Talent Search with his investigation on how metals bind to thiocyanate.

Tsien received the 2008 Nobel Prize in Chemistry,[897] for his discovery and development of the Green light-emitting Fluorescent Protein (GFP), what Tsien named as "molecular spies". Because GFP can be linked to other proteins, it becomes an important tool for studying biological processes in cells. GFP is recognized to be a powerful assistance for post-genome biological research, super-resolution imaging and multi-color imaging, which in turns bring research for genetic-based visualization techniques to a new height. As *Nature* described, he is the creator of a rainbow of fluorescent probes that lit up biology.[898]

---

896 https://www.cell.com/cell/pdf/S0092-8674(16)31329-0.pdf
897 https://www.nobelprize.org/prizes/chemistry/2008/tsien/facts/
898 https://www.nature.com/articles/538172a

Appendix 2

Life Sciences Fund Investment Logic

1. INVESTMENT MISSION

To pursue the meaning of life, people must have a mission. To ensure its survival and success, every company, be it large or small-scale, must have a mission as well. The mission of life sciences investment funds is aligned with humanity and longevity.

Throughout the history of global pharmaceutical industry, several outstanding leaders are well respected not only for their commercial success, but more importantly for their people-oriented virtues[899] and significant contributions to society. For example, in Belgium, Dr. Paul Janssen founded Janssen Pharmaceuticals,[900] later became a part of Johnson & Johnson. In the U.S., the Johnson Brothers founded Johnson & Johnson Pharmaceuticals. Putting people in the first place is the heart of its credo. George W. Merck, the Chairman of Merck & Co. once stated "We must bear in mind that medicine is used to diagnose and treat diseases, as well as to save lives. We must never lose sight of the fact that medicine is intended for the benefit of people, not profit, although profit will inevitably follow.[901] Profit will never vanish if we remember this, the more clearly we remember, the greater the flow of profit. We cannot simply stand back and declare that we have discovered a new drug. We cannot abandon our effort until the best outcome for all is achieved." These echo with the Chinese philosophy "do not forget what make you get started in the first place".[902]

A Life Sciences Investment Fund is a business entity for profit. A fund manager's core responsibility is to use professional knowledge and experience to evaluate investment returns and risks, to help invested portfolio companies maximize

---

899 The Chinese equivalence to be 以人为本

900 https://www.jnj.com/our-heritage/meet-dr-paul-janssen-a-legend-in-pharmacology

901 https://www.merck.com/company-overview/history/

902 The Chinese equivalence to be 不忘初心，方得始终

value, and in turn, pursue above-the-market returns for shareholders.

The author recognizes the importance of ensuring profitability of the fund and at the same time, improve humanity,[903] which means to improve people access to not only innovative medical supplies but also to basic medications, as well as longevity. The author also believes his investment logics stem from the Chinese philosophies and civilization.

Likewise to any other healthcare professionals such as doctors, pharmacists and nurses, fund managers in the life sciences shall be committed to improving humanity. Life is equal regardless of high-income or low-income countries. Life is the fundamental human rights, everything else is based on it. Therefore, the meaning of our role as a life sciences fund manager is to help other people live healthily and in longevity.

2. INVESTMENT OBJECTIVES

After determining the mission, the fund focuses on three investment directions:

1) Innovative or breakthrough projects to address unmet clinical needs or longevity

Humankind has historically been and will always be at a disadvantage in the fight against diseases. Despite technological advances, countless diseases remain as unsolved puzzles, including those that are currently incurable, difficult to prevent or diagnose, and can be prevented, diagnosed, or treated but with unsatisfactory results.

There are many examples of well-known but non-curable diseases presented in the previous chapters. In the future, some may become curable, with the tremendous efforts from global scientists, venture capitalists, doctors, and patients.

Other examples represent diseases that humankind have not made any significant breakthroughs even with countless global efforts and huge investments, such as neurodegenerative diseases associated with aging, certain ophthalmic diseases,

---

903 https://www.merriam-webster.com/dictionary/humanity

and Non-Alcoholic Steatohepatitis (NASH).

The term "breakthrough therapies" refers to treatments that have the potential to significantly improve this medical situation, making the treatment shift to the next paradigm, for example, CAR-T therapy. It is a game-changing innovation that offers hope to patients with some blood-related cancers. This technology heralds a new era in cancer treatment.

After reviewing the first three chapters of this book, we can summarize the following:

i. Drug or therapy targets have shifted from Proteins to RNA and DNA.

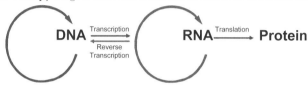

ii. The paradigm shifts from Chemical to Biopharmaceutical, now in the Life Sciences paradigm.

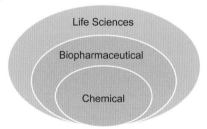

iii. Treatments have shifted from the General Medicine paradigm to the Precision Medicine paradigm, towards the final stage, namely Individualized Medicine paradigm.

General Medicine	Precision Medicine	Individualized Medicine

2) Projects allowing more accessibility to people in need, regardless of income level

Innovative and effective drugs and MedTech products are widely used in high-income countries and regions such as the U.S., some countries within the European Union, and Japan, Korea. However, even some residents in these economically affluent areas cannot afford some expensive drugs and treatments. The nature of capitalism and huge economic gap among classes make this situation an unsolvable problem.

For a variety of reasons, many patients in relatively middle-low-income countries and regions such as China, India, Southeast Asia, and Africa are unable to obtain or afford not only innovative medicines and treatments, worse still, in some cases, patients have no access to the basic medications for curable or preventable diseases. The huge global inequity in medical access is an overwhelming global issue.

This once-in-a-century COVID-19 clearly demonstrates that viruses, along with other diseases, are human beings' common enemy. Humans must be humble in the fight against diseases because the unknown of our body and diseases are much more than the known. If countries do not collaborate, humankind will never win the war against diseases. History has repeatedly proven this point.

This epidemic also illustrates that while high-income countries have a sizable vaccine stockpile, lower-income countries are experiencing severe vaccine shortages. There is no distinction between the rich and the poor when it comes to diseases, people are equal. Human life should be protected. As stressed repetitively, diseases are mankind's common enemy.

3) Projects addressing industry bottleneck problems

The industry has been facing the following bottlenecks for decades: huge amount of capital investments required for drug research and development, at least ten years plus in discovery and clinical trials time, high percentage of failure rate along R&D, high percentage of approved drugs resulting in less than expected drug sales, and the longtime debate on the innovation productivity in MNCs among industry and academia. All these elements prove that the existing business model has large room for improvements.

Fortunately, some start-up companies have identified industry problems and are attempting to provide solutions. For example, Artificial Intelligence (AI) and quantum technology have been used to boost the efficiency of drug research and development. Even though these companies are in the early stage, all their efforts are encouraging and can be considered as potential investment targets.

3. SYSTEMATIC ANALYSIS AND COMPETITIVE STRATEGY

Upon specifying an investment direction, the author suggests taking the following systematical analysis approach on the sub-sectors within the broad universe of life sciences.

Fund managers should focus on areas with high potential, at the same time, where the fund team remains focused and excels on areas with competitive strengths and tries to avoid unfamiliar areas.

There are numerous sub-sectors in life sciences which are highly diversified and forever evolving, echoing the Chinese saying, "a hundred schools of thought contending and a hundred flowers blooming." [904]

While inevitably, all investments have inherent risks, a systematic approach can help reduce the possibility of failure: 1) trends judgment, which relates to the evolution of the industry, including changes in the spectrum of human diseases, global R&D, and M&A progress, 2) market judgment, which relates to the indications for which the products targeted to treat and the market demand for such these products, knowing the major leaders in each sector, as well as their advantages and disadvantages, 3) technology judgment, it relates to selecting and working with potential winners in specific therapeutic areas, 4) trust and cooperation, it is critical to recognize that investment also requires chemistry between the company and the fund manager, who are willing to work together for win-win situation, 5) value creation, fund managers should figure out what value they can bring to this start-up, and help the business grow, 6) long-term objectives, since successful funds usually work with potential sector leaders for long term.

The traditional Chinese saying goes "the victors will remain victorious". [905] Investment funds should be able to select and work with, add value to with the potential winners.

---

904 The Chinese equivalence to be 百家争鸣，百花齐放
905 The Chinese equivalence to be 强者恒强

4. EVALUATING PROJECT DIMENSIONS

The author evaluates projects both objectively and subjectively.

1) Objective Evaluation includes the following aspects:

Addressing clinical needs through innovation or improved accessibility:

The fund takes a broad view of the industry and categorizes various sub-sectors to gain a better understanding of their global dynamics, such as which companies and products are in the clinical stage, raising funds, M&A activities, or making innovative technologies.

China has made significant progress on all fronts and has remarkably strengthened its overall national competitiveness. While examining projects of Chinese companies, one should also consider innovation standards from global perspective.

It is necessary to acknowledge that most global R&D projects are focused on a small number of therapeutic areas, resulting in an imbalance of inputs and outputs. As a result, investment in projects with higher accessibility would bring along more economic and social impacts, such as increasing biosimilar drugs, medications for respiratory system, and treatment products for infectious diseases and more.

The essence of life sciences industry is global collaboration:

Looking back at history over the past 50 years, all the major innovation milestones have proven one simple concept: no country can do it alone. Global collaboration is the only way to understand complicated mechanisms of the human body at all levels and identify the solutions to live longer and healthier, also as in clinical trials and development, product and technology commercialization, scientists, capital funding, patients, and markets.

The fund generally invests in the following types of projects: 1) products that already have a certain level of recognition in the global industries, 2) the founders of the company established some reputation in the industry, 3) start-ups with management team capable of exploring the international market.

China Value:

China is the fastest-growing market across the globe in life sciences, with the greatest potential for both market and innovations. Hong Kong benefits from its geographical advantage, becoming one of the world-leading financial centers.

The fund adopts the "investment + business development" approach to assist foreign companies investing in China with value-adding incubation, clinical trials, financing, listing on stock exchanges, and hiring qualified senior executives. All of these contribute to the invested companies' market value. Similarly, the fund assists China-based companies in establishing international partnerships, raising capital in Hong Kong, going public listing, and searching for capable directors and executives.

2) Subjective Evaluation

It is essential to primarily focus on the founders and key executives of the targeted companies since people are the key element of success. The evolution focuses on four areas: 1) the international business plan and leadership of the founders or controllers, 2) the professional skills, industry reputation and experience of the management team, 3) the company's value and missions, and 4) the ability to execute, since business plans are meaningless without timely and effective execution.

5. THE SUCCESS OF LIFE SCIENCES INVESTMENT FUNDS REQUIRES TWO CORE ABILITIES, NAMELY

i. **Professional capability:** indicates the insight into the global industry's trend and development, the capability to identify potential paradigm shifts, investing in rapidly growing areas, the accumulation of industry experiences and the connection of global contacts. A qualified fund manager is often a

Key Opinion Leader (KOL) with a sound reputation. Fund managers must develop distinctive investment strategies, choose directions based on the state of their own funds, ascertain the truth from the facts, and enhance their funds' competitiveness. Any business, even a small fund, should uphold a mission, an action plan, an investment logic, a process for implementation, and a habit to re-think.

ii. **Organizational capability:** indicates the efficiency in decision-making and execution, and mutual trust among General Partners (GPs), Investment Committees (ICs), and Limited Partners (LPs). These variables have a direct impact on the timeline and quality of investment decisions. GPs and LPs are both concerned with profit distribution, while ICs are closely involved with project investment decision voting. Investment in life sciences is a highly specialized field, hence ICs must be skillful professionals in the fields of life sciences, business, investment, and finance.

6. SUMMARY

Life sciences industry has the following characteristics: 1) high entry barrier, only for the most competent ones, 2) the powerful retain their dominance by capital means such as licenses-in, merges and acquisitions, business partnerships as well as legal actions such as lawsuits against biosimilars or generic makers to delay IP protection, 3) global collaboration is the essence of this industry that requires global allocation of talent, capital, market, technology and products. Therefore, for investments in life sciences 1) the investment rate of return is relatively higher, the risk is also high, and the investment cycle is comparably longer, and 2) stringent professional qualifications for fund managers are essential, requiring them to be multidisciplinary and international.

i. **Stay focused:** fund team must devote a considerable sum of time and effort to researching the industry, therapeutic areas, technologies and more. As a result, the capacity for project analysis is limited during a certain period, therefore, focusing on several areas would be more productive.

ii. **Stay humble:** fund team must recognize their own strengths and shortcomings. It is critical to partner with a knowledgeable and suitable co-investor in unfamiliar areas.

iii. **Stay disciplined:** fund usually makes handsome returns only on a part of portfolio companies, therefore, work and walk with winners.

Appendix *3*

Recommended Readings

1. *A Cure Within–Scientists Unleashing the Immune System to Kill Cancer* by Neil Canavan
2. *Blockbuster Drugs–The Rise and Decline of the Pharmaceutical Industry* by Jie Jack Li
3. *Conscience and Courage – How Visionary CEO Henri Termeer Built a Biotech Giant and Pioneered the Rare Disease Industry* by John Hawkins
4. *Genentech – The Beginnings of Biotech* by Sally Smith Hughes
5. *How to Prevent the Next Pandemic* by Bill Gates
6. *Inside the Orphan Drug Revolution – The Promise of Patient-Centered Biotechnology* by James A. Geraghty
7. *Medicine, Science, and Merck* by Roy Vagelos and Louis Galambos
8. *Moonshot – Insider Pfizer's Nine-Month Race to Make the Impossible Possible* by Albert Bourla
9. *Pharmaceutical Lifecycle Management – Making the Most of Each and Every Brand* by Tony Ellery and Neal Hansen
10. *Powerful Medicines – The Benefits, Risks, and Costs of Prescription Drugs* by Jerry Avorn, M.D.
11. *Science Business – The Promise, The Reality, and the Future of Biotech* by Gary P. Pisano
12. *Science Lessons – What the Business of Biotech taught me about Management* by Gordon Binder and Philip Bashe
13. *The 100-year Life: Living and Working in an Age of Longevity* by Lynda Gratton& Andrew Scott
14. *The Biotech Investor – How to Profit from the Coming Boom in Biotechnology* by Tom Abate
15. *The Gene – An Intimate History* by Siddhartha Mukherjee
16. *The Hot Zone* by Richard Preston
17. *The Structure of Scientific Revolutions* by Thoms S. Kuhn
18. *The Truth about the Drug Companies – How They Deceive Us and What to Do about It* by Marcia Angell
19. *The Vaccine – Insider the Race to Conquer the COVID-19 Pandemic* by Joe Miller, Özlem Türeci, Ugur Sahin

References

1. BCG Consulting —— 2022 年 5 月中国药企创新药出海总体趋势与挑战

2. Deloitte – Deloitte Insights —— 2021 年全球生命科学行业展望

3. 灼识咨询 —— 2020 年行业报告 —— 中国眼科医疗行业报告

4. 毕马威及医药魔方 —— 2022 年中国创新药企发展白皮书 —— 中国创新药企的起航、困局、突破

5. 中金公司 —— 2022 年 2 月主题研究 —— 细胞治疗开启肿瘤免疫疗法新时代

6. 中信建设证券 —— 2021 年 6 月证券研究报告 —— 泰格医药 (300347.CN) 从本土走向全球，持续拓宽业务边界

7. 中信证券 —— 2021 年 7 月投资价值分析报告 —— 信达生物 (1801.HK) 快速崛起的国际化 Biopharma

8. 中国银河证券 —— 2022 年 9 月行业周报 0918 —— 警惕美国生物法案重点领域「卡脖子」环节

9. 中国药促会及 L.E.K. Consulting —— 专题报告 —— 2019 保护创新 促进仿制 对中国建立药品专利保护体系的政策建议

10. 中银证券 —— 2021 年 12 月证券研究报告 —— 中国 CXO 行业跟踪报告

11. 中银证券 —— 2021 年 9 月证券研究报告 —— AI 新药研发 (AIDD) 行业系列报告 —— 洞鉴行业发展，把握投资先机：(一) AIDD 概览篇

12. 安信证券 —— 2022 年 6 月行业投资建议 —— 半年维度优先配置医药中游及下游，静待上游消化完成后的估值切换

13. 安信证券 —— 2022 年 9 月行业深度分析报告 —— 医药行业疫情导致行业整体业绩承压，静待下半年边际改善

14. 西南证券 —— 2021 年 4 月证券研究报告 —— 迈瑞医疗 (300760.CN) 「迈」向全球，「瑞」不可当

15. 西南证券 —— 2022 年 8 月证券研究报告 —— 金斯瑞生物科技 (1548.HK) 多板块协同加速成长，四位一体战略未来可期

16. 沙利文咨询（中国） —— 2021 年 9 月市场研读 —— 中国溶瘤病毒产业发展白皮书

17. 沙利文咨询（中国） —— 2022 年 7 月研究报告 —— 眼科药物市场发展现状与未来趋势研究报告

18. 沙利文咨询（中国） —— 2022 年研究报告 —— 关于创新药物独立市场研究报告

19. 沙利文咨询（中国）及病痛挑战基金会 —— 2022 年 2 月观察报告 —— 2022 中

国罕见病行业趋势

20. 沙利文咨询（中国）主编 —— 2022 年 1 月港股 18A 生物科技公司发行投资活报告

21. 招商证券国际 —— 2020 年 4 月公司报告 —— 诺诚健华 (9969.HK) 小分子，大前景

22. 招商证券国际 —— 2022 年 1 月公司报告 —— 北海康成制药 (1228.HK) 在快速增长的罕见病市场乘浪前行

23. 招商证券国际 —— 2022 年 5 月公司报告 —— 泰格医药 (300347.CN) 安全边际已现，四轮驱动开启增长新篇

24. 招商证券国际 —— 2022 年 7 月证券研究报告 —— 创新药系列报告（二）：海外临床篇

25. 东方证券 —— 2022 年 9 月公司研究报告 —— 恒瑞医疗 (600276.CN) 始终走在创新前沿，变革中期待突破

26. 东北证券 —— 2022 年 9 月证券研究报告 —— 医药行业 CXO& 创新器械2022H1 复盘

27. 东吴证券 —— 2022 年 2 月证券研究报告 —— 优质 Biotech 标的已具备战略性配置价值 —— 从发达市场看我国创新药 / 技术产业的发展前景

28. 东吴证券 —— 2022 年 6 月证券研究报告 —— 迈瑞医疗 (300760.CN) 仗剑前行，国产医疗器械航母路在脚下

29. 哈佛商业评论 —— 2021 年 5 月 —— 中美脱钩时代，该如何跟 14 亿人做生意？别说你了解中国

30. 海通国际 —— 2021 年 1 月行业研究 —— 小核酸药物：小分子和单抗后的第三浪，未来可期

31. 海通国际 —— 2021 年 1 月研究报告 —— 再鼎医药 (9688.HK) 首次覆盖：瞄准同类最佳与中国首创的 BioPharma

32. 动脉橙及蛋壳研究院 —— 2022 年 H1 全球医疗健康产业资本报告

33. 国金证券 —— 2022 年 2 月证券研究报告 —— 医药健康行业政策大梳理监事（2021）：拨云见日

34. 国盛证券 —— 2020 年 7 月证券研究报告 —— 君实生物 (688180.CN) 厚积薄发即将进入收获期，专注创新播种新冠 "特效药"

35. 国盛证券 —— 2021 年 1 月证券研究报告 —— 高景气时代下的创新服务商 CXO[CXO 行业投资手册 2021]

36. 华西证券 —— 2022 年 6 月证券研究报告 —— 眼科业务持续高增展，开启新十年高质量发展新征程

37. 华创研究 —— 2022 专题报告 —— 小核酸药物：剑指慢性病广阔市场

38. 开源证券 —— 2022 年 7 月行业深度分析报告 —— 从联影医疗拟 IPO，看创新推动国内医学影像产业向高端市场突破

39. 广发证券——2020 年 3 月证券研究报告——[广发医药 & 海外]微创医疗 (0853.HK) 高值器械龙头，创新引领未来

40. 广发证券——2020 年 3 月证券研究报告——疫苗行业研究专题之品种篇：从全球化视野看重磅品种市场空间

41. 广发证券——2021 年 12 月证券研究报告——[广发医药 & 海外]医药微创机器人 –B (02252.HK)

42. 广发证券——2022 年 6 月证券研究报告——[广发海外]信达生物 (1801.HK) 十年成果斐然，全球创新可期

43. 辉瑞中国医学部及艾昆纬市场调研团队——2021 年中国医药行业「患者为中心」理念指导下项目开展 （获批后）现况调研报告

44. 兴业证券——2020 年 7 月证券研究报告——君实生物 (688180.CN) 创新药赛道新巨头，PD–1 单抗头部玩家

45. 兴业证券——2021 年 10 月证券研究报告——创胜集团 (6628.HK) 拥有生物药研发, 临床和生产全平台能力的创新药新星

46. 国家药品监督管理局——2021 年 2 月——罕见疾病药物临床研发技术指导原则

47. 中央政府——「十四五」生物经济发展规划

48. B of A Securities–September 2021 Equity Research–*Tech–Enabled Drug Discovery: Primer on a fast–growing disruptor to BioPharma R&D*

49. BeiGene, Ltd (BGNE.US/688235.CN/ 6160.HK)–*2021 Annual Report on Form 10–K*

50. BeiGene, Ltd (BGNE.US/688235.CN/ 6160.HK) – *2022 Interim Report*

51. Berenberg Capital Markets–September 2021– *Biotechnology: At the crossroads of biopharma and technology*

52. BOCI–October 2022 Healthcare Sector Update – GenScript Biotech (1548.HK): *Rising in an era of cell gene therapy*

53. CIC China Insights Consultancy–2021 *Industry Report on China Ophthalmic Drugs Market*

54. Citibank–April 2019 Equity Research–Shanghai Junshi Biosciences (1877.HK): Initiate at Buy (1H): *Making Better Therapeutics Affordable*

55. Citibank–June 2020 Equity Research–Shanghai Henlius Biotech (2696.HK): *Initiate at Buy/ High Risk: First–Mover Advantage in Biotech R&D and Commercialization*

56. Citibank–*September 2016 Equity Research*–MicroPort Scientific (0853.HK)

57. Cloudbreak Pharma–June 2022 *Seeing Life Better Through Medicine*

58. CLSA–February 2018 Special Report–*Precision RX: Targeted medicine delivers freedom from one–pill–fits–all*

59. CLSA–July 2022 *China Healthcare Sector Outlook–Past the Crux. New, innovative landscapes beckon*

60. CLSA– *September 2022 Equity Research* – Innovent HK$27.15 –Buy Unlocking commercial potential

61. CMB Internationa l – *December 2021 Equity Research* – Airdoc Technology (2251. HK) *Pioneer in AI–based medical imaging industry*

62. Credit Suisse – *June 2019 Equity Research – CRO Industry Primer*

63. Credit Suisse – *May 2018 Equity Research* – BeiGene (BGNE.OQ/ BGNE US): *A star in a booming China biotech market*

64. Fierce Pharma – *March 2021 Special Report – The top 10 drugs losing U.S. exclusivity in 2021*

65. Frost & Sullivan – June 2022 Independent Market Research Report–*Consumer Genetic Testing and Cancer Screening Market Study*

66. GenScript Biotech Corporation (1548.HK) – *2021 Annual Report*

67. GenScript Biotech Corporation (1548.HK) – *2021 Annual Results Presentation*

68. Goldman Sachs – *April 2020 Equity Research* – Zai Lab Ltd. (ZLAB) *Unlocking the China value of global biotech assets*; initiate at Buy

69. Goldman Sachs – *April 2021 Equity Research* – CDMO/ CROs: *Robust funding backdrop supports solid 2021E/22E earnings outlook*

70. Goldman Sachs – *April 2022 Global Macro Research – (De) Globalization Ahead?*

71. Goldman Sachs – December 2018 Equity Research – Innovent Biologics (1801.HK): *Building a competitive edge in immune–oncology; initiate at buy*

72. Goldman Sachs – *October 2021 Equity Research* – Transcenta (6628.HK)

73. Hong Kong Special Administration Region of the People's Republic of China – October 2022 *The Chief Executive's 2022 Policy Address*

74. HSBC Global – *November 2020 Equity Research* – Mindray: Initiate at Buy: *Going from strength to strength*

75. InnoCare Pharma Limited (9969.HK) – *2021 Annual Results*

76. InnoCare Pharma Limited (9969.HK) – *2022 Interim Report*

77. Innovent Biologics, Inc (1891.HK) – *2022 Interim Report*

78. Innovent Biologics, Inc (1891.HK) – *2022 Interim Results*

79. IQVIA Institute for Human Data Science – April 2021 – *Global Medicine Spending and Usage Trends/ Outlook to 2025*

80. IQVIA Institute for Human Data Science – *Emerging Biopharma's Contribution to Innovation*

81. IQVIA Institute for Human Data Science – February 2022 – *Global Trends in R&D/ Overview Through 2021*

82. IQVIA Institute for Human Data Science – January 2022 – *The Global Use of Medicines 2022*

83. Jefferies HK Limited – January 2022 Equity Research – *CANbridge: Gearing up for rare disease opportunities in China*; Initiate at Buy; PT HK$20

84. KPMG & HSBC – *2022 Emerging Giants in Asia Pacific*

85. McKinsey & Company – August 2022 *Vision 2028: How China could impact the global biopharma industry*

86. McKinsey & Company – May 2022 *Unchartered Waters – Can European Biotech Navigate Through Current Headwinds?*

87. McKinsey & Company – November 2017 *Building Bridges to Innovation*

88. McKinsey & Company – November 2021 *China biopharma– Stepping on the global stage*

89. McKinsey & Company – September 2022 *Helix: Rewriting the DNA for the next wave of impact in biopharma*

90. MicroPort Scientific Corporation (0853.HK) – *2021 Annual Report*

91. Mindray (300760.CN) – *2021 Annual Report Summary*

92. Morgan Stanley – *April 2022 Equity Research* – InnoCare Pharma Ltd: *Initiate at OW; Potentially Safer BTK for the Oncology Market*

93. Morgan Stanley – August 2021 Equity Research – Keymed Biosciences: *Next– generation biologics from in–house R&D platforms*

94. Morgan Stanley – January 2022 Equity Research – *2022 Outlook: True Innovation as True North to Success*

95. Morgan Stanley – January 2022 Equity Research – CANbridge Pharmaceuticals: *Rare Strength in Rare Diseases*; Initiate at OW

96. Morgan Stanley – July 2022 Equity Research – *Positioning for a Potential Rebound in 2H22*

97. Morgan Stanley – March 2022 Equity Research – *Identifying Alpha Amid Volatility*

98. Morgan Stanley – May 2021 Equity Research – *Biologics CDMO survey: Market dynamics should remain favorable out to 2025/25*

99. N+1 Singer – March 2019 Sector Note – *Digital Health: A quantum leap for healthcare*

100. Nature Biotechnology VOL 40, May 2022 – *Reflections on Alnylam*

101. Park, H., Otte, A., & Park, K. (2022). *Evolution of drug delivery systems: From 1950 to 2020 and beyond*. Journal of Controlled Release, 342, 53–65.

102. Paunovska, K., Loughrey, D., & Dahlman, J. E. (2022). *Drug delivery systems for RNA therapeutics*. Nature Reviews Genetics, 23(5), 265–280

103. Pharma Research – 2021 Report Medicines in Development – *Rare Diseases: A Report on Orphan Medicines in the Pipeline*

104. RemeGen Co., Ltd. (9995.HK) – *2021 Annual Report*

105. Shanghai Junsi Biosciences Co., Ltd. (1877.HK) – *2022 Interim Report*

106. Sun, X., Gao, H., Yang, Y. et al. *PROTACs: great opportunities for academia and industry*. Sig Transduct Target Ther 4, 64 (2019). https://doi.org/10.1038/s41392–019–0101–6

107. The Lancet Global Health Commission – February 2021 *The Lancet Global Health Commission on Global Health*: vision beyond 2020

108. The Pharmaletter – August 2021 – *Incyte out–licenses tafasitamab to InnoCare for Greater China*

109. U.S. Food & Drug Administration – 2022 Center for Drug Evaluation and Research – *Advancing Health Through Innovation: New Drug Therapy Approvals 2022*, Novel Drug Approvals for 2022

110. Wedbush – May 2018 Industry Note – *Oncolytic Viruses: Multi–Modal Monotherapies*

111. World Health Organization – *2019 World Report on Vision*

112. World Health Organization – *2022 Global Vaccine Market Report – A shared understanding for equitable access to vaccines*

113. World Vision China – *2021 Annual Report*

114. WuXi AppTec (603259.CN / 2359.HK) – *First Half 2022 Results*

115. WuXi Biologics (Cayman) Inc. (2269.HK) – *2021 Annual Report*

116. WuXi Biologics (Cayman) Inc. (2269.HK) – *2022 Interim Report*

117. WuXi Biologics (Cayman) Inc. (2269.HK) – *2022 Interim Results*

118. Young, R. M., Engel, N. W., Uslu, U., Wellhausen, N., & June, C. H. (2022). *Next–generation CAR T–cell therapies*. Cancer Discovery, 12(7), 1625–1633.

Acknowledgments

This book is a collective effort of many professionals. They dedicated their valuable time to participate in chapters and help check facts and data. I genuinely appreciate their work. More importantly, this book is for the common good which provides basic information about the life sciences industry and shares life sciences investment from a China perspective. I hope it will be beneficial to readers.

There is a long list of respectful professionals to whom I would like to express my gratitude, specially Prof. Dong Sun, Prof. Yuk Lam Lo, Prof. Dennis Lo, Prof. Albert Yu, Prof. Dennis Lam, Prof. Jun Wang, Prof. Fang Hu, Dr. Michael Yu, Dr. Patrick Lu, Dr. James Li, Dr. James Xue, Dr. Dajun Yang, Dr. Qing Yang, Dr. Yiyou Chen, Dr. Lihan Zhou, Dr. Chun Wu, Dr. Dong Shen, Dr. Rita Shih, Dr. Li Zhu, Mr. Robin Meng, Ms. Lilian Cheung and many more.

I would also like to thank Joelle Lau, Kar Man Pang, Ming Hon Lu, for reviewing all syntactics.

Especially, I would like to thank my parents, my wife and two daughters for their wholehearted support. I have missed much valuable time with them during my writing.

I would like to end this book with the quote "**Competition is the law of the jungle, but cooperation is the law of civilization**" by Peter Kropotkin.

Let us work together for a better humanity, and combat diseases.